THE
NORTHWOODS
READER VOLUME 1
NORTHERN WIT & WISDOM

CULLY GAGE

CONTAINS THE COMPLETE BOOKS OF THE ORIGINAL #1, 3 &5

Avery Color Studios, Inc.
Gwinn, Michigan

©1999 Avery Color Studios, Inc.

ISBN 1-892384-02-7

Library of Congress Catalog Card Number 99-73715

First Edition 1999

Reprinted 2001, 2006

Published by
Avery Color Studios, Inc.
Gwinn, Michigan 49841

Note From The Publisher

This book is a combined volume of Northwoods Readers #1, #3, and #5. Numbers 3 and 5 have been out of print for a short time and because of the unbelievable amount of interest in those two volumes, we have decided to release this book combining the three. We hope the hundreds of thousands of Cully Gage fans will find this compilation as much fun and interesting reading as the rest of the Northwoods Reader Series. Enjoy!

Table of Contents

The Northwoods Reader - Book #1

Heads and Tales - Book #3

What? Another Northwoods Reader? - Book #5

THE NORTHWOODS READER

BOOK ONE

The Wooing

L ove came to Jaako Sonninen at exactly 9:15 A.M., Monday, November 3, 1919. It stopped him dead in his tracks like a pole-axed steer.

It happened right beside the middle counter of M.C. Flinn's store where Josette Bourdon, the new clerk, was assembling "Help-Yourselfs," little striped bags of assorted candies that sold for a nickel.

Forgetting the salt blocks he'd come for, the big Finn just stood there, transfixed, face blank, mouth hanging open. Only the deep red flush creeping up past the collar of his lumberjack shirt and into his shock of blonde hair betrayed a life within a body. Churning delight flooded Jaako in waves as he gazed at the tall French-Canadian girl, the loveliest vision of his life.

Josette was not particularly surprised to see her impact. Many men, young and old, had reacted similarly. She was strikingly beautiful as only a young French girl could be. Vivacious too, infectiously gay, and no more able to refrain from flirting than breathing, she fluttered her eyes at Jaako, smiled shyly, wiggled her tail and continued to make up the little bags of candy.

Jaako stood there red and helpless, jaw agape, unable to say a word when Josette asked if she could help him. She finally broke the spell by popping a red peppermint into his open mouth.

Then she burst into giggles and fled. Jaako turned, walking as if in sleep, making his way past the hardware section, the shoes and boots, the ladies garments… He backed out the front door, took one final look, got in his buckboard and drove away.

Down the wire from the screened balcony where that "old miser," M.C. Flinn constantly watched the whole store, came the little cash container to ring the bell at the candy counter. Josette hurried back to find a note saying, "No more of that, young lady, if you want to continue working here. I'm deducting five cents from your pay for that peppermint."

Josette took the yellow pencil from her hair and hurriedly wrote on the back of the note, "Yes, Mr. Flinn. I'm sorry, Mr. Flinn. I promise never to do it again. I'm sorry. I promise."

She put the note back in the canister, cocked the spring, pulled the lever and sent it winging back up the wire to her unseen boss behind the hole in the grating. She was scared.

Josette had good reason to be afraid. The job at Flinn's store only paid ten dollars a week, but it was her only hope of ever escaping the confines of the little forest village and a life of drudgery that she and her parents had always known.

The Bourdons were "dirt poor" and had been ever since Josette's father, Maxime, got hit in the back by a great chunk of iron ore while working in the mines many years before. Stooped and crippled by the accident, about all he could do was tend the garden, the cow and pig. The little pension of fifteen dollars a month from the mining company could stretch only so far so his wife took in laundry, mainly from the trainmen and section crews.

All her life Josette had known little at home except steam from the copper boilers atop the kitchen stove and the ironing board that was never taken down.

Before she entered primary school, Josette had learned to fold the sheets and shirts that went in the wicker basket she hauled on her sled to the trainmen's bunkhouse. Later, she had been put to scrubbing them on the blue corrugated washboard that leaned against the rim of the wooden tub, her hands and wrists growing red and rough from the harsh brown soap.

With high school came the ironing. It became a daily eternity of sliding the heavy sadirons back and forth, back and forth, winter and summer. Summers were the worst of all with the kitchen range going full blast. When haying time came, Josette almost enjoyed the respite, no matter how her arms ached from swinging the scythe. At least there was sun and air.

Until she entered high school, Josette hadn't really minded the drudgery so much. "You have to eat; you have to work." It was all she'd ever known. But in high school, because she was very bright and always brought home hundreds on her report cards, the teachers had given her books, magazines, catalogues and dreams.

Josette loved high school, the new experiences in learning, new boys to flirt with, new realization that there were other ways to live. The women teachers gave her some of their discarded dresses and showed her how to rip them apart, steam the pleats or wrinkles out, cut needed patterns from newspapers and sew them into colorful garments. There were no more skirts of dyed Gold Medal Flour sacks. Josette bloomed under their attention and the prettier she became, the more her teachers made Josette feel that she was destined for better things.

Occasionally, on an evening when she could escape the kitchen to join her friends down at the depot to "push out" the St. Paul train for Chicago, Josette would ache as she watched the well dressed people in the dining car eating leisurely with silver and porcelain on white linen. A red rose in a vase adorned each table.

With that ache came hope and determination. Somehow, someday, she Josette, would take the train too, away from this grubby little village with its never ending work, work, work. Someday she would go to Chicago or Detroit and if she ever came back it would be with diamonds on her hands and silk on her back. There were golden cities in her dreams.

But when Josette graduated from high school she found herself back in the kitchen, slaving over the tubs and boilers.

College, even Normal School, was out of the question.

Cut off from her beloved teachers with nothing to do but work all day, Josette became sullen and rebellious at home and almost hysterically gay when out with the boys at night, every night, but never all night.

Josette had made up her mind that no boy was going to get her knocked up. She had seen what happened to her older girlfriends. Fun in the haymow and the first thing you know, back in the kitchen! No, no. Not for Josette.

All the boys tried, of course, but Josette was tall and strong as well as pretty. She could fight like a wildcat and did. More than one young man came home from an evening with Josette with his face scratched or a lump on his head from the heel of her shoe. Marriage to any of them was not for her. She was already married to her dreams of escape, her dreams of golden cities and a life of graceful living.

That's why she was so frightened when M.C. Flinn sent her the note in the change canister. Money was the passport. Josette didn't care how long it took, how long she had to scrimp and save, but one day she would board that train. In the meanwhile she would take what fun she could, flirt with the boys, bedevil them mercilessly, and tease them out of their pants.

Jaako's situation was different. According to our standards he was rich. He had money in the bank - "bank raha" - the Finns called it.

He lived in a fine frame house with long sheds and a huge barn on a 160 acre farm north of town. It was the best land in the area with no stumps or rocks, with rich soil that spilled great windrows of potatoes on the ground every fall. He had enough cows to keep the cream separator busy filling the cream cans he took to the train each morning. All of this, (and the bank money), had come to him when his father died some years before. It had been hard-earned.

Jaako's father, Toivo Sonninen, came to our town straight from the "Old Country" in 1892, with three hundred dollars gold in his breeches.

Not knowing a word of English, he'd stepped off the train and talked his way up the hill street until he found a Finn to steer him to a boarding house. A big man like Jaako and a prodigious worker, Toivo found a job almost immediately, working as a lumberjack for Silverthorne and Company, cutting the virgin pine that covered our country.

Within a year he had learned English, had been promoted to woods-boss and had sent for his wife, Lempi, to join him in "Amerika." Another year passed and he was camp-boss with Lempi doing the cooking for the thirty men working under him.

Four more years and Toivo was riding-boss, running Silverthorne operations in five camps. He and Lempi saved every cent. When the pine began to thin out, Silverthorne and Company went bankrupt and the bank selected Toivo to handle the closing and cleanup.

There was some talk about how Toivo had "screwed the bank good" in the process, that he'd stashed away much of the logging equipment and kept some of the money from the rest he'd sold, but nobody ever proved it. All that was really known was that after the job was done Toivo was able to go into business for himself, first as a logger and then as a jobber, always doing very well and making enough raha to buy a good farm and have a big pile left over in the bank for Jaako and his mother when he died.

But Jaako and the old lady never spent any money either, except to make money. People said they were both "as tight as a whiskey keg," that "they sold their butter and ate pork grease on their bread."

Jaako certainly never went to the saloon on Saturday nights or to dances or even to the pay sauna. On Sunday he went to church. What he bought at Flinn's store he needed. There was no fancy stuff.

Some of the Finn girls did their best to catch him, for besides having money he was big and handsome, but Jaako showed no interest. He did a little logging, "worked the farm good," and stayed with his aging mother - until he fell in love.

Until Josette had popped the peppermint into his open mouth, Jaako had rarely "gone store" more than once a week and then only on Saturdays, like all the other farmers. Now he came every day right after he'd delivered the cream cans to the depot and picked up the mail.

In the beginning, Jaako would ask Mike Salmi to get him a bag of oats or chicken feed before awkwardly sidling up to the candy counter. Once there, he would stand, arms hanging helplessly at his sides, remaining mute until Josette, giggling, asked him to say what he wanted.

Blushing furiously, he could sometimes only point.

She had no mercy.

She'd roll her eyes, turn her seductive smile on him and pretend not to understand. "What do you want, Jaako?"

The sound of his name on her lips sent a shiver running from his scalp to his heels.

"What do you want, Jaako? Hard candies, licorice, chocolate, Jaako? Molasses kisses, Jaako?" Then she'd giggle.

Finally the big Finn would find tongue. "No, no candy. Two pounds of dried prunes for my mudder dis time."

Sometimes when she handed him the bag and their fingertips touched, Jaako would tremble uncontrollably, trying to haul out the huge roll of bills in his hip pocket to pay her. He always toted a big roll, big enough to "gag a goat." Not ones either, but fives and tens.

So it went, day after day. Hardtack he bought, dried apricots, cookies from the bins, Nabiscos in the box, almost anything from the counters or barrels or boxes or shelves in Josette's domain. Sometimes he even forgot his change. Jaako had it bad.

As weeks passed, Jaako began to suffer less noticeably in his contacts with Josette. One day he greeted her with a real, "Good morning," instead of the usual monosyllables asking for merchandise. She mockingly scolded him.

"Say Good Morning, Josette," she commanded. "Me Josette; you Jaako. You Jaako; me Josette."

He could only grin fatuously, but from then on he found he could talk to her a little more, mainly on safe things like the weather. Every day he bought a little more and stayed a little longer. Josette was amused.

Just before Christmas, Jaako surprised her by asking her to put up a big box of the best candies in the store. When she teasingly asked who it was for, he answered that he had a new girl.

"This present for her for Christmas. You make it good. Kinds candy you like maybe. My girl, she's very pretty. Nice girl too."

It was the longest utterance she had ever heard from the big man. It almost sounded rehearsed. As she assembled and packed the candies, Josette tried repeatedly to find out who the girl was, but Jaako just shook his head, smiling. After he had untied the rawhide from his roll of bills, the roll that always made Josette's eyes stick out, and paid her, Jaako made his move.

He picked up the box, pushed it across the counter and said, "This for you, Josette. You my new girl."

Then he fled and Josette pursued him.

"No, Jaako, no. Take it back. I'm not your girl. I'm nobody's girl. Take it back. Take it back."

But he was out the door and away.

M.C. Flinn descended from his cashier's cage on the balcony. He was a small man with thinning hair and rimless eyeglasses that pinched a pinched nose on a pinched face. As always, he was rubbing his hands.

"Now, young lady, some advice," he said, sucking his teeth at each pause. "Smile at customers. Don't flirt. You and Jaako bad mix. Oil and water, young lady. Finn and French. Good advice. Back to work!" He had seen all and heard all that had transpired from the beginning. Flinn felt that Josette had the makings of a good clerk. She was pleasant and pretty. She was good for business. He didn't want her marrying that big dumb Finn and leaving. He decided to "nip it in the bud."

Before the girl had a chance to reply, Mr. Flinn had returned to his screened box on the second level. Josette was furious all day at both men.

At closing time, 8 P.M., she left to make the long walk down the hill to Frenchtown and home. Jaako was waiting for her with his horse and cutter.

"Josette," he called. "I give you ride home."

She threw the box of candy at his head.

"You big dumb Finlander. I wouldn't ride with you if you had wings!"

She stalked off down the road with the horse and sleigh and Jaako following, single file in the ruts. It was a strange procession there in the dark. Midway down the hill she gave in, climbed in the cutter and laid it to him so he could get it clear. Josette wasn't his girl and never would be. She detested him. The big dumb ox was only half civilized, had been in the woods too long, had hay in his ears and manure on his shoes.

Jaako heard her out, grinning to himself in the darkness, delighted with her fire and spunk, listening to her voice and not to the torrent of her words. He was in complete bliss with Josette beside him under the bearskin rug with the sleighbells going ching-ching-ching. He could wait. She'd get used to it, but Josette was his girl. Let her yak.

The remark about the manure on his shoes filtered through however, and Jaako responded with the old Finnish saying, "Manure on shoes; money in the bank." That set Josette off again, and she flayed him with her tongue all the rest of the way home. Just before she jumped out of the sleigh, Josette slapped Jaako across the face as hard as she could. It was like hitting a chunk of granite and his grin grew broader, remaining that way for days. Jaako had a girl.

The next few weeks were miserable for Josette, but fun for the whole town, as twice a day the housewives peered through their lace curtains to see the procession with Josette struggling up or down the street, (no one ever shoveled their sidewalks in winter) and Jaako's sleigh behind her.

Nasty little boys would run out to offer their advice. "Jump in, Josette. Get a ride, Josette. Jaako won't bite you." Josette countered by getting some of her young men to walk her home from the store, a strategy that Jaako solved by noting who they were and, as soon as was convenient, knocking hell out of them.

Pow! Pow! "Josette my girl," he would say as he looked at them down in the snow. "You stay away. Hear?"

Raoul DuBois, one of those most smitten by Josette's charms, had to be clubbed down three times before he heard, but by the end of the month she was walking alone.

Josette finally gave in. Hoping with sweet reason to do what she could not with rejection, she accepted the rides. Besides, she wasn't having any fun; besides, it was a long cold walk in the winter storms, and besides, Jaako was always bringing her presents. Some of them ludicrous—a big ball of string, fully two feet across, that he'd tied and wound from bits for many years. This too she heaved at his head. But there were also little necklaces and bracelets and bright ribbons in the packages he slipped into her hand every evening. And on her birthday there were three rolls of brightly colored dress cretonne or calico that he had taken the train to Ishpeming to purchase.

On their rides up and down the hill, Josette tried in vain to make the big man understand that she was not for him or he for her.

"I'm Catholic, Jaako, and you're Lutheran. I'm French and you're Finn. We can't ever marry. I'm nineteen and you're twenty-six. You're too old for me. You're a farmer and a logger and will be all your life. Me, I must go to the city as soon as I save up enough, and I got sixty dollars in the sock already."

She told him her dreams of a better life, of the glimpses her teachers and magazines had given her of something other than the little village in the forest.

Jaako listened happily and clucked to the horse. "I got money," he said. "I take you Chicago, Detroit, maybe Niagara Falls even, so you marry me. No hurry. Friends now, OK. Sometimes more later."

He bought her some skis and they travelled cross-country over the back hills and had coffee and korpua together on a Sunday afternoon. He even took her to a dance or two in Le Tour's barn though he wouldn't dance himself and sat glowering at any man with courage enough to take Josette in his arms for a polka or waltz.

As spring approached, Josette began to admit that she was becoming fond of Jaako. He was so good to her, so big and strong and yet so vulnerable and sweet. No matter how mean she was to him, no matter how she bedeviled him, he just smiled. Maybe, just maybe she'd give in. Only once in all that time had he ever made a pass at her, once when his hand sought her leg under the laprobe. She had hit him and scratched him good on the face. It was too difficult to get at her shoe. All Jaako had done was say, "Ah, good. You fine good girl, I know now for sure. I marry you sometime, maybe summer." She told him again that he was just a big stupid, awkward ox.

"Ya," said Jaako. "You my girl."

They were together so often that the town began to talk and sides were chosen as always; Finns against French, along lines of the ancient feud which always seemed to exist in our town. Up to then no intermarriage had ever occurred between the two factions. The Finn girls only dated Finn boys with the French Canadians sticking to themselves as well. Oh, there was Old Hokkinen who had shacked up one winter with the widow Coreau, but he was a bit nuts anyway and that didn't count. He probably did it just to keep himself warm because he hadn't cut enough wood that fall.

Josette and Jaako both felt this growing social disapproval soon enough.

"What you want to go out with that frog for, Jaako? Don't you do it!" said his mother after Untilla, the preacher, had brought the news out to the farm.

"French girls not for Finns. Never go sauna. Just put on more perfume stink. Don't trust frog girls, Jaako. They loose. You find good Finn girl like Aili, Work hard. Many children, boys too. French girls lazy, dirty. You hear? Forget frog girls now. "

Jaako just went out to the barn without a word, and the next Sunday when the preacher raised hell about the Pope and the Catholics worshipping idols in their church and incense pots and Saint This and Saint That, Jaako got red under the collar and did not shake hands after the service.

In her turn, Josette got a workout despite her claims that she and Jaako were nothing more than friends.

Once when Jaako came by her whitewashed log house to pick Josette up, old Maxime limped out on the porch with his shotgun and told him never to show his face around there again. He also laid it on the line with Josette. "You bring zat beeg square-head to my 'ome again an' me I tell you one theeng. You can pack your sack an' hack." Josette's mother pleaded with her not to see Jaako. He would beat her. Finns worked their women to death. They drank without finesse. They were dour and sullen. No gaiety, no civilite. When Josette next went to confession, Father Hassel scolded her and talked of purgatory. Even her Godmother, Tante Moulin, who had always been her confidant, was rejecting. "I would prefer for you an Indian before a Finn, ma fille," she said coldly.

This intense hostility from both sides served only to bring them closer together. Many long talks and hard questions followed.

Yes, Jaako would take instruction.

"Ok. I go your church and see priest and listen hard, but no promise. Ya, you go your church, I go mine, maybe."

"What about children?"

"What about the children?"

"You decide,"

And over and over again. Did Jaako really mean it about taking her to Chicago and Detroit?

"Ya, even get job dere if you want. Sell everyting."

By this time they were kissing and hugging when they were alone, though Josette had to teach him how to do both.

Unfortunately, it was hard to be alone. Someone always came by no matter how far Jaako drove down the logging roads, and then the tale always travelled all over town, getting better with each recounting. One Sunday afternoon when they first drove to Wabik and walked down the railroad tracks toward Red Bridge, they were followed by a pack of dirty little kids chanting suggestive rhymes. Jaako wanted to kill them.

Despite the walks and talks and the fun she had teaching Jaako to make love to her, Josette was still far from being absolutely sure she wanted to get married. After all, her money sock was getting bigger each week from the pay she got at the store.

"Not yet," she would tell Jaako whenever he brought up the now frequent topic of marriage.

"Maybe later. I get sick of this little town and want to go see something else. I love you but..."

Such talk always scared Jaako into silence.

Late in May, Josette asked Jaako why he never took her up to see his farm.

"You ashamed maybe?" she teased him. "After all, I should see where you want me to live."

"OK. We go now. All I show you. Everyting." he answered, slapping his horse with the reins.

Though the girl had heard that Jaako's farm was the best in the county, she was unprepared for the sight of the long fields, green with new oats and alfalfa, or the great white barn and the herd of Jersey cows that dotted the landscape behind it. The large house was painted a spotless white. Jaako drove directly to the front door.

"All for you someday, Josette." he said proudly. When they entered, he called, "Aiti, Aiti, (Mother), I bring for you someone to see." There was no answer, nor was there any answer when they went into the kitchen and saw her. The old lady, stiff as an icicle, had turned her face to the wall. Jaako's face turned beet red with fury and he muttered something like "Saatana" under his breath. Then, collecting himself, he turned to Josette and said, "OK, OK. Never mind her. She get over it. We go see barn."

Leaving by the back door, Josette noticed a long line of sheets, curtains, clothes and blankets, fresh washed and hanging still wet. It was a very long line. And when they entered the barn she noticed the long row of "cow holders", the V-shaped yokes that hold the cows' heads when they are being milked.

"How many cows do you have, Jaako?" she asked.

"Maybe twenty five, but only milking fourteen now," he replied.

"Who milks the cows, Jaako?" Josette's voice was very soft.

"Oh, my mudder milks dem, but she's getting to old."

That night Josette emptied her money sock, packed a little bag and caught the train for Detroit. She never came back.

The Chivaree

I don't know if you had a chivaree when you got married. You may be unfamiliar with the custom. In fact, I'm not even certain how chiv-a-ree should be spelled, but that's how it's pronounced. Perhaps it's a French-Canadian word.

Anyway, when a man married in Michigan's Upper Peninsula, he had to save up a little "raha" (the Finnish word for money), for blackmail or endure the miseries of a chivaree.

My father said that when he brought his new bride up to our forest village in 1900, he only had $1.85 left in his pockets. Since a keg of beer cost two dollars and the cigars and candy another buck, they (the men and boys who met them at the train station) took what he had anyway and decided to settle for only half the usual chivaree. That meant they only raised hell outside my parents' new house until 2 A.M.

When I got married some 30 years later, the custom had about died out, but I still got a taste of chivaree despite the effort expended in bringing my young wife to our old hunting cabin, nine miles deep in the forest.

I should have known what was coming when I found our bunk piled high with logs and a dead porcupine stuffed in the oven of the old wood range, but it was still a shock when the damnedest caterwauling I'd ever heard rent the silence of midnight. The grown friends of my boyhood pounded on the galvanized iron sheets of the cabin roof. Then they broke in the door and demanded pie and coffee, and a jug, and money.

"Chivaree... Chivaree," they yelled.

With my new bride weeping under the blankets, I gave them five bucks and the only bottle of booze I'd been ambitious enough to lug the nine miles up the woods trail in my packsack. We drank all of it up quickly there by the light of a kerosene lamp while they offered plenty of detailed advice on how to mate thoroughly.

I had known some of them since childhood; others were total strangers, but all of them confessed to having a helluva good time. When they finally left, my bride had only one thing to say: "Take me back to Iowa!"

My tale here however, concerns the chivaree of chivarees; the best - or worst - that ever took place in our village. It lasted for more than a week, night after night. The old men still talk about it as a classic.

On the back road to the abandoned mine lived a widower, Old Man Putinen, and next door to him an old widow named Aili Pesonen. Both were in their sixties and they lived alone in their log houses though they shared the same log barn for their two or three cows.

They had worked out an arrangement whereby Old Man Putinen delivered milk and butter to a small number of customers in town while Aili did the milking and churning. They also had some joint chickens and the old man delivered eggs.

It was a sensible economic arrangement, but it stimulated a lot of gossipy clack about how far the sharing really went. Even the preacher suggested, gently of course, that they might be wise to get married if only to put a stop to all the bad talk.

Aili and Putinen both rejected the outrageous suggestion immediately. They were just friends.

Old Putinen said he didn't believe in all that ceremonial stuff anyway with licenses and everything. Said he'd never bought a license in his life for hunting or fishing or anything else. Said he'd fathered seven children by his first wife without a license and was damned if he'd start now
with all that nonsense.

Besides, he said, he wasn't about to put out any good money on any damned chivaree.

Putinen and Aili were both known for being tight. She reportedly saved her coffee grounds, drying them and putting them back in the can until they were completely blond, even after she shook them.

She wore shoepaks to church and they tell of the time she asked the butcher to cut the cheese with the ham knife: "I dearly love the flavor of ham," she said. They were both very frugal.

The talking and innuendo continued nevertheless. Their good neighbors made certain they heard the worst of it. One of Aili's married daughters came home to beg her mother to become an honest woman. The preacher prayed obliquely about them in church. The pressure grew.

Finally, Old Putinen was seen taking the afternoon train for Marquette. Aili had boarded the morning train. The rumor spread all over town, they had finally run off to get married.

When they returned on the evening train they were welcomed by a large and motley group, all primed for a chivaree.

Aili and Putinen both denied however, that they had been married. They had just been shopping. He'd bought a new currycomb and some other stuff, which he displayed. She showed the material she'd purchased for a new huivee (a scarf used by old Finnish women to cover their heads). Old Putinen walked up the hill first. Aili tagged many yards behind. No, they weren't married.

They were just being tight.

OK, they got a chivaree!

That night the men and boys waited until the lights were out in the two log houses before the din began. They banged pots and pans. They yelled and laughed and sang. They made lewd remarks
about Old Putinen's sexual prowess on his wedding night. Kids ran their notched spools against the windows and door, making an ungodly racket. All was pandemonium for about an hour, the crowd going from one house to the other, not knowing for sure where the old couple was bedded down.

Finally, since it was very cold, way below zero, the crowd dispersed. The men went to Higley's Saloon to warm their outsides and innards. The kids went home. All vowed to return again the next night.

And they did, night after night in that terribly bitter cold, but always they returned in vain. No matter how hard the men howled or banged on the doors or pounded their cans, no one came out. No one protested. Only the wind howled back.

After a week of this fruitless partying someone devised another tactic.

"Smoke 'em out."

A ladder was brought and erected. Large cans were fitted tightly over the chimneys and smoke soon filled Old Putinen's cabin. He didn't emerge.

OK! The buggers were in Aili's house.

The men took the cans over there and swarmed up the ladders again to plug the chimneys. Again smoke filled the house.

Nothing!

The men suddenly became scared. Maybe they'd murdered the old couple with their foolishness!

They broke in the windows and coughed their way through the rooms, frantically searching for the corpses.

No bodies.

No one was in either house.

They went to the barn. There, in the hay beside the cows, all snug under a down-filled comforter, were the two of them, sleeping peacefully.

Old Putinen was awakened and did the speaking through a snag-toothed grin. "You boykas make goot music," he said. "We no married. I jest helping Aili make hay."

Flame Symphony

It always seemed that our town had more than its share of assorted nuts, eccentrics and madmen, but perhaps the impression stemmed only from their greater visibility.

In our little village, everyone knew everyone else and everything about everyone else and about everything that had ever happened to them back through at least three generations.

And so we weren't particularly surprised when, after an apparently normal childhood, Elsa Gustafson suddenly became a rooster at the age of 17, crowing up and down the street at dawn. After all, her grandfather had become Jesus Christ at 62 and a couple of her uncles had been "stashed away" in the State Hospital for the Insane at Newberry. It ran in the family, that's all.

Our town was very tolerant of such deviancy. Unless the mad one presented some real danger to himself or the rest of us, we simply humored and enjoyed his antics. It gave us something to talk about and besides, most of us realized that on sanity's yardstick we each oscillated up and down the scale at times. We were just glad that the yardstick was elastic.

And so, we always enjoyed the news that old Mr. Hokkinen had shot up his outhouse again. He did it twice a year; in the fall when the lake froze over and again in March when it looked as though it would never thaw.

He didn't know why he had to do it.

"Comes over me," he said and that explanation was good enough for us.

The Hokkinens had the "holiest" outhouse in town and the neighbors said that Mrs. Hokkinen used a pail in the woodshed instead of the outhouse at these crucial times of the year, emptying it on the garden. She raised the best strawberries in town! Mr. Hokkinen was harmless though, everybody said.

So was our "Montana Kid" who became a western cowboy at age 12 and stayed that way the rest of his life even though he never got ten miles away from the village. He was quite a sight as he rode his imaginary horse down the street. Each evening he would bring the family cow home to be milked, twirling his lariat and hooting up a storm. But harmless.

Well, not quite harmless at that, for once, when fending off some invisible enemy with his left arm, the Montana Kid had pulled out a pistol and put a bullet through his own wrist.

"Take that, you dastard!"

My father took the pistol as payment for patching him up and dressing his wound, but that was all.

It was kind of nice to have a real western cowboy from the wide open spaces riding his imaginary horse down the streets of our town. It kept back the fear of the dark encroaching forest that isolated us.

You had to be really howling-mad-dangerous before they sent you to the Newberry Insane Asylum. Most of the eccentrics among us just remained in town, giving us something exciting to talk or laugh about when winter shut us in.

Two of our odd ones, Elly Engstrom, the Norwegian girl, and Carl Anters, our town's mad genius, managed to find in each other the understanding that they got from no one else. How their lives were linked together and later wrenched apart is not a pretty story, but it does illustrate the difference between our tolerance and acceptance, and it sheds some light on that wide gray band that marks the boundary between sanity and madness.

Most people agreed that Elly, her real name, was Elin, was warped into her strangeness by an embittered mother after Leif Engstrom, Elly's father, had deserted the family shortly after the girl's birth. He just wandered away and was never heard from again.

There were tough times, but Mrs. Engstrom had weathered them, making a meager living weaving rag rugs and knitting socks and mittens to buy her necessaries. Leif had left behind a good house and barn, a pig, some chickens and a heifer or two. These, along with a large garden and the help of the neighbors, made it possible for the mother and girl to survive. They still had to work terribly hard though.

At night, when all the yellow panes of the windows of the other houses had winked out, the kerosene lamps in the Engstrom house were still burning and you could hear the thump-thump of the loom inside. Even when Elly was a little tyke she always seemed to be working in the garden or going around town begging discarded clothing. Any kind of clothing would do: overalls, rags, flour sacks, anything that could be cut into strips, sewn together and fed into the loom. All of us saved everything we could for the Engstroms. There were no Aid to Dependent Children or Welfare checks in that day, so we brought them fish and game and did what we could. We did our best to take care of our own.

The thing that really set Elly apart from the rest of us though, was her silence. A little girl in school, Elly rarely spoke aloud or even cried with any voice. She whispered or didn't speak at all.

I remember her coming to our back door with a pail of wild strawberries or blueberries she wanted us to buy. She would just stand there, silently holding out the pail, never answering when we asked her how much she wanted and taking whatever we gave her. It was the same when she came to collect the rags for weaving; she'd just hold out the empty clothes basket and wait there with her wide eyes on us and no expression on her little face. Elly never played with the other children after school, perhaps because they used to tease and call her "The Ghost." A strangeling!

Even when teased, she just looked at her tormentor, a long disturbing look, then quietly disappeared, sneaking off by herself. Her teachers said that Elly understood everything and did very well in her written work even though she wouldn't recite. She quit school in the middle of the fifth grade though, to help out at home, according to her mother's note.

Her nickname, "The Ghost," stuck even after she'd matured, partly because of habit and because she was always pale, but mainly because she was a night walker.

Except for the few stragglers from the saloon downtown or when some school or church doings lasted later than usual, our streets were deserted after ten o'clock. It was bedtime... That was when Elly walked, especially when there was moonlight.

Charley, the night watchman, might meet her anywhere on the streets: uptown, downtown, even "way back Swedetown," walking slowly, smiling her strange smile. When he spoke to her, Elly would smile or nod, then glide off. She had even been seen in some of the surrounding fields at night. "Spooky!" She was so spooky as to be quite safe in her roaming. Not even the horniest French Canadian would have made a grab at "The Ghost."

Elly was 19 when her mother died.

She came to our house early one morning and knocked at the front door.

"Mother sick," she whispered. "Mother sick."

Dad took his bag and went over to find Mrs. Engstrom dead.

After a simple funeral, which was paid for by the village and which Elly didn't attend, my father and mother went over to see the girl.

They found the house filled with flowers. They tried to talk with Elly, but conversation was impossible. Dad finally asked what she would do, now that her mother was gone. Elly just smiled and shook her head.

My mother tried to say the right things, but she got nowhere either. Elly simply didn't respond.

As they left, my dad laid ten dollars on the kitchen table.

When we got up the next morning we found a cornucopia of birchbark filled with snapdragons in the space between the screen and our back door. There was a short note written on the back:

"Please don't worry. I'll get along. E." And the ten dollar bill was in it too. Dad shrugged helplessly.

After breakfast he went up to the store and told Flinn that in the future he'd pay the difference between what Elly got from the rugs and mittens she sold him and the amount of her monthly bills.

Elly changed a little after her mother's death. Not much, just a little. For one thing, she began to bring us flowers in the daytime: at least once a week and she continued to do so for several years. She did the same for other families which had helped her. Some were wild flowers: arbutus, addertongue, trillium. Others were from her garden, mainly asters and snapdragons.

Elly spent a lot of time in her garden and several people reported hearing her talking aloud and even singing to the flowers.

Elly would sometimes manage a few sentences aloud, though in a very soft voice, when my mother went to see her garden or brought her some small gift; a comb or ribbon or such. Mother had hopes that she might eventually be able to bring Elly out of herself, but she had to confess that the invisible barriers were very very high.

"A strange child. No, a strange young woman now. Maybe only a man can gentle her," mom said.

"Not a chance!" snorted my father. "She's sort of attractive in a pale way, but Elly would scare off any boy even if she weren't so scared of everyone herself. Who'd want to fool around with a night walker who won't talk? No, there isn't a man in town who'd think of it."

My father was wrong.

Even before Elly's mother had died, one of the kids had reportedly seen her up on Mount Baldy at dusk, holding hands with Carl Anters beside a tiny fire. Carl Anters was our village's other night walker, our mad genius and the composer of flame symphonies.

No one knew the story behind Elly's strangeness, but all of us had an explanation for Carl's - "too much old maid aunt and too many brains for his head."

Carl had been orphaned when he was four. "Galloping pneumonia," they said, had killed both his parents. That was why he came to our town to live with our music and art teacher, his aunt, Miss Anters, who took out papers, adopted him, gave him her name and raised him as her own.

Not a good raising, we felt.

She babied him, protected him, controlled his every action something awful. Carl never got a chance to play with the other children. He always had to go straight home after school to practice at the piano. He never had to do chores or even go to the store like the rest of us. His aunt even chopped all the wood. It was a very unhealthy relationship, some thought. Enough to make anyone into a queer duck.

Miss Anters repelled any comment to that affect with a fury which we felt was way out of proportion.

"Carl's a genius," she insisted. "I tell you, a real genius. Just you wait and see and you just keep your nasty thoughts to yourself. I'm going to help my son fulfill himself even if I do have to live with nincompoops in this ignorant hole in the woods. Carl's a genius. He's not like other boys."

It was tough to argue with her on the genius thing. Carl was far and away the brightest student we'd ever had in school. He was reading books and had mastered arithmetic before he entered first grade so they stuck him in the third where he spent the whole year bored silly. He also skipped the fifth grade and the seventh and then finished high school in three years.

All the teachers were delighted to see him go!

Carl wasn't silent like Elly. He talked all the time instead and Carl asked the damnedest questions: questions that no teacher could answer without making an absolute fool of herself. Most of us kids couldn't understand him most of the time anyway because of the big words he used.

I remember feeling a little sorry for Carl once and so I asked if he wanted to go trout fishing with me. He refused.

"Unfortunately, Gage, I have only a miniscule interest in fish of any variety. I have studied something of ichthyology and frankly, the species has little pertinence to my goals."

I never wasted the time feeling sorry for him again…

I remember Carl in a physics class when our teacher was presenting some information about atoms and electrons. Carl stood up suddenly, awkward and ungainly, but highly excited.

"Ah," he'd said. "Ah! I discern here an apparent universal. The atom is a miniature solar system. If all matter is composed of atoms, then behold! I shall shatter a million tiny worlds full of a zillion tiny beings by biting off just this one fingernail. Behold, catastrophe! I am God." And he fled from the room, talking to himself.

Yeah, he was odd all right.

He graduated just before his fourteenth birthday and instead of giving the usual oration that the valedictorian was supposed to deliver, Carl insisted on playing an original composition he'd written for the piano. It was a real ten-gallon flop, though my mother, who was an accomplished pianist, declared the composition a tremendous achievement.

It lasted far too long for me and most of the audience. Before Carl finished, most of us were looking around at the ceiling, thoroughly bored with the banging chords and Carl's sizzling fingers, prancing up and down the keyboard. What got the audience most, I think, were his fancy head nods and final bow. We sat on our hands solidly and there were even a few boos. We were "Turkey in the Straw" people.

Some months after commencement, Carl came to our door.

"Doctor, sir," he'd said, "Miss Anters, my aunt, has suffered a cardiovascular insult, I surmise, with pains in her thorax and considerable respiratory distress. We would appreciate a professional visit to our domicile."

Dad went down to see her right away. She was having difficulty breathing and she wasn't surprised when dad told her she'd had a heart attack.

"I know," she said, gasping. "My heart is breaking, mainly because of my son, I think, Doctor. Ever since he graduated he's become almost a stranger to me. He hasn't touched the piano. Won't talk to me. He's gone. Walks in the woods, day and night. Says he has to think."

She fell back on the pillow, exhausted. Dad gave her some nitroglycerin for the angina pains and on the way out the door he had a talk with Carl.

"Your mother's very ill," he began, "and she may die. She's spoiled you rotten and waited on you hand and foot all your damned life and now it's going to be your turn to do a little waiting on, YOU chop the wood and YOU go after the mail and YOU go after the groceries. She is not to lift a hand. Understand?"

But Miss Anters died that weekend.

It was several years before we saw Carl again, and again he came to our house.

"Doctor, sir," he begged, "Please, may I have an opportunity to discuss with you an insight which has come to me? I desperately need to present it to someone with some educational and cultural background. Please, sir."

Dad was not one to suffer fools gladly, but he'd just eaten a fine meal with apple pie.

"All right, Carl. Come into the living room and tell us what's on your mind."

I remember some of what Carl had said, but it didn't make much sense then. In essence, he'd claimed to have discovered a brand new art form, one that combined painting and sculpture and music and much more besides. He told us that he'd learned how to build fires so that he could predict exactly every color and contour of the flames from one moment to another.

"I arrange my kindling so it will produce a prelude, shaping the main theme of my composition. I've even learned how to create a counterpoint effect. I've composed three flame symphonies already and I can do them every time - if I have the same kind and right kind of wood. That's the hard part, and also trying to invent a notation that is adequate. I've just got it started, but look here, Doctor."

Carl pulled out a large sheet that looked like a musical score except there were no musical notes on it, just a set of complicated squiggles so far as I could see. He excitedly explained what they meant.

"This one refers to a forked flame, that one to a flame having single apex, this symbol represents the color and duration of the flame, and that's for the sound..."

He also had symbols for tempo. It was far too complicated for me to follow, even though he quit using those big words as he became more excited.

"And these little dots on the score are sparks, Doctor. By using osage orange or sumac wood, I can create a wonderful fanfare of sparks at just the right time. Just think, Doctor, here is the poor man's art form. All he needs is the proper wood and a match and the designs I can give him and a score he can follow from first flicker to ember. I think I've found it. I think I've found my meaning at last. My genius, as I learned at that horrible commencement, is not in music proper, no matter what my aunt told me. I was destined for greater - things to be the inventor and first composer of fire symphonies. Oh, there's much I still have to learn before I can let the world know of my accomplishment. The first new art form in a thousand years!

Carl suddenly stopped talking and looked my father right in the eye.

"Am I crazy, Doctor?"

My father was polite, but after he'd ushered Carl out the front door, he made his diagnosis.

"Nutty as a hoot owl," he said.

My mother didn't agree and argued that maybe, just maybe, Carl had stumbled onto something. Dad just smiled.

No one ever found out just how Carl and Elly first became acquainted. Perhaps they met on one of their night walks. I'd like to think that she'd watched from the shadows while he composed, building one little fire after another with different arrangements of sticks, talking to himself and scribbling on a pad, trying to get the notation just right and that one night she had simply walked up and quietly sat down beside him, maybe with a flower offering.

All we really knew was that they were seen together in many odd places and always beside a little fire, never at her house or his, and always after dark. They seemed to have two favorite spots: up on Mount Baldy on any night when there was little wind, and inside the ruins of the old iron furnace smelter in the valley when the wind blew. Long-dead artisans had smelted ingots of pig-iron there using charcoal. It was a spooky kind of place and dirty, but its isolation and draft made it a fine place for Carl to work out his flame symphonies. No one would have seen a fire in those old ruins and it wasn't too far away either, just across the field and behind the saloon.

Some of the kids were curious enough about what was going on to sneak after the pair when they wandered at night, but they reported that nobody was getting any and that there wasn't much going on. Carl just played with the fire or talked and Elly just listened and smiled. Sometimes they held hands, but that was all.

I don't think the grown-ups had any idea that Carl and Elly had been meeting clandestinely at night for several years, until the saloon burned down and ended their idyll.

That was a real humdinger of a fire!

It was almost midnight when the scary cry of "Fire! Fire! Downtown. The Saloon," was passed up the hill, house by house, each man responsible for waking his neighbor.

Men came running down the hill, from everywhere, each carrying a bucket. Others were tearing open the doors of the little tin-sheathed firehouse, pulling the chemical tank cart out and down the street. Men were chopping holes in the side of the saloon. Some were manning a bucket brigade, passing pails hand to hand from the well next door.

There was smoke and flame and hollering. Men began breaking in the front door and carrying out furniture and things like mirrors and chairs, but then they began carrying bottles and whole cases of booze. That wrecked the bucket line immediately as each took whatever he could salvage. There was never such a fire - Never such a long drunk. Half the town was plastered for months.

And of course the building burned up completely. It was almost customary. Our "community center" was a total loss. Sure was exciting!

The next morning the constable took Carl Anters into custody. A hearing was held before the Justice of the Peace upstairs in the Town Hall because there seemed to be some real evidence that the saloon fire had been set. Some charred sticks of kindling smelling of kerosene were found near the smoldering remains of the shed at the back of the saloon and the nightwatch who'd checked the building at 11:30 said he'd met Carl at about that time carrying an armful of cedar sticks. He had asked the young man what he was going to do with the kindling and Carl had said he was going to build a fire.

The Justice of the Peace interrogated Carl just long enough to get him talking about his flame symphonies and then demanded if he had an alibi. Had anyone else been with him at about that time? Carl said yes, that Elly Engstrom and he had created another one of his symphonies in the old iron smelting furnace. He insisted that he certainly hadn't set fire to the saloon.

They brought in the frightened girl and asked her to substantiate the wild story. Elly couldn't say a thing, not even in a whisper. She was completely mute.

The verdict was the same as my father's had been.

In our town it was all right to be nutty so long as you were harmless, but not otherwise. They put handcuffs on Carl and took him away on the next train to Newberry and the insane asylum.

The next morning they took Elly away too. After the hearing, she'd gone slowly home, got a scythe, cut down all her flowers and then started doing the same to all the other gardens in town.

Whitewater Pete

In the North Country, no day is so fair as a warm Saturday in late September. The maple hills are mounds of scarlet and gold with just a sprinkling of green from pine.

I remember lying out in the sideyard for an hour on one such Saturday, watching a late bumblebee dusting his bottom on the nasturtiums. He didn't miss a single one and he never buzzed the same one twice. I was picking off some of the orange and maroon flowers, sucking the trumpet stems to see if `Ol Bumble' had left any honey. I was pleasantly surprised to find that he had when my mother reproached me.

"Son," she said, "Please don't pick those beautiful flowers. They'll all be gone soon enough. I can't see how they possibly escaped that last frost, but let's be grateful." Mother dreaded the terribly long winters when all the world was black and white and she had to scrape the hoarfrost from the window with her fingernails each morning just to let a ray of sunshine into the house.

She loved all the flowers except wild goldenrod and that she hated with a passion simply because, when it appeared in late August, it meant that our brief summer was coming to a close.

After her protest I knew I'd better leave the premises to do what I'd been postponing for as long as I could. Besides, Mother had a knack for putting an end to would-be mischief by finding some chore for idle hands. Lord, she might even think it was the perfect day for cleaning the chicken coop!

I crawled through the backyard fence and took the back road out past Sliding Rock to visit my friend Pete.

I always thought of Whitewater Pete as "My Friend" - In Capitals - and would often whisper the phrase to myself for reassurance at those boyhood times when I found myself rejected and alone.

Other people in town thought less of him. In their view, "Mr. Pete was just another of the old lumberjack burns left behind when all the pine had been cut and the logging crews moved west to slash hell out of Oregon too."

Mr. Pete had just been too old when it was time to go along.

He was well over seventy when I knew him, tall and thin, but very wiry and he still had that curious spring to his gait that characterizes most of the men who walk in the forest. They were cat-like, ready for anything.

Most people didn't know Whitewater Pete at all. He minded his own business, trapped some, hunted and fished a little, sawed wood and sold it when he could, or built

---

19

an outhouse, shed or barn for someone who needed help and could pay him a few dollars. He lived in a tight little shack he'd built along the river bank upstream from the village.

Whitewater Pete was very proud. He wouldn't accept charity of any kind and there were times when my dad had to invent work for him so he could make it through another winter without starving. About the only steady income Mr. Pete had was the fifty dollars he got each year for sawing and splitting ten long-cords of maple for the stoves of the Township Hall. And that was a lot of wood for an old man like Mr. Pete.

But Mr. Pete was frugal. Twice a year he went to M.C. Flinn's store and bought a yellow pail of Peerless Tobacco, a pail of lard, a side of bacon, fifteen pounds of dried beans, a lug of dried prunes, some tea and sugar... the necessaries.

Oh yes, and he always bought some hardtack too. I remember that very well because whenever I visited he would break off a small piece of a large black rye wheel, dust it with a pinch of sugar and hand it to me. Hard as a rock, but for an always hungry boy, very very good.

I wondered how Mr. Pete, who had no teeth, could possibly eat it and once I was brave enough to ask him.

"Ho, son," he said, "I just slurp it around in my mouth for a while and then I goom (gum) it. My gooms are so hard now I could bite off a man's ear."

And then he told me a wondrous tale of a fight he'd witnessed between two rivermen, Bad Sam and Bignose Jack, in which each had bitten off one of the other's ears. Mr. Pete sure had some good stories.

I was eight years old when I first met Whitewater Pete.

I was playing lumberjack and riverman in Half-Way Creek, building a logging dam against the flow of one of its springs and floating sticks down into its holding pond.

It had been several decades since the townspeople had seen the last river drive down the Tioga River which flowed through our valley, but most of the old logging dams along the stream could still be seen and I visited them often.

I'd heard the tales of great log jams that formed down at the gorge below our village and how the rivermen stationed every half mile along the banks would give the long "Ai-ee" wail from one to another, summoning help to join in the task of freeing the key log at great risk to their lives. I had even tiptoed along the old log booms that shunted the pine into the sluiceways of the dams.

On Fourths of july, I had seen birling matches where a lumberjack on one end of a log, by rotating it fast and suddenly braking it, would try to dump another jack into the river. I had prowled the remains of tumbled down logging camps, and their old horse barns, hunting for such treasure as a bit of chain or a broken peavey. At the High Banks, I had relived in imagination, the story about how the great piles of timber had cascaded prematurely into the river, carrying ten men to their death. It surely must have been a rough and romantic time.

Anyway, I was completely engrossed in building a dam to recreate the river lore in that tiny rivulet when I was startled by an old man speaking to me.

"No, son," said the voice. "You've got that boom all wrong. Hell, the logs would break through it that way. Look! Slant it down this way..."

And Whitewater Pete got down into the creek and the two of us spent the entire afternoon in fantasy. It was one of the best afternoons in my whole life.

Mr. Pete was an encyclopedia of information about the logging days. One story after another kept spilling from the corner of his mouth where he squeezed the black corn-cob pipe. By the time we had finished building the dam we were both so soaked that Mr. Pete invited me to his shack to dry out before heading for home.

I'll have to admit that the place was kind of ramshackle on the outside, but it was spotless inside.

Hanging on the wall behind the long stove was an axe, a great double bitted one, and a one-man crosscut saw, both gleaming in the shaft of sunlight from the door. Mr. Pete showed me how sharp they were, shaving the hair off his forearm with the axe and letting me feel some of the saw's teeth.

A good man keeps good tools and he keeps then sharp. Remember that, son!"

Then he showed me some other logging tools: a pike pole, a peavey, used to roll the great logs, and a curious device called a "Comealong" which Mr. pete claimed, enabled a single man to do the work of five. And Mr. Pete held up his river boots with soles studded with sharp spikes—he called them "corks"—which enables a man to keep his balance while riding a log down a roaring river.

For me, that little one room shack was thereafter a treasure house and I visited as often as I could.

Mr. Pete and I had another special place where we spent many hours together. It was at the river's edge on a blanket of soft brown needles from a great white pine which towered above us. It was `OUR PLACE.' Some of his best stories of the old logging days were told there, but we sometimes just sat on a little knoll beneath the great tree, our backs to its bark, in silence and complete contentment. It was nice and quiet.

When I spoke to most people I stuttered pretty badly, but I could talk to that old man with very little trouble.

For one thing he listened.

If I'd ask a question, he'd take out his pipe, blow a smoke ring, cock his head in serious thought and only then offer his considered opinion. He never talked down to me like most big people and he never looked away when I stuttered. We were man to man and Mr. Pete was my friend.

I remember having a hard time talking when trying to ask how come the loggers had left our one big pine there on the knoll when they'd cut all the other ones.

His faded blue eyes never left my face during all my struggle to get the words out and he must have seen my tears for after a long pause he said gruffly, "Every man has his own devil to lick, son. Mine was booze. You got to wrassle 'em down a lot of times before they gives up."

Then he proceeded to answer my question.

He said it was because the big pine leaned too far over the riverbank and, unless you had a good man to fell it, into the drink it'd go. Mr. pete showed me just how a real sawyer would have angled the "kerf" just right so that the tree, "could be laid out right along the river, pretty as a French girl."

He showed me where you'd make the bottom cut and how deep the notch had to be and how high up the other side the final sawing should be done to, "make the hinge you need." Then he paced off the riverbank to show where the cuts would be made on the fallen trunk.

Squinting up at the great bole of the pine, he said, "And that top log hardly tapers a bit, son. What we used to call a riding log, the kind a man could ride on down the river a mile."

And then Mr. Pete patted the old tree and allowed as he was glad they'd left this last one for us.

But this Saturday afternoon I'd been fooling around watching a bumblebee and sucking nasturtiums, trying to put off going to see Mr. Pete to tell him that they were planning to take him to the county poorhouse.

I had overheard my parents talking about it and when I went to the post office for the mail, Aunt Lizzie was holding forth as usual with her latest gossip.

"Yes," she said, in her nastiest nasal voice. "We've just got to do something about that old bum, Pete. He can't make it through another winter in that disgraceful shack. Doc says he has heart trouble and he hasn't any money and now that we're going to use coal in the Town Hall he won't get his fifty dollars for cutting wood. So how is he going to make it? He'd be better off down there with the other old folks, I say. Won't be so lonesome, I say. He's getting so he won't talk to anybody... anyways to me."

Aunt Lizzie relished the news she was peddling.

"Yes," she continued, "He won't want to go and we may have to get the constable to take him, but the old bum's going to be a town nuisance once the snow comes and, and, and, and..."

I also remember hearing mother protesting to my father, asking him why the old man couldn't at least have the right to choose, but I was crying too hard in the other room to know how he'd answered.

I had finally decided to go tell Mr. Pete myself so he could light for some other place. The thought of it emptied me, but I had to tell him.

I'd shaken all the coins from my horsebank for him. I had over six dollars, but it was sure hard to go over the hill to his shack.

The door was open and I saw Mr. Pete, filing his crosscut saw. He took one look at my tear streaked face and made it easy for me.

"I see you've heard the news, eh son?"

I nodded speechlessly and began to sob.

The old man waited until the storm had passed and then said, with a crooked half grin that lifted my spirits, "But I'm not a-goin' to that poor-house. No Sir, not old Pete. Old Pete's got plans."

He refused my money and we ate some hardtack and drank some tea.

I was comforted. Mr. Pete could handle anything.

But when I left his shack he gave me his whittling knife and that bothered me plenty. He told me to take it and carve him something good.

When I got home and talked to my mother about what I'd heard and what Mr. Pete had said, she was most understanding. She told me that my friend did have bad heart trouble, that he probably wouldn't be able to last the winter if he didn't have real care at the county home, that I should know that this was Pete's only hope of sharing another summer with me.

Yes, they were going to take him down to Marquette on Monday, whether he wanted to go or not. I saw her aching for me.

But mother was wrong and Mr. Pete was right. On Monday he was gone when they came after him. Some claim to have heard him giving the old "Ai-ee" call as he rode the log through the rapids past town and into the gorge where they found his body.

All I know for sure, was that our great pine had been felled along the river bank and that the riding log was gone... And that Mr. Pete's shack was empty... And so was I.

The Reformation
of Billy Bones

Most small villages have their town drunk. Ours was Billy Bones. I don't think Bones was his real name, but everyone called him that and it fit.

He was the skinniest man I ever saw, about six feet tall with long gangling broomstick arms. One almost expected to hear him rattle whenever he walked—or staggered.

Everyone in town liked Billy Bones. He was always smiling. Not a silly smile like most drunks have when they're half plastered either, but a big, warm broad-toothed one that lit up his whole face.

Billy Bones was always polite too, always ready to say, "Good morning, my friend," to any man he met or, with a wide sweeping circle, to doff his cap to every woman. Of course, he sometimes fell flat on his face when he did it, but his intentions were honorable.

Then too, there were a few of us who liked him because he'd discovered a way to beat the system, to live without having to work for a living and still be happy.

That wasn't quite true actually, for Billy Bones worked pretty hard, if you could call it work.

He toiled in dandelion time, in rhubarb time or in apple time, gathering the ingredients for the wine he made, gave away, sold and drank. Billy made the best wine you could get, everybody said. It tasted good and had a wallop that would make your ears dance, to say nothing of your belly!

Some claim he fortified it with moonshine he made in a still he had hidden back in Buckeye Woods. If so, no one ever located it and Billy denied its existence.

He made plenty of wine though.

And we kids used to help him, picking dandelions or hauling apples from the wild trees that grew along the edge of the clearing. We did it partly to hear him talk to himself or to hear his town-famous temperance lectures, but mainly because, if we helped him, he'd give us sugar to put on the rhubarb that grew in a big patch behind his house. In the spring, we had a hunger for that rhubarb.

I entered Billy's house only once when my dad had told me to take a bunch of empty gallon jugs to the dump. Billy's rheumy eyes lit up when he saw me hauling my wagon past his house and he begged me to let him have the jugs.

"It'll save me a mite, sonny," he'd said. "I'll just have to get them from the dump anyways."

The inside of his house was something to behold. Two walls were lined with shelves of empty crocks, jugs and bottles.

"I kerlect jugs and bottles," explained Bones with an enormous wink. "It's me hobby."

When I winked back, he took a huge key and opened a six-inch padlock on a half-door hidden back of a curtain behind the stove and told me to take a look into his root cellar. At least another 50 jugs were stashed in there and, judging from the smell, they must have been full. Some kegs and a whiskey barrel were hidden there too.

"Jest a swaller or two to get me through the summer," said Billy. "Sonny, I'm a rich man. Richer than M.C. Flinn, down at the store."

When I hinted that I wouldn't mind having just a taste of all the wealth Billy slammed the door shut fast, sat me down on a big tub and gave me the temperance lecture straight. I'd heard it before, not just from Billy, but from some of my friends who'd memorized parts of it.

"I've got somethin' te put in yer craw, my friend. An' I hopes it sticks like a pork-erpine kill (quill). Drink, my friend, is evil...E-vil! The Evilist Evil. Stay away. Don't ya ever take that first swaller or yer a gone goose. One bitty drap an' yer done. Ya know wot likker does in the belly? It eats. It eats yer gizzard. Jest chaws away, chaws away till there's nuthin' north of yer arse but an empty gut. Drink is E-vil! Don't ya take that first swaller."

That was just the beginning. There was more, much more, and by the time he finished he had to drag a jug out from under the bed and drained it.

"Jest a little medicine fer me bowels," he explained.

But he never gave me a drop; never gave any "ta kids er Indians."

It wasn't that Billy was always drunk, but that he was never completely sober. If you went by his cabin about breakfast time, he was usually sitting on the stoop in the morning sunshine, talking to himself.

"Well, Mr. Bones," you could hear him say. "Gonna be 'nother fine day. Yessir. 'Nother fine day. Ya don't look so ver' good and ya don't feel so ver' good, so have yer mornin' coffee, Mr. Bones."

Then he'd pour a tin cupful from a jug, stir it with a bony finger and keep sipping till the smile came back to his face. If it had been a hard night, Billy sometimes needed three or four cups of jug coffee before the world got rosy and the smile returned again. These, with some "booster shots" now and then throughout the day, kept him happy and most of us had to admit that he was the smilingest man in town.

One sight I always treasured was old Billy Bones sitting among the yellow dandelions in the schoolyard each spring, picking them and carefully putting them in a sack as he talked or sang to himself. Sometimes he'd get so happy he'd fling a whole bunch of dandelions into the air and you could hear him laugh as they cascaded down around him.

Another familiar sight was Billy Bones going down the street every afternoon at 4:30 to meet the train. He always hauled a faded red wagon behind him in the summer and a sled in the winter. Everybody knew that under the gunnysack covering the wagon was a jug or bottle that he sold to the trainmen, his regular customers. All of us entered the pretense.

"Going to the store, Billy?" we'd ask.

"Yeah, friend. Got to get me groceries. Got to get me groceries." And then the monstrous wink.

Billy always managed the downhill portion of the journey fairly well, walking stiffly as though following an invisible chalkline. Coming back was another matter entirely. If he'd sold all his dandelion, apple or rhubarb wine, all was well. If not, he went around giving free samples.

"A swaller for you, me friend, an' a snort fer meself."

On these days Billy and his little red wagon navigated an erratic course back up the hill. We'd see him stop every so often, close one eye and take a bead on wherever he wanted to go next, heading carefully for that spot, always talking to himself. Using familiar teamster's directions, you could hear him steering himself.

"Little more 'Gee' now, Mr. Bones." — (Go to the right!)

"Now a little more 'Haw' (to the left) and watch out for the tilt, Mr. Bones."

Once when he staggered and sat down, a bystander heard him say, "Danged town anyway, built their bloody sidewalks too close to me ass, they did. Goin' sue 'em! That's wot Mr. Bones'll do-Sue 'em!"

Somehow he always made it back to his house. Year-after-year that daily journey was part of the rhythm of our days.

So long as Billy stuck to his wine he had the system beat, but as years wore by, the trip back up the hill became more and more arduous. To fortify himself for the ordeal, the old man began stopping off at Higley's Saloon, buying a drink from the day's proceeds and cadging several more from the other boozers hanging out there.

They'd say, "Billy, give us yer temperance lecture and we'll buy you a drink" or "Billy, tell us about the time the bear got you up a tree."

That bear story was a dandy because Billy always acted it out as he told it. How he was a-walkin' down by Hek's spring when this she-bear took after him and how he jumped up and grabbed that branch and swung himself up and how the she-bear began a-drinkin' the liquor from the jug he'd dropped and... They say that nobody could put on a drunken bear act so "natural".

The more polluted Billy became the better he preached and acted. He got plenty of free drinks too. Some were even on the house.

They say that once when he was telling the bear story and showing how he'd jumped for the limb, Billy had grabbed the wagon-wheel chandelier and pulled it crashing down from the ceiling in a shower of plaster. Didn't faze him a bit. Billy didn't even pause.

"Rotten branch," he said, and went on with the story.

The heavier drinking unfortunately took its inevitable toll. The smile left Billy's face and he began to stagger worse. He mumbled rather than spoke. Somedays he missed his daily journey down the street. Some nights he never got home at all or the night-watch would find him sprawled in the snow halfway up the hill.

Always skin and bones, he was now just bones, a sodden scarecrow. The whole town felt bad about what was happening and my dad went down to the saloon and told the proprietor not to give Billy another drink or he'd see that he wouldn't get his license next time around.

"Hell, Doc, I'm not giving him nothing," protested the saloon keeper. "Billy's been drinking moonshine and Lydia Pinkham's Vegetable Compound mostly. Them'll kill anybody, take it enough."

We all figured he'd be a gonner before spring.

Then one evening toward the end of winter, I was over with my father in his dispensary admiring Mrs. Saavonen's tapeworm, which he had described at suppertime in spite of my mother's protests. (Dad really liked to share some of the more gory details of his medical practice at mealtimes.) He was telling me about it.

"These Finns from the Old Country like raw fish and even when they boil them they don't cook 'em long enough, no matter what I try to tell them. Well, Mrs. Saavonen's been doing poorly for some months now, getting thinner and thinner at the same time she's eating more and more, so I suspected what was wrong with her. Gave her a hell of a purge - a concoction of castor oil, calomel and a squirt of croton oil. Sure enough, fifteen minutes later there was the end of that tapeworm in her stool with more hanging out her tail. Well, I wanted to get the head so I just kept tugging at it, hauling it hand over hand like you pull in a pike on a line. Must be six, seven yards of it in that jar."

It looked to me like a long, tangled yellow-white noodle and I was about to ask if he'd got the head out too when someone screamed in the hallway and in came Billy Bones, flinging himself at dad's feet.

"Got to help me, Doc! Got to help ol' Billy. Got the snakes awful bad. Watch out, Doc! There's a red one a comin' over yer shoulder!" He screamed again.

Billy's eyes were as white as a scared horse's. He was shaking all over, jerking in stark terror.

I'd never seen delirium tremens before and I hoped that I'd never see anything like them again. Dad gentled the old man and gave him a shot of morphine. We hitched up the horse and took Billy to the jail in the Town Hall where the constable could keep an eye on him until he sobered up. The constable helped dad lay Billy on a cot. He was out cold.

Dad was quiet all the way back from the jail, but he kept biting his lip the way he always did when he was mad about something or when he was really determined.

Things began happening pretty fast the next day.

Legal or not, dad got some men to clean out every jug and bottle from old Billy's house. They hauled them to the dump and smashed them, but we later learned that they hadn't found the half-door to the root cellar behind the curtain.

Dad got Mrs. Jensen who took in boarders, including our preacher, to agree to give Billy a try-out.

"We'll sober him up and clean him up, but you and the preacher have got to 'feed him up' and keep him that way," dad said, paying her generously.

Then he marched over to Flinn's Store to try and persuade Mr. Flinn to give Billy a job as a delivery boy. It was a hard sell situation.

"You're crazy, Doctor," said Mr. Flinn when dad proposed the idea.

"That drunken old bum couldn't take an order, let alone deliver it somewhere."

"I promise you that he'll be clean and sober," said dad. "Let him go along with your regular driver at first. We'll get him dried out and I'll pay his salary."

That offer did the trick and Billy had a chance for a job and a fresh start.

Dad went to the ladies who ran the Methodist Ladies Aid and the Catholic Order of the Eastern Star to get them to organize what came to be called the "Billy Watch."

If any of their membership saw Billy Bones with his little red wagon or his sled, going after his "groceries" or staggering, or heading for the saloon or hanging around the depot, they were to round him up and take him back to the boarding house immediately. If he gave any of them any trouble, they were to get the constable to take him. Billy wasn't to go any further down the street than the schoolyard and certainly nowhere near the saloon or the depot. Dad was emphatic and hinted strongly that if any of them ever wanted his medical services in the future they had better cooperate.

Dad finally called on the preacher and the priest.

"Damned if I know what religion Billy belongs to, if any, but somehow I want you to get him started going to church even if you have to kidnap him to get him there. Get him on the wagon and save his bloody soul!"

They both laughed and promised to do whatever they could.

This done, Dad marched on over to the jail and proceeded to give Billy "blue-shirted hell."

He told him, in no uncertain terms, that he'd never save him from the snakes again, that he'd never get out of jail unless he swore never to take another drink. And there was a lot more. He told Billy what he'd done with his jugs and about the new life he'd arranged for him and then he left him in jail "just to think about it" for a week before going to see him again.

The whole town was agog and they did a lot of talking during that week Billy was in jail. Most were pretty pessimistic. So was dad, privately of course.

"Oh, I don't really have much hope," he said "but that poor old fellow ought to have one chance anyway. Maybe the town can pull it off. We'll see."

And we saw. There were miracles still in the land and the reformation of Billy Bones was one of them. Oh, there were some pretty shaky moments at first and a few times when the "Billy Watch" had to go into action, but it soon became apparent that Billy was really changing his ways and becoming a new man.

For one thing he was eating right, probably for the first time in his life, and his job brought him into all the better homes of the community where he found great interest and approval and encouragement for the change that was occurring. Everyone asked him how he was doing and they all smelled his breath to make sure.

"Not a swaller," he'd tell them proudly. "Haint had a swaller o' likker since I quit. Old Billy Bones knows better now. Not goin' take that first drop neither, no sirree."

Billy had become sort of a civic project.

Basking in the glow of our acceptance and interest, Billy bloomed. Pink returned to his cheeks, fading the purple from his nose. M. C. Flinn fired the other driver and let Billy take the orders and make the deliveries all by himself - at smaller wages than he'd paid before of course. Flinn's only complaint was that Billy took longer enroute than he should have. Everybody knew why though. Billy couldn't just take an order and leave. He had to pass the time of day, had to do a little preaching on the e-vils of drink and he had revised and improved his old sermon by personalizing it.

"Yep, friend, jus' look at old Billy Bones here now an' 'member how he wuz-Jus' a old bum, stinkoed up day 'n night, a lyin' in the snow so snockered couldn't even git up, a-fearin' them snakes an' goin' ta jail. The e-vils of drink, my friend. Don't you never take that first swaller."

He often let one of us kids make his rounds with him and he'd lecture us all over town.

Billy also got religion real bad. After visiting both the Catholic and Methodist-Episcopal churches, he chose the latter.

Perhaps he was influenced by his fellow boarder, the preach mainly, according to Billy, "Because them Mefordists holler louder and lay it on me stronger-like."

Billy never missed a church service or a Men's Bible Class. He liked going. Liked being dressed up. After a couple of months he even joined the church and got baptized, an experience that affected him greatly.

"Been washed in the blood of the lamb, friend," he'd tell anyone who'd listen. "Washed clean as the driven snow, friend. Ol' Billy's bin saved."

One Sunday, Billy came to church in a brand new blue-serge suit, clean as a whistle from a long Finnish sauna the night before, and very solemn. He was to take his first communion.

When the old organ began to shake the church and the choir sang,

> "Break Thou the bread of life
> "Dear Lord for me
> "As Thou didst break the loaves
> "beside the sea,"

the tears began rolling down Billy's pink cheeks as he and several others walked slowly up front and kneeled on the step below the altar to receive the sacrament. He wept even more when the preacher intoned the ancient words of comfort:

"Ye that do truly and earnestly repent of your sins, and are in love and charity with your neighbors, and intend to lead a new life..."

The service droned on until the preacher broke the bread and put it to Billy's lips and gave him the cup of wine, saying, "Drink this in remembrance that Christ's blood was shed for thee, and be thankful."

Billy hesitated for only an instant.

He didn't go back to the boarding house after church and he didn't show up for work at the store next morning. Billy Bones simply disappeared. No one ever saw hide nor hair nor bone of him again.

Oh, someone said that someone had told them that someone had seen an old bum lugging a packsack and a jug up the railroad tracks way over by Nestoria, but whether it was Billy Bones or not we never knew. The great forest that hugged our village had swallowed up more than one of those who had wandered in it drunkenly. Most of the people in town figured that was what had happened to poor old Bones. It was too bad.

The truth often provides a miserable ending for our personal tales even when they seem to be ending happily and this was probably the case with Billy Bones. So I deliberately made up another ending for the story because I didn't like the probable ending. I've told it over and over and over again until even I believe it. It goes like this:

Billy didn't go back to the boarding house after church and he didn't show up for work the next morning either. Instead they found him in his old place in the schoolyard, sitting in a patch of yellow dandelions with an empty jug beside him.

"Yep, friend," he said, flinging a dandelion over his shoulder happily, "Like I allus say, don't you ever take thet first swaller. For drink, it is E-vil!

Bats

Long before I read "Dracula" or explored some of the caverns of Kentucky, I was fascinated by bats.

Every summer evening about dusk the air would be full of them, swooping and soaring in blurred circles as they fed on mosquitos that infested the little town where I lived as a boy.

My friends and I tried to catch them by flinging our caps high in the air. Only one did I actually catch, doubtless a deaf one, for their sonar is incredibly efficient. We kept it out in the barn for a week in a screened box, hidden secretly, for my mother and grandmother were deathly afraid of the "critters." My father didn't like them either. He said they had rabies.

The bat I had was a quaint little creature, covered with fur, (and a few lice), except for black leather wings. His face was like that of a tiny human and when I held him, I could feel his heart throbbing so fast it seemed to buzz. He wouldn't eat the houseflies or mosquitoes we caught. He evidently had to catch them on the wing, so he died. For two minutes I grieved deeply for my little friend, Oscar.

As I mentioned, my grandmother Gage was petrified by bats. She loved to sit out on the front porch in the evening and watch the children, the buggies going by or Old Billy Bones staggering home from the tavern. She'd cluck her tongue at him, call us to her side and give us her temperance lecture.

"See that man, children?" she'd say. "He'll come to a bad end. That likker is eating holes all over his insides right now. Mark my words, now, someday he'll spring a leak and all his giblets will come oozing out of the holes."

We used to follow Old Billy, hoping to witness the puncture, but it never happened. He just disappeared on his way home from church one Sunday.

When the bats started flying near the end of July, grandma Gage no longer dared sit on the porch. Neither did my mother. They were afraid the bats would get in their hair. "Bats always go for a woman's hair," Grandma said, "They lay eggs in it."

Once she tried wearing the long hood with the isinglass peepholes that we used when the temperature went down to 30 and 40 degrees below zero. The hood was just too hot and she had to be content with peering out the bay window. This made her so irritable that we had to be very careful whenever we got near her.

Grandma was the sweetest old lady in lavender and lace that ever graced a rocking chair, but she had one little eccentricity. She liked to stick needles in the hind ends of

---

anyone who came within striking distance when she was sewing. Then she'd chuckle to herself for hours. I should tell you about the time the preacher… but back to the bats.

Occasionally, really very rarely, a bat would get into the house. Then pandemonium! My father would get the broom and start swinging, getting madder with each miss. The women would scream and throw something over their hair - anything. I remember seeing my Grandma's legs for the first time when she pulled up her long skirts and ran from the room, looking upside down. Another time she tried to burrow under the rug, and I remember hoping the bat would try to go up her pantaloons. It was always very exciting.

Finally my father, exhausted from his efforts, would yell at them to shut-up, insisting that bats didn't get into women's hair, that it was all nonsense, that he'd wait until daylight and then he'd pick the damn thing off the ceiling or wherever the bastard went to roost. More screams and tears and profanity.

Very, Very exciting - almost as good as the Fourth of July. I remember leaving the woodshed door open some evenings in the hope that a bat would enter.

The morning after one of these encounters, while the women still lay abed with the sheets over their heads, it was our job to make a complete search of the house. Supervised by father, and with a dime reward to the kid who first spotted the little beast, we usually managed to locate the bat. We never did find it hanging from the ceiling. It never made any sense to me that it might. There was no toehold. It was usually hanging upside down from the upper corner of a door frame or one of the windows.

Father would kill it, the women would get up, and finally we had breakfast. There was just one time when the bat completely disappeared. We searched and researched that house, basement to attic, but no bat. There were no open windows through which it might have escaped. No one had opened the door. It was in the house! A long hunt and a longer night followed. We looked again for it next morning.

Everywhere.

No bat.

Finally my father went to the bedroom, threw the covers off my trembling mother, commanded her to get the hell downstairs and make him some breakfast. He should have been at work two hours before. She wept and shook all through the meal. My father felt some remorse at his roughness, but he was "full fed" by this time.

"Now look, dear," he said with an enormous patient sigh, "Let's be reasonable. That bat will not get in your hair. Bats don't get in people's hair. They sleep all day. They will not move all day. I'll try to find it again after I get home at noon. Let me say it again - BATS DON'T GET INTO PEOPLE'S HAIR." He left the house.

When my mother finally stopped sobbing and shaking, she went to my grandmother's room while I eavesdropped in the hall. I heard my father's argument all over again as mother tried to persuade Grandma to come out from under the covers. "Bats don't really get in people's hair. They sleep all day. He'll kill it when he gets home. Bats don't get in people's hair." Well, Grandma did get up eventually and had her breakfast, though she wore a kerchief. I went out to play for a bit and when I returned, my mother and grandmother were getting dressed to leave.

"We'll be back in an hour or so," my mother said. "We have to go see Mrs. Duggan, poor thing. She's ailing and I'm fetching her some broth."

"Yes," said Grandma, "and we're getting out of this bug bat-house."

She went into the hall, put on her hat and let forth with the scream of screams. The bat was in her hat.

Mrs. Murphy Gets A Bath

It was after 4:00 p.m. when my father stumped heavily into the house and dropped his two black bags; the pill case and the instrument satchel, on the floor.

He wrestled out of his heavy beaverskin coat and hung it with the black fur hat on the hall tree.

"Cully," he said to me, "I'm bushed. You'll have to unharness Billy from the buckboard and feed and water him. Give him an extra scoop of oats. He's had a rough day too. He's out front."

I was glad to do it because it gave me a chance to drive around to the barnyard. I never usually handled the reins unless dad was with me. I was only twelve. That afternoon the old horse was so tired that I had no trouble with him at all except when I went to back the buckboard into the carriage shed. Billy wanted to go to the stable right away, buckboard and all, but I finally managed to get him unharnessed.

I unhooked the tugs and led Billy into the big box stall, but not until I'd removed the bit from his mouth and put on the halter. It's tough trying to put a halter on a horse when he's eating oats, but you can take off the harness and horsecollar all right. I had to jump though to put these up on their hooks, high on the wall. I climbed up into the hayloft and pitched down an extra big pile of hay through the hole in the ceiling of the box stall. I had to pump and carry five pails of water before Billy was satisfied and ready to let me rub him down.

When I returned to the house, dad was in his Morris chair with his feet up on the hassock, talking to my mother. He was making entries in a little black notebook.

"Did pretty well today, Edith. Took in $23. Of course, fifteen was from Einer Pesonen for that breach baby case two years ago. He was out by the road at Halfway Creek and had the money in his hand. Said he'd just got paid for a carload of pulp."

My father never sent out a bill in his life, but he recorded all the money that was owed him in the pages of that little black notebook and he knew who hadn't paid.

I remember that he'd once pointed to a grown man walking up the sidewalk in front of our house.

"See that bugger? He's not paid for yet!"

But he never dunned any of his patients. He served a territory as large as Rhode Island, most of it wilderness, and it seemed to us that he was always tired.

Dad certainly was that day for he'd been out half the night on a baby case. He'd just leaned back in his chair when there was a knock at the front door.

"Another damned wart," he growled. "Why don't they come at office hours? If it's old lady Pascoe with her usual Monday afternoon headache, I'll give her short shrift!"

But dad's face lit up when he opened the door. It was Father Hassel, the Catholic priest, hoping for his weekly chess game, a stout glass of whiskey, a good cigar and some good conversation. In the barren wilds that both of them served, educated people could be counted on one hand. The need to share insights above the bread and butter level was almost a craving.

So whenever they could manage it, my father and the priest got together. Sometimes dad would go down to see Father Hassel, but more often the priest came to our house, hopefully he teased, to convert my father away from his avowed agnosticism, but mainly to escape his parish duties and his housekeeper for the procession of priests who served our village. Not that Father Hassel was very vulnerable... He was about sixty, red cheeked, white haired and did his utmost to serve his people.

It was said that he didn't holler much about purgatory or pass out tough penances or ask for more money than the French Canadians and Indians who came to Mass or confession could spare. Dad and Father Hassel had met often at the bedsides of dying patients, had ridden cabooses to far away junctions and they had genuine respect and affection for each other.

One of the house rules was that when Father Hassel came to visit we had to clear out to the kitchen so they would be undisturbed in their chess game and so they could speak freely. I used to like to hear them talk though, and would often sneak up the back stairs and tiptoe down the front ones to sit on my dad's bed behind the curtains where I could listen. On this particular occasion they were talking about old Bridget Murphy who lived uptown in one of the mining company's old houses.

"Father," said my dad, "You've got to do something about Mrs. Murphy. Yesterday her neighbors heard her cow bellowing, probably because it hadn't been milked for some time, and after they looked in on her they called me. She was moaning and a bit bloated when I went in. Bowels hadn't moved for almost a week, she said, and she was sure she's going to die. I gave her castor oil and calomel and she'll probably be all right in a day or two, but you'd better go see her.

The priest nodded.

"I'll go up after supper," he said, "even though she hears only one Mass a year at most and comes to confession only when there's an eclipse or something. Which is all right with me, Doctor. The only sins she ever confesses are thirty years old and she uses my time to revel in her old memories of fornication. But I'll go see her."

I grinned, hiding there behind the curtains. I knew what that meant.

Old Bridget Murphy was a true character in a village filled with them. She was loud and profane and we boys used to like to go sit on her porch on a summer afternoon to hear her tell of the glorious "loving" she used to get from her late husband, "Misther Michael Murphy, God rist his black sowl."

The old woman would sit there in her rocker, always wearing a pair of faded scarlet shoes, rocking away and chuckling evilly as she told her tales. It was educational.

"Ah, me late husband, Misther Michael Murphy, he was a man," she'd say. "That he was, that he was. A hard worker, he was, and a fighter to be sure and when the whiskey was in him, a mean divil, but ah me bhoys, he was a booger in bed. He'd grab me, he would, and nail me a yellin' to the floor. That he would. Sivin times in a row once. Sivin, I tell you and I felt ivery last one a shakin' me teeth. Did I ever tell you bhoys 'bout the time...?"

Of course she had, but she told us again and again anyway. Mister Murphy must have indeed been quite a man.

Bridget Murphy also liked to sing and she taught us some noble bawdy ballads... And woe to the youth who took his girl past her house when old Bridget was on the porch. Keeping time to their steps, the lewd old woman would chant in a voice you could hear a quarter mile away, "Take down yer pants, Colleen, and give the bhoy a chance. Take down yer pants and give the bhoy a chance." How embarrassing!

Sometimes, on St. Patrick's Day she'd paint a bright green stripe around the back of Paddy, her pet pig. Sometimes she painted its hind end a bright orange. Bridget liked color. She always had a red geranium in her window, summer or winter.

My father continued, "Well, now," he said. "I'm not concerned with the old girl's bloody soul or sins, or even her health, for all that matter, but in all my life, Father, and I've been in some pretty terrible homes, I've never seen such a dirty place or such a dirty old woman. Why, I could hardly bear to lift her nightgown to palpate her abdomen. Father, she's a crust on her so thick it almost shines. And the stench! I've got a strong nose, Father, but I could hardly wait to get out of there. I'll bet she hasn't bathed for years. You've got to give her a bath, I tell you. And clear out and clean out that whole place. That damn pig of hers was in and out of the room constantly and, God help me, so were the chickens. I had to shoo away one old hen that was roosting on the headboard. It's terrible.

The priest moved his Queen's knight to the Bishop's fourth and puffed his cigar thoughtfully.

"The Irish do not have the same feeling about dirt as we do, Doctor. I know she smells pretty high. Had to aerate the confessional last time she came. But surely this is your province as the health officer and not mine."

Dad moved a pawn up to challenge the knight.

"Do you want me to sic Aunt Lizzie and the Methodist Ladies Aid on poor old Bridget and shame all the good Catholics in this town who ought to be taking care of their own?" dad asked. "Aunt Lizzie would love the job and so would all the other Protestant women."

"You're right, Doctor.

"Check!

"I'll talk to Mrs. LaFon and see if the Sisters of St. Mary won't tackle it. But if I know Bridget, we may have to call you to anesthetize her so we can get her in the tub - if she has a tub, which I doubt. And besides, she's sick, isn't she, Doctor? Could she stand the shock of such a bath? And if she could, what about the pig and those chickens? If I know old Bridget, she'll go right back to her old ways.

"Check again."

"Tell you what we'll do," my father said, moving his King out of danger. "I'll tell Bridget that she's very sick and in danger of dying and that she has to go to the hospital in Ishpeming immediately. They'll give her the bath of her life there and you can even administer the last rites before she goes if you want to. Bridget's really not that sick, as

I said, but that'll get her out of the house so I can get some men to fix up the barn and pig and chicken house. Bridget says the only reason she lets the pig and biddies into the house is because the outbuildings are so cold and drafty now with winter coming on so fast.

You get your women to clean that house from top to bottom and I'll take care of the rest. Have you ever been in her house, Father?"

The priest shook his head.

"Well," said my father, "all the buildings are inter-connected. Mike Murphy bought that company house when the mine shut down, added a woodshed to it, added a log barn to the shed and there's where Bridget keeps her cow, added a pig house to the barn, and ended the string with a chicken house. They're all connected, though there are doors for each part. Seemed like a good idea in this land of forty below winters. Anyway, that's why the pigs and chickens come into the house proper. I wonder that the cow hasn't!"

The next few days were busy ones with dad supervising the men repairing the outbuildings and Father Hassel overseeing the Sisters of St. Mary as they cleaned the house. Dad grinned when he got the phone call from the hospital.

"Well, Bridget's had her bath," he told my mother. "The nurses down there say they won't ever forgive me. They found a slight impaction in the bowel, but nothing serious and the old gal's all right now and yelling to come home. By tomorrow everything should be spic and span. The barn, pig shed and chicken coops are all as tight as a drum. What a job! Good thing it's only the first week in November. Bridget and her brood should be snug all winter."

Two days after Mrs. Murphy returned home, Father Hassel knocked on the door early in the morning.

"Doctor," he said, "I'm afraid our good deed has had an evil ending. The shock of that bath and the clean house were probably too much for Bridget to take. Her neighbors say there's no smoke coming from her chimney and the door is locked and nobody answers their calls. Will you come up with me, please?"

When my dad returned, mother ran to the door.

"Is it true? Is the old lady dead?"

Dad shook his head ruefully then roared with laughter.

"No, Bridget's fine. She told us she'd got to feeling too lonesome for her pig, Paddy, and all her biddies. We found her wrapped in blankets out in the barn with her cow and pig and chickens all around her, and she was happily smoking an old corncob pipe. Said she couldn't bear to dirty up that nice clean house... Hell, you can't ever get the best of the Irish!"

U.P. Bakkaball

There was very little to do in our small forest village during "the long white," those nine months when snow and ice covered everything. Hunting and fishing stopped when the deep cold set in and great drifts smothered the land. But we did have bakkaball (basketball). The Finn kids never seemed to be able to handle the pronunciation of the *'sk'* sound although they could put it together pretty well in one of their favorite epithets "buskan hosu" (shit pants).

Anyway, football and baseball were strictly summertime things diddled at by little kids, but of very little importance. Bakkaball was our serious sport.

All of us played bakkaball. We played in the snow until it was packed down solid. It never did get hard enough to dribble on, not that we ever had a ball that anyone could dribble with anyway. We 'created' our own balls, rolled-up burlap bags tied with a string, a ball of rags some mother had planned to use for weaving a carpet... In a pinch we used ten-inch snowballs, packed tight, but these weren't very permanent and when you caught a teammate's pass it usually knocked you on your tail. Once we used a blown up pig's bladder, but it was too light to go through the potato-basket hoop nailed to the barn door.

Our games rarely had more than four players and more often only two. It was one-on-one and devil take the hindmost. No referee! No fouls! We took turns throwing the ball up in the air and then fought like wildcats in the snow until somehow the "ball" went through the hoop. Then we threw it aloft again and fought some more.

Slug, bang, slash; get the ball anyway you could. Body contact? Of course! Knock him down and wrestle the ball away. There was only one thing you couldn't do: no fair kicking in the crotch!

We played bakkaball even when it was thirty below. We sometimes even got up a sweat running around in our heavy clothing and swampers. As I remember, there wasn't a lot of team play even when we chose up sides. Oh, you might occasionally pass the ball to a teammate if you knew some opposing player was about to knock you down, but otherwise you tucked it under your arm and charged over your opponents until you got close enough to the barn door to have a chance to shoot. Without referees there was no one to toss the ball in the air after a basket was made so the opposing jumpers held the ball jointly as the rest counted - one, two, three and then they were supposed to toss it straight up. No one ever did and we had more good fights as a result of those jump balls than at any other part of the game. It was mayhem in the snow. Finn kids, Indian kids, French Canadian frogs; we all played bakkaball throughout the winter.

The only ones who played bakkaball indoors were members of our town team. Each of the villages had a team of big men in their twenties or early thirties - lumberjacks, miners, farmers - all with monstrous muscles. They had no gym suits, but played instead in their long winter underwear, red or dirty white, in the large meeting room of our Town Hall. How they could bear to practice once a week and play once a week after their terribly strenuous labors each day was beyond my comprehension. Perhaps bakkaball provided the only opportunity to fight like hell, legally. All of us kids, used to sneak down to the Town Hall to watch them practice and, if we could manage an extra ten cents which was seldom, we'd go to see them play some team from another town.

Play?

It was slaughter!

At these team games there was always a referee, a very brave, or very stupid, or sometimes just half-drunk fellow. No man in his right mind would want to take such an assignment. I remember one referee throwing up his hands and quitting on the spot after getting knocked down twice, first by a member of one team and then by someone from the other. The referee had failed to recognize the limits of his authority and made a mistake by calling a couple of fouls. Referees were there to throw jump balls, not to call fouls. After they'd heaved him out an open window into the snow the game continued with a new referee shanghaied from the crowd of onlookers. They had six referees that night.

Many of the games were never completed, but ended in a gang fight always won, if that's the word to use, by the home team and their loyal fans who had broken through the chicken wire barrier that separated the stage from the playing floor.

The hall had a low ceiling too, so no one ever arched a shot. The players aimed directly at the basket, expecting to miss it, but hoping that someone could put the ball through from the melee beneath the hoop. They took that first shot from the far end of the floor, shooting the ball from between their legs, then rushing in to clobber the nearest opponent.

Hazardous to the health too was the big pot-bellied stove at one side of the playing floor. The men made a wide dribble around the red glow of its cast iron hulk if they could and there were four men stationed nearby who were supposed to heave back any player who might be flung against it. The guards often failed in their duty when it seemed pretty certain to be their asses that got burned. They'd flinch or step aside at the last moment and you'd hear the agonized howl of a roasted half-breed Indian or a broiled Finn.

And another brawl would always begin whenever that happened...

Our town constable, Charley Olafson, was six feet tall and three feet wide and he came complete with silver star on his massive chest. Charley usually did his best to maintain some semblance of order or at least prevent murder at those games and most of the time he succeeded to some degree.

A very strong man, Charley would pick up a combatant in each hand, lift them from the floor and bang their heads together. He always felt bad when he had to do it twice. He prided himself on being able to get it right the first time. Charley was a man of peace. He just wanted to render people helpless, not unconscious. He wasn't always able to do so, though. When eight or ten men were slugging it out with each other at the same time, Charley regretted only having two hands.

I remember one real bad riot vividly. The other town team had come with a sizeable contingent of burly supporters and they hogged all the best seats on the stage behind the chicken wire next to the basket. Our team was ahead by just a few points when one of their fans began aiming his miner's carbide lantern, one with a big bull's-eye lens, right into the eyes of our players every time they were ready to shoot. All hell broke loose. The chicken wire was ripped down and the whole place became a madhouse of fighting men with me and the other kids cowering bug-eyed in a corner.

Out came Charley, this time with gun in hand, and he fired a shot through the open window to get their attention. "What's the trouble, boys? What's the trouble?"

Our team went over to answer his question. They took away his gun, pitched it and Charley out through the open window and returned to the fray. I don't know who won because I ran home. That's how they played bakkaball in the U.P. when I was a boy!

Civilization Comes
To Our Town

Culture, 'with a capital C,' came to our forest village in the lissome form of Miss Lorelie Young, the new English teacher.

Miss Lorry was from Boston and fresh out of Bryn Mawr or some other eastern finishing school.

How she happened to end up in our town I never found out, but I know that she, an incurable romantic, was hunting for adventure out west among the cowboys and Indians and such.

We had Indians and half-breeds, all right, but the closest thing to a cowboy she ever saw was me riding Billy back from duck hunting on Splatterdock Lake with my shotgun slung over my shoulder. Miss Lorry didn't seem to mind that ours was not the Wild West of her dreams. It was wild enough with bears coming into town to raid the apple trees and the wolves chasing deer on the hills behind the schoolhouse, shattering the night air with their howls. To her, everything was primitively fascinating, completely different than anything she had ever known.

Miss Lorry said she had travelled extensively in Europe and even to Egypt, but that she'd never seen anything like this. Intensely curious about how we lived and completely unafraid, she immersed herself in our activities.

All us high school kids, boys and girls alike, fell in love with Miss Lorry almost immediately. A strange white being from outer space had come to our town and wanted to know how we lived. We told her and showed her and she in turn told us of life in the big city and foreign lands... Not that there wasn't some testing.

The Finn girls parboiled her in a sauna, made her whip herself afterwards with cedar branches and jump naked into the pond. They showed her how to churn butter and grinned when her arms almost broke from pushing the plunger up and down. The Indian girls taught her how to make a moccasin out of deer hide by chewing the leather until it was soft and supple. The French Canadian girls taught her bawdy French songs and took her to Mass and into their homes to eat crusts smeared with bacon grease instead of butter. She even learned how to milk a cow.

The high school boys gave her a few rough times before surrendering to her charm and enthusiasm. I remember a nature hike she sponsored after school to gather material for an English theme. About 15 of us boys and girls, but mostly boys, took her past Sliding Rock, had her climb the rock face of Mount Baldy along the ledges, jump ditches, hop on clumps of saw grass across a swamp and go through the tangle of a cedar swamp to get to Fish Lake.

Scratched and soiled, Miss Lorry loved every bit of the ordeal and squealed like the other girls when we boys stripped and took a swim.

On the way back along a well trodden path, she asked about everything; the names of the trees and shrubs and flowers, how you snared rabbits, the habits of grouse.

Was it true, she asked, that you could boil water in a birch bark basket without having the bark catch fire?

We showed her that it was - that the heat went into the water and wouldn't char the bark. We had her taste the pulp of a Jack in the Pulpit, setting her mouth on fire, and then we showed her that when boiled in that birch bark basket it was sweet as a potato. Once she picked up a rabbit dropping, well dried, and asked if that nut were good to eat. Of course we assured her that it was. She nibbled it delicately, saying that it was a little bitter and offering the rest of it to Okarri who gallantly chewed it down - much to our admiration and amusement.

About half way back to town, we jumped a deer that bounded gracefully away, a sight which triggered all the boys into aiming imaginary guns at it. Miss Lorry was appalled.

"How can you kill such a beautiful creature!" she exclaimed.

We thought she was asking for information...

"Why," said one of us, "You aim for a spot just behind the front shoulder, or the neck if you're close enough. Or, if you got a miner's carbide light, you can shine 'em at night and shoot them between the eyes. Old Man Kalla has built himself a perch up in an elm tree by the lake clearing and he shoots them in the back when they come out a dusk to feed. Or, if you can steal some telephone or telegraph wire, you can make a big noose out of it and put it across a runway fastened to a strong maple sapling."

"Yah," said another boy, Pierre Rameau I think, "mon granpere, he told me that when he was a young man, he used to make pits in their runways and have some sharp stakes that the deer would fall on and kill themselves. My granpere, he said he never had money for shell and you got to eat.

All of us nodded, boys and girls alike. Without deer meat how could you make it through the winter?

Miss Lorry tried to understand and jotted down a few sentences in the little notebook she always carried. She said she might write a book about us someday.

She certainly kept gathering material for such a book. She learned some words and phrases of Finnish and found ways of getting into some Finn homes for coffee and korpua or fish-eye soup or their delectable soft cheese and smoked fish. After word got around that she wasn't "stuck up" and knew all the ancient Finnish epic of the Kalevala and had even visited Helsinki, doors were opened to her that had never been opened to any but another Finn. She went several times to the Finnish Lutheran church and talked at length with the preacher who said afterwards that she was a good woman. Miss Lorry even attended a Holy Roller (Holy Jumper), service once in their little white church, amazed and delighted by the religious frenzy of those who writhed on the floor, regretting their evil ways, or those climbing the pillars of the church porch, yelling to God to let them into heaven. She even tried to sing the strange hymns and put a whole dollar in the collection plate.

Miss Lorry loved our autumn days with the scarlet maple and yellow birch leaves against a background of green pine and firs. Every Saturday she walked in the forest and by the blue lakes, usually with three or four of us tagging along. I remember once that we took our lunch along over to Horseshoe Lake and stopped in to see old Arne Nevola who had a cabin there.

Arne was pretty close to being a hermit.

He was a short man with faded brown eyes, half hidden by a tangle of hair and beard. We were fixing to share our sandwiches with him, but he refused. He'd just caught a handful of trout, he said, and was about to cook them. He offered us coffee. Miss Lorry looked aghast as old Arne put a chunk of salt pork into the pan on the stove, waited till it sizzled, then took each trout, squeezed it hard (they were uncleaned), and dropped it into the pan. He said something in Finnish and we translated for Miss Lorry.

"Arne says you gotta always squeeze 'em till they squeak before you cook 'em."

The old man ate the trout like we eat sweet corn. No fork. Arne didn't believe in forks.

"Forks leak," he told us.

Miss Lorry took notes.

Miss Lorry was an excellent though highly unorthodox teacher. Appalled by the dog-eared texts in English and American Literature that were provided by the school board, she sent home for huge boxes of her own books and placed them in the assembly room for all to read. One of them was "Bartlett's Quotations," which got more use than any other since no one could come to class unless they came with a quotation they had memorized. We prowled through that book over and over again, looking for one that would please her or that would make the class laugh. I collected one of the latter from Shakespeare: "Phew, methinks I smell of horsepiss!" The class roared. Miss Lorry never batted an eye.

She soon discovered that most of the kids had never willingly read a book and she spent much of her time reading to us.

She was an excellent reader and she chose passages that whetted our appetites. There were adventure stories; Jack London, Kipling, Thoreau for the boys, and love stories for the girls, always followed by an exchange of comments.

There was even poetry. Not Longfellow or Swinburne, but poets like Vachel Lindsay or Robert Service...

> "Fat black bucks in a wine barrel room,
> barrel house bucks with feet unstable,
> reeled and roared and pounded on the table
> hard as they were able..."

> "I saw the Congo cutting through the black,
> cutting through the jungle with a golden track,
> and all along the river bank a thousand miles,
> tattooed cannibals danced in files..."

Hell, before that class was over we were all prancing around the room chanting, "Boomlay Boom."

Miss Lorry even got us interested in writing. Instead of the horrible theme topics of past years; things like, "What I did last vacation," or "The Beauty of the Sunrise," she told us to write of what we knew so she could put it in her book someday.

Those she liked she read aloud to the class:

"How to Skin a Skunk Without Getting Polluted"
"How Old Man Torault Wrestled the Buck"
"How to Make Saffron Buns"
"My Father May be Head of the House,
but My Mother is the Neck that Turns the Head"

That sort of thing...

Why, we even wrote poetry of sorts, usually couplets or limericks. They didn't have to be very good, but they had to rhyme like:

"Eino and Aili went to the well,
But what they did there I better not tell."

Or

"When my old man takes off his socks,
We plug up our noses with a bunch of rocks."

Still, Miss Lorry encouraged more noble sentiments. Once, I remember, when we entered her composition class, she was dressed as a member of a Sultan's harem.

"Shh!" she said softly. "Today I'm going to play you Victor Herbert's 'Natoma, The Dagger Dance'. You will watch and listen and then write down your thoughts and feelings about what happens."

She cranked up her Victrola and the music flooded the room while she danced, a wild eerie performance ending with that last vicious stab in the breast with a real knife. We screamed and wept until she rose from the floor and showed us that she was I right.

"Now write for me," she said, and left the room to change her clothes. Shaken, we did our best.

You must remember that this all happened more than 50 years ago in a very isolated little village in the deep woods of Michigan's, Upper Peninsula.

Living there was surviving. No one had any money to amount to anything. Nothing new ever happened. There was no television, no radio - just gossip. Everything was known "about everyone-by everyone." Horses and cows, meat and potatoes, fish and hunt, hang out the laundry and bake the bread, live and die; every day - every month; the seasons held no surprises.

With Miss Lorry's coming there was suddenly something new to talk about and oh, the cackling that went on. Nosy old Aunt Lizzie was the worst. She collected every choice morsel of Miss Lorry's daily doings, stopping kids on their way home to quiz them and to cluck with outraged shock at what was going on.

Finally, just before Christmas she went to the superintendent and told him that Miss Lorry must go, that she was a bad influence on the children and the community, that half the high school girls were shortening their skirts all the way up to three inches below the knee the way Miss Lorry wore hers. Some were even plucking their eyebrows. She continued interminably.

"They say she smokes in her rooming house and then hides it with perfume. And...Annie, the post mistress, says she got a parcel the other day that gurgled when she shook it so she probably drinks too. And she wears those red and orange dresses, with her legs showing even. Not proper for a schoolmarm that. And she reads dirty books and doesn't mind it if the boys say hell and damn in class. And what does she and those high school boys do when they go walking in the woods? Tell me that!"

Aunt Lizzie's sniffing grew louder. "I tell you she's a bad influence and she's got to be fired."

The superintendent didn't give in.

"Miss Young is the best damn teacher we've ever had come to town," he answered, "and you, my friend, are the nastiest old busybody I know. I'm running this school and I'll thank you to keep your evil thoughts to yourself hereafter."

But he told Miss Lorry about the confrontation and that she should know that they each now had a mortal enemy in Aunt Lizzie.

"Try to be as discreet as you can, Lorry," he begged, though he knew she couldn't be.

He was right. The next day Miss Lorry made a formal call on Aunt Lizzie, engaged her in very polite conversation and made her a present of a bottle of very fine wine. The gauntlet was thrown and accepted. Aunt Lizzie went to work in earnest, travelling all over town stirring up trouble, gossiping, spreading innuendo, inventing outrageous lies always prefaced by, "You know what I heard today? They say…

The more we tried to defend Miss Lorry the more certain some of our parents were that she had indeed made us her captives and was not a good influence. Our peaceful little village found itself divided in two camps and everyone was relieved when the Christmas holidays came and Miss Lorry took the train back to Boston.

My mother, who liked Miss Lorry very much and who had been greatly distressed by Aunt Lizzie's machinations, said she almost hoped that the teacher wouldn't return, though she would miss her greatly. She added that she doubted whether we would ever see Miss Lorry again.

She didn't know her woman. Miss Lorelie Young came back on the St. Paul train on New Year's Day, the day before school was to reopen. Three huge trunks came with her and the host of kids who met her lugged them up to her boarding house on their sleds in a triumphant procession.

Miss Lorry was back!

There was a steely look in her eye when she visited my mother that evening.

"Mrs. Gage," she said, "I almost didn't come back, but then I thought of those fine children and the terrible poverty of the lives of their parents and I knew I had to. I'm going to civilize this town, Mrs. Gage, or die trying. I'm going to bring it beauty; the arts, music, and the dance, and painting, and sculpture and drama.

My mother, who had had a gentle upbringing complete with finishing school, gasped and murmured something about Lady Quixote. Miss Lorry jutted her Yankee jaw.

"I'll make a beginning at least," she vowed. "You'll see!"

We saw.

She was a whirlwind of energy, a fountain of innovation. That was the liveliest winter our town ever had, before or since.

She put on some kind of program in the school gym almost every other week, begging us to make sure that our parents came to them.

She put on a lantern slide show of the great paintings of the world.

She held concerts "via Victrola."

She published a weekly town newspaper, all handwritten, with twenty copies made by us to be passed around from house to house.

She tried to organize a dancing club, offering to teach us how to waltz and do the fox trot.

She started a bridge club, complete with lessons, tables and refreshments.

She made an abortive attempt to create a mobile library, taking her own books to the homes of her students so that the parents might find one they would like to read.

She organized a barbershop quartet.

Miss Lorry failed, abjectly and completely. Everything she attempted ended in fiasco and frustration.

The lantern slide projector yielded only fuzzy gray ghosts of the pictures she so wanted to share with us - And besides, Mullu Ysotalo came reeking of skunk and a helluva fight ensued before Charley Olafson, the town marshal, stopped it. He went through his usual routine of simply picking up the participants, one in each hand, and banging their heads together. Charley was an artist at head knocking. Said he could "tell by the tonk' when he'd banged 'em just right. But the session was a shambles and Miss Lorry wept. All who attended the soiree said they had a fine time.

After the first concert, despite her enthusiastic interpretation of the classical music that emerged from the scratching old Victrola, few parents returned. In fact, Aunt Lizzie was the only one that did and she was there to hunt for trouble.

In desperation Miss Lorry shifted from records to home talent. She had discovered somehow that Old Three Toe Jack could play the violin and Bill Shipley the bugle and somebody else the harmonica. I played the flute, a cracked old wooden monster that took so much air that I was always dizzy after two minutes of coping with the leak. We also had vocalists and the barbershop quartet. All of us had planned to rehearse several times before the announced concert, but one rehearsal was enough to scotch the project.

Miss Lorry learned that the only tune Three Toe Jack could play was "Turkey in the Straw" and that he had no sense of rhythm at all.

Bill Shipley had a busted lip from a fight at the saloon and he couldn't hit more than a few notes of "Taps" on his battered old bugle.

The barbershop quartet came thoroughly plastered. One was so drunk that the other three had to hold him up; the vocalist flatted and the harmonica player was so nervous that he kept sucking in when he should have blown out. Miss Lorry was devastated.

Her weekly newspaper was a hit at first. Complete with items like: "Bill Mager says his horse hurt his leg skidding pulp yesterday" and "Church services will be held in the M.E. Church, Sunday at 11," (which everyone knew anyway), it even contained an extensive article on the Pyramids of Egypt by Miss Lorelie Young herself.

The paper died after three issues because it became obvious that there wasn't anything new in town and nothing in the paper, except for Miss Lorry's articles, that everyone didn't know about already.

The only adult who came to her bridge lessons was Old Lady Viehema, the Holy Jumper. She stormed in with an axe and a torrent of Finnish, smashing the tables and denouncing the entire affair as the work of Satan himself. She had eyes of fire and all of us, including Miss Lorry, fled.

Perhaps Miss Lorry's biggest disappointment was her dancing club. Surely, she thought, her devoted boys and girls would enjoy learning to waltz and fox trot. The girls showed up, but not a single boy came.

My mother helped her understand.

"You see, Lorry," she said in her soft voice, "It isn't that they don't want to come. It's that they don't have shoes. Haven't you noticed that they wear their swampers, those rubber bottomed boots, always? A few have moccasins for summer, but those boots are all they have and it would be pretty hard to dance in them."

The trouble, though my mother didn't mention it, was deeper rooted than that. Miss Lorry just didn't understand that everything always stopped during the long bitter winter. We didn't leave the house any more than we had to. Forty below and four or five feet of snow on the level and mountainous drifts had conditioned us to hibernation like the bear and the others of the seven sleepers. You conserved your energy all you could and waited for spring so you could change your underwear. At the time of the long sleep Miss Lorry's strange enthusiasm made little sense.

All of us felt sad to see the light go out of her eyes. She became thin and my mother would invite her to our house each week to give her a good meal and lift of spirit. My mother knew how she felt. She too had tried and failed many years before to find some fun in the bleakness of winter.

"Lorry," I remember her saying, "This is the time to wait. The Finns have a good word for it - "sisu" - the ability to endure anything. This is the time of the long night. Try again in the spring and everything will be different. But sisu now."

Miss Lorry finally took her advice and confined her energies to planning and writing the musical comedy that was to be the highlight of her sojourn with us. She scheduled the show for the week before the end of school, the first week of May.

Our school ended earlier than most because the boys had to help plant potatoes and that was when the walleyes and northern pike were spawning in the rivers. We had to fill the fish barrels for marinating and salting down or smoking and do our beaver trapping if the snows lingered.

Miss Lorry finished her musical about the end of March and all of April was spent learning the songs and lyrics and rehearsing and making costumes.

It was good to see her come alive again and her enthusiasm fired us all. A real live show just like they had in the big city -

> Singing and dancing,
> Chorus girls,
> Her Magnum opus,
> Her last gallant try...

Oh, how hard we worked making the sets, rehearsing lines and lyrics until they were letter perfect, making the signs that advertised the play, sewing the costumes.

I don't know how much money Miss Lorry spent, but it must have been considerable, far more than the miserable salary she got from the school board.

I remember how she and my mother made the sewing machine hum night after night, putting together the golden panties the chorus girls would wear, a task Miss Lorry didn't dare farm out to their mothers lest all hell break loose. You must remember that none of those loggers or farmers or miners had probably ever seen a live show or a line of chorus girls come kicking out of the wings. That chorus line was to be the final number, the grand finale. We were sworn to secrecy and we never told a soul.

Tickets were free, but we made them and covered the countryside passing them out and explaining what they were for. The show was called "Out Where the West Begins" and it has cowboys and Indians and a love story and fine music. That's what we told them. An event!

"Going show?

"Yah."

The school gymnasium was overflowing, balconies and all, with people sitting on the steps that led down to the basketball floor on that "night of nights."

Never had there been such a crowd in the place. Everybody was there, even old shaggy Arne Nevola from Horseshoe Lake. There were trappers and lumberjacks that no one had seen for years.

Even though everybody had had their spring bath, the place stank with hot crowded bodies and the bear grease on the shoepacs.

Finally the fanfare came from the Victrola in the wings and the curtain went up. You could hear Charley Olafson sniffing and grunting as he cranked it off stage.

Out marched a mixed chorus to the recorded strains of "Mademoiselle from Armentiers. "They were garbed as soldiers returning from the war. Back and forth they marched across the stage singing, "Over There," but with Miss Lorry's words, ending with "It's good to be back from being over there."

Very stirring.

Applause.

Then a dramatic scene in which the heroine, in nurse's costume, tells her parents that she can't settle down now that the war is over, that she's leaving home again, leaving to go west, to The Frontier.

From the wings the chorus bellows loudly, "How you Gonna Keep Em Down on the Farm Now that they've Seen Paree?"

The curtain comes down as our heroine bids her parents farewell.

Loud clapping.

And Gascon Barbassou, one of those who had seen Paris during the late war, gets up and yells from the back row, "Sacre Mo Jee, she's right, mes amis. It hard to come back to ze bush wen you see Paree."

Laughter.

The next scene opened with the chorus dressed as lumberjacks and miners singing, "Out Where the West Begins."All I can remember of the lines -

"Where cows meander the streets complacent,

Where all the movies are wild and ancient,

Where the doctor kills every other patient..

That's where the west begins."

We sang it loud and clear and everyone in the audience nudged his neighbor and looked at the doctor, my father. When he threw back his head and laughed too, the crowd went into uproarious clapping and One-Eye Foulin hollered from the back-

"Yah, and them cows they sheet all over the sidewalk too."

Ah, we had grabbed the audience.

It was going to be a success!

From the wings came the sound of chopping and sawing as the chorus disappeared. Out staggered a lumberjack covered with ketchup and pseudo blood, moaning loudly. Enter our heroine, the nurse, to minister unto him, bandaging his wounds, wiping up the ketchup and singing some song of comfort.

Some old lumberjack hollers from the audience, "Hell, put some tobacco juice on it and he'll be all right!"

Great gales of laughter.

I forget much of the rest. There was a barroom scene with a painted woman doing some eloquent bumps and grinds on a table while the chorus sang, "Every Little Movement Has a Meaning of Its Own," and which ended in a helluva realistic fist fight, complete with authentic black eye for Sulu Virta, and an Indian being tramped on the sawdust floor.

Again our nurse appears, does her good deeds, heals the hurt and reproaches the roisterers for their evil ways in a song entitled, "Drink is E-vil," followed by another chorus of "Out Where the West Begins," whereupon Billy Bones, our town drunk, takes a snort from his bottle and passes it around to his friends in the balcony.

"Yeah," he shouts down, "Drink is E-vil to be sure, but Wahoo!"

That rotgut whiskey he bought for a buck a pint down in Wasek always made you yelp!

Then there was a moving love scene in which Howard Lemond and the nurse sang to each other tenderly. It ended with a clinching embrace into which Howard threw himself so enthusiastically that our heroine, Millie Lapin, howled with pain and yelled, "Howard, you hug like a bear! Let me go, you bastard!"

The lines weren't in the script, but they brought down the house Out Where the West Begins!

Then came the final scene, the Grand Finale, the one all of us had kept secret for so long. All the characters on the stage were singing. Out from the wings came the pony chorus, girls linking arms and kicking high in unison. Lots of bare leg below the short golden panties.

Wahoo!.

Uproar.

From the front row of seats, most of which had been taken by his wife and eleven children, jumped Pete Floriot, his eyes bulging.

In a voice that shook the building, he roared, "Maggie! Have some decent! Cross yer legs below!"

He had spotted his daughter, Marguerite, kicking high.

Outraged, Pete leaped to the stage, grabbed the weeping girl, gave her butt a resounding swat and yanked her down over the footlights, through the aisles and up the stairs. You could hear his voice giving her French hell until the front door of the school slammed shut.

Catastrophe!

The chorus line was broken, the girls were in tears, confusion was everywhere.

The air was electric, like it always is just before a good fight breaks out.

But out of the wings swept Miss Lorry, her head held high.

The show must go on!" she shouted, and go on it did. Inserting herself in Maggie's place, she danced them off and then back in again, kicking higher than any of the girls.

Defiantly!

Proudly!

The whole ensemble sang the theme song lustily and the curtain came down Out Where the West Begins.

That night the school board met in executive session and fired Miss Lorry. No formal charges were presented, but everyone knew what Aunt Lizzie had long suspected. Miss Lorry didn't wear any panties under her skirts and she had kicked too high and too revealingly.

As one of the board members succinctly put it, "You just can't teach here after you've shown the whole town yer twat!"

Miss Lorry departed on the train the next evening and all of the kids and half of the town's adults were there to see her off. As the train pulled away from the station most of them were weeping as Miss Lorry waved from the back of the sleeping car… But I'm sure that what she remembered most was that we sang to her - "Out Where the West Begins."

Redhanded

For many years no one in our village ever locked the doors of a house at night or even when the family left for several days at berry picking time. The possibility that evil persons might enter our houses or barns to take something that didn't belong to them never entered our heads. If we shut the gates of our barnyards it was only to keep our cows inside or someone else's cows or horses out.

Oh, you might shut the doors of the chicken coop tight, but that was because of the skunks and foxes. There were plenty of odd people in our town and, after their fashion, a lot of sinners, but no thieves.

"You don't take nothing that don't belong to you," was drummed into every child's head as soon as he could listen.

I suppose this community-wide honesty was partially the result of our village's isolation and smallness, for surely there's a bit of thievery in all men.

It was just that if you took something, you couldn't use it anyway for everyone would know instantly who it had belonged to. And besides, most of us were poor and we knew very vividly how difficult it would be to replace something that was stolen. When you had to wage the battle of survival yearly, when you had to scheme and scratch to make it through the next winter, you just couldn't take away the tools or things that your neighbor needed to help him do the same. If you needed a particular tool all you generally had to do was ask to borrow it - and make sure it was returned in better condition than when you got it.

Then too, since all of us were in about the same boat as far as possessions were concerned, there was very little envy. If your neighbor had a better pair of skis or a bigger stack of wood than you, he had gotten them by his own labor and you could have them too if you wanted to work badly enough. If we had any real unsatisfied wants, they were not for things, but for opportunities - like for a chance to do more hunting and fishing!

Anyway, that's how it was in our forest village until the Trader came to town and moved into one of the company houses that had been vacant since the iron mine closed. Jim Olson, caretaker for the mining company, said the Trader had signed the year lease under the name of Mordecai Jimson, paid his twelve dollars and agreed to repair the house as required.

The mining companies owned all the land on which our town was located. You could buy one of their houses or build your own and the annual lease-rent was very cheap, but you couldn't buy a bit of the land since the company hoped to reopen the mine someday. Or so it was said.

This arrangement did have some advantages. For example, if some undesirable character came to town or someone didn't keep his place up, the lease was simply not renewed and he had to move out. We always sized up any newcomer by watching to see how he fixed his place up.

The Trader sure did. For a month he worked like a beaver on his house and barn. He even painted the windowsills and doors bright red when he got everything else done. Finally he started trading. He'd drive into your barnyard with his long wagon, one with a big box on top, knock at your backdoor to ask if you might be having some old jug, copper bottom boiler, tools or junk that you might like to trade for what he had. Always polite and sweet talking was the Trader.

Since it was kind of hard to resist taking a look at what he had in the wagon, you'd usually find something in your house or barn that you didn't really need and then the Trader would open

the padlock on the long box and let you take a look. He always had quite an assortment of things in there, nothing new, but all carefully repaired or in good shape - tea kettles, hammers, axes, a couple pairs of boots, a shovel or two, all kinds of things, even toys.

Anything he had that was made of wood or metal was always painted the same bright red as the trim on his house and barn. Sometimes the things in the box looked better than they really were, but generally most of us felt we'd gotten the better end of the swap.

The Trader would usually haggle just enough to make it interesting, but usually he'd give in and you'd feel good getting a sound 10 gallon crock, maybe, for that old broken rocking chair that you were going to chop up for kindling anyway. It was really kind of exciting to have the Trader come to our house.

I remember that once I got a pretty fair jackknife in exchange for some empty Mason jars that we had discarded because the meat in them had spoiled. Sometimes, if you didn't think you had anything to trade he'd ask if he could take a look at your barn or shed to find something he wanted so he could make an offer and, of course we always let him.

I don't know how long it took after the Trader came to town before we began to suspect that he might be a thief. Quite a while, if I reckon right.

The first things we began to miss were from our hunting camps: a bucksaw, a coffee pot, a blanket or two.

In those days, no one ever locked his hunting camp either and anyone was free to use it when the owner wasn't there. We also left our cabins stocked with a few cans of beans, coffee, sugar and hardtack so that anyone who was lost or who needed a snack before making it back to town could help himself. It was sort of an unwritten law of the woods. But none of us would ever take anything away from a hunting camp and certainly not the kinds of things that began to disappear. You just didn't take axes or coffee cups or frying pans. At first, the men suspected that some of us kids were furnishing one of the many shacks we were always making, but they looked them over and concluded that we weren't.

Then other things began to disappear too, from our barns and sheds and even our houses. It might be a rake, shovel, even a crowbar or perhaps only a file.

The set of Victor mink traps that Arne Ysamaki had boiled one evening and hung up on the sauna to dry was gone the next morning. A whole row of Pere Moulin's potatoes had been dug up overnight. When cutting marsh hay down in Beaver Dam Swamp, Eino Sonninen had left his rake and pitchfork on the haycock Saturday night as he had every summer for years. On Monday morning they weren't there. Another time 'Sier Broussard's sledge was missing. Mrs. Salo's cow, newly freshened after the calf was born, had been milked almost dry between morning and evening right out in the clearing back of the grove. Some dried fish hanging on the back of Atitila's shed disappeared. A length of chain left outside the blacksmith's shop was gone. There were many happenings of this sort.

It was bad. When one of the French Canadians down in the valley had something taken, he blamed it on some Finn up on the hill and vice versa. Neighbors began to watch each other's kids suspiciously. After they turned out their kerosene lamps at night, people stayed awake as long as they could, peering out of their darkened windows.

In one month, M.C. Flinn sold more of his old padlocks than he had in twenty years.

Arne Hutilla left a new pitchfork sticking out temptingly from the haycock next to his barn and set two bear traps under some straw beside it, but all he caught was Piiku's big hound dog.

Charley Olafson, our constable and night-watch, almost went crazy checking out the complaints.

"When I ketch that varmint I'll bang his bloody head on a rock," he threatened and he would have too. Charley was big, but he was slow and not just slow afoot either. He was very good for banging heads together to settle fights or for hauling drunks up to the cage in the Town Hall to sober up, but not much for detective work. We sure had a lot to talk about that summer and winter, but it was mostly bad talk. Too much suspicion hung in the air.

We gradually began to discern a pattern in the thieving. It usually happened at night and more in the summer. In the winter things were stolen only when we had a bad blizzard to cover the tracks. Every so often we would have a spell when nothing was taken. I don't know who it was that noticed that these times seemed to coincide with the Trader's occasional absence. You see, about once every month or six weeks, he'd take a trip to one of the other towns in the vicinity and be gone for a week and then return with fresh trading stuff in the long box.

Some had been suspicious of him right from the start, he being a newcomer in town and having had the chance to look over our premises, but since he seemed like such a nice, honest sort of man, people hated to air their suspicion out loud. Nevertheless, once spoken, it became almost a certainty. The Trader must be the thief. It made sense.

"Bet that barn of his, the one he keeps padlocked all the time, is just full of our stuff," someone said at the post office.

"Yeah," said another, "and then he takes it to the other towns and trades it there, steals their stuff and trades it here."

"Yeah, and fixes it up and paints it red to keep anyone from finding out," added a third man.

People began to wonder how much of the stuff we'd gotten from the Trader actually belonged to someone else in our village. We somehow hated to use any tool painted red because anyone who had lost one like it would be sure to come and look it over.

Pitu Angeaux, for example, was sure that the red hammer his neighbor Marcel DeForet had traded for was the one taken from his wagon one night.

"Me, I know by ze heft. Eet was ze only hammair I ever have I like," he said. But he couldn't prove it.

As you can imagine, we watched the Trader pretty carefully from then on and although the thefts continued, they weren't quite as frequent.

There were also some who tried to visit him when he was working in his barn, but the Trader always refused to let them in. He even got kind of nasty about it and nobody ever got to see the inside of his house. He told those who tried that they should mind their own business same as he minded his.

When he went on one of his trading trips, even around the village, every door of his house and barn was double padlocked and the curtains were always drawn. The Trader had the only barn in town that had curtains on the windows.

Someone asked him about it once and he answered again, "None of your business, but that's my workshop where I repair the lousy stuff you people stick me with when I trade with you."

Kind of surly, he was.

As you can imagine, the town soon soured on the Trader once the suspicion took hold and he began acting the way he did. People refused to let him bring his wagon into their barnyards. They wouldn't trade or let their kids trade either. Some even called him thief to his face.

Finally, Jim Olson, the mining company caretaker, went up to see the Trader and told him that he'd have to clear out, that his lease would not be renewed and warned him of bad trouble that was brewing.

"Whether you're our thief or not, Trader," he said, "you'd better get the hell out while you can."

The man nodded and said he reckoned he'd have to. He'd have to get his things together and probably have to make three or four trips. He planned to go to some place up the line where people weren't so goddamned evil minded, he said.

When the news of the Trader's impending departure spread around town, the response was more anger than relief.

"That son-of-a-bitch is a-going to cart away half our belongings," said Olie Anderson angrily. "Are we going to let the bastard get away with it?"

Wiser heads counseled good riddance and there probably wouldn't have been any violence at all if Mrs. Murphy's pet pig hadn't been taken the very next night. Some still say it was a bear, and the way the pig pen had been shambled it could well have been, but whatever it was, it triggered off a real doings.

A bunch of men just walked up to the Trader's house that next evening after dark, busted in his door, took him and put him in his outhouse and nailed the door shut. Then they shot the padlock off the barn door, took everything out of it, spread it in the yard, and did the same to everything in the house, beds, blankets, curtains - even the stove. Setting a guard to make sure the Trader couldn't get away, they passed the word around the village to come next morning and claim anything that had been stolen or missing.

Well, come daylight you'd have sworn there was an auction going on there in the yard. People were scurrying around and looking everything over and talking like sixty. Only Charley Olafson, our constable, was absent. He was too sick to carry out his duties, but to look close for a pipewrench with a nick in the handle.

That pipewrench wasn't found in all that display of things in the Trader's yard. What's more, there were only a few people in the crowd who felt strongly enough that something was theirs to take it away.

"Oh, old Lemi claimed that the red hayrake was the one that had been stolen from his shed and he showed us where the Trader had fitted in a new peg before painting it. And Pete Lafollete took away some traps that were his, pointing to where one side of each had been filed away, the place where he had always put his notch. There were a lot of people who thought they recognized something that belonged to them, but it had either been painted or repaired or dented in such a way as to keep them from being certain. It's hard to tell one camp frying pan from another. So, to their credit as honest folks, they couldn't bring themselves to claim something they thought 'might' be theirs.

They just weren't sure enough. You would have thought they couldn't have acted so noble, but it wasn't so much being noble as their long habit of being honest. In our north country you just didn't take anything that didn't belong to you.

When the crowd dispersed at last, the Trader's yard was still plumb full of all sorts of things. The men who had run the whole show were plenty frustrated. They didn't have a shred of guilt though… They were sure they'd done the right thing. Everybody who had come that morning was still convinced that the Trader was the thief, even if he had been smart enough to alter and disguise the appearance of the things he'd stolen so much that their true owners couldn't recognize them.

People were really frustrated and mad until someone came up with the idea of painting everything red as a reminder that the people of our village weren't to be trifled with.

They put red paint on the horse's back and on the Trader's wagon and on the stove and chairs and tables and blankets and curtains, on every single thing that wasn't already painted. When everything from a coffee cup to an undershirt was daubed with at least one big splotch of scarlet, they opened the outhouse door and dragged the Trader into the yard. There they painted his shoes, then his hair and finally his hands. And then they all went home and had a very satisfying cup of coffee.

About a year later we were talking about the Trader and my father summed up the whole affair pretty well.

"No," he said to my mother, "I'm still not certain that the Trader was our thief. If he had been more people would have been able to claim their stuff, but, whether he was or not really doesn't make too much difference now. What happened to him sure made it mighty clear once again that you don't take anything that doesn't belong to you. Far as I know there hasn't been a thing taken from anyone since he left. Why, the kids didn't even swipe any of the apples from our trees last fall, and that's the first time they haven't since we've lived here."

Old Napoleon

My father discovered the lake that now bears our family name in 1901. He said he'd gone deer hunting for the first time in his life, had gotten lost and was heading southwest when he cut across some huge tracks and decided to follow them a little way. "Big as the hoof prints of a two year old heifer," he'd said.

"Big as your hand."

The tracks led him north, over a hardwood hill where he'd jumped the buck, but he never got a shot.

"I saw him clear," my dad would say, "Looked as big as a horse and he had a rack like a brush pile."

Dad named that buck "Old Napoleon" and spent the rest of his life trying to shoot him.

Of course no deer ever lived as long as my father who died at the age of 94, but in every forest area there is usually one gigantic buck, wise enough and wary enough to become part of the legend of "Old Napoleon."

I've seen an Old Napoleon four or five times in some thirty years of hunting and I've seen his tracks much more often. I can understand my father's obsession with that majestic animal.

And an obsession it was, almost of the nature of Ahab and Moby Dick. Dad thought and talked about Old Napoleon every week of the year - even when he was trout fishing and e-v-e-n when

they were biting. No matter how many deer he killed, and he shot a lot of them, the end of each deer season left him with a profound sense of respectful outrage. Old Napoleon had out-smarted him again.

Dad always returned from deer hunting with a tale of another encounter.

One year Napoleon had circled the camp at night, coming close enough to look in the cabin window.

Another time dad retraced his steps after lunch and found clear evidence in the fresh snow that Old Napoleon had followed him to the knoll where he was sitting, had watched and pawed the ground not thirty yards away.

One year, standing on the ridge at the end of the escarpment, dad heard the big buck coming right toward him - crunch, crunch, crunch breaking the new snow crust, getting closer and closer in the heavy brush to the little clearing where the gun could cover well enough to shoot. And then a damned red squirrel had sounded off in a maple right above dad's head. A long silence - then crunch, crunch, crunch - the big buck back-tracked and got away, leaving nothing but his huge footprints behind.

Another year, dad said he almost had him again. He came across Old Napoleon's tracks at the edge of the forest opening we called Beaver Clearing. It's an odd place with a big bluff surrounded by a few acres of open plain through which a small spring creek meanders. The big buck had crossed the swale and bounded up the bluff. Cautiously, dad had made enough of a circle to see that no tracks descended on the other side.

What to do?

Where to sit or stand?

Dad finally decided to follow the tracks up to the base of the bluff and then to run, as fast as he could around its side, hoping to get a shot as the deer came down.

Dad did all this.

Nothing stirred.

Not a sound.

Finally, he went back to where the buck had climbed the bluff, the only easy place to get up, and there he found Old Napoleon's tracks coming down.

"Walking!" my father had said with rueful admiration.

"That old buzzard had been watching me all the time.

Walking! He was probably watching me all the time. And probably laughing at me. I'll get him next year."

That year he'd found Napoleon's bed in some cedars just north of the lake, still warm and steaming in the frosty air, but the tracks showed no alarm. They also showed that the buck was feeding as he strolled, a cluster of huge prints revealed how he had reared to reach an especially succulent looking sprig of cedar ten feet from the ground. With his heart pounding in his ears, dad had tip-toed down the fresh trail, finger on the safety, ears and eyes straining. The tracks led into a big blow- down of fallen spruce, miserable stuff for a man to make his way through though the big buck had leaped the windfalls easily.

When dad was halfway through the tangle, Old Napoleon snorted, so near and so loud that dad said he almost fell off the log he was balancing on. Again the buck snorted. And again. As dad said, "The old devil had me right by the balls. He knew exactly where I was and try as hard as I could, I couldn't spot him. And he circled me, snorting every minute or so while I stood there frozen on the windfall. Finally Old Napoleon was back there by his bed where I'd come from and he gave me one last big blast and took off in bounds that were twenty feet across. I suppose he had to get back there before he got wind of me, but oh, those were some of the longest minutes I've ever spent. I'll get him yet. I'll get him next year."

That year dad vowed to get Old Napoleon or bust. He'd hunt no other deer. He'd run him down. He'd follow his trail till hell froze over. When my father came back that year he was chastened, He told us that he hadn't even seen the big buck's track till the day before they had to break camp, but then he'd taken off after him, trailed him from nine in the morning until almost dark.

Dad had returned to camp, got some food and a blanket, returned to the trail and slept beside it until dawn. Then he took up the chase again.

"Lord, what a rounder," dad said. "Old Napoleon led me east to the Oxbow, then northwest around to the third lake, then over to Rock Dam, then back not fifty yards from the cabin. I think he was trying to tell me something. Saw him twice, but never got a shot. I'm bushed right down to the bone, but I'll get him yet. I'll get him next year."

And so the tales went - year after year.

Looking back, it seems as though Old Napoleon became almost as much a part of my life as of my father's.

In my childhood, the opening of the November deer season was as exciting as Christmas or the Fourth of July.

The week before was spent in preparation, gathering supplies, targeting the rifle, cleaning it, polishing it, hearing the tales of big bucks again and again.

In the kitchen, the baking was going on and butter was churned for the big crock. The big hampers were filled with Hudson Bay blankets and the foodstuffs were checked off against 'The List.'

I still have 'The List,' though the writing is faded: One bushel of potatoes, two slabs of bacon, one ham, sixteen loaves of bread, flannel nightshirt, extra compass, handaxe... and fifty other items.

Then the great day would finally come. Dad's four hunting cronies assembled - Cap Keys, Lou Touloff, Swede Ackman and Tony Marchetti, the tough Italian timber cruiser who could sling a deer as big as he was across his shoulders and carry it two miles.

They were all big men, stomping into the house in their red caps and red-plaid Mackinaws, gay and carefree as children unexpectedly let out of school.

Then up the street would come Pete Tario with his great brown horses pulling the lumber wagon or sleigh up to the back door. Then there was more joking and man talk as the hampers were loaded. Old Napoleon's name always danced around in the frosty morning air.

I remember running alongside the rig as far as I could, reminding dad that this was the year he was to come back with the big buck... He needed no reminding!

The years of my youth slipped past and I was finally granted the occasional privilege of driving the buckboard or cutter up as far as the bridge and walking over the hills to deliver a message or a packet of Chicago Tribunes to the cabin. I never did find my father there. He was always out hunting Old Napoleon, but the other men made me welcome. As they continued their poker game, they would tell me to help myself from the big stewpot on the box stove and invite me to admire their deer, already hanging from the buck pole outside. Big, rough men, they made me feel grown-up.

I never had the chance to join them, indeed to even go deer hunting, until many years later when I finally got a job that permitted me to take off that week in November. I always managed to get up to the old cabin for a short time every summer, however. I brought my young bride up there on our honeymoon and later led or lugged my children in a packsack and I wandered the forest and lakeshore in July or August, always looking for Old Napoleon's tracks. One place or another, I always found them.

And dad, who sometimes joined us, would sit in the old rocker and retell the stories of the hunt.

As his old cronies died or grew too feeble to hunt, a few of my friends and I took their places in the cabin with dad in deer season. One year the bridge over the river went out in a great flood and hat-snatching alders gradually crept across the logging trail up which the teams had hauled the supplies. For some years we had to pack everything in, but the annual hunt continued. In his seventies, dad hunted like a man possessed. At four in the morning he would begin clicking his watch-cover in the top bunk, turning on the flashlight to see if it was time to get up. He would always rouse us at five-thirty with his cry of "Daylight in the swamp! Today I get Napoleon!" And then we'd have to sit around after breakfast, waiting for daylight.

Dad was always the first to leave camp and the last to return. He rarely came back for lunch. We worried about him. He'd stagger in at dusk so exhausted and trembling so hard that he could barely hold the shot glass of whiskey to his lips. Sometimes he'd fall asleep in his chair, cleaning his rifle, and we usually had to help him up the birch ladder to sleep for an hour or two before the evening meal. At night the ache in his old bones would make him moan aloud in his sleep, but he could never wait to get going again next morning.

Napoleon, Old Napoleon! Without quite saying so, he'd made it clear that the great buck was his alone and that no one else should shoot him.

None of us would have.

We got a lot of spikehorns those years of dad's seventies.

During that decade dad shot only one buck, though in other years he rarely failed to get both the camp deer and one to take home. He was a very good hunter.

Dad saw plenty of deer he could have shot, but he was after Napoleon. No other deer would do. I think he was 75 when he made that one mistake.

I worried about him and had made it a practice to trail him discreetly and so I was able to join him shortly after I heard the shot. He'd dropped a monster buck, 280 pounds at least.

"You got him, Dad. You got Old Napoleon!" My father shook his head.

"No, no," he said. "It's a good buck, but just a baby compared to Old Napoleon. Look, only sixteen points and look at these tracks. Not half big enough. Well, I'll get him next year."

He seemed depressed.

Lord, it was a big deer. I broke two ribs trying to lift it over a windfall on the way back to camp.

When dad was 79, he insisted that I take my 14 year old son, John, out of school so he could join us up at deer camp, so I bought the boy a gun and a license. In our state, a boy John's age could only hunt deer in the company of a supervising adult and dad insisted on taking over that role.

He filled the kid with so much hunting lore that I was afraid John would sicken and never want to hunt again. Moreover, dad was a stern taskmaster, impatient with hunting error.

Once, after the old man had given him bloody hell for moving his head before moving his eyes while overlooking a runway, John had become sullen and asked to hunt with me.

I said no.

Old Napoleon

The last day of the season he asked to go hunting alone and I let him take the trail up to Porcupine Bluff and hunt by himself. Dad didn't approve, but when he heard the two shots he was on the bluff almost as soon as I. And there the two of us shared that curious atavistic experience of watching a boy suddenly become a man. John was alternately elated and sober, excited and depressed. He insisted on cleaning the buck himself and on dragging it back to camp without any help from us.

From that time on he chopped the wood without being told, carried a bigger pack without protest and joined in our man talk around the stove.

Only recently did my son tell me that his grandfather had taken him down to the lake later that same day, told him that all that land would someday be his and confessed to the boy that his own hunting days were over.

"Maybe I'll not be able to get Old Napoleon after all," he told John. "I'm not the man I was, but if I don't get him, then by God, you do! Then he swore the boy to secrecy.

The next year, when dad passed his eightieth birthday, for some utterly important reason that I now forget, I was unable to go deer hunting. Dad bought a license and made an attempt to walk up through the tangle that by then had completely covered the river road, but he got so worn out before he reached the place where the bridge had been that he barely made it back. For the first time he admitted that he was getting old. The next year we packed into the cabin and hunted, but it wasn't the same without dad. His rocking chair was always empty. No one wanted to sit in it. It was not a good deer season either. There were only a few small deer around and no sign at all of Old Napoleon.

After that we stopped coming up to the lake except in summer and then we portaged in by canoe from the west through the second lake, up the creek, over the beaver dam and finally into dad's lake. He didn't want to come with us. Too old, he said, too hard work, but over and over he expressed the wish to see his lake and the old cabin again.

When dad turned 92, my brother John and I decided to fulfill that desire. A new crop of loggers had cleared the river road, built a new bridge and were hauling pulp down from the headwaters. Knowing that the old man could never walk in, we hired some contractors to bulldoze, grade and gravel a new road to the lake. It cost us plenty and a lot more to build a fine new cabin on the rock point below the old cabin.

The old one was in really bad shape by this time. The bottom logs had rotted so much that we could only open the door part way and the inside was a shambles, thanks to the porcupines who had taken up residency and lived riotously for some years. Nevertheless, we had the men make a side road to it on the chance that dad might want to visit it again. My children and their children cleaned the old cabin up as best they could.

Dad was 94 when everything got done...just before deer season. By this time he was very frail and we were very upset to learn from his housekeeper that he had gotten himself a hunting license. He was polishing up his rifle between naps. When my brother, John and I arrived the week before the opening, we tried in vain to dissuade the old man.

"One last hunt," he said. "Got to get Old Napoleon. Just put me out on a log somewhere and let me be."

His voice quavered, but he looked us hard in the eye. So we brought up his things, got the new cabin warmed up, and scouted around for a good place beside the road where he might sit for a few minutes for auld lang syne and his ancient dream. I found a good spot overlooking the bend in the new road before it started up the hill, a place where a heavy deer trail crossed. And I wrestled one of the old camp chairs out of the cabin and put it in place behind a blind I'd built of branches. Sneakily, I scattered a few apples on each side of the road where the deer trail crossed. Dad would have shot me for doing it, had he known.

We brought him up the evening before season opened. He kept looking out the car window, watching for tracks in the inch of freshly fallen snow. Once he asked us to stop and back up to where a deer had crossed.

"Naw," he said, "That's just an old doe. A big one, but the toes are too pointed. Old Napoleon's tracks are bigger and blunted from long pawing the ground during rutting time."

He was excited and remained that way. His hands trembled so much that when he drank his tea at suppertime he had to use both hands to lift the cup. After the meal we sat him in the big chair in front of the fireplace and there he reminisced, telling of old days and good times in the old cabin.

How he and his cronies had once spotted a spikehorn through the window, trotting up the trail right toward camp and how three heavy men got stuck in the door trying to get out to shoot it.

And the night Touloff went out to take a leak and yowled like a lynx and had laughed at the rest when they'd run out in their underwear and bare feet to try to get a shot at it.

And the time dad painted Tom's huge nose a bright crimson with the newfangled mercurochrome dauber, telling him that it was a new cure for the sniffles and later that it would never wash off.

Or drawing a straw across the open mouth of a snoring bedmate and squeaking like a mouse.

And, of course, the tales of Napoleon.

The heat from the roaring fire and his cup of Old Crow finally put dad so sound asleep that he barely roused when we took off his boots and got him into bed.

We had already finished breakfast when the old man awoke at eight-thirty, but he still managed the old "Daylight in the swamp. Roll out, you buggers," cry. Too excited to eat much bacon and eggs, he let us help him on with his boots, fetch his old rifle and drive him up to the place I'd prepared. We had to help him walk over to the chair in the blind overlooking the deer trail. Then we bundled him in blankets and told him that whenever he had had enough or got too cold to just shoot his gun and we'd be right back to get him. When I left, dad was sighting down the rifle barrel at the deer trail. Somehow I almost wept. He seemed so frail and feeble.

I returned as soon as I'd taken the car back to the cabin, walking very carefully until I got to a little knoll where I could see dad and the deer trail very easily. I must have watched there twenty minutes before I heard a twig snap on the far side of the road where I'd scattered the first bunch of apples. I don't think the old man heard it, but a few moments later he certainly saw the huge buck that bounded across the road. He raised his rifle.

"Shoot! Shoot," I prayed silently. "He'll be in that brush. Shoot. Shoot now. Now!"

But the deer had smelled the other apples and began to feed on them broadside to my father, right in the open, not thirty yards away. Dad's rifle shook wildly as slowly, ever so slowly, he raised it up and I watched him steady it against the sapling that held up the blind.

"Shoot! Shoot! Now!"

I wanted to scream the words, but I couldn't.

The great buck suddenly looked up at both of us and the booming report of dad's gun echoed through the hills.

Old Napoleon didn't fall. Two magnificent bounds and he was out of sight and I knew why. Dad had raised his rifle and fired into the sky.

I made my way back to the road and joined my brother who had heard the shot. When we reached dad he just shook his head.

"You bundled me up too good," he said. "I must have dozed off for a moment and when I woke up there was Old Napoleon, going over the hill. I took a quick shot, but I missed. That derned old bugger outsmarted me again. I'll get him next year."

There was no next year.

But I vividly remember the little smile that crossed dad's face when he said it.

The Paddygog

Several summers after my father's death, my daughter and her family were vacationing with me at his old house in the village where I spent my youth. One morning, Jennifer, then eight, found me on the porch when she returned from playing with the village's current crop of youngsters.

"Grampa," she said. "We kids found a great big paddygog up there by the grove. What's a paddygog, Grampa?"

I had to confess that I didn't know, but that I would sure like to see one if she could lead me to it.

Up the old familiar street we went, hand in hand, Jennifer chattering all the way.

"It's awful heavy, Gramp, and big like this." She held her hands together in an arc above her head.

"And there's a big long chain on it and it's in the leaves by a big tree and it's kinda dirty, and that's what the other kids called it. A paddygog, Grampa."

She led me to the vacant space where our Town Hall stood before it burned down and then to a big maple tree.

"See! See! There it is, Grampa."

Jennifer pointed to a huge rusty iron triangle that lay half-hidden in the leaves and grass.

I recognized it immediately. It was Paddy's gong, the one he beat with a crowbar to celebrate the top o' the mornin' on St. Patrick's Day. It brought back a host of memories.

Patrick Feeny, Paddy as he was called by all the kids who adored him, was our village blacksmith.

My dad always claimed there were only two indispensable men in town: him, the town doctor, and Paddy, the blacksmith. The preacher and others were way down the list.

Dad fixed up the bodies.

Paddy repaired the things. He was not only a blacksmith, but a gunsmith and mechanic of great competence. He could fix anything from a watch to a broken logging derrick 30 feet tall. Moreover, his services were cheap. Paddy never set a price.

"Sure, and you can pay me what you think it's worth," he'd say. "Pay Paddy when you can."

That's how he operated and it was a shame how many people cheated him or didn't pay at all.

The Paddygog

M.C. Flinn, the stingy old proprietor of our general store, probably took advantage of Paddy more than anyone else. Flinn used to say disapprovingly whenever his name was mentioned in connection with Paddy, "No way to run a business. No way to run a business." But Paddy never seemed to mind even when some of his customers complained about his being too slow.

He certainly worked terribly hard, not only in the smithy, but late at night in his home. Any evening a passerby could see him at the workbench by the front window, taking a gun or clock

apart and putting it back together again. He especially liked clocks. His house was full of them. Said they kept him company. No one else did. People only came to see Paddy when they needed him.

But the smithy was his first love. I can see him yet, a huge man, built square to the floor from the shoulders down, in a sooty leather apron and ragged under shirt, his heavy hammer clanging a piece of white hot iron, fresh from the forge, until it turned cherry red. Then Paddy would plunge it hissing and smoking into the water barrel. It was almost as good as the Fourth of July to visit the blacksmith shop.

A single man, Paddy dearly loved children and always made us welcome though he'd built a bench back by the stanchions to keep us out of the way of sparks and bits of hot metal that sometimes

shot from his anvil. Once in a while he'd even let us help pump the huge bellows on the forge until the fire roared, but we had to keep out of his way when he was shoeing one of the great draft horses the loggers and farmers brought in.

Paddy had a way with those horses. He'd lead them in, half crooning to them all the way till they were in place. Then he'd shove up his stool, take a monstrous hoof in his lap and start paring it with a knife as our eyes bugged out. The horses never seemed to mind a bit.

First he'd measure the hoof with big calipers then sort through a barrel for a new shoe, heating it red, bending it over the anvil. Then he'd cool it and nail it home with mighty blows, rarely more than two whops to a nail.

After the horse had been led away, Paddy would give us the hoof parings for our dogs or he'd save them for the trappers. They claimed you couldn't find better bait for wolves or coyotes than those parings.

Then Paddy would come over to our bench to give us a ginger snap from the big tin on the shelf, He'd pour himself a cup of tea and tell us wonderful tales of the wee people, the leprechauns of the ould sod of the Ireland he had loved, but left as a boy.

Like many powerful men, Paddy had a soft voice. His had a special "lilt to it" though, like he was talking music. This, along with his brogue, made us hang on every word lest we miss something.

He'd tell us gory tales of the wars between the old kings of Ireland from whom he claimed to be descended

"Sure it is, me bhoys, that ivery Irishmon has a wee bit iv king's blood in him, that he has."

It was a little hard to imagine Paddy wearing a crown. His face was always so covered with soot that his eye holes gleamed white, but you could sure feel some hint of strange royalty just the same, especially when he told his tales about the slaughter of

Shannon's Ford and stories of castles and dungeons. Paddy loved the land he'd left and he opened the windows of our isolated little world when he told of tinkers with high wheeled covered carts, long stone walls that curved across soft green hills and the smell of "taters" baking in the ashes of a peat fire hearth.

Perhaps it was because several generations had sat on that bench that no one protested when Paddy went on his week long St. Patrick's Day spree.

At daylight he'd crank the chain that held the huge steel triangle that we called Paddy's gong down from the rooftree of the smithy. Then he'd take a sledge or crowbar to it till the reverberations woke half the town. I can hear the sound of it still, half boom and half clang, echoing from the hills that nestled our valley.

St. Patrick's Day!

Paddy Feeny was making sure that no one forgot the Irish.

But just the gong's great clanging flood through town wasn't enough.

Paddy always got out his big goose gun, at least an eight gauge with a barrel so big it was terrifying, and he'd shoot that off: first downtown, then in front of the post office and finally at the uptown post office. It sounded like someone had touched off a cannon! Everyone in the village knew then that it was St. Patrick's Day!.

After he'd fired the goose gun, Paddy would visit old Mrs. Murphy. They'd have a cup of tea and talk about old times and maybe they'd sing a few Irish songs together. Then Paddy went to Higley's saloon, bought 10 bottles of rye whiskey and proceeded to get "polluted to the gills" for a whole week. Paddy never drank at any other time, but he sure laid a real drunk on then. He didn't do a lick of work either, just sang Irish songs or keened between bottles. Anyone who needed some iron work or horse-shoeing done made sure it was finished before St. Patrick's Day or they put it off till the week after. Year after year, Paddy "cilibrated" in the same way.

It was early February when people of the village suddenly realized just how important Paddy was to them and stopped taking him for granted.

He was doing something he'd done hundreds of times - fitting a huge steel rim on a heavy wheel from a logging wagon - and his knees just sagged and he fell on his face there on the brick floor of the smithy. Some men slid him onto a couple of boards and carried him over to his house while others ran for my father. The news spread swiftly through the village and dad had to shoo people out of the house before he could get to feel Paddy's pulse and put on the stethoscope.

"A massive heart attack," he concluded. "Go get the priest."

Unfortunately, Father Hassel had gone to Marquette that morning to see his bishop, but when he returned that evening, Paddy had rallied considerably. He still got the last rites and the lights of the Catholic Church burned all night as Masses were said for a soul that had seldom seen the inside of the confessional.

For three weeks Paddy lay abed. He received more attention then than he had in thirty years. He was never left alone for a minute. One or another of the neighbor women took turns hovering over him day and night. Dad said it wasn't so much their nursing as his digitalis and nitroglycerin that pulled Paddy through, but he was finally able to totter over to the smithy to offer advice to a strapping young lad who was clumsily trying to fill in.

"Now don't you let Paddy do a damn thing," my father warned. "He isn't even to lift a hammer. If he wants to sit on the bench with the kids for half an hour or so at a time, that's all right, but he's got to take it real easy for a long time or he's a dead man."

We made sure there was always one of us to sit on the bench with Paddy, but he didn't tell us any stories. He would run out of breath if he tried to talk very much.

Even after Paddy could get around, the townspeople made sure he was cared for. They cooked his meals, cleaned his house and,watched over him constantly, showing in a thousand little ways how much they really cared. He couldn't even go to the outhouse without someone watching to make sure he came out again after a reasonable time. Paddy gradually improved enough to joke with the women about nagging him back to health.

According to dad, however, who examined Paddy almost every day, his apparent recovery was not a true reflection of Paddy's condition.

"Paddy's in bad shape," he told my mother. "I don't like what I hear in my stethoscope and his pulse is still none too regular. He could go anytime."

I sure felt bad when I heard him telling her that.

When the middle of March approached, the whole village began to worry again, especially after they heard that Paddy had sent Jim Pillion to bring his usual 10 bottles of rye from the saloon.

Dad blew his top, went over to Higley and read him the riot act for sending the whiskey and he tried to find it in Paddy's house.

"You drink half a bottle of that rotgut, Paddy, and you're dead. I tell you, you can't touch a drop of it. Now where did you hide it?"

But Paddy wouldn't tell.

"Now, Doctor," he said with that wide old grin of his, "a wee bit from the bottle nivver killed an Irishmon yet. An Irishmon will cilibrate the day, that he will, so long as he has a heart in him, will he not?"

Dad managed only to take away the goose gun.

"If Paddy tries to climb that hill, he'll be gone before he gets a quarter of the way up it," he told the neighbors. "And if he tries to take a sledge to that triangle gong of his, that'll do him in too. You watch him now. Paddy just can't do that kind of thing in his condition. I tell you he's got to take it easy for a long, long time."

But dad knew the nature of the Irish and he worried. So did the rest of the village.

I don't know who first got the idea, but I think it started in school. Some kid, probably a regular on Paddy's bench, thought that if we could hold a real slam bang St. Patrick's Day celebration in Paddy's honor the night before the day came, then he wouldn't feel he had to go through his old routine and kill himself.

"We'd calibrate' for him."

The idea caught hold and grew so fast and spread so far that no one could stop it. My dad felt all the excitement might be more than Paddy could stand and he still worried.

"Well, I don't know," he told us at the dinner table. "It might just keep him from banging that gong and drinking that booze if he sees all of us sharing his Irish insanity. At least he'll find out that the whole town likes and respects him after all these years of neglect and Paddy's sure got that much coming. I just hope it don't hurt him. "

Well, we really celebrated that St. Patrick's Day Eve and Paddy didn't even know that the whole doings were in his honor until he got out of Old Man Marchand's rig and entered the Town Hall.

It was full of people cheering him. It was full of green streamers and paper shamrocks three feet high. And it was full of Finns and French-Canadians, Indians, Swedes and "mixed stuffs," each with a bit of green on him to show he was Irish too. School kids were parading across the stage singing, "Where the River Shannon Flows" and other Irish songs.

And the speeches, too many of them, all telling Paddy how much he'd meant to the whole town. Old Mrs. Murphy was even trying to teach a bunch of little school kids how to do an Irish jig for him.

At the end of it all, Paddy was presented with a huge grandfather clock, a token of our esteem.

Paddy Feeny weathered it all and enjoyed every minute of it. After the clock presentation, he stood up, held out his arms to all of us and shouted, "Erin Go Bragh," and was driven home.

He went to bed and died in his sleep.

Everyone felt terrible, but the next day, St. Patrick's Day, the men hauled Paddy's big triangle up to the Town Hall, hung it by a chain to the roof piece and rang it till sundown. They rang it again the next year and on St. Patrick's Day every year after until the Town Hall burned down.

After my grand-daughter showed me her paddygog, I got a crew together and we hung the huge triangle from a big limb of the maple tree. Since Jennifer is half Irish, I lifted her up so she could be the first to bang it with a hammer and I gave each of the other kids a dollar so they would remember to ring it next St. Patrick's Day.

The Prophet

His name was Pierre Rousseau, but nearly everyone called him "The Prophet." Oh, there were some who called him fool and a few more who'd nicknamed him Paul Bunyan because of his enormous size, but they were all careful to address him as 'Sieur Rousseau or Prophet to his face.

Rousseau did indeed look like Paul Bunyan must have looked. Way over six feet tall and three feet across the shoulders, he was far and away the strongest man in our village, even stronger than the blacksmith. His bushy black eyebrows, full beard and a voice that rumbled like thunder in the hills had terrified me when I was a kid.

But The Prophet, like so many giant men, was gentle and easy going. He never fought in the saloon on Saturday nights and he never beat his wife, Minna, a tiny half-breed Chippewa who shared his cabin on a little farm out by the charcoal kilns northeast of town.

They had no children and that made The Prophet's heart ache for he loved them almost as much as he scared them... And he only scared them because he was so darn big and loud.

The first time I met him, I was about six years old. My dad and I were going into the post office to get the mail.

"Ah, my friend," he roared when he saw my father. "You 'ave a fine boy dere."

Then he bent down to give me a closer look and shouted, "Mon petit, you like to fly like a bird, no?"

I must have nodded as I shrank away because the next thing I knew he'd picked me up and thrown me ten feet in the air above his head. He caught me gently and put me back on my feet with a gale of laughter that sent echoes down the valley. I was terrified! I clung to my dad's leg until we got back to the horse and cutter and I had nightmares for weeks about a big black bearded monster coming out of my bedroom closet up there under the eaves.

"Tres formidable," was how the French Canadians described The Prophet!

The Prophet's predictions were legend in our town.

Once he'd foretold a great forest fire that would start in the Buckeye on August 14, and threaten our town - And it did!

There were some scoffers who'd said The Prophet had started the fire himself so the blueberries would be better the following.year, but then there'd been the time he told Joe Hamel that his bay horse would die in the harness that day - And it did! And then The Prophet had nearly killed his own horse, racing half the night to warn Eino Ysitalo out by Wabik, one of his detractors, against going into the woods that day lest something evil happen to him. Of course Eino laughed and went anyway and, perhaps un-nerved by the warning, had chopped a big gash in his leg. And another time he warned everyone against butchering their hogs after the second frost as they usually did. He said the meat would spoil. Those who failed to heed his advice regretted it too, because that was the first November that anyone could remember when not a single lake froze over and not a single snowflake fell.

The Prophet had made a lot of predictions and enough of them had come true that the townspeople now consulted him about the best time to make hay or when the pike would make their spawning run up the river or whether the M. E. church should have its Sunday School picnic on such and such a day.

Still, The Prophet knew his limitations. When Raoul Deforret, after fathering four daughters in a row, asked him to come and see his pregnant wife and tell him if he'd have another girl, The Prophet flatly refused.

"Women and cards, cards and women, women and cards ... I don't perdick," he roared.

He specialized mainly in the weather.

Every day, except Sunday, The Prophet drove to town to give his weather prediction. He came to the post office at nine o'clock, just before the morning mail was "disturbed." You could hear him coming half a mile away, singing to his old mare Nanette at the top of his voice. She didn't seem to mind the singing as she pulled the wagon in summer or the sleigh in winter; rain, snow or shine. The Prophet had a lot of songs too; some English, some French, mostly both. The only one I can remember went something like.

"Oh ze wind she blow from ze nort'
And ze wind she blow som more,
But you want get drown on Lak Champlain
So long as you stay of ze shore..."

And everyday, as he entered the crowded anteroom in front of the mail boxes, a hush fell over the townspeople as they awaited the oracle's pronouncement.

"Ah, mes amis," The Prophet would begin, "You want for me to tell wot ze wethair will be, yes? Me, I say dat she will be..."

It was sort of like the "My broker is and he says that" commercial on modern television - except that The Prophet told them. No hedging either. No ten per cent chance of showers or snow flurries, or this or that, like they tell us today, but "It would rain that day, half a pailful; Or it would snow four and a half inch, oui!"

Then he predicted the weather for tomorrow and sometimes for a more extended time. It took a very brave or skeptical or foolish person to doubt him. The message seemed to come down from on high. From where I stood, it did!

The Prophet was remarkably accurate. Rarely did he miss calling the shots. Indeed, my father was so impressed by his uncanny ability to predict the weather that he made a trip out to his farm 'ust to find out how The Prophet did it. He returned even more impressed.

"You know, Edith," he told my mother at the supper table, "The Prophet really studies the weather. He's got a real feel for science in a crude sort of way. I don't suppose he's ever heard about barometric pressure, but he showed me a marked stick - keeps it in his well - told me that when the water level went up that stick, even a little bit, that it meant rain. And he's got a whole woodshed full of calendars, thirty years worth of 'em, with notations for every single day. He told me he studied them and the clouds and the birds and a whole mess of other things before he made his 'perdickshuns'...

Anyway, we had no other source of information in our town during the first two decades of this century. There was no WLUC, no radio stations, no weather satellites... And the weather was important to us in a way that the modern city dweller would find hard to understand. A farmer or a fisherman might still understand, but most of you wouldn't.

Only a few families received a daily paper, *The Chicago Tribune* or *The Mining Journal*, and they were usually delivered several days after publication so the weather... had already happened.

So we appreciated 'our' Prophet's predictions. We believed them. And we relied on them. Through the workings of that curious communications grapevine that characterizes small villages, his weather news came to almost every house in town within an hour after The Prophet had spoken. Any discussion of the weather always began with, "Prophet says..."

All dogs have fleas, perhaps, as David Harum has suggested, "to keep them from brooding on being dogs."

Terry O'Hara was The Prophet's flea.

A feisty Irishman, barely five feet tall, aggressive, obnoxious and too small to hit, he heckled the giant unmercifully whenever one of his predictions didn't come true. He too was always at the post office when the morning mail came in, ready to rub it in. Even on the days when The Prophet's predictions for the previous day proved correct, Terry was there to yap at him.

He would pull out a small black notebook and read off past blunders in his little squeaky voice.

"And how about last Wednesday the fourth, big man? How about it now? Ye said it would rain, you did, and there wasn't enough rain to make a good spit."

The Prophet, towering above him, never answered. Once though, when Terry had gone too far with the spite of his tongue, The Prophet had picked him up with one hand, lifted him until he touched the ceiling and then quietly seated himself, dangling the little Irishman like a babe on his knee.

Only once in the 20 years of my adolescence did the people of our forest village lose faith in Their Prophet and they did a bit of crucifying... That always seems to be the lot of the seer.

It happened, if I remember correctly, in 1914-1915 or thereabouts.

The Prophet had stopped giving his daily and weekly forecasts, but concentrated instead on warning 'his' people about the terrible winter he saw coming.

Everyday in the post office, he would tell of the winter to come, of the miseries in store. It would be the year of 'ze long winter' - from October to June - it would snow - snow above the windows and be so cold that if you sneezed it would crack your nose.

"I tell you, my friend, make the wood, make the wood now or you run out by New Year. She's going blow an' she's going snow lak you nevair see before."

Terry O'Hara and his followers scoffed, but most families took The Prophet's warning seriously enough to build up their woodpiles, salt down an extra barrel of fish and smoke or can as much venison as they could get before the regular deer season came 'round.

The Prophet was really worried and showed it by divulging some new bit of weather predicting evidence each day.

The wasps had built their nests higher, much higher, off the ground. Ants were walking in straight lines instead of roaming around. A rooster had crowed at bedtime and the hen had molted in August month. The milkweed had opened its pods three weeks early. Northern Lights had been seen in July, way in the western sky too. The beavers had built their dams earlier and bigger than ever before. Squirrels were taking hazelnuts deep into their burrows instead of burying them in the leaves. The fish were not on the surface, but winter deep in the lake and the trout were already slimy in their spawning. The brown middle band of the wooly caterpillar was twice as wide as usual. A dry summer makes a deep snow winter. The lakes were open, but the geese had gone south.

"Buy a new suit of wool underwear," The Prophet suggested, "and grease your boots good."

All that warm, lovely September he preached his gloomy gospel, not just in the post office, but to almost every house in town - except O'Hara's.

The snow began to fall in the first week of October, just as The Prophet had predicted, and by mid-month there was more than a foot of it on the level.

"Start banking your house," The Prophet ordered. "Pile the snow high above the foundations. Get the hay-cocks out of the swamp and into the barn while you can. Forget the game wardens. Shoot your deer now. Butcher your pig and young steer. Cut some extra wood because it will soon be too late."

By the first of November, it was blatantly clear that The Prophet had been right.

Blizzard after blizzard roared down from Lake Superior, heaping snow in huge drifts. You could almost see it creeping upward to cover the tops of the picket fences. No one shoveled their walks except O'Hara and his looked more like a tunnel.

One of the trains got stuck in a great drift out by Red Bridge and you could hear its lonesome whistle calling urgently for help from the crew at the roundhouse by the station. The telegraph wires whined in the wind. Dogs, let out in the morning, floundered belly deep and were soon howling at the back door. Hoar frost so covered the door and window panes as the bitter cold clutched the houses, that the kerosene lamps were kept burning all day in the kitchens.

Waist deep, we tramped down a narrow trail to the outhouse and barn only to find it blown shut again within the hour.

With the schools closed, the sight of a man struggling up the street on skis, scarf over face and bending into the wind, was event enough to bring us all to the window. Only a few of the strongest managed to get to the store or the post office. Even The Prophet had been in only a few times on snow-shoes.

When he came, he reminded us of his prophecy in that voice like thunder. "ie, I tell you she's going to be a bad one. Like this till June, mes amis."

But toward the end of November the blizzards stopped.

The Prophet

It was still very cold, way below zero, but the sight of the sun at least gave us energy enough to stop huddling by the kitchen range and start living again.

Once the company team had compacted the four feet of snow on the street with the huge roller, Flinn's store bustled with people again as they replenished their necessaries. Every chimney lifted a tall exclamation point of white smoke into the cloudless, windless, cold blue sky. We had survived!

The fir trees still sagged with their burden of white, but the world seemed cleansed and bright again. Sometimes it was almost too bright... The surface of the vast drifts sparkled as though dusted with crystals of ground glass and the brilliance hurt our eyes so much that the children were given knitted face masks with slits to see through. But our spirits were high. We had survived. The worst had to be over. We'd never have a full month of storms again like those we'd just endured.

What was The Prophet saying now?

The news coming from the post office wasn't at all reassuring. Day after day The Prophet came, saying the same thing, that soon the snow would begin again, that the wind would blow again, that more storms were on the way, that winter would last until June. We began to hate our Prophet. The very thought of seven more months of frigid misery was just too much to bear. O'Hara' gained some companions in his giant badgering campaign.

But it came to pass just as The Prophet had foretold. December was bad; January was worse; and never before had February gone by without at least one short thaw.

The days limped along, each like every other, with snow, wind or both and a gray, gloomy sky. Our bones ached from the cold no matter how many sweaters we wore or how close we huddled to the

open oven of the kitchen range. Depression seeped into and through all of us as fathers anxiously scanned diminishing woodpiles and mothers watched the Mason jars of meat and fruit disappearing from cellar shelves. No one left the house unless it was absolutely necessary. People stopped talking to each other — even husbands and wives. The women cooked and knitted in silence; the men did the chores or just sat around, looking into space.

That was the winter I read the entire collected works of Charles Dickens - even "Martin Chuzzlewit" - hating every page of every volume, but having nothing else to do.

The horses in the barn, shaggy in heavy winter coats, refused to lie down on the cold floor no matter how much straw we put down in the stable. They locked their knees and slept standing up. The chickens stopped laying and the cows gave little milk. None of us even tried to scratch the frost from the window panes to see outside anymore. Even the sun, when it made a rare appearance, was ghost pale, not worth looking at.

Damn The Prophet, anyway!

We began to blame him for our woes.

We hardly cared to turn over the calendar when March came.

March - April - May - And The Prophet said we'd have snow in June.

Four more months of the same. Four more months to hunch down and sullenly survive.

But miracle of miracles, The Prophet was wrong!

It suddenly turned warm. The mercury climbed past the zero mark on the thermometer, then into the tens and the twenties. The days were cloudless, windless and the sun shone again. Over the barrier of 32 degrees inched the mercury.

A little thaw," The Prophet said, but day after day the mercury rose further up the scale. It even stopped freezing at night!

By March 12th, we were having temperatures in the sixties. It was unheard of. Impossible. We always had terrible storms in March. Rarely did spring come until May.

We were almost afraid to hope and then the crows came back on St. Patrick's Day. Word of their arrival swept through the village like a crownfire in a spruce forest.

"The crows are back. No, not the ravens, the crows!"

We heard their ancient cry, a sure sign of winter's end.

No one who has not lived in the north country can possibly understand what the coming of spring can mean to those who have suffered the long cold, endured the bite of winter.

Oh, to watch the hill streets become rivers as great banks of snow sink and sag; To see the tops of fences again; To hear the great booming - shuddering echo across Lake Superior as the thick pack ice cracks and groans; To walk again down the railroad tracks on a Sunday afternoon; To walk, not to ski or snowshoe but to walk and without heavy clothing; To find the first patch of arbutus on a sunny bank; To catch that first sight of green grass!

The horses shared our exhilaration. Blinking and hesitant when first led from the barn, they were soon rearing and prancing or rolling over and over on the bare ground, kicking their legs in the air - just like we were. And the cows mooed and played bull with each other before munching the new grass so their butter would turn yellow again. Mrs. Haitema threw away the can of old coffee ground she'd been saving. Catholics went to early Mass again. The clotheslines blossomed with color all over town, long johns dancing in the breeze. Ponds, everywhere ponds, where we could sail little boats made from wood shingles, or wade, or just fall in and get soaked for the hell of it. Sparrows fought over fresh horseturds and boys fought over anything at all. Spring, Spring, Glorious Spring! We'd made it through the winter!

It was a tough time for The Prophet as you can imagine.

"What do you perdick today, Prophet? Snow till June, Prophet? Got your long underwear on yet, Prophet?"

O'Hara and his followers were in their glory.

Little children would run along beside The Prophet's rig, chanting, "Prophet, Prophet, you're way off it" or You make us sick with I perdick." The big man ignored them mostly.

One weekend in early April, he predicted that a terribly heavy snow would cover the land the next Monday. He got the amount of precipitation right, but it was rain, not snow.

By the middle of the month the ground was dry enough to be plowed and potato planting began. Over and over, The Prophet pleaded with the men to wait at least until the usual time, Memorial Day, but by then the temperature was in the seventies, the pike had completed their spawning, violets and adder's-tongue and trillium were everywhere in the woods and it was summer-like. So they laughed at The Prophet and reviled him... so much that he stopped coming to the post office.

May came and the peonies bloomed in the yards. Maples shed their red buds and leafed out. Even the tamaracks in the swamps sprouted new green pinfeathers. By the third week of May, men were sharpening their scythes on the grindstones. It would soon be haying time.

The week before Memorial Day, The Prophet appeared again at the post office. He was in no mood to accept any of O'Hara's nasty mouth and sent him sprawling in the corner with the back of his giant hand.

"You make fun for me, no?" His voice was like thunder and his eyes swept the room.

"But I tell you something now you weel remembair! I perdick she will get cold and freeze an snow yet. And in June month I tell you too."

No one laughed - and it was just as well too, for the next day it turned bitter cold. A wild wind swept down from the northeast, blackening the flowers and the potatoes, shoving the people back inside their houses and the animals into the barns. And it got worse and worse. And it snowed and snowed and snowed through half of June.

But we got our Prophet back!

King Of The Poachers

This story is about Laf Bodine, King of the Poachers, the most skillful violator Michigan's Upper Peninsula ever produced.

That honor really meant something special in our land of great granite hills, brimful lakes, deep snow and huge forests, a land where the game warden was generally regarded as a mortal enemy because he threatened the very survival of half the populace.

Most of the men of that time were violators of the game laws mainly because they had to be in order to survive and partly because they enjoyed the sport of outwitting the conservation officers.

With the iron mines closed down and the logging activities uncertain after most of the giant white pine had been cut, there was little money for anything. Certainly there was none for "store meat" when the streams were full of trout, the lakes teeming with pike and the forests with rabbits, partridge and deer.

It's a bit hard to view the illicit activities of that time in proper perspective. The dynamiting of a beaver pond full of brook trout seems outrageous today, but back then those trout, carefully salted down in a barrel back in the woodshed, made the difference between eating or going hungry when March came. It's even difficult for me to remember the urgency connected with making sure the cellar shelves were crowded with jars of venison or canned wild berries - how important it was that there be a huge crock of sauerkraut, slabs of bacon and plenty of smoked or marinated fish on hand when the leaves turned gold and red.

Make it through the winter! Make it through the winter! That "command" was heard by all of us. Every autumn there was fear. Spring brought triumph, but with that triumph returned some of the urgency to start getting ready for another winter. The old bitter jest about, "Nine months of winter and three months of rough sledding," was not very funny to the people of the U.P. at the turn of the century.

There were years when every month brought a frosty night and I remember sleeping out once on the shore of Goose Lake in a heavy snowstorm... That was on August, 3rd.

What I'm trying to say is that we needed all the fish and game we could get and we didn't particularly care how we got it.

The State Legislature, 400 miles away in Lansing, could pass all the game laws they wished, but we had to survive. They could send their game wardens north to catch us, if they could. Sometimes they did and sometimes they didn't, but all of us poached without the slightest sense of guilt.

Poor old Belanger was the laughing stock of the entire community because he always got caught. Whether haying or potato digging time, he always carried enough fine money in his pocket when he went shining deer because he had to stay out of jail long enough to get the crops in. Most of us were more adept.

The king of the poachers, though, was Laf Bodine. He was our hero, the most cunning and resourceful of all the violators in the Upper Peninsula. He'd made a career of it. Except for the month in the summer when he made pocket money guiding around a bunch of rich bastards from Chicago up at the Huron Mountain Club or when he was trapping, he probably did some violating every day of his life. His exploits were legend in our land. We admired him greatly. Moreover, Laf Bodine was sort of a Robin Hood. Any family that was having a rough go of it could expect to find a mess of fish or a couple of ducks or a haunch of venison on their back porch come daylight... especially if they were out of season!

They always knew who the giver was too, though Laf never mentioned it. You see, he always left his trademark - a slip of birch bark with a cedar twig stuck through it. Once or twice our family even found such an offering on the back porch. We found a big pike once and six blue winged teals another time, both gifts complete with birch bark and cedar. The reason my dad, the village doctor, was sure it was Laf was that when he saw him the next day, Laf had asked if he'd ever received payment for Mrs. So and So's medical bill. Dad grinned and said yes and Laf grinned too.

And there was the time when the Juntinen's horse got struck by lightning down in the Company Field. That horse had made a living for Toivo Juntinen and his eight young kids. Seven prime beaver hides, all skinned out and fleshed, enough to buy a new horse, the birch bark and cedar twig... All this they found in their outhouse the next morning.

When anyone got a present of illegal game or fish, they knew it was Laf's doing. Some winters they said he kept half the village alive. In return, for our people were very proud in their own way, Laf could always count on an occasional loaf of homemade bread, a dish of fresh butter or some Mason jars of canned blueberries to vary his meat diet. I remember once going out to Laf's cabin at Fish Lake with a friend of mine whose mother had knitted Laf some socks and mittens after she'd found a hind quarter of venison in their sauna building. The family hadn't eaten meat in over a month.

Laf's real name was Lafferty, named so as a slight gesture of affection - of revenge - by his mother Sarah, a full-blooded Menominee Indian, after Laf's probably father, a wild Irish mining engineer who had graced and raped our town for a few months in 1909. Perhaps that was why Laf had that shocking red head of hair that lit up the forest trails he strode. There were nine or ten other people in town with that same red hair and all were about the same age and fatherless, though that made little difference to anyone. You just had to be careful about whom you called a bastard! We took care of our own and a child was a child and always seemed to be welcome.

The original Lafferty had been a giant of a man and smart, according to those who'd known him. He didn't drink or smoke, but he sure must have screwed everything in sight. He'd gotten himself fired after four months in town when the mining superintendent caught him with his seventeen year old daughter in the mining office. She too had a red headed baby, but had married a guy in Ishpeming and left town.

Anyway, Laf was a big man and as red headed as his father, but not so fond of women. He stayed pretty much clear of them.

They say Nellie Bodner almost had her hooks in him once, but that broke up when Laf found out he'd have to buy a license. That went against his principles! A wife and kids would have just interfered with his life's chosen work anyway - poaching!

Much of what I write is hearsay because I only had one personal encounter with the king of the poachers and that was when I was only about nine years old.

It was on a Sunday afternoon in early spring. I'd hiked down the railroad tracks to see how far over the banks the Tioga River had flooded, thinking that I might try fishing there next day. There's a little feeder creek that parallels the tracks just above Red Bridge and below the tangle of an old beaver dam that plugged it, I saw the silver flash of fish.

"Ah," I'd said to myself. "Here's the time to learn how to tickle trout."

I'd heard how from my elders that, if you were very careful, you could put your hand in the pool, hold it there for a few minutes and then, if you rubbed your hand backward along their bodies, it would mesmerize them long enough to let you grab them by the tail and heave them up on the bank.

I sneaked down the bank very carefully, put my arm in up to my shoulder and almost yelped it was so cold, but I waited. A fish about a foot long did swim over my open palm several times, but whenever I tried to stroke it backwards, it fled. I remember almost weeping with cold and frustration when Laf was suddenly there beside me.

"No, boy," he'd said gruffly. "You're going about this all wrong. Here, let me show you."

He stripped to the waist revealing a massive chest covered, like his arms, with a mat of red hair. Then he lay down on the bank beside the little pool, watched and waited until one of the fish swam over his hand and stayed there, undulating in the current. I watched enthralled as Laf ever so slowly brought his palm upward and forward from tail to head, stroking the fish ever so lightly. Then, suddenly, up came his hand with the fish held firmly by the gills. It was a big sucker, not a trout, but I almost clapped.

"Well, that's the way to do it, boy," Laf said. "Hell, if you start at the head end like you were, you'll always scare 'em. You were also stroking too fast and too hard. Easy does it. Slow... Slow...

Under his watchful eye and slightly bloodshot from a swallow of rot-gut he'd offered, I managed to catch two more before my arms became almost paralyzed from the icewater. Laf noticed my uncontrollable shivering and built a little fire of dead willow twigs. I remember that it gave off plenty of heat and almost no smoke at all.

"Here, boy, arch your belly over the fire, like this, and you'll warm up fast, even your frozen arm. I'll go get an ironwood branch and show you a better way to catch suckers."

Laf disappeared as silently as he'd come, returning shortly with a black club, stripped of bark and all but one branch. Laf whittled the branch with a monstrous sheaf knife until it had a sharp point. The whole outfit looked like a four foot fish hook. Then he cut a notch just below the sharp point and hardened the sharp end of the stick in the glowing coals until it was charred black. Thrusting the contraption into the pool, he quickly snagged out another sucker, an even bigger one.

"Do it the same way," he said. "Come up from the back end, but jerk quick and hard!"

I soon caught on to the knack and had four of them on the bank before he took the stick away from me.

"How many you need?" he asked. "Every one you catch you got to take home and I figger you've got ten, maybe twelve pounds already. We don't waste 'em. We don't waste anything…"

He walked every foot of the three miles back to the depot to make sure I didn't throw any of those damned suckers away!

I thought my arms would fall off, but I learned a lesson; several of them. One was that Laf Bodine was quite a man.

Even the game wardens agreed to that.

We had a whole series of them, one after another, a new one almost every year. Some said the Conservation Department used our town as a training school with Laf acting as the teacher for new game wardens. He certainly bested them, ran rings around them and made them look foolish while the townspeople cheered.

For one thing, Laf's fame was such that any new game warden always concentrated on catching him, leaving the rest of our poachers free to fill their larders. It wasn't true that the State sent only new recruits to our town either. Some of their very best men came.

They watched Laf's cabin; tried to follow him in the woods, tried to anticipate what he'd do or where he'd strike next. Laf made monkeys out of them.

The best of it was that Laf had a left-handed way of bragging about his skill at outwitting game wardens and it kept us abreast of his exploits.

Almost every evening from eight to ten, he could be found by the potbellied stove in the depot waiting room or at a table in Higley's Saloon, telling tales about his Uncle Joe. There would always be a group of men around him, sharing the lore and lies of hunting, fishing and violating adventures, but when Laf spoke, after a couple of hookers of rotgut, they mainly listened, with awe and respect.

They knew, of course, that Laf never had an Uncle Joe and that Uncle Joe was him, but they learned a lot about the way to poach and not get caught, from the "master."

"My Uncle Joe," Laf would begin, "knew all there was to know about catching trout, but he used to claim he never et one in his life that was legal size. He liked the sweet little ones, five and six inchers, fried crisp in the pan till you could eat 'em bones and all.

"Oh, sometimes he might get him a glass jug, put some carbide in it, put a little hole in the cork and then wire it down good before heaving it into a beaver pond. Uncle Joe used to sometimes bring half a sackful of trout and give 'em away to them that might be a-hungerin', people like Miz Olson up in Swedetown.

"You see, when the water leaks into the jug and the miner's carbide begins to fizz enough, boom goes the jug and there's your trout right on the surface. Just scoop 'em up. All sizes, but Uncle Joe he only kept the small ones. Said they were sweet as apple pie."

It didn't take much checking to find out that Mrs. Olson's kids had dined on trout the day before - and that they were small ones.

Whenever Laf voiced his opinion, not his Uncle Joe's, he was virtuous as hell.

"I don't approve of my Uncle Joe, that old reprobate," Laf would say. "The law may seem unreasonable, my friends, but them game wardens must do their duty, even if it means taking from the tables of the starving, the poor and the downhearted. Let me say it to you, my friends, any low down, no good son of a pup that'd violate them there laws should be hung from the nearest birch tree. That goes for my Uncle Joe too."

All the men in the saloon loved to listen as Laf supported the game wardens he bedeviled constantly.

In his depot and barroom tales of the exploits of Uncle Joe, Laf revealed many artisan secrets. He told how to use a set line in the spring when only a ring of water circled the shore, well before trout season opened; how to make a snare out of telephone wire for a deer runway; where to make a scaffold and how high up so the deer would walk right under it; when to dynamite pike during their spawning season; where to hide a deer you'd killed - in the outhouse, a dry well or under the hay in the barn.

I know one of his tales was true because I checked it out myself. There was always a deeryard over by Goose Lake when the snow got deep. Maybe a hundred or more deer wintered there and, as the game wardens found out, many of the families in our village relied on the area for their winter's meat supply.

It was hell trying to dodge the wardens once the snow came. You either went out hunting at the beginning of a blizzard, hoping the snow would cover your tracks, or you didn't go out at all. But, according to Laf, his Uncle Joe had solved the problem simply enough. He reversed the straps on his snowshoes and learned to walk with them that way.

Any game warden would think Uncle Joe was going south when, in fact, he was trudging along north.

I knew Laf and not his mythical Uncle Joe had actually done this because, one winter when I was snar'ng rabbits by Horseshoe Lake, I saw him going by down the trail and was amazed to see his tracks leading off the other way. The game wardens never caught on to the trick and you can bet none of the townspeople ever told him. You had to make it through the winter and it was good to know that Laf Bodine was not in jail!

Only once did Laf "almost" get caught.

Seventy year old Francois Perine, who had already reared one big brood of children, suddenly found himself saddled with another batch of kids when his youngest son and his wife had both died. All seven of their children had come back to town to live with the Perines in a cabin far too small for them. It was really rough going for the old man and Denise, his wife.

One December day, Laf came upon old Francois, lying in the snow completely bushed alongside a deer he'd dragged for half a mile through the snow. He still had to miles to go.

Laf knew the game warden was in the area, but he built a fire for the old man, boiled a can of water over it and inserted a sock with a handful of tea in the toe. When the water turned copper colored he gave some to Francois along with a lump of sugar.

When he was sure the old man had revived, Laf tied the fore and hind legs of the deer together, flung it over his shoulder, and made his way to town with his backward snowshoes.

He dumped the deer off in Father Hassel, the Catholic Priest's carriage house so Francois could pick it up later. Then he went back to see how the old man was doing. There he found the game warden who promptly arrested Laf for removing the corpus delicti. The case never came to court though, because Father Hassel had found the deer and had hastily removed it...the corpus delicti.

But it was a close call.

Shortly after this incident, the State paid Laf Bodine the ultimate compliment. They formally offered him the job as game warden, $150 a month and a uniform.

All our townspeople waited anxiously while Laf made his decision. How would they dare violate if Laf were warden? How would they make it through the winter? Who would bring them meat when the children cried? They had no cause to worry. Laf didn't betray his people.

Laf never answered the game warden who offered him the job, but he acknowledged the compliment. He left a big chunk of venison, one trout and a partridge on the warden's doorstep - complete with a wisp of birch bark and a sprig of cedar.

Valentine's Day

"Paul," my mother said, as dad finished his breakfast, "Don't run off to work like you usually do. Listen to me. Did you know that Aunt Lizzie is setting her cap for Bill Trager? It's outrageous! Why she must be, let's see, 54 - 55 and Bill can't be more than 33 or so. But there's no mistake. She's out to marry him. Poor Bill, such a nice man - weak maybe and he drinks too much sometimes, but a real nice man."

My father grinned. "You know, she just might pull it off at that. Bill can't say no to anything or anybody. Everyone takes advantage of him. But how do you know she's after Bill?"

My mother ticked the items off on her fingers:

"1. Aunt Lizzie has her hair 'frizzed' fresh on Tuesday and again on Thursday, instead of only on Saturday, when she used to curl it for church.

"2. She bought raisins, brown sugar, some yeast and some flour at the store and she never had before. Going to bait Bill with cookies and homemade bread.

"3. Mrs. Casey saw Aunt Lizzie stop Bill Tuesday morning and bring him into her house - back door - and when Mrs. Casey just happened to take the opportunity to return the cup of sugar she'd borrowed, Aunt Lizzie was plying Bill with cookies and flirting outrageously, primping and being coy, as they had coffee together, tete-a-tete.

"God!" growled my father. "Everybody knows everything that happens in this town. Mrs. Casey borrows sugar from all her neighbors just so she can horn in any time she wants. Has she borrowed any from you, Edith?"

My mother made a little face and nodded.

"OK, buy her a sack so she won't find out when I cut my toenails!

"But how about Bill? Is he falling for the snare? I always thought he was kind of sweet on Annie, the postmistress."

"Oh, that was a long time ago," replied my mother. "I still think it would have been a good match, but they're both too sweet and kinda shy. Neither would take the first step.

No, Aunt Lizzie sure knows how to handle a man like that. Lead him by the nose right up to the church door… Like she did her other two husbands," continued mother.

"Yeah, and killed them both," said dad. "Nagged them to death! Any man can't tell

---

80

a woman to shut up deserves his fate. Well, anyway, there goes Bill Trager. Old Aunt Lizzie's got him!"

I was very upset. I bent lower over my Cream of Wheat.

Annie and Bill were special people in my life and Aunt Lizzie sure wasn't. I couldn't stand that old hag, the old simpering fake. I couldn't bear her bossiness at Sunday School or the horrible way she whined those high notes off key on the hymns. A nasty woman. She mustn't trap poor Bill into marrying her. If she did, he'd have to leave the little 40-acre homestead that he'd hewn out of the forest down by the lake and go live with her and those pictures of her dead husbands that hung in her parlor by the horsehair sofa. Those pictures had the pupils of the eyes dead-center so they seemed to follow you wherever you went in the room.

And Bill wouldn't be able to have any time for a small boy like me to help him know how to hitch up a horse - or to plow - or to whittle - or to listen to the wonderful tales of his Navy experiences... Like the time he found "Waterloo, Iowa" tattooed on the hind end of a girl in Marseilles.

Hell, Bill Trager would die, being married to someone like Aunt Lizzie. She'd make him dress up and shave every day like Silly Billy, the village idiot. If he married her, Bill wouldn't be able to keep his chickens and pig or his old horse that he treated to a big handful of oats every Fourth of July, saying, "Eat till ye bust!"

And I liked Bill's log cabin. It was halfway to the lake, a good place to stop, all full of junk - padlocks, magnets, tools and bits of old harness. I dropped in often in the summer on my way for a swim, but even in the winter I would make my way down to his homestead for a pleasant afternoon. Bill seemed to like me. I certainly liked him.

I also liked Annie, the postmistress. You see, I helped deliver the mail.

Old Man Marteau who was responsible for bringing up the mail from the depot by sleigh in the winter and buckboard in the summer, lived right behind our house. Once he'd operated a livery stable, a flourishing one, but he was down to just a couple of horses and rigs by the time I got to know him. Nevertheless, every day - rain, snow or shine - he met the Duluth, South Shore and Atlantic (trainmen called it the DSS&A, "Damned Small Salary and Abuse"), every morning and evening, hauling the mail bags to the downtown post office and then to the uptown post office where Annie presided.

Old Man Marteau had arthritis pretty bad.

I remember my father calling me one hot summer's day to come see the old man buried to his neck in a manure pile and holding a little pink umbrella over him to fend off the sun.

"A good treatment," said my father. "Moist warm heat and pressure. My pharmacopoeia has nothing better."

Anyway, Old Man Marteau was glad enough in his surly way, to have me help him with his chores. I'd ride down to the station with him, get the mail bags when they were thrown down from the mail car, load them in the rig and carry them into the two post offices. I was also elected to use the long buggy whip to keep the other kids from hitching rides with their sleds and wagons.

The mail bags usually weren't too heavy for me except at Christmas and seed catalogue time, and I would bring them into the inner sanctum sanctorum of Annie's post office with real pride, because there was a sign on the door that said: "Private

Property of the United States Government. Unauthorized Personnel Forbidden to Enter."

Once inside and behind the wall of pigeon holes and lock boxes, Annie would let me unlock the mail bags and do some of the preliminary sorting. It sure made me feel important.

Annie was a rather plain woman, about 30, but she had a sweet smile and a very soft voice. I liked her. Everybody liked her, though some suspected that she steamed open letters and read their mail. She certainly knew a lot about all the people in town.

Anyway, I decided to pay Bill Trager a visit one afternoon. He was sharpening a scythe with a long hone. It seemed a bit odd since it was only the first week of February with drifts higher than a man"s head everywhere. I'd had a hard time getting down to Bill's place even with the trail well broken.

I found Bill morose and without any good stories. He just kept sharpening that scythe, zing - zing, spitting on the hone to make it work better.

Being only eleven years old, I just couldn't keep still any longer.

"Bill," I said, "They're saying old Aunt Lizzie is going to marry you. You aren't going to let her do that, are you?"

Bill put down his scythe and lit his pipe.

"Well," he said, "She's got me scared, I'll admit. Every time I go past her house on my way for the mail, it's 'Mister Trager, would you kindly fix this poor widow's doorknob - or help move her settee' or she's out shoveling snow and asks for just a little help. And then she feeds me good vittles - Damned good vittles. A lot better than my bacon and beans and coffee-pail-bread. Of course, she's old enough to be my mother, but what's wrong with having a mother? Ah, that's crazy talk. Enough."

He fell silent and I eventually left, really worried. But what could one small boy do?

I decided to try to do something, nevertheless.

I went down to Flinn's store and bought a bunch of store valentines. I had to rob my businessman bank, the one where you put a coin in the little seated man's hand and he'd drop it into his vest packet. Anyway, I bought seven valentines, addressed three of them to Annie and three to Bill and signed their names appropriately. I forget now what I wrote on the lacy things all full of hearts and flowers, but it was something like, "I've kept loving you all these years," for the first card, then I progressed to, "I hunger for you, my dear" and "I'll be at the post office tonight at eight-thirty. Please come, my true love."

It was hard for an eleven-year-old to write that doggone mushy stuff, but I did and I wrote the same on each pair of valentines, one for Annie and one for BILL. I felt a little guilty signing their names like that, but I had to do something to stop Aunt Lizzie.

Then, each night after dark, I'd walk down to the post office and drop the letters with the valentines in them into the slot of the locked door. I sure worried hard about the whole business.

Finally, about a week after Valentine's Day had come and gone, I went back to delivering the mail bags again. I don't really know what happened, but Annie was looking almost pretty and she kissed me. Blaugh! Wet lips! I wiped them off as she turned to the teakettle on the potbellied stove and held up the envelope against it impishly.

"You're a good boy and you had a marvelous idea and it worked!" Annie flushed. "But it was the seventh valentine that helped most of all!" she said.

I knew what she meant. It was the one I'd bought for Aunt Lizzie and signed Bill Trager's name to. Lord, it was a horrible one, an old fashioned comic valentine, featuring an ugly old woman with warts and wens, and bearing a verse inscribed with a blackened heart:

Lizzie,
"Roses are red and violets are blue,
But How in the hell could anyone love you."
Bill Trager

Grampa

This is a story about the biggest trout ever taken from the Tioga River. You may not particularly like trout or stories about them, but you sure would have liked my Grampa Gage, and I can't tell about the one without telling about the other.

There is a special sort of relationship that exists between grandparents and grandchildren which can be curiously close and rewarding. Perhaps it exists because they share a common enemy, the generation in between...

Grandparents have little compulsion to pull the onion to make it grow. They feel no great responsibility for shaping or molding the new clay. Grandchildren are to be enjoyed. So too are grandparents, since they aren't always saying do this or do that. Still, I feel there is another more important reason for the affinity. Grandchildren share a common secret with their grandparents and that is that the way to live is to suck the present moment for all the juice that's in it and nuts to the past and future!

Anyway, Grampa and Grandma Gage came to live with us from spring to autumn during the two years when I was nine and ten. They were two of the most delightful years of my life, not because of Grandma (she was a nasty, razor-tongued old she-devil), but because Grampa Gage was mine, all mine. He was my 74 year-old playmate, mentor, model and constant companion. A boy of 9 or 10 has a deep hunger for identification and association with a man, a hunger that my own father had neither the time nor the inclination to satisfy. I was lucky, very lucky to have my Grampa Gage.

He was a short man, but very wiry and tough. He had been a farmer, lumberjack, teamster, grocer, banker and bankrupt, in that order. He'd gone bankrupt because his best friend, the cashier at the bank, had absconded to South America with most of the liquid assets. All that Grampa had left after the inevitable run on the bank were his sense of humor and his dignity. It was a bit surprising that he had managed to retain either because Grandma Gage's tongue never let him forget the bank failure, even though she had lots of money and stocks of her own and the house in her name. Perhaps it was because she felt compelled to constantly humiliate Grampa in public that he found the relief and escape he needed in our relationship, but I don't believe it. Grampa Gage just liked being with me.

Each day began at 5:30 with Grampa shaving in the bathroom beside my bedroom. He'd be lathering his face (and often a bit of mine), with copious suds, twisting it into a hundred contortions - all funny ones - as he stroked at it with the gleaming straight razor. Next, he'd comb the gray mustache that always had a smile flickering beneath it and he'd turn to me. "Well, Mr. McGillicuddy, shall we do our exercises?"

He had a new name for me every day and he used that name all day except when other people were around. Then he just called me "Boy."

So we'd do our exercises, then go down to the kitchen, make a pot of coffee and share some toast and conversation before any of the rest of the family woke up. Grampa Gage never talked down to me the way most grown-ups did.

"Mr. McGillicuddy," he would say, "I would appreciate your opinion, sir, on the prospects for another nice day" or "Mr. Gallupus, what, sir, is the a-gend-a for our morning adventure?"

His blue eyes always twinkled, but his face and manner were completely serious. Whatever I gave would be considered gravely.

If, for example, I would say that we might start building a shack hideaway down in the grove behind the chicken coop, Grampa Gage would give it some long, silent thought, pursing his lips, furrowing his brow and nodding before replying, "Well, Mr. Anderanderanderson, I agree. Let us indeed erect a Taj Mahal this fine day. Where, sir, do you think we might find the necessary and appropriate equipment, sir? A hammer perhaps?"

Grampa used lots of big words which he never explained unless I asked, but he would sound them out now and then.

Some mornings when it became time to decide what to do, Grampa would say, "Enjoy. Just enjoy!"

Some days all we would do would be to collect different shades of green, or taste plants like soursap, nettles and Indian tobacco, or just feel rocks. Other days we would hunt holes and hide treasures in them for another day; a sugar lump, a piece of gum, or a note to Mother Earth.

Perhaps the most important thing I learned from Grampa was to have a gay spirit and not to be afraid of fantasy or afraid to do or say nutty things.

For one thing, Grampa was always rhyming.

He'd point to a sapling and say, "I'd like to be that birch. Wouldn't have to go to church."

But most of the time he made Grampa Goosers, as he called them.

"Fiddle Dee Dee, Fiddle Dee Dee, Grandma sat down on a bumblebee. The bee stung her twice. Now wasn't that nice? And her bottom's as red as can be. Tee Hee! Her bottom's as red as can be."

Or he'd suddenly ask me if I'd ever seen a frog cry and proceed to tell me a long tale about a monster frog he once saw rocking back and forth on its haunches just dripping with tears and moaning, "Why am I the only frog in the world who doesn't know how to jump?"

Well, Grampa said he felt really sorry for the varmint, especially when the other frogs in the swamp, not half his size, were teasing him and calling him "Kindergarten baby, slopped in the gravy."

So Grampa said he got down beside the frog, told him how to jump and showed him how.

"And then, Boy, you know what I did? I took out this here pencil while he was thinking over what I'd told him and I give that old frog the goosiest goose up the hind end you ever did see. An' he took off like a projeck-tile, he did, right up straight in the air, and lit on a tree branch. I had a devil of a time getting him down and told him to take it easier next time, but he didn't. Just kept jumpin' and jumpin' and jumpin', higher and higher every time, and one moonlit night he scrunched down and took off and nobody ever saw him again. Some say there's a man in the moon you can see if you look right close, but 'pears to me it looks more like that there frog. I'd 'preciate knowing what you see, Mr. O'Flaherty, next time you get the chance."

Grampa always told the best stories after he'd had a snort or two from the little black bottle in his hip pocket. He never let me taste it though.

"Save something for your old age, Mr, O'Flaherty. Save something for your old age," he'd say.

Sometimes I just had to ask him if his stories were true.

Like the time he told me about General Gage, who during the Revolutionary War, while in command of the British troops after they captured Boston, had seduced a fair young American maiden under a rose bush.

"And from that issue, Mr. O'Toole, all the Gages have come, including you, Mr. O'Toole. Though you bear not the name, yet that noble blood runs in your veins, as you shall know one day when with girl under a rose, Mr. O'Toole."

Grampa looked at me hard. "And what's more, Boy, I put upon you a command. You are not to divulge, which is to say, tell any female relative of mine what I have imparted to you this day. I mean both Grandma Gage and her daughter, your mother, or your own daughter or her daughters, but you shall tell your son and your son's son this thing."

I was very impressed, especially when he insisted that I swear to do his bidding by "the immortal grace of the daisies" in which we were sitting at the time, but I still couldn't help asking if it was really true.

"Should it be true?" roared Grampa. "Should it be true?"

His question has beset me all the rest of my life.

Wild and wonderful as our conversations were, there were times when our actions were just as zany.

Like the time we had been on safari, hunting lions in deepest Africa, down in the meadow. Not real lions, ant lions, those curious beetles that make a funnel in the sand to trap any unwary insect that ventures along its slope.

Grampa would say a magic word like "Oogalalamot.," tickle the side of the funnel with a straw and out of the hole would come the ant lion, clicking its jaws. Then we'd run like hell and Grampa would have to take a swig or two from his black bottle to "regain" his courage.

"Out of the jaws of death, it's hard to catch your breath," he'd say.

I think that was the time, too, that he taught me 'The Dance of the Wild Cucumber.' I can still see Grampa doing it, crossing his arms in the air and chanting the refrain ecstatically, "O Tweedle Dee and Tweedle Dum, All Hail Immortal Nose and Thumb" -always with the appropriate gesture on the final word. I got pretty good at it finally.

It was always difficult for me to understand or accept the drastic shift in role that took place in Grampa Gage's behavior when he returned to the house. As soon as he entered the door, he suddenly became another person; quiet, dignified and solemn. No more jokes. No wild flights of fancy. He was just very polite and reserved.

What was worse, he became Grandma's slave and whipping boy.

"Arzeeeee!" she would screech (his name was Arza), "Fetch me my scissors. Fetch me this. Fetch me that. Quick now, stonefoot, stonehead! Why did I ever marry a slug like you, Arzeeeee? I said fetch my scissors."

"I'm coming, Nettie. I'm coming. I've found your scissors."

Grampa wouldn't hurry, but he always did her bidding. And then she lashed at him with all the caustic invective she could muster while he just stood there calmly and waited for her to stop. She'd humiliate him so much that I wanted to throw the coal scuttle at her sometimes. Grandma Gage was not a nice person and she caused quite a strain in our household. Just to give one minor example of her irritating ways - At the table she would never ask politely for something she wanted like Grampa always did. Instead, she'd snarl, "Have you got a mortgage on that butter?"

She was a female hellion and how Grampa took it and bore her clacking all those years was a mystery.

I explored the matter with him once and he told me the story of Socrates and his shrewish wife, Xantippe. How once the philosopher had come home late from drinking with the boys to find the door locked. At his knock, Xantippe poked her head out the window above and gave him blue fits, getting angrier and angrier with every nasty word, finally to a point where she emptied the chamber pot over his head. Grampa paused and relit his pipe.

"And then, Mr. O'Hallahan, Socrates proved, sir, that he was indeed a true philosopher. He wiped his brow and said, 'After the thunder comes the rain.' I, Mr. O'Hallahan, am not a philosopher, but even I know that even the widest river runs somewhere safe to sea."

I had another glimpse that shed some light on their curious relationship. It came right after I'd done something very bad. I don't remember what it was, but it was bad because even Grampa was upset with me.

True to character, however, he never mentioned it directly, but while walking down the back road to the lake, he began talking about the trees and bushes as though they were people.

"Now that lovely birch sapling there, that's your mother. And that fine spruce is your father. A bit hard to climb up on, and scratchy, but a good stout tree. Now look at this young maple seedling, Boy. It's beginning to grow crooked, growing all wrong. Let's straighten it up, Boy."

I understood immediately that I was the young maple and I began to cry. Grampa comforted me, and to distract me from my woe, pointed out a large hawthorne full of thorns and red haw berries. I put one of the haws in my mouth and began to nibble at it.

"Cannibal, Cannibal!" Grampa hollered. "Stop eating Grandmaw."

I burst into laughter, thinking how thorny she was, but then Grampa interrupted in a wistful, far away voice, "But, ah, that hawthorne was lovely in the spring, Boy."

I've probably told you too much about my Grampa, but you still can't really know what he was like unless I tell you about that big trout.

At that time, no one in the Upper Peninsula ever fished for anything but northern pike and trout. We preferred the latter.

My father, who lived to be 94, attributed his long life to the fact that the only days that counted were those on which he didn't go trout fishing! He had the fever - but he was a meat fisherman, counting a trip successful only when he returned with his basket full to the brim.

Grampa was different. He was a fly fisherman and perfectly content to bring back just a fish or two, usually those that had been injured in the battle with the hook and line. The rest he returned to the water with a long and proper admonition about things not being what they seem.

One of the aches I remember from childhood was that my dad wouldn't ever take me fishing with him. When he did manage to steal a few hours from his work, he preferred to fish with his cronies, wading up to his armpits in the big river, dunking his worms and always after as many trout as he could get. He used to twit Grampa about fly fishing, telling him that all he'd ever get on flies were the baby ones, that any decent trout wanted the biggest night crawler that could be found.

That didn't bother Grampa any and he was bound that I would learn to fly fish. So for about a month we'd walk down Company Field Hill and across the swamp to Beaver Dam Creek so I could practice with his flyrod. It was hard to get the knack of it until Grampa had me practice putting a green apple on a stick and flinging it off suddenly. After that it was easy. When I even caught a small trout or two from the pond, Grampa said I was ready for a real fishing ex-ped-ition.

And so, one fine summer afternoon, there we were in the buckboard, riding up the logging trail that runs alongside the Tioga, the old horse stepping lively under the slap of the reins. We even had a little adventure when old Billy suddenly began to snort and rear and refused to take another step.

"Now what the tarnation has got into him?" asked Grampa. Then he sniffed. "Oh, oh. Smell it, Boy? Bear smell. One must have crossed here short time ago."

Grampa got off and led Billy past the place and I got a whiff of it, rank and strong.

There wasn't any more trouble, but I was a bit scared going down the steep incline of Campbell's hill. I remember the song the old loggers had about it.

"Going up Campbell's hill, coming down,
"Going up Campbell's hill, coming down,
"With the horse standing still and the wheels going round
"Going up Campbell's hill, coming down."

It was steep, but Grampa sure knew how to handle a horse.

When Grampa finally stopped and unharnessed Billy to feed him some oats and a chunk of hay from the back of the wagon, I was almost jumping with excitement. We gathered our gear and made our way down a narrow trail that angled kittycorner along the bluff to the river bottom and the lovely pool below the broken old bridge. It was a long pool bordered by reddish gravel from the overhanging cliff. There was plenty of room for the back cast.

Grampa was in no hurry as he put the gut leader to soak in a little pool beside the log where he sat. He even refilled his pipe before he assembled his bamboo flyrod.

"Now, Boy," he said observing my impatience, "let's just wait a mite till you calm down or you'll forget everything you've learned. Where would you say, sir, that you would be a-lying were you a fat, hungry trout?"

I pointed to a foam circled eddy at the head of the pool.

"Mebbe so, mebbe so," replied Grampa, "but let's save that for later and begin casting down at the tail of the run. You'll often find a lazy one in such a place just awaiting for you. Mind though, that if one takes your fly, you keep him out of those old beaver cuttings."

Then he took a leather covered fly box out of his inside coat pocket and asked me to pick out two of the wet flies, one for the dropper and one for the end of the leader. I selected the brightest ones, a red and white Parmachene Belle, and the blue and white Silver Doctor. Grampa raised his bushy eyebrows questioningly, but tied them on.

"Whose turn first?" he asked as we finally rose from the log.

It was hard, but I managed to say that I thought it ought to he his turn first so he could show me how to do it, that I might throw a sloppy line and spoil it for him. Grampa gave the decision some thought then said no, he'd take his turn later.

"Now Boy," he admonished, "I'm going to say only three things and, may God help me, not a word more. Cast a little bit upstream as slow and easy as you can. Take up the slack as it drifts down so you'll have a tight line. Any trout will hook hisself then. And DON'T HORSE 'EM IN or I'll beat your damned tail off."

He almost scared me, he sounded so ferocious.

Well, I didn't do too badly the first two casts. Caught a trout on each of them. Not very big ones, maybe ten inchers, but I switched hands and played them off the reel just like Grampa had shown me until I had them near the shore. Then I swung them back on the, gravel for him to take off. I had just begun the backcast for the third try when I remembered about taking turns and I made a mess of it while I was telling Grampa I'd forgotten and was sorry. You just can't talk and cast a fly at the same time. As I handed him the rod, he told me we'd have to wait a bit because the splash of the rod tip along with the tangled line had surely put the trout down.

"Let's just contemplate and enjoy," he urged as he lit his pipe and puffed for the longest time, sending pale blue rings of smoke drifting past me. I cleaned my two beautifully speckled trout and put them in the basket.

"Is it time for me to try again, Grampa? It must be an hour."

He was amused at my impatience and showed me on his gold watch that only 13 minutes had gone by.

"Well," he said, "I see the fever's on you, Boy, so why don't you take the rod up to the head of the pool and cast there at the base of that riffle while we're waiting for these to calm down. But first, here's one for the gentleman!" and Grampa pulled out the black bottle from his hip pocket, took a hefty gulp, then dipped both flies in the liquor. "That's for luck. Go catch us a sloib, as the Finns would say."

Grampa's nose was hovering over the bottle again so I went along the gravel upstream about a hundred feet, made a couple of good back casts and let the line go out. A perfect cast for once! The flies lit on the water like eiderdown and had barely sunk beneath the surface when WHAM! The rod was almost pulled out of my hand and the tip bent under the water as the reel whirred under my hand. Something terribly heavy tore my line downstream toward Grampa - then over across to the other bank, then back almost to my feet, then up into the riffle where I saw it for the first time. A monster fish! I wish I could remember what actually happened, but I couldn't then and I can't now. All I recall is Grampa running up and down the gravel, hollering and praying.

"Keep the rod up! Oh, dear Lord, turn him, turn him, quick, before he gets in that snag! Boy! Let him have it! Let him have it! Crank, crank, crank! Take up the slack!

Take up the slack! Tight line, Boy! Tight line! Let him wear himself out. Lord, oh Lord, don't let him get off!

I know I did everything wrong. I even slipped on a rock once and sat down hard with my butt in the water, but I kept the rod high even then. I don't know how long the battle lasted - a minor eternity - but the big trout finally began to tire and I started to move him in closer to the sandbar where I was standing, knee-deep in the stream.

Grampa was still hollering at me.

"Now back up, Boy! Back up slowly! He's coming in. Oh Lord, don't let him get away now! Back way up on the bank, Boy. No, no, keep the rod high. Easy now..."

Grampa waded in behind the fish, and with him splashing behind and me pulling, it thrashed and wiggled and slid right up on dry land. Grampa leaped upon it, pinning it safely to the gravel while I put the rod down and came shakily over to see what I'd caught.

"Never was such a trout. Never!" yelped Grampa, panting as he un-hooked the fly.

"Look, it won't possibly fit in the basket. Good thing we brought the wagon! Here, Boy, here's your fish. Put him way up there in the shade."

It was even hard for me to lift it, it was so heavy. I had to use both hands. Grampa sat down on the log, his hands trembling. He could hardly get the little black bottle to his mouth.

"C'mon here, Boy! This calls for a celebration."

He rummaged in a pocket and brought out a collapsible tin cup which he filled with river water, then he poured a little liquor in from the black bottle.

"A toast to the King of the River!" he said. "Drink it down, King! Drink it down!"

It tasted like river water and I spit it out as I went back to admire the big fish and allow Grampa to get over the shakes.

He must have gotten over them for he suddenly gave a great yell and there he was, doing the 'Dance of the Wild Cucumber' all the way up to the bridge and back.

"You're turn Grampa, your turn." I motioned to the rod.

"Dunno if I have the strength to hold it," he replied. "But I'll try her a couple of times and then we'll go home and show your folks what the King of the River has caught. Don't worry about the trout. He's safe. I tunked him over the head with a rock and he won't get away. You'd better go up to the rig and put a lot of ferns under the seat so he'll keep fresh and won't lose color on the way home."

Up on the hill beside the road I found enough ferns for several armsful, but between carries I went partway down the trail to see how Grampa was doing.

Hey, he had a fish on too. And a big one. Another monster. Bigger than mine? Yes, it was! I had an empty sinking feeling in my stomach. But why was Grampa doing everything wrong?

He was jerking the line, horsing the fish, trying to lead it into the snag! And why was he fumbling for something in his pocket?

A moment later he slid the great trout up on the bank, cut the leader right at the fly and gently shoved the fish back into the water with his foot.

Carrying my trout, he met me coming down the trail. Grampa pointed to the broken leader before I could say anything.

"Let's call it a day, Boy. Snapped off my leader on a snag and lost the flies. Let's go home."

It was a long ride home behind the old horse clomping down the road, but it was worth it when dad, mother and Grandma Gage came out to the barnyard to see how we'd done.

"How many you get?" asked dad.

"Only three," I answered.

"But there's only two here in the basket," he said, peering into it.

Then I showed him what was in the ferns under the seat.

"Well, I'll be damned. Never saw such a trout. I'll be damned. Go four pounds. On a fly too? Impossible!"

"And how about you, Arzee?" demanded Grandma. "How about you?"

"Aw, I got skunked," said Grampa happily.

That's the kind of man he was.

Old Blue Balls

A violent war between the 'Uptowners and the Downtowners' had been waged sporadically for many years in the little village where I was born and spent my childhood.

The town had two centers, each with a store and tiny post office. One was in the valley, the other at the crest of the hill. A straggle of houses lined the one street that joined them.

The railroad station and a community of French Canadians and a few half-breed Indians were situated in the valley. On top of the hill lived the Finns, a few Swedes, three or four Cornish ex- miners who hadn't left when the iron mine closed, and the rest of us. The school with its playground battlefield divided the two areas.

It was Catholics versus Protestants in a neighborhood war of the roses or bloody noses. You had to fight to survive. I had more black eyes and puffed lips in my day than any prize fighter, but so did all the rest of the kids.

Every school day produced a few fights, individual or gang. The chip on the shoulder was reality.

"I kin lick you!"

"Let's go down and get the Frogs!"

"Pass the word. The Suomalinas (Finns) are coming. Get your clubs."

There were no Marquis of Queensbury rules - only one: No fair kicking in the crotch! We fought until they ran or until we ran, bloody from the field.

The mayhem peaked twice each year: in the fall when the first snow packed well enough to make iceballs and in late spring when the snow was almost gone and we could take off the itching underwear - usually May. Hell, in the spring you just had to do something outrageous. We fought. It wasn't enough to just piss in some other kid's maple sap buckets. You had to raise real hell. Like young bucks, we had to lock horns and charge. Spring always had the best - or worst - battles royal. Like the sap, blood had to flow. It was tradition!

Oddly enough, now 50 years later, the fighting has stopped. The Finns and the French have intermarried. The kids nowadays make love and play organized baseball. The towns have come together, become one, are homogenized and pasteurized. The old tradition of battle is ended. This is the tale of how that war finally stopped and how peace came to the village at last. It's the tale of the big shit fight and how we got the best of Old Blue Balls, the school superintendent.

Old Blue Balls

To understand, you would have had to know Old Blue Balls Donegal. His 'real name' was Mister Donegal or Old Man Donegal, but everyone called him "Sininen Pollu," a Finnish phrase meaning dark blue testicles, and we used the English translation...Behind his back!

To his face it was always, "Yes, Mr. Donegal. No, Mr. Donegal."

Old Blue Balls was tough. In his late fifties when I knew him, he was in perfect physical condition with a wrestler's torso. He was short and looked thin, but oh, was he in shape.

When he looked at you hard with his electric blue eyes, the impact was almost that of a physical blow. He had gray bushy eyebrows and two deeply engraved furrows on each side of a widely slit mouth which eventually joined a 'utting lower jaw. There was a spring to his walk and he always appeared half ready to pounce, probably because he kept his great clubs of fists slightly in front of his thighs and didn't alternate his arms like most people do when they walk. Donegal looked tough and he was. In that rough land and time he had to be.

The story of how he was hired and how he took charge illustrates the point.

Our school had been in some trouble because a minor depression had halted most of the logging operations for a year or two. Ordinarily, when a boy got big enough to lick the teacher or the superintendent, he was big enough to start cutting pulp. Few ever finished high school, but since there wasn't any work in the bush, the big boys stayed in school and made life miserable for all of us and especially for the teachers. The matter came to a head on opening day of the fall semester when a new superintendent and two or three new teachers arrived. The old ones had quit to nurse their bruises.

Among the new teachers was a Miss Crough who looked like an old black broom. The first morning session went well enough, but when the teachers came back to school after lunch, they had to walk the gauntlet of boys sitting on the fence that lined the schoolyard. All of them were being ominously quiet and polite - until Miss Crough came along. Then every boy on the fence cawed like a crow. They cawed in time to her steps. When she hurried, they cawed faster; when she lagged, they slowed down. She became angry and slapped one of the smaller boys, a mistake, for she then found herself leading a procession of cawing boys up the board sidewalk and into the building. And that wasn't the end of it. Caws were heard all over the school intermittently, for the rest of the day. Even in kindergarten! The superintendent called the constable who came and laughed and left. At seven-thirty that night, when Miss Crough, the other new teachers and the new superintendent boarded the train for Green Bay and Chicago, the school board met in emergency session to make plans for their replacement.

Anyway, that's how we wound up with Old Man Donegal, an honors graduate from the University of Chicago who loved to fish and hunt and who was so broke when he arrived that he had to borrow three dollars for food.

He sized up the situation instantly and made his presence felt by calling each and every pupil into his office. He began with the biggest ones. These he thrashed thoroughly, one after another, using his fists on the older tougher kids, a razor strop on the middle sized, a ruler for the smaller children and a gentle swat with the flat of his hand for the tiniest ones. Only the last ones got an accompanying grin.

The rest heard the same roar:

"Now take this and this and this! And let me tell you something. If I ever hear of you making any trouble around this school for anyone or if I catch you at it, I'll tan the tarnation hide right off you!"

Donegal meant it too. He demonstrated year after year. He ran a tight ship, terrorizing pupils and teachers alike. He'd often invade a classroom, watch what was going on for a moment and then take over the teaching himself if he didn't like what he saw. Loitering in the halls was even dangerous. He'd appear unexpectedly and accost you with questions:

"How much is eighty-seven times forty-three?

"What's the capital of Constantinople?

"Who was Daniel Boone?"

If you couldn't answer, you had to find out pronto and report in his office on the third floor of the three story frame building that was our schoolhouse. It was so old it swayed in the wind gusts. Anyway, no one ever entered that horror sanctum on the third floor without trembling, guilty or not.

Old Man Donegal was also very patriotic. All of us had to know every word of the Star Spangled Banner by heart and be prepared to sing it anywhere, on command. I recall one time during World War I, when the classroom door suddenly burst open and Mr. Donegal poked his head in to yell, "Forty Thousand Germans Killed. Hooray, Hooray, Hooray!"

When we failed to join in on the last hurrah, he entered and had us yell it for fifteen minutes.

He was also his own truant officer, not loathe to invade a home and drag a crying youngster out from under the bed. He always knew where we'd sneak off to go fishing or swimming and often as not he'd get to Fish Lake and be hiding in the bushes at Big Rock before we got there. He'd always wait though, until we'd taken off our clothes, before jumping out and whaling us. He was omniscient, omnipresent and omnipotent. We feared and hated Old Man Donegal intensely, but we sure respected him. He was always one move ahead and he always got the best of us -

Except once.

I was in the eighth grade then.

The year before, someone or something, maybe lightening, had burned down the old wooden school building and some of our classes were being held in my father's hospital across the street. That was where Donegal had his office.

Behind the hospital were two outhouses, each divided into two compartments with a hole in each. One of our favorite tricks was waiting for some unsuspecting soul to sit down to do his duty and inserting a switch under the hole in the other compartment and banging the kid's ass. I remember such experiences vividly.

Well, one day at recess, Old Man Donegal entered one of the outhouse doors and some kid came up with the ingenious idea of telling Sulu Lahti, who'd just come out, that Emil, his worst enemy, was taking a crap - and here's a good club, Sulu.

Sulu fell for it and whopped Old Blue Balls' ass a good one. When his terrible roar shattered the silence, we all fled... All except Sulu.

Old Man Donegal charged out of the outhouse, holding his pants up with one hand and reaching for Sulu with the other. Oh, was he mad! And he got madder, trying to hold, hit and keep his pants up all at the same time.

Old Blue Balls

Under the stress, Sulu's command of the English language failed him:
"Exercise me, Mr. Donegal. Exercise me!" (He'd meant "excuse me").

The superintendent's bellow echoed over the hills:

"I'LL EXERCISE YOU ALL RIGHT! I'LL EXERCISE YOU LIKE YOU'VE NEVER BEEN EXERCISED BEFORE!"

Wow! What a walloping! Sulu wasn't able to sit down for a week, but he was a hero to all of us, Uptowners and Downtowners alike. He was the only one in the world who had ever gotten even with Old Blue Balls Donegal, the only one who had given him a good crack on the ass Sulu, the avenger.

So now to the end of the hill war. The battle that was to end all battles took place at dusk one day in late May, 'ust before school let out for the year. It had been a long bitter winter and the harsh discipline of the classroom was becoming unbearable. Individual fights and group skirmishes were increasing. Without snow, we had turned to fists and even stones. Blood really flowed. One boy was seriously injured when he got hit in the head with a chunk of iron ore. Old Man Donegal decided to step in right then. He visited every classroom and delivered the same message. Anyone who threw a stone, a big one or a small one, in the schoolyard or elsewhere, and hit another child with it would be dealt with severely.

"I'll scrape every bit of skin from his hide!" was the way he'd put it.

That put sort of a crimp in our plans and a damper on our anticipations. Plans had already been made for that evening's mayhem with challenges made and accepted. But then some kid came up with a bright idea.

"OK," he said. "No stones. Horse turds. They're almost as hard as stone's anyway after a day or two in the sun."

Agreed.

We went ahead with our preparations.

God, but we were ingenious! Warfare was the mother of invention! There was always a way to get around any rule!

You have to remember that this was in the day before automobiles. There were only two in town then and the farmers were still bringing their teams up to smell my dad's Ford so they wouldn't bolt and run away when they met him on the road.

There were lots of horses in town and lots of cows. They roamed at will. Every night, while I lay abed, I could hear the clomp-clomp of some old nag making its way up the pine-board sidewalk that ran along one side of the street across from the house. And there was always the tinkle of cowbells.

The cows and the horses both preferred the sidewalk to the street for some reason - perhaps because they liked the sound of their reverberating hoofs. Anyway, I could never figure out why they always shit more on the way up the hill than on the way down, but they did. Maybe it was the extra effort. Anyway, they seemed to produce more manure on the steepest part of the grade, right in front of Old Man Donegal's house, opposite the school.

There was one old bay mare named Nellie who used to climb the hill every day just as school was being dismissed and she religiously left a pile in front of his gate. We used to watch for the ceremony and were never disappointed.

Nellie would begin to twitch her tail at the bottom of Donegal's property line; then she'd let out a monstrous fart or two; then her sides would begin to heave; her tail would be hoisted high and out of that collapsing rose of a hind end would cascade the aromatic nuggets of the day. Some said Nellie was the reincarnation of some poor teacher that Old Man Donegal had bedeviled to death. Anyway, we had plenty of ammunition!

That afternoon we gathered bags of horse turds: old ones, new ones, big ones and little. Our sidewalks had never been so clean, but only because all the horse manure was gone. The big, round, soup-plate-like mementos left by the cows were still everywhere. We called them cow-pasties.

We Uptowners were still assembling when the Frogs attacked. They had outflanked us, coming from the side road by the Methodist Episcopal Church, which wasn't fair. They gave us quite a trimming at first and those horse turds hurt like the devil when you got one in the ribs or the side of the neck. But the French and Indian kids spent their ammunition too hastily and ran short, whereupon the tide of battle shifted as our runners brought up new bagsfull. Then they overran our position and stole a lot of our turds. It was a real melee with about 40 kids from 9 to 14 taking part in the frenzy; crying laughing and screaming.

A new tactic suddenly appeared.

Someone got a stick, put it in one of the cow-pasties and flung the soft manure at his opponent with a most satisfactory result. Splat! You could see where the brown stuff hit and clung. In an instant, all of us were using sticks and slinging cow manure. Moments later, the sticks were forgotten and we grabbed up handfuls of the crap and flung it. Oh, what a mess. Someone slammed a whole round saucer against the side of my face and I could only see out of one eye. It was one of my own comrades who had mistaken me for the enemy in the growing darkness. I gave him a fat handful right in the kisser! In moments all thought of sides was forgotten. We fought anyone near enough to be a target.

That was when Old Blue Balls Donegal made an error in judgment. He was suddenly in our midst, roaring and bellowing, knocking heads together and commanding us, in that terrible voice of his, to stop instantly and go home. A great juicy chunk of cow manure suddenly came from nowhere. It flew through the air and hit him square on the nose. Oh, what a noble splatter!

Our fighting stopped and all of us attacked Donegal. The air was literally full of cow-pasties and he was the one and only target.

He couldn't take it. He fled and we chased him, screaming with joy, down the street and right to his gate. We hugged each other; Uptowner, Downtowner, Finn, French and Indian. We danced and hurled epithets - and anything else we could find - at his house. It was a noble moment in all our lives... We never fought each other again.

Omnium Aureum

Every two or three years nowadays, my wife, The Madam, fixes me with a steady brown eye and lays down an ultimatum:

"Clean out your study or I will. It's throwaway time."

I can't blame her. I have to admit that the place is a disgrace with the piles of books teetering on the desk, stacked on the floor in the corners and all those papers, helterskelter everywhere. I even get a bit overwhelmed by the clutter at times So, a few hours ago I got some cartons around and began

discarding ruthlessly. I made some real headway too, until I found that old copy of Virgil's 'Aeneid' that my dad had given to Old Man Coon 50 years ago.

Coon was an old hermit who'd spent most of his life trying to find gold and had a mine of sorts up there on the headwaters of the Tioga. The old book's leather binding was ragged and broken and it still showed the tooth marks of the porcupine that had chewed it after the old man died. There was no point in keeping it, but I glanced through the pages briefly before throwing it away.

Inside the cover, in my father's Spencerian hand, was his name and the date, June, 1910, but what grabbed my attention was a slip of paper tucked tight into the final few pages.

On it was written, "Amicus medicus. Morturite Salutamus. Omnium aureum est in umae tres divisa. In aqua sed non in fluvia." And it was signed, "H. J. Coon, March 14, 1918."

I haven't been able to think about anything else since I discovered that slip so I'd better put everything down on paper that I can remember about the circumstances while the memories are fresh in my mind. It's been over 50 years since Old Man Coon died.

H.J. Coon was always a mysterious figure. He wore his hair long, way below his shoulders, carried a pistol in his belt and came to town only twice a year, in September and May. Annie, the postmistress, said that there was always a registered letter waiting for him and he signed for it without comment and left. Then he took the train to Marquette, returned, bought a pile of groceries and a three gallon jug of whiskey, had a long sauna at Lahti's and went back into the woods.

My father said he was probably a remittance man, some black sheep from a wealthy family out east, who they paid to stay away, far away.

Dad probably knew Mr. Coon better than anyone else in town because they shared the same curious hobby. They both had an interest in Latin literature.

As I've mentioned before, my father was a country doctor in a wilderness land, one of the few persons with any education thereabouts. His interest in Latin stemmed, he said, from the eight years of the language he'd taken in high school and medical school. He knew it well enough to be able to use some phrases when he talked with the Catholic priest and he often liked to make some comment in Latin when he was treating his patients. He said it helped in the healing process, that 90% of all medicine was humbug anyway and that a little incantation was almost as good as calomel or castor oil. Anyway, most of the townspeople were impressed by his learning and they had great faith in his medical skill.

Once, when Mr. Coon had come to town with a great boil on his neck, Dad, in the course of lancing it, had uttered some ancient Roman proverb, whereupon the old hermit capped it with another, also in Latin, much to dad's surprise and delight. He said that they then had a hell of a good conversation and that Mr. Coon was really a highly educated man. Dad thereafter insisted upon his having dinner with us whenever he came to town hopefully only after he'd had his sauna and gotten rid of the half-year camp stink.

I don't remember much of what they talked about at the table - mostly philosophy and stuff, but never about gold - and they were always quoting things in Latin to each other.

Old Man Coon would never talk to anyone but dad, though, during those meals. He completely ignored my mother's attempts to engage him in conversation. She didn't like being shut out of the table talk and dreaded his bi-annual visits even though she had to admit that he had excellent table manners even if he wasn't polite to her. Anyway, on what was to be his last visit, my father gave Mr. Coon one of his two copies of Virgil. He said it should help him make it through the winter.

It didn't do it. Half way through February, the cruelest month of the north country winter, a timber cruiser for the Silverthorne Land Company had dropped in at the old man's cabin for a cup of java before snowshoeing the rest of the way back to town. He'd found the old hermit very weak from starvation. He'd been living for almost a month on oatmeal and buckfoot soup, made from deer hooves and horns. The timber cruiser told dad that a bear had broken into Coon's shack in late November and had just about cleaned the old man out except for one deer which he'd shot shortly afterward and on which he'd been living ever since. He said the old man was in bad shape.

Well, dad went right down to the store of course, and bought a good bunch of vittles - a bacon slab, beans, flour, tea, sugar and the like, maybe 40-60 pounds - enough to bulge a packsack to its seams anyway. But he had a terrible time trying to get someone to lug it up to Coon's homestead. Dad tried everywhere, threatened and begged, but no go. He said to my mother that he really couldn't blame them for refusing: 16 miles, four feet of snow on the level and no crust, rough country in that granite, 18 below zero at noon. It would be a bitter journey all right, but a man's life was at stake so dad, true to form, decided to go himself. When Jim Olson, caretaker of the mine property, heard he was going, he said he'd go along too, but at the very last minute dad had had to hop the caboose of the noon train. A woman up at Sidnaw had been in labor for two days and the baby was stuck crosswise, according to the telegraph message. So dad took off his hunting clothes, grabbed his black satchel and caught the train.

He gave Jim Olson a ten dollar bill to hire someone to carry the provisions up to Old Man Coon. That was a heap of money in those days.

Anyway, everything got all fouled up and I forget how, but they let this half-breed, Will Twofeather, out of the village pokey where he'd been sobering up from a two-week bender, gave him dad's money, loaded him up with the groceries and put him on snowshoes headed for Coon's place. When dad finally returned from the Sidnaw confinement and they told him what they'd done, he was furious.

"Why the hell did you give that Indian bum the money first?" he hollered. "I'll bet he's over in a Nestoria saloon right now drinking it up. You never give an Indian any money until the job's done!"

Wow! Was dad ever mad. He was even biting his lower lip again. He stormed at the handful of men he had summoned.

"Damn the whole cowardly pack of you. Just wait till you get sick and call me next time. I'll cut the black gizzard right out of your guts and give you a taste of the stuff in the black bottle on the top shelf!"

Though they all agreed, the men didn't go that day or all the rest of the week because we got clobbered by a terrible blizzard with high winds and deep cold. It was reported that someone had seen Will Twofeather getting in an empty boxcar on the 7:29 train for the Soo or points east.

All that time dad kept worrying about Mr. Coon. When the blizzard finally ended, he got up another smaller box of groceries and hired three men, including One-Eye Foulin, to take it up to Coon's place, pulling the grub on a toboggan. They started at daybreak and returned about midnight that night. When they pounded on our back door, dad let them into the kitchen and made them a pot of coffee. I sneaked down the back-stairs and hid behind the kitchen door so I could hear what they had to say.

"Yeah, we made it all right, Doc," said One-Eye Foulin.

"Coon's dead. Frozen stiffer'n a preacher's prick. Was sittin' there in his rocking chair with a long log under his arm that come through a hole in the door. He had the other end stuck into the open door of the stove. Pretty slick idea, Doc. Thataway Old Coon don't carry any wood, just rock forward and nudge the log a bit more into the stove. But the fire was out, Doc, and there was Old Coon, just sittin'. He was friz so hard we couldn't unbend him no how. Just roped him onto the toboggan sitting up and drug him back that way."

The men said that it was kind of scary sometimes, hauling him that way, what with him sitting back there like he was driving a team in the moonlight. They said One-Eye had given them a bad start when he suddenly grunted "Giddyap" and the others who were pulling thought it was the corpse that had spoken.

"Where'd you leave the body?" asked my father.

"Hell, he's right there by your back stoop, Doc. Take a look."

I ran back upstairs and saw the sight. There indeed was Old Man Coon sitting hunched up on that toboggan with the box of groceries between his legs. The ropes that held him ran around his body and then forward to the curve of the toboggan and they did look like reins. Pretty eerie! Old Man Coon, with his long hair, looked like a girl fixing to go on a sleigh ride. Scary!

I returned to my eavesdropping behind the kitchen door.

"No. No sign of new groceries in the cabin, Doc. Everything bare as Tobey's butt. Nothin' to eat. The old man, he starved to death, for sure."

"Same as murder," my father said. "Take the body down to the depot and put him in the baggage room and tell the agent to ship it to the Ishpeming morgue as soon as he can. I don't want that hanging around here for the family to see in the morning. I'll make out a death certificate."

The men left, dad blew out the kerosene lamp and I heard the squeaky rasp of the toboggan as the men hauled Mr. Coon away - still driving the team.

That spring, about May break-up time, I got wind of an expedition my dad and Jim Olson were planning. They were going up to visit Old Man Coon's place. I wheedled and begged until they promised to let me come along. It was going to be pretty miserable they told me. We'd have to wade through icewater up to my neck in the flats. I'd have to carry my own blanket and food. Yes, and a fishpole too. There should be some early trout in the rapids. We might even have a chance to get into Old Coon's gold mine. I was so excited the night before we left that I couldn't sleep a wink.

It was a tough trip. Snow was still lying deep in the shadows of the north side of the hills and in the swamp pockets. That water in the flats flayed me with icy fire. I got soaked to the gills. Dad and Jim didn't walk slowly or wait for me at all. They just strode along up the endless trail while I had to run in spurts to keep them in sight. I remember thinking at times that I would try to make it to 'that birch tree' and then I'd die. I finally made it somehow, only to find them already in the cabin.

It was an unholy mess. The front door with the hole in it had been left ajar and the porkies had taken over. Dishes and pans were on the floor, chairs were overturned and gnawed and there were droppings everywhere on the floor, bed and table. An axe handle had been chewed almost through. A few books were squashed on the floor and they had torn pages.

Others had been there besides the porcupines.

"Look, Jim! They've already been up here hunting for the old man's gold," my dad said, pointing to a pile of earth on the floor.

When Jim pulled up the trap door we saw how someone had dug around the supports of the cabin beyond the confines of the square cellar, with its flattened, musty potato sacks. I was still shivering and shaking so much that the men told me to make a fire in the stove and sweep out the crap and corruption while they scouted around outside.

That's when I'd found the chewed copy of Virgil's 'Aeneid' with my dad's name in it, the one I'd just re-discovered this morning. I took it out to him as he was examining and explaining to Jim the operation of Coon's crude handmill for grinding up the quartz and greenstone ore.

"Yeah, that's the book I gave to H.J. last fall," he said. "What a mess. Stick it in the fire, Son. I've got a better copy at home."

But I put it in my pocket instead, along with a few chunks of ore as souvenirs. I wanted something to show the other kids to prove that I'd been all the way up to Coon's gold mine.

After supper I had some time to get outside and explore a bit myself. It was apparent that old Mr. Coon must have done a tremendous amount of work in the years of his hermitage. A four foot shaft had been sunk into the side of a solid granite bluff along a seam where the quartz gleamed white. I was scared to go into it. It was very dark and even I would have to bend my head. A grown man must have had it very hard, drilling and blasting and hauling rock in such a narrow shaft. There was also a large windlass made out of a hollow pine stub that Mr. Coon had set on a log frame. I could see that it could be turned by its large handles so he could pull up a bucket of ore or tailings from the shaft. I couldn't turn it myself.

What impressed me most was the hermit's rock pile. It ran for about 40 feet, out into the cedar swamp and it was almost seven feet high and about that wide. Every chunk in that causeway had been hewn or blasted out of solid rock. Surely Mr. Coon must have found something to have worked so hard.

I hunted for scraps of ore with yellow threads or pieces that were especially heavy. One chunk that I could hardly lift was full of little yellow cubes and I was sure I'd found some gold, but the men laughed when I lugged it to them excitedly.

"Fools gold! Iron pyrites," they said. "Not worth a damn. Look instead for little greenish threads in white quartz or yellow speckles on the green-gray stuff."

I didn't find any.

That night the men gave me the old man's bunk while they slept on some balsam branches by the stove. I fell asleep hearing them talk about gold and the men who sought it. They talked about the two real gold mines, the Ropes and the Michigan, both on this same formation of Old Man Coon's. They'd taken more than a million dollars worth of gold out of each mine they said, but even more from the pockets of those who'd bought stock in them. No placer mining in this country. Any gold was always scattered in quartz veins and pockets. Dad told the tale of Bedford, the station agent at Clowry, who once got lost while trout fishing and how he cut cross-country to get home and found a chunk of quartz so rich it assayed $50,000 to the ton. And how Bedford spent the rest of his life hunting for the mother lode. He even hired him a prospector from out west one summer but never

found it again. Jim told about the old shaft in the granite up there by Silver lake that no one knew anything about. The shaft was sealed people said, with an iron door. Jim had been there and it was true, he said. If Old Man Coon had been here for 30 years blasting and chunking and grinding, he must have found some gold and salted it away, they insisted. He had no heirs so far as they knew so now the land would probably go back to the state. Would it be worth buying at tax sale time? Hell no. Too hard to get in and out of in that kind of country. If old Coon had really got some gold and hidden it, where would he have put it? God, in all this forsaken country his cache would stay hidden forever. Maybe he left a will. We'll look for it in the morning. I fell asleep, listening to them talk.

In the morning, the men were drinking tea and eating hardtack when I awoke. They gave me a cup of it too, black as tar and with a coppery taste so strong I choked. Dad laughed and told me to go get a drink at the spring to take the fur off my tongue.

"You'll find it," he said. "Look for a square wooden box just to the left of the path leading to the creek. It's about halfway."

I found it easily, took off the square board lid and tried to get enough water by lapping it up with my cupped hands, but they leaked too much. I finally put my head down through the opening so I could drink directly. A precarious position, but while I was upside down there drinking, I noticed the tops of three jugs back behind the log framing of the spring. Curious, I tried to pull one out to see what was in it, but I couldn't budge it. Awfully heavy! It seemed to be anchored in stone. Oh well, who wants to lug home a heavy jug. I had another drink of water and forgot all about the jugs for 50 years. Until this morning cleaning my study, when I found what Old Man Coon had written on that yellow slip of paper in that copy of Virgil, the one I'd brought back as a boyish souvenir. "Amicus medicus." (Doctor, my friend.) "Moriturite Salutamus." (We who are about to die salute you.) "Omnium aurcum est urnae tres divisa." (All the gold is divided into three urns.) Urns? Jugs! Three jugs in that spring! "In aqua." (In water.) "Sed in fluvia non est." (But not in the river.) In the spring! In the spring!.

I fear I must confess that I haven't made much progress in obeying The Madam's order. I keep looking at that old broken book and the yellow slip of paper. I keep remembering those three jugs in the spring. I keep wondering if I could possibly find a trace of Old Coon's mine again and its three urnae. I'm getting pretty old. There's no trail left up there. It's all grown over by now. Yet...

HEADS
AND
TALES

BOOK THREE

Gypsies

"The gypsies are coming! The gypsies are in town! Lock your doors! Hide under the bed!" Every August that cry ran up our hill street long before they appeared in their covered wagons in route to their usual camping grounds beyond our long closed mine. Little shivers of delight and fear beset me as I watched the little procession. First came a man with gold rings in his ears, swarthy as an Indian, leading the way with long steps. Then came the covered wagon hauled by one horse with a boy holding the reins. Inside the wagon we could see people, in colorful clothes, behind the puckered opening and sometimes we heard them talking or singing. Tied to the rear of the wagon was a string of horses, three or four of them, some carrying packs. Most years there were two or three of these gypsy wagons but this particular August there was only one. Perhaps others would be joining them later.

My father scoffed at the belief that all gypsies were thieves or that they kidnapped little children. In other years he'd treated some of them up at their encampment for various hurts or illnesses and never charged them anything for his services. "They're poor folk living by their wits," my father said. "They're wanderers by nature and there've been times I've envied them. No moss on those rolling stones. They're free. I like 'em!" One of Dad's favorite possessions was a big yellow calabash pipe some gypsies had given him.

The gypsies spent about a week working over our village. The man was a tinker and scissors grinder, and since these services were in much demand, he was given work at some of our houses even though we wouldn't ever let him come inside. My mother, who had a leaky tea kettle, a pan whose handle had come off, and a big copper wash-boiler with a hole in it, let me watch the gypsy man repair them. After sanding around the holes, he'd light a little alcohol lamp and blow a jet of flame at the spot till it was hot enough. Then from his pack, he got out a soldering iron, heated it too, put it in some kind of paste and quick as a wink, the thing was fixed. He knew his stuff all right, but he didn't say a word to me or smile. When he was done, he motioned to me to get my mother who thanked him and asked him the price. In answering, I noticed that he had a thick, odd accent but we gathered that he would settle for two pounds of sugar, a peck of potatoes and twenty-five cents. She gave them to him and he went on to the next house.

That afternoon, two gypsy women in colorful dresses with huge sleeves came to our back door. They also had gold rings in their ears, and wore gold necklaces and bracelets. Their English was even harder to understand but they were selling ecru lace and silk scarves of very bright colors. The gypsies wore these scarves around their heads, layer upon layer, and it was sure pretty to see them laid out on the green grass beside our back step. Mother bought some lace and an orange scarf but had trouble when they kept wanting to haggle and insisting on more money. Finally she put down a five dollar bill and indicated that was all she would pay. They jabbered some more, then took it, but they also snatched up the orange scarf before they left. Mother felt cheated but was glad to get rid of them.

I suspect the gypsies got a more hostile reception at most of the other houses on our street than they did at ours. They had a bad name for stealing and cheating and they were slick at it. People claimed they could steal the shoes off your feet and your socks would never know it. And speaking of socks, that was why M. C. Flinn, when he heard the gypsies were in town, hired Charley Olafson to be at the door of the store to turn them away if they tried to enter. He had good reason. The year before some gypsy women had put up a commotion back of the grocery counter and then, after they left, M. C. had found that their kids had swiped three pair of men's work socks. Mr. Flinn knew they had because he'd put out six pairs that very morning and no one else had bought any. Of course, he charged them twice as much for the dried apples they'd bought but M.C. Flinn didn't like to get taken. Anyway, Charley turned them away when this bunch tried to come in.

Somehow the gypsies fascinated me and so one evening when they were still camping up at the mine, I tried to get Mullu to go up there with me to hide in the bushes and see what they were doing. He was scared but came along and we watched them eating their supper meal. There were six of them altogether sitting around their fire, eating something from a big black kettle hung over it. They'd take their bowls and dip out some stew or goulash or something, then break off a chunk of bread to dip in it. No forks or knives. Not even spoons. Sometimes they'd tip the bowls up to their faces to get the last of it. We'd heard that gypsies would play the fiddle and dance but we did-n't see any of that -just people eating and jabbering together. Mullu and I left feeling disappointed.

Gypsies were known far and wide for being smart horse traders and you had to be pretty careful or they'd skin you good. In our town we had two men who fancied them-selves as being pretty slick traders, not just of horses and mules, but for almost any-thing. Their names were Pete Hummel and Herb Anderson. I've always had a hard time remembering Herb's real name because everyone called him the "Deacon." Not that he went to church much, if he ever went at all, but he sure looked and acted like a deacon, pious as hell. They say he was swapping things even when he was a kid - pencils for jackknives, jackknives for a batch of marbles, and so on until he came up with a pig and a heifer even before he quit school. Just a natural trader, the Deacon was. He'd swap anything for anything. They told a tale about him that once a fellow over by Michigamme so much admired a feisty white mare the Deacon had, he said he'd give his wife for that horse. The Deacon didn't bat an eye. "All right," he says, "how much to boot?" That probably was just talk but the Deacon had done right well by his trading. Had a barn and barnyard full of stuff he'd traded for - an old mule, pigs and chickens, horse collars, a cutter, oh there were piles of things.

The other trader, Pete Hummel, mainly specialized in horses, cows and mules. He knew a lot about them and the tricks that people used to skin you, when swapping. That's why the Deacon asked Pete to come along with him when he went up to the gypsy camp. As they rode up there in the buggy behind his old horse, the Deacon explained. "I seen them going up the street when they come in," he said. "And they was leading three horses behind the wagon. Two of the horses were dogs not worth a handful of oats but there was one big brown one that looked pretty good. Maybe worth trading for. I figure they got too many people to be in that one wagon and I got an old buck board to home they might be a-needing."

"You mean that one with the broken spring that you painted over, the one with the wobbly wheel?" asked Pete. "Yah, I know it. But if that horse is as good as you say he looks, you ain't going to get no Gypsy to go for it. What you going to throw in for boot, Deacon?"

"Oh, I dunno," answered the Deacon. "Best wait and see what's up there. I been skinned before by gypsies. Once long ago I traded a good heifer for a mule they had and come to find out it was a moonie - went nigh blind ever so often, specially in the dark of the moon. You know the tricks, Pete, better'n I do, so if I trade for that horse, you look it over good for me."

"Aw, hell, Deacon," Peter replied. "You know the tricks pretty good yourself. I see you've sheared and trimmed old Betsey's mane and pumped air in the hollows above her eyes and colored the gray hairs with permanganate potash soaked in coffee. Thought you had a new horse when you first drove up. I bet you filed her teeth too."

The Deacon grinned and nodded. "Yup! Old Betsey's got the teeth of a seven year old now." he said. "Not bad for a fifteen year old mare."

When they got near the mine the Deacon touched up the horse with his whip and they trotted briskly into the campground. The two men got out of the buggy and went over to the gypsy man who was sitting on a stump by the grazing horses.

After the usual preliminaries of looking at all of the other horses and explaining that he could use a spare horse but didn't really need one, the Deacon asked if he could look over the big brown one if it was for trade. The gypsy nodded and the two men sure gave it a going over. They looked in its mouth and found that the teeth were sound with good crowns and hadn't been filed. Probably five years old or less. The hollows above the eyes were firm. They fanned a hand past the eyes and it blinked so it wasn't blind. They went over the body for knots and spavins but found none. They lifted both hind hooves to see if it was a kicker or if there was anything wrong with the frogs but there wasn't and it had a fairly new pair of shoes. Pete even smelled its breath to make sure it hadn't been given a spoonful of dynamite with its feed. No, no acrid odor. It had good hearing. It was alert. Good front legs, too.

Pete took the Deacon aside. "Gawdamighty!" he said. "That's the best horse I seen for years. Nothing wrong with him but you'd better know if he can stand hitching. Ask to take him out for a little ride."

The Deacon nodded. "Might still be a kicker bad enough to stove in the buggy or break the cross tree," he said. "And maybe he's a heaver though I don't see the sign. Or maybe he'll go lame. That damned horse is too good to be true.

With the gypsy's permission, they hitched it to the buggy and drove to Flinn's store and back. The big brown had a fine gait and responded to the reins and whip as a good horse should. They stopped at the store to see if it would stay put or start creeping. No! That horse would stand without hitching. They trotted back swiftly and the horse wasn't even breathing hard when they unhitched it.

"Damn my bones, Deacon," Pete said. "If you can get that horse, you sure better. Never seen a better one. For ten cents I'd start trading for it myself."

Then the haggling began and it lasted two or three hours before they made a deal. The Deacon would trade his horse for the brown one and throw in a buckboard, three sacks of oats, and give twenty five dollars to boot. He'd be back next morning bringing the buckboard and oats. If the gypsy man didn't want the buckboard, he could have the buggy. That was the swap.

All that night the Deacon worried about the trade. There must be something wrong. That horse was just too good, but scratch his brain, he wasn't able to think of a thing that might mean he was getting skinned. Except dealing with a Gypsy horse trader. Of course, the gypsy was getting a pretty fair deal, too. He'd have a good old sound horse and a buckboard to relieve the crowding of six people in that old covered wagon. That made sense. Nevertheless ... Finally he got to sleep.

The next morning the Deacon, after rubbing old Betsey's coat with oil to make it gleam, hitched her up to the buggy, tied the buckboard on behind it and made his way to the campground. As he approached it he was relieved to see the big brown horse still there. The thought had come to him that maybe Pete had beaten him to it. And he was relieved again when the gypsy took the buckboard with the broken spring and the wobbly wheel instead of his buggy. He said goodbye to old Betsey, hitched the brown horse to his buggy and sped down the street to his home. A pleasure to drive. The Deacon could hardly believe his good fortune.

But that afternoon everything fell apart. He had fed the brown horse well and currycombed and brushed him until its hide glistened. An easy horse to put the bridle on, too. Some horses fought the bridle but not this one. The Deacon drove to Flinn's store and then decided to return by the back road to Lake Tioga. Gad, that was a good horse. A keeper. No trading him.

But on the way back when they came to the first little hill, the horse balked! Just planted all four feet solidly on the ground and wouldn't move. The Deacon whipped him and pleaded with him. He tried to lead him by the bridle. No! The brown horse, damn him, wouldn't budge. "Oh God," prayed the Deacon. "I've got a real genuine ten carat balker, I have. What the devil will I do now?"

There wasn't anything to do except wait and hope to hell that the horse would start going again. The Deacon knew that you could beat a balky horse with a two by four until he'd roll his eyes back so you could see the white of them but it wouldn't move until it got good and ready. It took the Deacon three hours to get back from Lake Tioga - just a mile. Odd thing was, the horse would trot on level ground, but give it a little hill and he'd stop and you couldn't move him if you'd build a fire under him. There was no cure for a real bad balking horse. He'd been skinned by gypsies again.

Luckily no one had seen the brown horse balking so the Deacon figured on trading him as fast as he could, and he thought, of course, of Pete Hummel. Twasn't a nice thing to do but in trading, as in love, all is fair. Caveat Emptor! Let the trader beware. After all, Pete had looked the brown horse over and had said it was a good trade. Maybe it was his turn to be skinned.

So, for about a week, the Deacon made a point of driving over to Pete's house or past it every day with the new horse because fortunately it was all on the level. He sure didn't try to go up our hill street. Then, toward the end of that time, he stopped to dicker with Pete about trading for Pete's buckboard. Not trading the horse, mind you, but maybe Pete would trade his buckboard, which was almost new, for that heifer the Deacon had in his barnyard. No, Pete wasn't interested in the heifer, nor in the cutter, nor in anything else. But maybe, he said, if the Deacon would consider trading the brown horse they could dicker. He'd been mighty impressed with that horse.

The Deacon said he wasn't interested. He'd never had a horse so easy to handle or so easy to drive. While, as a trader, he'd never say no to any deal if it were good enough, he felt he had the horse he always wanted. So it went day after day with Pete Hummel grudgingly raising the offer. Finally, the Deacon gave in when Pete said he'd trade his own horse and his new buckboard and throw in fifty dollars to boot. Pete's horse wasn't much better than old Betsey had been but she was a lot younger so the Deacon felt he'd got the best of the trade. At least he'd got rid of that balker. He gloated a little.

That was why he was a bit surprised when a couple of weeks later Pete Hummel drove up with the brown horse and suggested they take a little ride to Lake Tioga and back. Pete didn't seem to be at all upset over having been taken either. "Never had such a fine horse," he said. He thanked the Deacon for trading with him.

Off they trotted down to the lake and then, on the way back, when they came to the little hill where Brownie had first balked, the horse began to slow down a bit and the Deacon knew it was about to balk just as it had done with him there. But Pete merely tickled the brown horse's tail with his whip, didn't really strike it at all, and the horse lunged forward. That same thing happened two more times and then finally Brownie really did balk. Stopped right there and rolled back its eyes. The Deacon couldn't help grinning a bit even though he knew it'd be a long time before they got home. He waited for Pete to start cursing both him and the horse.

But Pete didn't. He got out of the buggy and went over to the horse, touched it on the tail with his whip and then whispered something in its ear. Brownie took off in a hurry and Pete had to run to jump back in the buggy.

"I don't have him quite broke from that little balking habit yet," he explained. "But he's coming fine. Give me another week and he'll never balk again." The brown horse didn't balk once all the rest of the way home.

The Deacon was sure mystified and a bit upset. Nobody could break a real balking horse of the habit. What was it Pete had whispered in his ear? Unable to stand it, he finally asked him.

"I say the secret words," Pete replied. "Learned 'em from my pappy. They always work on a balky horse and all you got to do is tickle him with a whip just before you say 'em. Then after that you don't even have to talk to him. Just use the tickle. That's all you need, once he's trained."

Well, the whole business sure mortified the Deacon and he kept puzzling over those secret words of Pete's. They'd sure be handy. The Deacon knew other people had balky horses he might trade for. Could make a real profit knowing how to cure a balky horse. And it sure garred him to see Pete trotting that fine horse up our hill street day after day. Finally, he couldn't bear it another moment.

"Pete," he said. "Tell me what you said to that horse and I'll pay you five dollars."

"Nope," said Pete. "Won't tell you them secret words until you give me back my boot - fifty dollars."

It took some weeks of brooding before the Deacon finally gave in and handed over the money.

"I say, 'Screw the Deacon!' three times and blow in his ear," Pete said with a grin. "It's the blowing that does it. A horse can't stand that. Balk or no balk, you blow in his ear and he's got to get up and go. My pappy taught me."

The Haunted Whorehouse

As Mullu and I emerged at dusk from Hatsnatcher Swamp, having followed the old river trail along the Tioga. We saw a speck of firelight by the big slough. We'd had a long day trout fishing and were both very wet and cold. There had been places along the river bank where the alders were so tangled it was easier to wade in the water even if you had to go in up to your armpits and put your worm can under your hat. Yes, we were cold, it being early in September when more sensible fishermen had long quit the streams. Mullu and I had hoped to catch a few of the big spawner brook trout that often showed up at the first hint of frost but all we'd caught were a few little ones. Wet butt and no fish again. A fire would sure feel good.

When we reached the fire we found Dick Duggan, a very old former miner, tending his trot line for bullhead. A black coffee pail hung from a bar between two forked sticks and it boiled over just as we got there. "Want some coffee, boys? You ain't got no whiskers to strain the grounds but she'll hot you up all the way down yer gizzard." The old man poured some coffee into a dirty soup can that had seen better days.

"No thanks, Dick. Just want to warm ourselves before setting out for home. Had any luck yet? We almost got skunked." Mullu's voice shivered as much as his knees as he turned his back to the flames.

The old man was glad of the company. "Ah, yer crazy going for trout so late in the season," he said. "Even if you get a few, they'll be slimy at best. It's bullhead time, boys, bullhead time. You can't catch a better eatin' fish than a fall bullhead, no siree."

Just then a cowbell clattered. "That makes three of 'em I've got on the line," the old man said. "Better bait up again." Hand over hand, he hauled up the clothesline and laid it in loops on the bank as three bullheads kicked around on the ground. We were interested because although we'd done a lot of fishing, we'd never used a trot line. Dick had strung about eight droplines from his clothesline, each with a worm covered hook, and at the end of the clothesline were two heavy horseshoes. After rebaiting, Dick grabbed a length of clothesline, whirled the horseshoes around his head and then let them fly way out into the slough. He then propped up and tightened the line with a big forked stick, reattached the cowbell and poured himself another can of coffee.

"That's pretty slick," I said. "I've only caught one bullhead in my life and the bugger horned me when I took it off the hook. My hand was sore for over a week and I never did clean or eat the fish. How do you clean a bullhead without getting hurt, Dick?"

"Nuthin' to it, boy. Nuthin' to it. I take the hook out with pliers like you see and when I get home I nail the head to my barn door. Then you cut 'em around the gills and they skin out right easy. Nuthin' to it."

"Are they really good eating?" Mullu asked, looking at the ugly fish squirming in the pail.

"Are they good eatin'? They the best. No bones. All white meat. You got to fry 'em crisp, though. Crisp brown." Dick smacked his lips. "I be feeding good tonight," he said.

The old man saw that we were getting ready to go and wanted to hold us a little longer. "Bullheads is good for more than eating," he said. "They keep haunts away, too" he said.

"Aw, I don't believe in ghosts," said Mullu. "There aren't any."

"The hell they ain't. I tell you I know. Maybe you can't always see em but they there."

"How do bullheads keep ghosts away, Dick?" I asked.

"Why you nail one on top each door of the house. Haunts, they won't pass a bullhead door. You boys got a lot of larnin to do yet, saying there no haunts." The old man was indignant. "I seen 'em and heerd 'em and feeled 'em. I know. Tell you what you do. You go down to the old haunted whorehouse back of the depot and hang around some night and you'll hear one a-yelling. Though she be dead and buried long ago, her haunt can't leave the place."

"What's the story, Dick?" I asked. "I never heard of any whore-house in town."

"Ah, I s'pose it was afore yer time. Yeah, afore you boys were born even. Maybe twenty, thirty year ago, when they were still driving pine logs down this river. Every spring, a madam and her whores come up on the train from Green Bay to take care of them lumberjacks coming out of the camps, horney as hell and hungry for she-meat. Well, that madam and her girls would bed 'em down in that old house till their wages was all gone. Oh, they'd screw some of the farmers and iron miners too as a sideline, but it was the lumberjacks and rivermen as was the best pickings. Then when they'd cleaned up plenty, the whores would go back to Green Bay to wait for next spring. You boys never hear about that? Everybody know that whorehouse."

"No," I said. "That's news to me. Where is the old whorehouse and how come you know it's haunted?"

"It's the last house on the road out to the slaughter house," Dick replied. "The one that's all boarded up with a big hole in the foundation. You've probably gone by it. On the railroad side of the road."

I nodded and the old man continued. "Here's how it come to have haunts. I was a-working for Henry Thompson then. He was the mine superintendent. Lived in the big house beyond yours, he did, and I did his chores. Well, so long as the whores minded their own business and kept out of sight, nobody minded them much. Fact is, some felt having that old whorehouse there kept the jacks from tearing up the whole town when they come out of the woods. But one afternoon, when their madam was away, three of the girls, all painted up like Injuns, had the nerve to walk all the way up the street giggling and carrying on fierce like, a-wiggling their butts at any man they passed.

Couldn't much blame them, it being a nice spring day, but the people sure got plenty mad and they told Thompson something had to be done about it." The cowbell clanked again.

"There's another old bullhead swallered a hook for sure," he said. "Well, as I was a-saying, something had to be done so Henry Thompson, he strapped on his forty-five an' told me to come along down there with him about the time the St. Paul train was due. He just bust in the door and laid down the law. Told the madam and the whores he was putting them on the train for Green Bay. Right then. No stalling. Wouldn't let them say a word, come as they were. Leave everything. Henry, he give the madam a hard slap across the face when she tried to give him some lip and we had no more trouble. Got'em on the train and waited till it pulled out. That Henry Thompson, he were quite a man, yes sir. They used to call him King of Tioga..."

"But the haunts, Dick? What about the haunts?"

"Coming to that," replied the old man and he filled and lit an old corncob pipe, knowing he had us hooked good.

"Well, 'bout a month or so after that, Henry Thompson, he got some men and sent them down to board up the house tight so there'd be no more trouble. Nail down the windows too, he said, before you board them. Well, the men could nail down the windows downstairs from the outside but they had to go in to do them above. When they climbed the stairs they smelled a helluva rotten stink coming from a locked closet, and when they opened it, a dead women was there, all in a heap. I suppose the madam had locked her in to punish her. Maybe she was fixing to run away. I dunno. Anyway, she was left in that there closet and died there. They buried her out back of the house and nobody said nothing, knowing Thompson would get them if they did. You never hear that story boys? Well, it's true. I was one of them men and I know."

Dick poured another can of coffee before he went on. Well, her haunts been hangin' around the place since. I hear her ascreaming one night when I passed by and there's been others too as has heard her. Ask Old Pullapin. Damn near scared him out of his shoes. He said he saw lights in the house too, lights shining through the cracks in the boards but he'd been drinking so I dunno. I never seen no lights. No haunts, hey? You boys go down there some dark night and you'll find out. That old whore, she'll still be a screeching so loud you'll pee in yer pants."

As Mullu and I left, we could hear him muttering, "No haunts, hey? No haunts? They's lots of haunts every place."

The next afternoon Mullu came over to our house and made me a proposition. "Let's you and me go explore that old whorehouse tonight, he said.

"You bring your dad's claw hammer and pry iron and I'll bring a candle and some matches. Nobody has to know. It'll be dark by eight o'clock and it shouldn't take long just to look it over. Maybe we'll see or hear that ghost."

I confess I didn't much like the sound of it but he shamed me into saying yes. So down the street we went and out along the slaughterhouse road till we came to the last building on the right. Sure dark by then and black as tar. I jumped four feet when the board Mullu was prying off the back door let go with a screech. Sure spooky. We had a hard time getting all those old boards off and the door opened but finally we got in. Couldn't see anything until Mullu lit the candle and that made it even spookier, it flickered so. The house smelled of mildew and camp damp. Rats or porcupines had sure messed it up something awful. I was all for getting out but no, Mullu said, we had to go upstairs and see that closet where the whore was locked.

He led the way up the creaking stairs. When I stepped on some loose plaster that had fallen off the stair well and it crunched, I jumped again. Then I heard something. "Mullu!" I whispered. "There's something down there below us. I just heard something moving. Listen!"

We listened hard, holding our breaths. "Aw, you're just imagining," Mullu said. I knew I wasn't. I'd really heard something rustling. Probably a rat but it sounded bigger. All my nerve endings were quivering.

"C'mon. Let's go, Cully." Mullu began to climb up the rest of the shaky stairs and I followed the candle he held before him.

There were several bedrooms up there, all interconnected by doors, and each had a cot and a chair, not much else. Some of the mattresses had fallen off and split open, or had been chewed open, for the wood shavings that filled them had spilled out of the openings and were all over the floors.

"Where's the closet?" Mullu whispered. We groped around trying to find it and finally did between the last two bedrooms. We had just stumbled over its fallen door and were trying to look inside when suddenly we heard a woman scream.

Geez! We were petrified, frozen in our tracks. I felt the hair on my scalp crawling. Then it screamed again, a woman in mortal agony. Mullu dropped the candle and it went out"

I still don't know how we managed to find our way down those ramshackle stairs in the blackness. Then, just as we were bursting out through the door, we heard a third scream - and a rifle shot so close it almost split our ears.

I don't know who ran faster, Mullu or me. All I know is that there were two exhausted kids panting on the platform of the depot trying to catch our breath before we started up the hill for home. Old Dick Duggan was right. There were haunts. And when I got home I went straight to bed with the covers over my head, trying to forget what had happened.

The next day we had to go to, school. Mullu and I didn't look at each other. Sure was hard to concentrate, the memory of that woman screaming was so vivid. I found myself shuddering, just thinking about it.

It being the opening day of school, we didn't have to go in the afternoon so when Dad suggested I go with him as he made his calls, I was glad to accept even though it meant a lot of waiting in the buggy while he was in the houses. When he came out of the last one after a long, long time, Dad said, "Mrs. Laroux just told me that LaSeur shot a big Canadian lynx last night. Let's go over and see it. I've only had a glimpse of one in my whole life. They're getting scarce but I've heard them several times when I've been out hunting or fishing. They sound like a woman in childbirth who's having a rough time of it. A real screech. Once Jim Johnson and I were sleeping overnight up by the Hayshed Dam and had our baskets of trout hanging from some bushes by the fire when a lynx let out a howl and screech that sure jumped us out of our blankets. I suppose he was after the fish but you've never heard a scream like that, I'll bet."

When we got to LaSeur's cabin, Dad explained that he wanted me to see the lynx. LaSeur led us out to his barn. The animal looked like a gigantic grey and white cat with a big head and whiskers. In the middle of its brow, right between the eyes, was a bullet hole.

Dad grinned and so did LaSeur. "Yeah, Doc. I know what you're thinking. Yeah, I was headlighting for deer last night over by the slaughterhouse and I see green eyes, not yellow like deer, but I shoot and get this cat. A big one, eh Doc?" Dad agreed.

I told Mullu about it next day and he said maybe so, maybe what we'd heard was that lynx. But he also said later that he had gotten a bullhead from Dick Duggan and nailed it over the door of the haunted whorehouse when he went back there to get our claw hammer and pry bar.

Aunt Lizzie: Evangelist

Ithink it was in the fall of year 1913 that we got William Decker, the new young preacher from down below. Before he'd run out his time with us they were calling him Decker the Wrecker. That wasn't really fair because he was a nice young fellow with plenty of good intentions and enthusiasm. The trouble was mainly that he didn't know us or how we lived or what we expected from our preacher.

For one thing, Parson Decker didn't preach much hellfire and damnation, nor did he try to scare the devil out of our dirty souls as our other preachers had always done. Instead he tried sweet reason with us, tried to show us that sin didn't pay. Now that was all right, of course, but the folks kind of missed the drama and fury the old preachers always put in their sermons. No, the feeling of being scared green and then relieved each Sunday just wasn't there any more. When you came out of church at the end of the service, you no longer felt that you'd been snatched just in time from the jaws of hell. It was more like you'd come out of Flinn's store with a pound of good cheese.

For another thing, Mr. Decker was too evangelical for most of our folks. Often he seemed to be more interested in saving other people's souls rather than our own. Our congregation felt that if they paid a preacher, he should take care of their souls exclusively, not start trying to persuade old Pete Halfshoes, our half-breed Indian, to quit drinking and come to church. They knew that if Pete did come, he'd bring his pet skunk, Mabel, with him and they'd both be snockered good.

Nor did his parishioners like it when Mr. Decker tried to raid the congregations of the other churches in town by getting their kids to come to his Sunday School so they could play baseball on our team Saturday afternoons. That wasn't right! Over the years our village had achieved a fairly stable truce between the Catholics, the Lutherans, the Methodists, and even the Holy Jumpers. A man's religion, if he had any, was his own business, and if he didn't have any religion at all, well, that was all right too. Live and let live!

When I got home one evening singing a new song we'd learned at Epworth League, even my father was a bit upset. "That man's going to make trouble in our community," he said to my mother. Mother hadn't heard me singing it so I sang it again. It had a good tune.

> "Oh, the foxes they got holes in the ground,
> And the birds got nests in the air.
> And everything's got a resting place,

But a sinner ain't got no where.
Oh, there's great trials,
Grand tribulations.
There is great trials,
I'm bound to leave this land.
"Oh, Methodist, Methodist is my name,
Methodist'till I die,
I'm going to join the Lutheran Church,
But I'll die on the Methodist side.
Oh, there's great trials,
Grand tribulations.
There is great trials,
I'm going to leave this land."

When some of the elders tried to calm Mr. Decker down on his proselytizing, they just made him more determined. So one Sunday, he announced from the pulpit that three Sundays from that date, they would have a very special service, an evangelical one. Every church member was to bring another person to church with him. Mr. Decker said he would prefer that we bring persons who had never gone to church in their lives or who had dropped out, but it would be all right to bring someone who belonged to some other church too. There would be stars in the crowns of those who brought two or more. You can imagine how that shook us up. Not Aunt Lizzie, though. As a pillar of our church, she wanted that star and that crown. She'd bring her quota, she said. Mean, old gossip that she was, Aunt Lizzie had always been a consistent church goer. Never missed a Sunday. Some people said it was only so she could do her bloody screeching in the choir. Aunt Lizzie was awful on those high notes, clinging to them, flatting or sharping them, torturing the hell out of them till all of us shriveled in our seats. I don't know why they didn't kick her out of that choir, she made us suffer so, but probably they feared her nasty tongue. Lately, she'd been singing solos only once in a while and that was a mercy. At least she didn't spoil the grand old hymns, thanks to Annie, our organist, who drowned her out. Aunt Lizzie did a lot of thinking before she settled on Eino Tuomi and Emil Olson as the two sinners she'd bring to church that evangelical Sunday of Sundays. Lord knows, they qualified! Those two old whiskey drinking eprobates had never been to church in their whole lives. Probably hadn't even been baptized either. Aunt Lizzie realized that it would take some real careful scheming to come to church with those two trophies.

The next morning when I brought her the weekly copy of Grit, Aunt Lizzie had notes for me to deliver to both old men. Since Emil couldn't read and I knew I'd have to read his note to him anyway, I unfolded it. "Dear Mr. Olsen," it said, "I have some work I need done. If you can help me on Wednesday and Friday mornings I will pay you. Sincerely, Mrs. Elizabeth Campton." Eino's note was the same but she'd asked him to come work for her on Tuesday and Thursday mornings. That puzzled me a bit as I walked down to their houses. Those two old buggers were almost like brothers. They were inseparable. Why, they even ate together although they lived in separate houses side by side at the bottom of the hill. They shared their garden, the milk from Eino's cow, and the eggs from Emil's hens. You never saw one of them without the other - even when they were out poaching deer.

Emil and Eino sure needed the work. Winter would soon be coming and the potato crop had been poor that year. They wouldn't have had any potatoes at all except that they'd gone up to the town hall and emptied all the spittoons to make bug juice. Oh, they had enough turnips but you can get sick of turnips day after day. Worst of all, neither of them had been able to store up any whiskey for the long winter. All they had between them was one bottle of red-eye and that was being saved for New Year's Eve if they didn't break down and drink it before. In other years, Emil and Eino had always counted on the money they got for sawing the wood for the Town Hall's stoves to buy their booze, but this year the damned Township Board had given the contract to Sam Ysitalo. The thought of a long winter without whiskey was unsettling. Therefore, promptly at eight o'clock that next Tuesday morning, Eino was at Aunt Lizzie's house ready to do whatever she wanted done. She greeted him more warmly than he'd expected she would. "Thank you, Eino," she said. "I hoped you come help a poor widow lady. Come in and have a cup of coffee while I tell you your job this morning." She also gave him a big slice of homemade bread with wild strawberry jam on it to go with the coffee. Eino hadn't had anything taste so good for years.

"I've got a lot of work that takes a real man to do," she said, "but first, I'd like to have you saw up that long cord of maple wood in the back yard. Stove length and split and piled in the shed." When Eino suggested that maybe he'd better go get Emil to help with the sawing she vetoed it. "No, Eino," she said. "Just you. You're a big handsome man and can do it yourself. There's a one man crosscut saw in the barn and you'll find the axe there too."

Eino shrugged. Didn't make any sense. Two men could saw a lot more a lot faster than one man could. But what the hell! The job would just last longer and he'd make more raha, more whiskey money. Eino worked hard all morning and had the logs cut up by noon even though that saw sure needed filing. When he came to the house for his pay, Aunt Lizzie inspected the woodpile, praised him effusively, and again had him in for coffee and fresh doughnuts. "No matter what they say about Aunt Lizzie," Eino thought, a damned good cook." But a moment later, when she put only a fifty cent piece in his outstretched hand, he was shocked and disappointed. He looked at it with his mouth open.

"Not much pay for a full morning's work," he said. Hell, that wasn't enough for more than a good snort or two.

Aunt Lizzie saw his unhappiness. "Yes, Eino. That's not enough wages, I know. But I'm a poor widow lady, Eino, and that's all I can afford." Somehow she squeezed a tear out of one eye while watching him with the other. "You're a good man, Eino. Help me if you can." The old Finn put the fifty cent piece in his pocket and left.

When Emil found out how little Aunt Lizzie had paid his friend, he was outraged. "You too easy going, Eino," he roared. "No man work all morning for fifty cents. Tomorrow I tell her one dollar or she can stick it. We never get whiskey money that way."

And Emil did tell her, too, next morning. Told her one dollar or nothing doing. Aunt Lizzie surprisingly gave in right away. Even gave him an extra fifty cents for Eino. Moreover, she also had him in for coffee and doughnuts after he'd split the chunks Eino had sawed the day before.

Well, that's the way it went for the three weeks before Evangelical Sunday. Aunt Lizzie got a lot of work done out of those two. They cut up another long cord of wood and stacked it; they took down her stovepipes, shook the soot out of them, and put chains up and down her chimney. Emil cleaned her chickencoop and put down fresh fall leaves for the hens to scratch in. Eino made a big stack of new cedar kindling.

But Aunt Lizzie was good to them. The two old men had never had such good eating. Why, sometimes Aunt Lizzie even had a big slab of apple or blueberry pie for them after work and she didn't seem to mind interrupting to get them to talk about themselves and their past lives. Somehow she seemed to be able to weasel out of them stuff they'd never even told to each other.

Of course, Aunt Lizzie talked too - often about church and religion and such. She seemed surprised, almost shocked, when they told her no, they'd never been in a church. She said that was too bad, that everyone ought to go to church at least once, that they were sure missing something. Finally, toward the end of the third week, after she had fed Eino a batch of cinnamon rolls fresh from the oven, she suggested that maybe he and Emil might go to church that next Sunday. She was going to sing a solo, she said, and she'd really like to have her boys hear it. Aghast at the thought, but trying to be polite, Eino said that he couldn't go because he didn't have any church clothes. Aunt Lizzie didn't argue. She understood, she said. "Have another cinnamon roll, Eino."

The next day she also brought it up to Emil who said the same thing, having been forewarned. Then Aunt Lizzie invited both her boys to come to have supper with her Saturday night. She'd really appreciated their help and wanted to do something special for them. Pot roast and all the fixings, she said. They accepted.

Ah, that was a good meal! Eino and Emil hadn't had one like that in their whole lives. Not only pot roast with browned potatoes and mashed rutabagas, but a side dish of chicken salad too. And then a big hunk of delicious coconut pie. A feast! But that wasn't all. Aunt Lizzie went to the back room after the meal was over and brought out two men's coats, two pair of pants, two neckties, and two pair of men's shoes. "These are for you, dear boys," she said. "They were my past husbands' and they've been in the closet for years now. I've noticed that both your mackinaws and pants are pretty thin and with winter coming, you ought to have better ones. Besides, you said you couldn't come to hear me sing in church because you had no church clothes. Well, now you have them, my dear boys. You be there to meet me at the church door tomorrow at 10:45 or I'll come get you." Boom! Just like that!

Emil and Eino had been able to stash away five bottles of whiskey by that time and they emptied one of them that night. Still a bit hung over next morning, they had a terrible time putting on the new clothes, especially those neckties around the collars of their old lumberjack shirts. They didn't even tackle the shoes. Splay footed from years of wearing clompers, they couldn't even get their toes in them. When Emil came over to Eino's house at ten-thirty, he found his friend all dressed up but sipping another hair of the dog. "I can't go, Emil," he said. "These damn store clothes driving me crazy."

But the two old men were at the church door at ten-forty-five, mainly because the thought of old Aunt Lizzie leading them up the hill was too horrible to consider. She was outside when they got there. Triumphant, she looked them over, straightened their ties, then led them in to shake hands with the young preacher. I was an usher that day but when I tried to lead them down in front, Emil said, "No, Cully. We sit in back!" And they did, in the last pew nearest the door, so I put Charley Olafson along the aisle in that pew to box them in. Emil and Eino really looked kind of nice in their new church clothes, but their eyes were sure seared. I couldn't help sneaking glances at them all through the service to see how they were doing.

Eino was slumped down, almost hiding, in his part of the pew but Emil was looking all around. When Annie Anderson started playing the organ, they both were so startled they jumped and Emil got to his feet to see better what she was doing. (He told me later that it was the first time he ever saw a woman walking while sitting down. He was referring to her pumping the foot bellows.) Then in walked our choir, three men and three women, and Aunt Lizzie. The two old men nudged each other but it wasn't time for the solo yet. Our choir's first number wasn't too bad. Billy Timmons, the bass, had a strong, low, vibrant voice and the tenor hit the high notes true enough. You couldn't say that for Aunt Lizzie but Annie managed to cover up those high screeches of hers pretty well. Then came the Call to Worship and another hymn. That presented some problem. Emil and Eino had trouble knowing when to stand or sit, always doing both too late. Sort of out of sync. They watched the others pick up the hymn books and did so themselves but they didn't try to sing, of course. Emil couldn't read English, let alone music. Then after the preacher read a long passage from scripture about brother-hood, he said a long prayer about being each other's keepers and ended by blessing all the newcomers who were there that day. Emil and Eino hadn't been blessed before and they sort of liked it.

Next came the offering while the choir sang again. Emil looked startled when he saw the plates being passed around. "Hey, Eino! You got any raha?" he said in a loud whisper that made the people in front turn around slightly. Eino passed him that first fifty cent piece of Aunt Lizzie's to put in the plate and then didn't have anything else to put in, so he just pretended. A quick learner, Eino. Then came the Doxology with all the congregation saying it good and strong, another hymn, and finally the sermon.

Mr. Decker's text was something about bringing in the sheaves and he sure brought in too many of them. The sermon lasted a good half hour too long and before he was half through, Emil and Eino were wriggling around on those hard pews trying to get comfortable. Yes, and crossing and uncrossing their legs. They'd drunk too much whiskey the night before and had too much coffee before they got dressed. I could see them fighting for self control. It gets harder as you get older.

At last, at long last, when the preacher ended his sermon with another prayer, he announced that Mrs. Elizabeth Campton would render the solo entitled "Whispering Hope." She rendered it; she sure did. To the organist's surprise, Aunt Lizzie began in a key three notes too high. Annie did her best but she had a tough time trying both to transpose and to blot out with an organ blast those high notes of Aunt Lizzie's. It wasn't too bad on the first "whisper my dreams" but the second time around Annie just stopped playing altogether and Aunt Lizzie really butchered it good. Then, frowning, she stopped abruptly, waiting for the organ to catch up.

In that merciful moment of silence every person in the congregation heard Emil's hoarse whisper. "Excuze! Eino and me we got to go pee." Charlie Olafson moved his number fifteen shoes out of the way and out of the pew the two men shot, out of the church door, and around the back for relief.

But they didn't go to their houses right away. Instead, they went up to Aunt Lizzie's place, took off their ties and their coats, and after a moment's hesitation, the pants that had belonged to the husbands she had buried. Dumping everything on Aunt Lizzie's back steps, the two old buggers loped home down the long hill street. Fortunately, they'd got beyond the church when the people started coming out but I got a good look at them as they high-tailed it around the corner. Quite a sight they were in those lumberjack boots and long underwear!

When Emil and Eino got to their cabins they felt so virtuous they opened another bottle. That left three for the winter.

Dr. Springer

"The crows are back! The crows are back!" The joyous shout echoed up and down our hill street. It had been a terrible winter, much worse than usual, with one great storm following another. Drifts piled upon drifts until some of our lower windows were half covered and our sidewalks were more tunnels than pathways. No January thaw had come our way that year, nor did February or March bring relief. LaTour, the oldest man in our village, said he'd never seen the likes of it in his lifetime.

But the crows had returned at last and there was joy in Tioga. "We've made it through the winter! We've made it through the winter!" That was what we said to ourselves over and over again, and what we said to everyone we met. Those unfortunates who have never experienced an Upper Peninsula winter cannot possibly understand the sense of triumph, rebirth and renewal that always was ours when spring finally came.

Day followed day with blue skies and warm sun. The drifts sagged, you could even see the tips of the picket fences piercing them. Saucers formed around the base of the maple trees; great loads of snow shuddered off the heavily laden firs. Although it still froze hard every night, rivulets and then torrents of water ran down our hill street. We kids made snow dams, across it and were delighted when they broke and carried our stick boats away. All of us were wet to the bone until we went to bed but no one spanked us. It was spring, spring, spring, and everybody was smiling. The whole town of Tioga was full of laughter.

With the release came a great burst of energy. The men took down the storm windows and the storm sheds from in front of the doors. They cleaned out the barns and chicken coops. They tapped the maple trees. They trapped beaver and fished the open edges of Lake Tioga for trout or they dangled their lines from the railroad bridge over our river for the pike that were going up to spawn. They split summer wood. They greased their boots.

The women stopped counting the mason jars of venison and fruit in their cellars and went into a veritable orgy of housecleaning and baking. Mrs. Mattson was the first to hang out a line of clothes to flap colorfully in the soft breeze even though she had to wade in snow three feet deep to manage it. Other wives were soon doing it too.

Horses rolled in the barnyard with their feet kicking the spring air. Cows bellowed incessantly, and often played bull, mounting each other. Chickens began to lay again once they were freed to scratch in patches of brown grass outside their coops. Dogs roamed the yards in groups with lust in their souls. It was spring.

We kids were erupting volcanoes of energy too and our parents had to catch us to get us to sprout the rest of the potatoes and to haul them up from the cellar before it filled with melt water. We made snowmen and snow forts where we fought viciously with hard packed snowballs. We cleared out a space to play marbles. Out of shingles, we made boats with little paddlewheels powered by a rubber band and sailed them across the ever growing puddles. Why, we even enjoyed chopping big cakes of ice off the sidewalks with the splitting axe. Hard work, but each big chunk we could slide off the walk brought us closer to summer. School became almost unbearable. To be jailed inside when the birds were singing in the sun was torture. By the time the breakup was over, we had known more spankings for misbehavior than at any other time of the year. Who cared? Whoops! it was spring at last.

But there was one house in our village still filled with winter's gloom. In it lived Jacques and Marie Conteau, both in their late sixties. They were waiting to die. Not that there was anything really wrong with their health, my father said after a neighbor asked him to visit them, but they had no reason for

living. The fall before, Jacques had sold his cow, and killed his chickens and two pigs because he was tired of tending them. "My strength, she is gone," he said. All Jacques had left was an old horse. He would have sold her too but no one wanted to feed it through the winter. Jacques had nothing to do nor any urge to do it.

Marie, throughout their forty years of married life, had often had spells of depression accompanied by mild and vague ailments that my father could not cure. Her husband, Jacques, like most French Canadians, had always been a gay spirit but it had been a long hard winter (tres doloureux) and he too had been down in the dumps for a long, long time. The two of them rarely spoke to each other any more. After forty years, what was there to say? Silently, Marie prepared the meals, and silently they ate them without appetite or enjoyment. Jacques went to bed early and got up at dawn; Marie went to bed late and rose long after sun-up so they could escape each other. They slept on the edges of the bed as far apart as they could get.

Partly because the Conteau's house was the last one on the road to Mud Lake and the snowplow never went that far, Jacques and his wife had been pretty snowbound all winter. No one came to see them and Marie never left the house. Jacques did snowshoe into town once every two weeks for groceries or to get the mail but that was all. Usually they got a monthly check from their only child, a son who lived in California and hadn't been back for seven years, and this was what they lived on. Not that they ate much or needed much. The Conteaus didn't feel lonely; they just felt angry and depressed. Marie no longer braided her hair but wore it in a straggly bun and didn't care how she looked. She also sighed frequently and every time she did, it irritated her husband so much he thought of popping her one if she ever did it again. So he went out to the barn, fed and bedded the horse, and whittled fire sticks until he had enough for ten winters. The evenings were the longest and the worst. She read, or pretended to read, her Bible and he the Farmer's Almanac. Neither had smiled since the summer before.

Finally, about the middle of May, they had their first visitor. It was Francois Bourdon with whom Jacques had often fished and hunted. "The walleye are running, Jacques," he said. "Untu caught seven big ones last night off the railroad bridge. I got plenty of chub minnows. You come with me." But Jacques refused. He was not feeling well, he said. Francois was appalled to see how the two of them looked. Thin and sallow, with droopy mouths! The winter had been hard on them. They really looked sick so he came to our house and asked Dad to go see them.

When Dad returned he went down to see Father Hassel, the Catholic priest. "Father," Dad said, "what's the policy of your church about suicide?"

"It's a major sin, Doctor. Why do you ask.?"

"Well," said my father, "two of your flock seem determined to commit it by slow attrition. The Conteaus. They're in bad shape, deeply depressed, not eating enough. Nothing really physically wrong with them but…"

"Come to think of it," interrupted the priest, "they haven't been to church or confession for over a year. I'll go to see them right away, of course, but what do you prescribe?."

"I deal with the body, Father," said Dad. "You deal with the soul. Their souls are sick, deathly sick. They'll never make it through the summer to say nothing of another winter. I've seen it happen. They've got to have some reason for living. They've got to have something to care for and love and they have nothing. I told them I'd send them some medicine and if you're going to see them soon, you might take this bottle with you. It's my own special concoction for a spring tonic. I call it the Elixir of the Root of the Royal Banyan Tree. Mostly alcohol, of course, and it tastes pretty good if I do say so, myself. You might try a nip of it yourself, my friend, if only to help you bear that ugly housekeeper of yours."

The priest grinned and accepted the large bottle. "I may just do that, Doctor." he said. "Or call upon you for another one for me."

As my father left, he said, "All foolishness aside, I'm really worried about the Conteaus. They've got to get some meaning and loving in their lives."

And so it came to pass that about a week later when Jacques went out to the barn to whittle some more fire sticks, he found in it a little springer spaniel puppy wiggling a tiny stub of a tail. Jacques rushed back to the house. "Marie, Marie!" he called. 'Come see! A little puppy is in the barn."

"A dog in the barn, a horse in the barn, you in the barn, so?" She didn't look up from her Bible and her voice was a listless monotone. It was the longest utterance he'd heard from her in months.

"I show you then." When Jacques picked up the little puppy to bring it into the kitchen, the dog licked his face and he noticed for the first time that there was a note with writing on it tucked under the collar.

"Marie, see what I find out there in the straw? You got glasses on. What this paper say? "He handed her the note. She read it twice before she answered.

"It say 'Dear Jacques and Marie: My name is Willie. I am six weeks old. I would like to live at your house. Also I am very hungry, please. A friend sent me to you.'"

"No," Marie said. "No! We will have no dog here. Put it outside or take back to barn. This no place for a dog. Or for you or for me. We too old and sick to have a young dog."

But Jacques put the puppy in her lap as he went to the cupboards. "We give Willie something to eat first," he said. "What you have for him. We got no milk, no meat, no bone. Two egg here. And bread. What we fix for Willie, Marie?" He noticed that she was holding the little dog in her arms as though it were a baby and that it was licking her thin hands.

I fix something," she replied but when she gently put the puppy on the floor, it whined softly so she picked it up again and began stroking him. "Willie scared, I think," she added. "I hold him now some more. You make mash of egg and bread and canned milk and put in saucer." Willie began to climb up her body to lick her neck and as she brought the little dog down to cradle and cuddle him in her arms, Jacques noticed that she was smiling. He hadn't seen that smile for years. Old as she was, Marie was almost pretty when she smiled that way.

Willie was hungry and lapped up every bit of the food in the saucer. Then he went over to Marie's feet and promptly went sound asleep. The Conteaus looked at each other.

"What you think, Marie? Who bring the dog?"

"I don't know. Maybe Francois, eh? Or the Dumonts, may be so?" The puppy stirred and she stroked its back. Willie sighed and went back to sleep. "'What we going to do? We don't want dog here. How we take care, when we sick?"

Jacques thought for a long time and tried to keep from looking at the pup. "Yes," he said finally. "We go to town this afternoon and find out where he come from and give him back. You come too, Marie, to hold dog in the buggy. And put on that pretty pink dress and blue jacket so you look nice. I going to shave even."

Jacques spent most of the morning cleaning up and curry combing the old horse who was well caked with manure from the long winter. Marie washed and braided her hair. As they drove down the road to town in the warm spring sun, they both felt better than they had for a long time.

Francois wasn't home but his wife, Elsie, made them welcome. Of course, they had to have coffee and cinnamon rolls. The conversation was gay but no, Elsie was sure that Francois hadn't brought Willie. She made much of the puppy too and Willie loved the attention. Then the three of them went to the Dumonts and had to have coffee and cake again. No, no one in town had springer spaniels they were told. Lots of hounds but there wasn't a dog in town that looked like Willie. They visited several other old acquaintances and got the same story. At the last house, old Dewarre offered to take the puppy. "That's a fine dog," he said. "The best there is for partridge. I give you five dollars for him."

Jacques looked at his wife. "No," she said, "we'll find who give Willie to us or we keep him ourselves." The little puppy wiggled his tail and nuzzled her arms. Both of them hid their relief as they got in the buggy to go home. Neither said anything but it was decided. Willie was their own.

They stopped at Flinn's store and cashed one of their son's checks to buy a big pot roast with a marrow bone in it, some milk, eggs and butter and a big bag of flour. As Marie gathered up the supplies, Jacques wandered around the store. "Marie, you come here. I buy you new hat so you look pretty, yes?" He held Willie while she tried them on. When they left the store, she was radiant and both of them were almost happy. As they clopped, clopped along the road home, Jacques found himself humming the old song: "Oh, zee wind she blow from zee north/and the wind zee blow some more/but you won't get drown in Lac Champlain/so long as you stay on zee shore."

That night Jacques suddenly awoke to find that Marie was not in his bed. Nor was she downstairs. He found her in the barn sitting on a bale of hay rocking Willie. "I hear him crying," she said. "He scared and much alone so I come. Look, he sleep now." Jacques went back to bed but it was a long time before Marie did too.

Thanks to Willie, the summer was a delight to both of them. He changed their lives completely. For one thing, there was always something to talk about. Willie had chased a bee and got stung. That was why he'd come ki-yiing back to the house. He also got burrs in his ears that only Marie could remove as she bathed him in sweet talk. Willie had brought back a stick Jacques had thrown into a puddle. Should she, Marie, give Willie a bath? He was scratching a lot. She was concerned. Willie had got so far down in a fox hole only his tall was showing and Jacques had found it hard to get him back out. That sort of talk. There was always something to say to each other.

Now that they were going to church and confession again, they hated to lock Willie in the barn when they were gone. Jacques just had to build a fence, Marie said. And a doghouse too where she could put the sleeping pad she'd made from an old quilt. It was good to hear the sewing machine going again, Jacques thought, and to have his socks mended and buttons sewed on but he sort of hated to fence Willie in. Such a gay spirit in that dog. And how affectionate he was, always ready to run in JOYOUS circles when it looked as though Jacques was going to take him for a long walk. Always ready to jump into Marie's lap if she sat on the back steps or on the cellar door. Willie was getting bigger now. Big feet and long legs. Soon he'd overlap that lap of hers.

When the Conteaus had to have a fence or stay home all the time, Jacques repaired the woven wire surrounding the old pig yard and pig house. Marie didn't approve even though a heavy crop of grass and weeds had come up in it. "Willie too nice a dog for pigpen," she said. She didn't give in until Jacques had cut the weeds and grass with his scythe and put a new floor in the pig house. But Willie didn't like it either. He didn't like it at all! He ran around the enclosure and howled so long Marie had to go inside the fence to comfort him. And then he howled some more when she left. "He get used to it," said Jacques.

Marie was delighted when the howling suddenly stopped and discovered a very proud but dirty Willie on the back steps wagging his tail. He had dug a hole under the gate so Jacques buried a length of fencing and put Willie back. How the dirt flew between the mournful howls, but finally the puppy lay down in the sun and slept. A half hour later, however, he was back on the steps again. No, Willie hadn't dug his way out but the gate was open. Jacques put him back again and pecked around the corner of the barn. The dog was pushing up hard with his nose against the bent wire latch and soon had dislodged it from its staple. "He's smart dog," Jacques told his wife, "But I'm smarter." He installed a throw-bolt on the gate. "Now, let's see you get out!" he said as he went back to the house. Oh, the walling! But ten minutes later, there was Willie on the steps again even though the gate was still locked. Impossible! Jacques put him back and watched again, this time to see Willie climb that five foot fence and flop over its top. That was the end of his being fenced in. Thereafter when the Conteaus left the house, Willie was first shut up in the barn, then later, in the summer kitchen.

Feeding was no problem. Willie ate what they did except for fresh peas which he picked out of the dish and dropped on the floor. An egg beaten up with milk and bread was his favorite so Jacques bought a cow and then chickens. A lot more work, but somehow it seemed enjoyable. Willie went along when Jacques drove the Jersey to the pasture and again when he went after her. At milking time the dog sat beside Marie, waiting for his saucer of warm milk. Both Jacques and Marie talked constantly to the dog, Willie cocking his ears and listening intently. He even understood French Canadian and would come immediately when Jacques whistled with forefingers between his teeth and yelled "Venez, Willie, Venez!"

As his second teeth began to come in, the dog chewed anything it could find. Chunks of wood, a tin can, anything. A new soup bone was soon whittled down to a scrap. Marie rubbed his red gums with a forefinger. Willie didn't bite. In August month Jacques went hunting again and shot an illegal deer so Willie could have plenty of bones and meat and Marie canned the venison for the winter. When Francois brought them a fine mess of trout, they discovered that Willie couldn't get enough of the

pink meat so Jacques began to fish again, too. The dog wasn't much good when Jacques had to wade the stream for it loved the water and would spoil the holes with its splashing so Jacques borrowed Francois' boat and trolled for pike in Lake Tioga. Willie would sit on the back seat, stiff and erect, as Jacques rowed. "Mon Capitain!" Jacques called him. When a pike was thrashing in the bottom of the boat, the hills around the lake echoed with Willie's barking.

Willie also put on a frenzy of barking when Jacques cut down a tree for the winter's wood. As it fell, the dog would run around it in circles, then climb up on the fallen trunk and bay almost like a hound. "That dog, he think he chop it down himself," Jacques told Marie. And on the way home from the woods, Willie would sit on the wagon seat close beside the man, occasionally licking his face. Good company, that dog.

The spaniel was very affectionate. Willie loved everybody who came to the house and the Conteaus had a hard time for a while trying to stop him from getting in their laps too. They were having a lot of visitors once again by this time, not only the older people who stopped in for coffee and a chat, but a lot of kids too. Willie loved children of all sizes, especially when they'd throw a stick or chase him around the yard. "He's no watchdog, Marie!" said Jacques, but then of course, none of us needed a watchdog. No one in town ever locked their doors.

Soon it was fall and the pink fireweed and yellow goldenrod were in bloom everywhere. A few maple trees were gowned in scarlet. Jacques then took Willie hunting partridge, wandering the edges of hills and swamps where the yellow poplars grew. The dog roamed back and forth before him and when it spotted a grouse, it first froze and that stub of a tail vibrated swiftly. Then Willie began to jump stiff legged until the big bird flew up in a flurry of noisy wingbeating. Unlike most springers, however, Willie barked. Jacques was delighted. You need a barking dog because if you have one, a partridge will fly up into a nearby tree and sit there looking at the dog and become an easy shot. Ah, that Willie was a treasure.

By October, when the nights became cold, Willie was living and sleeping in the summer kitchen. There had been no problem with housebreaking either. Both Jacques and Marie just made sure that one of them always took him outside first thing in the morning and last thing at night, and always a half hour after he'd been fed. Only once had Willie had an accident and then he was so ashamed over the lapse that neither Jacques or Marie had the heart to punish him. Not that they ever had, for that matter. He was a good dog, Willie was. He never tried to enter the kitchen even when the door was open. He'd come to the threshold and look at them with his sad brown eyes but he wouldn't come a bit further. Indeed, when the weather got really cold, the Conteaus had a hard time convincing Willie that it was all right to go to his bed quilt under the kitchen table next to the big kitchen range. Somehow he seemed to know that it was a real privilege and was careful not to abuse it. Willie never begged for food at the table and when they snapped their fingers he always went right to his bed and lay there. Un bon chien!

One of the things that Willie had never mastered was climbing steps, even those that led up to the back stoop. If Marie was sitting there, he'd leap them to nuzzle her and beg to be scratched, but he wouldn't climb. Since the Conteaus rarely used the living room off the kitchen, Willie never entered it. Nor did he ever attempt to climb the steps in the open stairwell that led from it to the bedroom loft under the roof where they slept.

That was why, one very cold midnight in November, that Jacques was so surprised when he found Willie nudging him over from the edge of the bed towards its middle. Full of sleep, Jacques threw the upper blanket over the dog and found himself next to the warmth of Marie's body. For the first time in many years, he took her in his arms. They lived happy ever after.

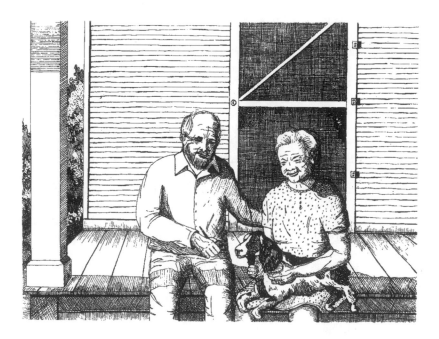

Spitting

When I was a boy in the old U.P., spitting was an art, a science, and a necessity. It was a necessity because almost all of our men chewed tobacco or took snuff and you don't swallow the juice of either or you'll turn green. Most of them also smoked but not on the job. Filling and tamping and lighting a pipe wasted too much time. "Taking a five," our phrase for a short rest, was not particularly approved of by most straw bosses. A man was supposed to work hard and to keep at it until quitting time.

So our miners always carried a plug of chewing tobacco in their hip pockets, biting off a chunk now and then throughout their hard day to keep the chew going. So did our lumberjacks, although most of them preferred loose tobacco, mainly Peerless, that they bought by the pailful. It made a bigger and better cud, they claimed, one that could last half a morning of sawing pine. The snow around every stump was speckled with brown from their saliva. Those who worked on the railroad were about equally divided between chewing plug and loose tobacco.

But even some of the professional people were known to chew tobacco or indulge in snuff. My father, the doctor, said he started in medical school to counteract the stink of formaldehyde that came from the cadavers he had to dissect. Our school superintendent used snuff and so did one of the itinerant preachers who held services in the Methodist Episcopal Church. What I'm trying to say, I guess, is that spitting wasn't considered particularly vulgar back then. If you chewed tobacco, you had to spit. It was as simple as that, and as necessary.

Of course, there were limitations. You weren't supposed to spit on the floor. Every public building had signs in gold letters: "No Spitting On The Floor By Order Of The Board of Health." And, unless you couldn't wait another instant, you didn't spit in the presence of lady school teachers or such. Also, you didn't spit on another man's shoes unless you wanted to fight him. I can't say we were always discreet about our spitting, but there were rules of sort, and we followed them.

When the brown juice got to flowing strong and the men were inside a building, they looked for the nearest spittoon. Our word for spittoon was "gabboon" and I don't know why. They were everywhere except in church. Every house had one. Some were brown colored steel with an originally white mouth but the best were made of brass. Cleaned and polished, you can't find a prettier sight than a big brass gabboon gleaming on a sunny floor. Some families even used them occasionally as flower pots. But the best thing about brass spittoons as compared to the steel ones was that they rang when you hit them fair and square. Not a big noise, but it was a clang just the same. You didn't hear it if you hit the outside of the gabboon - only when you pinged the top around the hole. That was always the target.

Usually it was only the men that chewed tobacco and needed the gabboons. Some of the old Finn women did smoke their corncob pipes of Peerless as they rocked beside the warm kitchen range and a few of them also chewed Copenhagen snoos, as snuff was called. I used to like to visit the Haitemas to see old lady Haitema daintily spit in her special blue coffee cup. (All the others were white!) There'd be a big bulge behind her lower lip as she nursed her snuff, and then, when it was time, the old gal would pick up the blue cup from the floor beside her, hold it up before her mouth at arms length with little finger delicately extended, and let go. Never missed once.

All of us boys, of course, had to imitate our elders, first by chewing the fluffy white flowers of Indian tobacco, and then later the real stuff. It was a rite of passage to manhood. A lot of us, including me, tried as hard as we could but never managed to make the grade. I could handle Indian tobacco, but every time I tried snuff or cut plug, I wiped out. Awful tasting stuff and, no matter how fast I kept spitting, the taste lingered for hours in my mouth even if I chewed rhubarb afterwards. In my desperate experimentation, I twice swallowed some of the juice and almost lost my insides. Although I've been smoking a pipe now for sixty-five years - a dirty, filthy habit that I love - I never did acquire the ultimate merit badge of adulthood.

I said earlier that spitting, in addition to being a necessity, was an art and a science in the old U.P. Yes, we admired a really good spitter. The distance champion in our area was a big Swede who lived over by Half-Way named Sven Anderson. His record was thirteen feet and eleven inches - achieved on a windless winter day. The best any other man managed was a mere eleven feet which was plenty good. Sven had a mouth big enough to hold a cud as large as a baseball and he also had good teeth. You've got to have good front teeth as well as a strong tongue to spit well.

However, a lot of our men didn't have good teeth because they'd cracked too many hazelnuts in their youth and because there was no dentist nearer than Marquette. Filling a cavity was unknown and if you got a bad toothache, you either put some cotton soaked with oil of cloves on it, or you endured it, or you had someone pull it with a pair of pliers. No anesthetic! I vividly remember my father putting his forceps in my mouth and yelling, "Cully, hold onto that porch pillar tight and stop yelling."

Anyway, many of our men didn't have the dental equipment to be a real spitting champion. Henry Nyman, though, was a fair to middling spitter and he hadn't had a tooth in his head for years. His gooms (gums) had so hardened that he didn't need teeth. I myself once saw him bite off a chunk of a black rye hardtack and chew it down without even wetting it. Some people claimed that one time Henry got in a fight and bit off the fellows ear with those gooms. So I don't know if teeth really had anything to do with being a good spitter. Maybe it was just an art, handed down from father to son.

But it was also a science of sorts, especially when you tried for accuracy instead of distance. You had to calculate the right quantity and thickness of the juice in your mouth, how much air pressure to store up, and how suddenly to let it go. It wasn't just the velocity or the trajectory either. Often you had to figure in the windage.

Spitting

The most accurate spitter we had in our forest village, but only at a distance of four feet, was Eric Niemi, who lived in a shack by Mud Lake. He's the one who never cleaned his trout. Just squeezed them till they squeaked and put them in the pan. Anyway, old Eric sure was accurate in his spitting. We kids liked to go down to his shack in the summer just to watch him nail flies to the panes of his one window with a good squirt of tobacco juice. Didn't have much of a view out of that window anyway because it looked over a swamp.

Because of the skill involved, all of us boys did a lot of spitting and we had to practice religiously to be good at it. We'd get a board with a knothole, draw a line on the ground to stand on, and try to spit through the hole without spattering the board, or we'd get a can to serve as a gabboon. For some reason, Mullu was usually more accurate than most of us and that was surprising because he spit a curve. He couldn't help it, he said, but he sure could hit the hole or the can most of the time. Most of us spit straight for the target but I found I could do best by lobbing it.

We also played a spitting game called Spimoryette. If a naive or newcomer boy came to play with us, we initiated him. "It's an old French Canadian game," we'd tell the poor devil. "Put your cap on the ground, turn around and cover your eyes and holler "Spimoreyette" seven times, and then we'll hide and you have to find us. Anyone you catch will be IT next time around." So the poor gullible kid would put down his cap and as he said "Spimoryette" (spit more yet) we'd follow his orders. We also had a game called "Peemoryette", but I won't describe that!

And, of course, in school we had spit balls. We usually didn't spit them though. We either used a blowgun made of a hollow elderberry stalk or a little gun of the same material with a spring made of a corset stay. You sure could make another kid yelp when he got hit in the neck by a spit ball from either of these. We also used to make a juicy spitball and plaster it onto the ceiling over the teacher's desk and watch with innocent anticipation until it dried and fell down on her head.

We even had a song about spitting. It went like this:

Oh, I'm a 'olly consumptive,
Hawk, hawk, ptuie!
I do not work; I do not play.
All I do is spit all day,
Hawk, hawk, ptuie!"

But I've got to tell you about Maggie O'Conner, the cleaning lady at our railroad depot. All of us in Tioga were proud of that depot because it was a good sized one, being at the junction of the north-south and east-west railroads. There were four rooms in it. The western room was the place where all the American Express or Wells Fargo packages were stored as they came in. The next room was where the station master reigned and the telegraph operator worked and listened to the constant clattering of his keys. Then came the passenger waiting room with seats, the ticket window and the board that told which trains were due and when. Finally, at the eastern end, was the baggage room. Only the two middle rooms were heated by potbellied coal stoves.

Maggie's job was to keep all of these rooms reasonably clean. The express and baggage rooms weren't too bad for Maggie but the middle two rooms were, especially the waiting room. Plenty of snow and dirt was always being tracked in there but the worst part of her cleaning job was due to the regular evening spitting competition to see who could hit the gabboon.

You see, there wasn't much to do in the evenings in our town. No TV or radio and few newspapers or reading material. Our men, if they had biting money, nursed a long beer at Higley's Saloon, but if they had none, Callahan's Store or the depot were about the only places they could go.

Somehow the men who regularly hung out at the depot in the evening started a spitting contest to see who could hit the top of the brass spittoon and make it ring. Every night there would be four or five of them, each of whom would put a penny in a can for the privilege of making a try for it. Whoever made the spittoon ping got the pot. At first they started from a chalked line about five feet away from the gabboon and then each night thereafter the distance was lengthened a foot. As you can imagine, there were more misses than hits and Maggie got sick of having to clean up the mess when the doors were locked at 9:30 after the last passenger train had left. She usually cleaned and mopped the floors of the express and baggage rooms first, then the station master's room and last of all the waiting room where the contest was held. When Maggie gave the spitters a piece of her mind for spitting all over the floor, the men said, "Aw, shut up, Maggie. That's yer job!" And when she appealed to the station master, he said the same thing. It was not a woman's world down there in the depot.

Finally, one night there was a lot of misses. In fact, because none of the men were able to hit the gabboon from seven feet, there were thirty-five pennies in the can. Maggie, who had been watching them, waiting with her mop, suddenly said, "Let an Irish woman try it!" and on the first attempt she let fly and pinged the gabboon right plumb on its top. As the men's mouths hung open, she picked up the spittoon and the can with the money, and left in triumph.

As you can imagine, the news of her feat spread throughout the village. For once, a woman had showed up the men in their most macho sport, and that without even having any tobacco juice to spit. "How did you do it Maggie?" one of her friends said. "Ah, it was easy," she replied. "I practiced a bit after closing time before I scrubbed the place and last night when I won the pot, they never knew I spit a raisin!"

That was the end of the evening spitting contests in the Tioga depot.

Callahan's Store
(Parental Guidance Requested)

Besides Higley's Saloon and the depot there was only one other place in our town where our men could go sit on a winter's evening. That was Callahan's store which kept open until nine or ten at night, the store where the Last Man Under the Table poke club used to meet before they held that wake with drunken Dinny in the coffin. It was always warm there by the big pot bellied stove and usually four or five men could be found around it, sitting on boxes or cracker barrels, passing the time till Mike Callahan kicked them out and closed up for the night. Some wild stories were sure told around that stove.

There was the one about how in the old days the lumberjacks used to try to leave their mark on the low ceiling of the bunkhouse by jumping and kicking it with their sharp caulked (corked, they called it) boots. It took a good man to do it and many tried and failed. But there was one jack named Long Legs Poulet who gave a great leap, turned a somersault in the air, and planted both boots up in the pine boards so deep that they left him up there for three days to cure.

"Yah," someone said, "They was real he men in them old days. Had to be. A rough life that, logging the big pine and hauling them back over them hills. Why, there was one hill over beyond Hell's Canyon so steep they had to run a big rope over the top and hitch three span of oxen to pull the teams over the top."

"Yeah," said one of the listeners, "I heerd of that hill. My pappy called it the five fart hill, because it took that many from his horse to get his buckboard over it."

"Speaking of farts," another man said. "Ever hear about how old man Mullen married him a young wife, 'cause he wanted a kid so bad. And he tried and she tried but nothing happened for a long time. And then she began to swell up good and the old man was sure proud and happy. Sure was nervous though when her time came due. Old man Mullen, he was a pacing up and down front of the bedroom door until Dr. Gage finally comes out. 'What 'tis it, Doc? Boy or a girl, Doc?' The Doc he give it to him straight, he did. 'Mr. Mullen,' he said, 'you sir, are the father of a ten pound fart!'"

"Yeah," said another man. "Doc Gage tells it to you straight. No beating around the bush or using ten pound words. Like the time the young preacher come to him with gonorrhea and tells him he caught it in an outhouse. 'Young man,' Doc sez,' That's no place for intercourse!"

"Speaking of preachers or priests," the first man said, I once got a young priest to save his soul, I did. I was coming up on the train from Milwaukee. Been visiting my daughter down there. Well, any old how, this young priest, still wet behind the ears, he gets on at Green Bay and sits down besides me. So I sez, 'Howdy, Mister. Nice day' just to be sociable like. But he wasn't having any of it. Didn't even nod. Just set there reading his Bible or something. Didn't say a damned word and kept way over on the end of the seat. I seen though that when any gal or woman walks up the aisle he looked 'em up and down and all over. Well, when we come to Iron Mountain, and he gets ready to get off, he turns to me and sez 'I fear I have not been a very good companion, sir, I am a man of the cloth and must do my devotions.'

"I give him a terrible glare, rose up from my seat and sez, 'Mebbe it's just as well, young man. For you see, *I AM THE DEVIL!*' Gadamighty, you should have seen the squirt gallop down the aisle a-crossing himself. Why, he was still doing it out on the platform when the train pulled out. Done a good deed, that day, I did!.""

Of course, there always was a Paul Bunyan story or two. Like the one about how when Paul Bunyan had to take a crap, he always wiped his tail with thirteen porcupine. Damned near cleaned them out of the country in blackberry time. Once Paul could only find twelve so he sits down in the middle of Lake Tioga to clean himself and the water in the river runs upstream and spilled over the divide of land into Lake Superior. Damned poor trout fishing for three years.

The room was cooling off and one of the men began to put a big chunk of coal in the stove. "Hey, you!" hollered Mike Callahan. "Don't put that coal on. It's nigh closing time. If you're cold, go home.'"

The man put the chunk back in the scuttle. "Jeez, for stingy!" he exclaimed. "Bad as that McGregor feller from Scotland who used to live in Republic. Stingiest man ever hit the bush, he was. They say that when his wife was in labor he got an old Finn midwife instead of the Doc. And when the baby starts coming, the Finn woman hollers at him, 'Turn up the lamp. I can't see!' So he did and the baby was born. Then McGregor turned down the wick again. 'Wait a minute, Mister,' she yells at him. 'Here comes another!' And out comes its twin, so he begins to turn down the lamp. 'Hold it!' she sez. 'Mebbe there's another!" 'Like hell,' says McGregor. He blew out the lamp and lit a candle. 'Damn light seems to attract them!'

It was time to go home.

Fly Time

Paradise had its snake and the U.P., that lovely land, has its insects: mosquitoes, black flies, gnats, deer flies, fish flies, horse flies and no-see-um-big-feelums. Often it didn't seem quite fair to have made it through a terrible winter only to have to endure fly time, that elastic period from the middle of May to the middle of July. Fortunately, there usually were a short few weeks after the break-up when we could roam the woods and streams unbedeviled by the flying hordes that would beset us later.

A good time that! Though little patches of snow still remained on the north sides of our granite hills and in the cedar swamps, the skies were bright blue and you could feel the warmth of the sun on your back as you knelt to smell the arbutus. We always knelt, perhaps as an unconscious posture of thankful prayer, but mainly to make sure that the arbutus we picked was

truly fragrant. The pink kind was usually best but the white occasionally was most fragrant of all and there was always some arbutus that had no scent whatever. So we knelt and buried our winter faces in spring and brought home great bunches to give to our mothers or to sell to the passengers at the railroad depot.

Depending upon the season, this grateful period lasted only two or three weeks. Then, after a few warmer days, came the black flies, hordes of them, to swarm over our necks and faces, to climb up under our sleeves or pants, and sit there chewing away until, heavy with our blood, they dropped off to let others take their places. In a good year, according to Slimber, he'd counted one million to the acre in the open and more in the swamp.

Not only did black flies leave a bloody crust along your hairline, they also found their way into your nostrils, ears and the corners of your eyes. And your mouth, too. There were times when we inhaled through clenched teeth to prevent their entry when clouds of them surrounded our heads. Old Eric Lampi, who had a homestead on Mud Lake, almost went crazy when some black flies got inside his ear canal and fluttered there until my father squirted some peroxide into it and drowned them. Couldn't really blame those black flies for getting in his ears. There was nowhere else to bite. Eric had hair down to his eyebrows and a heavy beard over the rest of his face. Actually, he looked like a very dirty teddy-bear. The flies probably tried his nose and hands first but these had a lot of yearly layers of dirt so hardened that nothing could penetrate the armor. Eric didn't believe in saunas or washing. "Water's for kalla (fish)," he said.

Those that got up your nose couldn't be wiped out; you had to blow them. My Dad was good at it. He'd take his nose between thumb and forefinger and with a mighty snort, would fling the contents to the ground. No handkerchief! Dad didn't use handkerchiefs except when there was company around. He always said that a rich man put in his pocket what a poor man threw away.

When the black flies were really thick, you also had to be careful when you took a leak out in the woods. The best way was to unbutton your pants and poke your pecker just a little way out through the slit and keep fanning the air with your other hand. Must have been tough on the women.

Since black flies, unlike mosquitoes, gave no warning and would be sitting and chawing on your neck before you knew it, most of us who wandered the woods developed a curious stroking gesture to clean them off our hides. You wiped your fore-head, then the back of your neck and ears on one side with one hand, then did the same on the other side and you'd do it about once every minute. Got to be almost habitual after a time. They said that Jacques Poulin got so he was still doing it when snowshoeing.

Most of us wore a couple of large bandannas when we were trout fishing even though it was considered a sissy sort of thing to do. Sometimes we'd hide them in our pockets until nobody was around and then we'd put on one bandanna so it hung down from our hats in the back and on both sides, with one corner coming out in front till it hit our noses. Since it wiggled when we walked, that also discouraged any stray mosquito from settling too. The other bandanna we wound around our neck up to the chin. That gear really did seem to help but we always took it off when we got back to town. Like our parents, we kids in the U.P. were expected to be tough.

The gnats and no-see-ums came next. Gnats never really bothered us too much because they didn't bite. They swarmed all over us, of course, and got in our eyes and ears and we often inhaled them, but they were more of a nuisance than a real problem. Moreover, they didn't appear until after the sun got warm and they always went away at sundown.

No-see-ums were a different breed, however. So tiny they were almost invisible, they could bite like a chigger. Wiping them off didn't work; you had to scrape them. Even the bushiest beard didn't help for they worked their way through the underbrush and dug into the skin beneath. Fortunately, they too left at dusk, leaving their stings behind them to pester us for hours afterwards. Their surname of "big-feel-um" was sure deserved. Both gnats and no-see-ums bothered us worst when we were sweating and during the middle of the day. The only way we found to cope with the critters was to smear white zinc oxide over any exposed area and that made us look like Zombies. Most of us just endured them as the price we had to pay for being outdoors.

Mosquitoes came next, but I shall postpone telling about them until later. Some of our worst flies were deer flies. Looking like innocent house flies, except that they were gray, they didn't just drill us; they took out chunks of flesh. As we walked the trails up the Tioga River, they'd buzz around our heads in circles, and if you were quick enough you could catch them in the palm of your hand if you held your arm above your head. My brother Joe could catch them every time but they always seemed to light on the back of my hand rather than the front. Deer flies are at their worst in July and prefer hot, sunny days to do their devilment. They seemed to inject an anesthetic so that you never felt their biting until after they've taken out a hunk of flesh and flown up onto a tree limb to digest it. No, deer flies don't hurt when they're biting, but they sure do afterwards. Deer and dogs as well as humans suffer a lot. The deer cope by splashing around at the edge of a lake and the dogs just rub their ears and nuzzles with their forepaws, moaning softly. No fly dope seems to deter deer flies.

In July, the fish flies arrived and they pestered us all summer long. They look just like ordinary house flies and perhaps they are but they bite like hell when you're in a boat or cleaning fish on shore. We usually carried fly swatters along when bass fishing because fish flies aren't hard to swat.

When I was a boy in the U.P. there were always a lot of horses and cows and therefore also a lot of horse flies. They could gouge out a real hole in your skin before you knew it. Almost an inch long and glossy black, it's impossible to swat them. In the old days, farmers or anyone else who owned horses covered their backs with a fringed leather netting that flopped around and dislodged them when the horses shook themselves. You can tell horse flies by their sound too. They have a booming buzz as well as a vicious bite.

But it's the mosquitoes for which the U.P. is most famed. These are not the namby pamby dwarfs that inhabit Lower Michigan or Wisconsin. Our mosquitoes are a different breed! They possess a hybrid vigor acquired over many generations of having to pierce the tough hides of tough people. They're a lot bigger too and we take a sort of perverse pride in them. To survive the bites of thousands of these super mosquitoes annually is to breed real character.

Unlike the sneaky black flies and deer flies, mosquitoes sound a warning before they attack. They are flying rattle snakes. At dusk by a lake or swamp you'll hear them howling like coyotes for blood, creating a universal tone that a musician friend of mine identified as C-sharp, but in a cabin at night a single mosquito as it zooms around your bed will vary its pitch. When the tone gets lower and louder, it means that the bugger's located its target and is ready to come in for a landing and to start drilling. It's almost impossible to swat or shoot them on the wing for they zag when you expect them to zig. You've got to wait there in the darkness with your skin quivering with tension until the skeeter finally lights and then you wait some more until it's too loggy to dodge when you slap at it hard. One mosquito in a bedroom is a lot but there will always be another one once you've thought you've got them all and have closed your eyes to sleep.

One of the first commandments every U.P. child learns at its mother's knee is not to scratch a mosquito bite no matter now much it itches. Scratching only makes the itch worse and often results in a swelling that can become infected. As boys we used to have competitions to see who could stand a drilling mosquito the longest. We'd bare an arm and then when one lit, we'd start counting. I remember one big black devil that drilled for a count of eighty-three and turned pink from my blood before it staggered away. Often, when we'd swatted a mosquito, you'd find a little patch of blood in your hand. We liked that; it was revenge! No wonder the people of the U.P. had sisu, that Finn word for being able to endure anything.

Oddly enough, mosquito dope was not taboo, although most of our men never used it. The basic standby was oil of citronella, a thin yellow liquid that you smeared on your ears, face, neck and wrists. My father used to buy it by the gallon and dispense it in four ounce bottles. We rarely put in on our foreheads because any sweat might run down to our eyes and the citronella in it would set them afire. Dad also had a big bottle of oil of pennyroyal for those who preferred that in their home-made concoctions. The worst fly dope was that used by LaTour, the oldest man in our village. He brewed up the worst smelling stuff of all, consisting of hot tar soaked in kerosene mixed with tobacco juice from his spittoon. He claimed that it kept the mosquitoes away completely and I believe it. Sure kept us away too.

Some of our families had smudge pots smoking by their front and back doors. They'd fill a large can with coals from their kitchen ranges and then stuff green grass on top of them. Somehow, no matter how you tried to place the can, a lot of the white smudge smoke always got in the house and then you'd have to go outside and get bitten until it cleared. When we kids would sleep overnight on a fishing trip up on the headwaters of the Tioga, we'd make smudges too by throwing sawgrass onto our campfire and then when the mosquitoes got too fierce, we'd sit in the smoke for a while. That sure worked but pretty soon our eyes were watering and we were coughing so hard we couldn't stand it. Then we had to suffocate under a blanket, if we had one, or pull our jackets over our heads if we didn't. Those were long nights up there in the bush. Oddly enough, when the trout were really biting, there didn't seem to be many mosquitoes. Probably we were so intent on hooking the fish we just ignored them. One of the best smudges I ever saw was outside a huge hollow pine stub with an Indian in it. He was sitting back in the hole and the smoke was going straight up the bore and never touched him. Pretty slick! I asked him if I could try it for a moment and he grunted "No!"

Many of us kids tried to smoke to keep the mosquitoes away but the only pipes we could afford were corncobs that burned our mouths. Moreover, the Granger or Peerless tobacco we'd steal from our fathers was so strong that we only smoked when we couldn't bear the biting mosquitoes a moment longer. Also, you had to keep puffing almost constantly to keep the skeeters off and that usually made us sick. It was better just to endure. People who have never lived in the U.P. when the mosquitoes are at their peak cannot possibly understand the viciousness of these bugs when they're out in full force. Hardened murderers who escape from the State Penitentiary at Marquette rarely were able to spend more than one night in the woods at fly time without begging at the gates to be let in again.

We joked about our mosquitoes, of course, as we did about all calamities that came our way. Jules LaPorte went around with a sponge tied on the top of his hat, explaining that he'd found a sure fire way to keep the mosquitoes from biting. "Me, I soak dat sponge weeth the blood of a lapin (rabbit) and the flies they go for dat and not for me." He was delighted when a few others fell into the trap and tried it. Another French Canadian with a very bald head claimed that the mosquitoes didn't bother him at all so long as he kept his head bare. "Zee mosquitoes, zey sit on my head and bend their stingers on bone and so can't bite no more." Another man claimed that he solved the problem by putting a bare arm near the inside of a screened window and then, when the mosquitoes poked their stingers through the holes, he'd hit them with a hammer and clinch them to the screen. When he got enough of them anchored there, he said, he'd go out to collect them for soup. Better than fish-eye soup, he insisted.

A lot of lies were told about the size and power of our mosquitoes. At Higley's Saloon there were always arguments about which area had the biggest (it was Goochee

Swamp) or the strongest. "I had one that went right through a sweater, two flannel shirts and my underwear and dug into me so deep I couldn't pull it out. Had to cut it off with a hacksaw." That kind of thing. Pretty crude stuff, most of it. I could tell you a better yarn - the one our town liar, Slimber, told about the four mosquitoes, big as pigeons, that sat on a maple limb outside his cabin at Mud Lake waiting two weeks for him to have to open the door, but I won't. The truth, the whole truth, and nothing but the truth has always been my motto. The biggest mosquito I ever saw stood only two inches tall in his stocking feet. Of course, if he stood on his head when drilling for paydirt, he was a lot taller but I don't think that should count. My father, the village doctor, was also a truthful man. He told us often about one time when he spent a night up in Thompson's camp at the Boilers so he could be sure to fish for trout in a beaver pond at dawn. "Never saw the mosquitoes so bad in my whole life," he said. "Almost drove me crazy and I knew that by morning there'd be nothing left of me but bones. So I used my brains, opened the cabin door wide so the hordes could come in, then when they were all inside, I ran out slamming the door behind me. Slept on the grass ten feet away and never got another bite."

Speaking of the truth as being stranger than fiction, Norman Beritti who lives on Easy Street once told me that the mosquitoes in Goochee Swamp were so large they had fleas. Orange fleas, he said. Now Norman is a virtuous man and I have never known him to tell even the smidgen of a lie. He is trustworthy, loyal, helpful, friendly, courteous, kind, obedient, cheerful, thrifty, brave, clean and reverent, but mosquitoes so big they had fleas? Hoping to sustain my faith in his integrity I made a standing offer of five bucks to anyone who could bring me such a mosquito and damned if Denny Visserink didn't. It was a huge critter and sure enough on the back of its head was a little orange speck, a mite, that moved. Maybe it wasn't literally a flea but it was close enough so I paid up, reciting the old rhymes:

> "The flea is wee and mercy me,
> You cannot tell the he from she,
> But she knows well. And so does he"

> "Greater fleas have lesser fleas
> Upon their backs to bite 'em,
> and lesser fleas have lesser fleas
> And so an infinitum."

Norman accepted my apology for doubting him. "They're hard to see, those orange fleas, but you can tell them because they have blue eyes," he said.

People seem to differ not only in their vulnerability to mosquito bites but also in their ability to attract them. Perhaps it's the body odor. I do know that perfume attracts them. We used to mix it with fly dope and when we smeared that on some fishing buddy, the mosquitoes would come from a mile away to nail him while leaving us alone. White or yellow clothing also seems to bring them so we never wore it. (We never had it.) Those sad souls who always get a bump when bitten (we called them swellers) always got more bites than those who don't. We sure liked to associate with them in fly time. But the best of all things that can keep mosquitoes from biting you is to have a companion from Down Below. Or a fat little baby.

Santa Claus Du Bois

It was the day before the day before Christmas and all of us were merry and full of the holiday spirit except my father. Upon returning from seeing his last patient, he was glum and depressed all through supper. And afterward, he didn't even read the Chicago Tribune; just slumped in the big Morris chair and stared into space. Finally Mother couldn't stand it another moment.

"John, what's the matter? Are you worrying about one of your patients again?"

"Yes, I suppose so," he replied, "but I'm also worrying about Santa Claus." He grinned at her astonishment.

"I've just been down to see Henri Picotte," he explained. "He's the logger who had that bad compound fracture of the leg when the leaning tree he was cutting sprang back on him as it fell. They call those trees widow makers and they're always dangerous. Anyway, it was a nasty double fracture with a piece of bone coming right through the flesh. I've had him flat on his back in a cast for more than a month now and, although I'm pretty sure the bones are knitting, the wound isn't healing. Ulcerating - a lot of proud flesh and some oozing pus on the wet dressing every day. Oh, it's better than it was two weeks ago but I don't like the looks of it. I keep wondering what else I might do. Henri's a fine big man and a proud one. Keeps telling me he'll pay me as soon as he can get back to logging again. Of course, I told him to forget it, that he could pay me any time, but it bothers him."

"You said you were worrying about Santa Claus, too," Mother interrupted.

"Oh, yes, that too," said Dad. "While I was down there seeing Henri, I heard his wife Marie explaining to the two children that there wasn't any Santa Claus and that there wouldn't be any presents this year. Henri heard it too and tears went down his face. It's hell to see a strong man cry. 'Fix me up, Doc. Fix me up soon as you can,' he said."

Mother had tears in her eyes too when Dad fell silent but she was thinking hard. "We've got to do something for those children, John," she exclaimed. "How old are they?"

"Let's see. I think it was five years ago that I delivered Pierre, the boy. Florette, the girl, must now be about three. Nice kids."

"I'm sure I can get up a bag of toys and some candy from Flinn's store for them." Mother was full of the Christmas spirit. "You can take them down to the Picottes tomorrow when you make your calls."

Dad thought a moment. "No," he said. "I told you Henri is a proud man. He'd resent it. He feels too much in debt to me as it is. That's why I wish there really was a Santa Claus."

The next morning at breakfast Mother was radiant. "John," she said, "I think I've found a way to help those Picotte children have a good Christmas. Let's hire somebody to play Santa Claus and take them the presents I'll put together. Henri wouldn't have to know who sent them."

Dad was intrigued by the thought. "Yeah," he said. "That might work out. But who would we get to play Santa Claus and where would we find an outfit? There isn't a Santa Claus costume or beard in the whole town..." Then he began to laugh. "Just thought of someone who could play the part," he explained. "Old Du Bois could. He's got the white beard and he's short and fat. But that old bugger is the worst scoundrel in town. In his youth he sired half the illegitimate babies in this village and he's spent more nights in our jail for fighting and drunkenness than anyone else. And he's not much better now either. Still drinks like a fish when he can get his paws on a little money. No. Du Bois playing Santa? Gad!" Dad laughed hard again at the thought. He was still chuckling as he went out to hitch old Billy to the cutter.

But Mother was not to be discouraged. She wrote a note and asked me to deliver it to Mr. Du Bois. When I knocked and he told me to come in, I found him eating potatoes and salt pork from a skillet on the table. He really did look a little like Santa Claus, sitting there with his red flannel underwear tucked into his pants, and with a bushy white beard on top of a fat beer belly. "Wot you want wiz me, garcon?" he roared.

I explained and gave him the note. He read it word by word, tracing each one with his fork, until finally he understood. Then he laughed.

Oh, how he laughed, sounding and looking more like Santa Claus every minute.

"Your mere, she wan' me be Santa Claus for ze Picotte kids, oui? Sacre mo Gee! An' she pay me ten dollaire for dat? Ho, Ho, Ho! For ten dollaire, I bit ze nuts off a bear, I got so beeg a thirst. You tell her I do eet. I come up see her zis afternoon. Du Bois Santa Claus, Ho, Ho, Ho!"

Oh how my mother scurried around after I brought her back the message. She went up to Flinn's store and brought back a lot of candy and boxes of animal crackers, a doll, and a little red wagon. Then she went up to our attic and came down with some of our old toys. All of these she wrapped with Christmas paper and put in a burlap bag I got from the barn. She also wrapped one of Dad's undertaker cigars for Mr. Picotte and a box of chocolates for his wife.

"Does he really look like Santa Claus?" she asked me. I said that he really did except for a big brown smear on his white beard at the corner of his mouth, probably from chewing tobacco. I told her about the red underwear and how his belly shook when he laughed.

"Oh, but he can't go out in this weather in that red underwear," Mother said. "Ah, I know. I'll give him that old red deer-hunting coat of father's. I'm giving him a new one for Christmas anyway, the old one was so ragged. But what can we do about a cap? I've only seen Mr. Du Bois a few times and all he ever wore was a disreputable old hat. Let me think."

"How about my red stocking cap?" I asked. "It stretches."

"That's it!" she replied. "We'll give Mr. Du Bois a new hat and coat as well as money for playing Santa. Now let me put some red ribbon on that burlap bag."

When Dad got home that noon and Mother told him what she'd done, he was pretty dubious. It wasn't that he was afraid that the Picottes would resent the gifts coming from Du Bois but rather that he would probably steal some of them, or take the ten dollars and head straight for the saloon. "You don't know these drunks," he told my another. "Maybe you ought to give him the money only after he's done the job. Also, ten dollars is too much. Five would be plenty."

Mother was glad that my father was still making calls when Du Bois showed up late in the afternoon. With that old hat and a fleabitten old bearskin coat, he just looked like a bum and a dirty old bum at that. However, once she had him put on Dad's red hunting coat and my stocking cap, he did look a bit more like Santa Claus should. Mother then told Du Bois how he should act.

"You are to knock on the door and say 'Ho, Ho, Ho, here comes Santa Claus' and then you go in and sit on a chair and invite the children to sit on your lap as you take the presents out of your bag. And give them those candy canes first, then the other packages. I have them all labeled. And keep saying Merry Christmas and laughing a lot. Here's your ten dollars and you can keep the red hunting coat and stocking cap. So, Merry Christmas to you and make those children believe in Santa Claus, Mr. Du Bois."

Du Bois felt like a fool going down our hill street in that get up and carrying his old coat and hat as well as the red ribboned burlap bag. He soundly cursed some kids who began to follow him chanting, "Lookit! Lookit! There's Santy Claus. Naw, that's old Du Bois."

He was relieved when he got back to his cabin. There he opened the bag to look at the contents. Maybe there'd be something worth stealing. He felt each of the gaily wrapped packages but they were probably just kids toys so he didn't open them. Indeed, the only thing he took were two of the four bags of candy. After all, he was about out of sugar for his coffee and they'd do in a pinch or he could just suck on one now and then to get the bad taste of rotgut whiskey out of his mouth. Du Bois rubbed his hands with anticipation. After he took those presents to the Picotte kids, he'd head straight for Higley's Saloon and really get polluted. Putting one of the stolen peppermints in his mouth to ease his parched throat, he walked over to the Picotte's house, glad that it was too dark to have anyone see him making a fool of himself.

Outside the door, he rehearsed his opening lines until he had them right. When he knocked and it was opened, he found a very surprised mother and two delighted children. "Santa Claus! Santa Claus'" the kids screamed. They flung themselves on him, grabbing his legs and asking to be picked up and hugged. Du Bois had originally intended just to dump out the stuff in his bag on the floor and leave immediately but he sat down on a chair with a child on each knee and started distributing the presents while Mrs. Picotte went into the bedroom to tell her husband what was happening.

"An' here one for you, little girl and one for you, boy. Ho, ho, ho' See wat Santa he bring you. Open up! Merry Christmas, open up!" First there was a doll for Florette and some jackstraws for Pierre. There a pretty red hair ribbon for the girl and a box of alphabet blocks for the boy. The children hugged Santa and tried to kiss his whiskers, then rushed into the bedroom to show their father what they had gotten. "Merry Christmas! Merry Christmas! Ho! Ho.! Ho!" Du Bois was really enjoying himself.

"An here, Madame, I find something for you. Open up!" It was the box of chocolates. Santa got one too as little fingers put it through the white whiskers into his mouth.

"An' for votre pere, too, we'ave someting, oui! You take it to 'im and tell me wot it is, eh?" he told the children.

"It's a cigar, a big cigar," the boy said when he returned. "My father, he says thank you very much, Santa Claus, and he say to tell you he was almost out of Peerless for his pipe."

There were other packages with more hugging and kissing. Then finally, at the bottom of the sack, were two bags of assorted candies. Du Bois felt a twinge of guilt, thinking of the two other bags he'd stolen but then he remembered the two candy canes he had in the pockets of my Dad's hunting coat and gave them to the kids. Somehow, he hated to leave when he had to go. He couldn't remember a time when he had felt so warm and happy.

"Ho, ho, ho! It's time to go," he roared. "A Merry Christmas to all of you and bon nuit!" Then, picking up his empty sack, he went out into the night.

Two days after Christmas, Father Hassel, our Catholic priest, came up to play another game of chess with my father and as usual we kids had to clear out. Mother told me to haul in a load of kindling and wood for the breakfast fire but then I went upstairs to listen through the register to the men talking. Most of it was chess talk and it was evident that my father was taking a licking for a change.

"Well, Father Hassel," my dad said. "It looks like you've got me on the run. Two moves to checkmate. Okay, I resign."

"A miracle!" the priest exclaimed. "A miracle'"

"Oh, don't go raising your eyes to heaven, you old devil," Dad replied "You know you sucked me in to taking that Queen's Bishop's pawn. No miracle that; just my damned stupidity. Trouble is, that you look so damned saintly I forgot your cunning. No matter, let's have another glass of whiskey. There'll be another day."

"I never argue with an agnostic, Doctor. About three fingers, please, if you will. But speaking of miracles you and your family performed one last Christmas Eve."

Dad was puzzled. "What do you mean?" he asked.

"Well, it probably won't last," the priest said, "but yesterday Du Bois came to confession for the first time in forty years and he sure had plenty to confess. He told me your wife had hired him to play Santa Claus to the Picotte kids and that he had stolen some of the candy that was theirs and came to realize how rotten he was. He even gave me ten dollars for the poor box. Merry Christmas, Doctor, you old agnostic, you old fraud!"

The Miner

Ever since he was a tiny lad Tim Trevarthen had wanted to grow up to be a miner. Mine talk had always been part of his daily life because his grandfather who had come from Cornwall, and his father were both hard rock miners. The old man had died but Tim could still remember the gory stories he used to tell, the tales of hair breath escapes when the timber of the tunnels gave way, the frantic climbing of ladders when the handing wall of the stope let go, the heroic deeds done in the bowels of the earth. The deep tone of the mine whistle at six o-clock morning and evening, the muffled blasts that sometimes shook the earth, the roar of the crusher, these had formed the pattern of Tim's days. And at night, as he lay abed, Tim could hear the ore trains thudding and clanking, and blowing their whistles as they rounded the curve before being switched to the main line that led to the ore docks at Marquette on Lake Superior.

Every morning when we arose in Tioga, we checked the wind. If it was strong and came from the southwest bringing with it not only black smoke from the tall stack, but also clouds of dust from the crusher, all of us closed the windows and shut the doors tight. There would be no hanging of clothes on such days because they'd be covered in an instant with the blue particles of the specular hematite for which the Tioga mine was famous. It was choice ore, in great demand from the smelting furnaces of Gary, Indiana, and other places down below because, when mixed with ores of lesser grade, it made better iron and steel.

But that dust was sure hard on our mothers. In the winter, it wasn't so bad although our snow-filled yards were colored blue, but in the summertime the ore dust collected in the grass and we tracked it into our houses or shook it off our clothing everywhere we went. At that, it wasn't as bad as the soft red hematite ore that came from other mines, like those that made the Carp River run opaquely red all year around. No amount of boiling and scrubbing could ever get all the red stain from the miner's work clothes that flapped from the clotheslines of those mining locations. We did a little better in Tioga but it was still hard to live with.

Tim didn't mind the dust. As a child, he collected it for the sand pile beneath the big spruce tree where he built little shaft houses over holes in the earth. Heaping up sand to serve as ore piles, he then ran strings over spools to pull up the tin can skips full of the dust. Always he day dreamed that when he was grown up, he would be a hard rock miner too. Sometimes he'd get a chunk of ore that had fallen beside the railroad track and with his father's hammer and a spike, would pretend to drill a hole in it. Then,

---

with some firecrackers saved from the last Fourth of July, he would try to blast off a piece. Once Tim spent a whole day contriving a play carbide lantern out of a tin can and candle, one that he could wear on his cap like the miners did. Yes, when he grew up, he'd be a miner.

But Henry Trevarthen, his father, had other ideas. He'd always made a good living in the mines and now was shift boss on the three lower levels, but he was determined that his son would not also spend his life in the dark depths of the earth as he and his father before him had done. "It's not right for a man to live like a mole or a rat away from the sun," he told Tim. "A miner's work is hard, heavy work. You're nothing but a mule; you're an animal down there underground. Ten or twelve hours a day, six days a week of it and you'll hardly be able to eat, you'll be so tired. Then on Sunday when you might think you could go hunting or fishing in the sun, you'll still be too bushed to do anything but lay around the house like I do."

"And it's dirty, dangerous work, too," he continued. "Miners die young even if they don't get killed on the job, or maimed to be cripples the rest of their lives. I don't know how many a fine big man I've seen all done in. There's always danger around. You keep watching, listening, smelling for it all the time. That's no way to live, lad!"

Tim had heard that sort of thing too all his life but it hadn't made any difference. Whenever he thought he could get away with it, he'd sneak up near the shaft house to watch the huge wheels bringing up the skips full of ore. He liked to watch the little cars shuttling back and forth along the top of the ore pile discharging their ore. He loved the powerful sound of the crusher grinding those big chunks into bits. But most of all, he dreamed about going down, down, down into that mysterious dark hole and making his living like a real man. Tim resented his father's refusal to let him go underground to see what it was like down there as some of his friends had done.

"No!" said his father, whenever he'd asked. "No! If I can help it, the only time you'll go underground is when you're dead. No!"

The conflict came to a focus when Tim graduated from High School. Because he had done very well academically, he gave the Valedictorian's speech. It was entitled "The Rule of Law" and Tim had thought about it for some weeks. He began by saying, "All things are governed by law," dropping a heavy book from the rostrum to startle the audience with the law of gravity, and he ended with a quote from Emerson or somebody saying "To thyself be true!" To Tim this meant becoming a miner, though he didn't say so up there on the platform.

He said it to his father later. "Look, I'm nearly eighteen and it's time to be earning my own living. I'm strong as most men even if I can't hand wrestle you down yet. I know you've saved for years to put me through college but I've had my bellyful of books. If I can't get a job in the mine here I'm going some other place. There's lots of mines in the U.P. I'm set on being a miner and nothing's going to stop me."

Henry Trevarthen didn't say anything for a long time; just held his head in his hands. Finally he spoke. "The curse of the Trevarthens!" he said. "Ay, we're doomed, all of us, to muck out our days in the dark. I ask only one thing of you, Tim. Don't close your mind tight on this. I'll help you get a summer job here in our mine so you can see what it's really like and then in the fall if you'd rather keep working than go to the Michigan College of Mines up in the Copper Country, well I'll say no more. If you were a mining engineer with an education, you'd be close to the mines all your life, but with none of the grubbing and mucking. Well, enough of that." Tim promised to keep his mind open.

True to his word, Henry Trevarthen went to the mining office the next day and explained the situation to Captain Trelawney. "The boy's bright and he'd make a good mining engineer but he's bound he's going to spend his life in the pits. I know it isn't done, but could you fix it so Tim can get a real taste of what it's like to be a miner? He's strong enough to do a man's work, I think. I don't want him abused, but I don't want any special mercy for him either. Let him see what it's like, that's all."

Captain Trelawney agreed. "Just start him on surface, Henry," he said, "and tell the shift boss what you've told me. If Tim's a bloody nuisance, the deal's off, of course. I'll pass the word down about him."

Although it started easy enough, that first month turned brutal before it was over. Tim spent his first week in the big stone machine shop building where one of the two huge horizontal steam engines that ran the generator was being overhauled. The work wasn't hard but it was often very dirty. He swept and polished and once caught hell from the straw boss because he hadn't filled the grease cups on the governor tight enough. "Get your goddamn hands in so there ain't any air pockets left," he yelled. "Poke it tight! Poke it tight!" As punishment, he gave Tim a day in the coal bunker shoveling coal into the chute and about ten minutes spelling a fireman who had to throw the coal through the furnace door into the firey blast. That was awful. Tim's face burned for days afterwards and his eyes kept watering.

Then for two weeks, Tim unloaded logs, lumber, and lagging from a railroad car, a lot of it very heavy stuff that made his back and arms ache so much he could hardly sleep no matter how tired he was. Next, he spent a week with pick and shovel helping dig a ditch to hold a detour steam line from the boilers to the hoist. His partner there was an old Irish miner named Mick Hanley who'd been transferred to surface when he couldn't hold his own underground any more. Mick taught Tim how to muck. "Slow and easy and never jerk'" he said when Tim almost pooped out after two hours of the hard labor that first day. A small man, the Irishman had a rhythm about his shoveling that Tim admired, but found hard to acquire. "It'll come to you, me boy. It'll come to you. Lift with yer legs." He also told Tim to rub lard in his hands when the blisters broke. Mick's own hands were so calloused he didn't need gloves, but it took a lot of hurting before Tim's hands hardened enough so he could forget them.

It was a good thing he'd had the experience because his next job was shoveling ore that had spilled out of the crusher. He had to put the rock into a heavy wheelbarrow and move it away from the base of the structure where it had built up into a huge mound. Five other men were also on that job and Tim was ashamed to find how many more wheel-barrows of ore they could load and move than he did no matter how hard he tried. Also, his boss kept giving him hell for his slowness. Once one of the other men ran him down with his barrow. "Get out of the way, you son of a gun, and let a man work!" There was-n't any comradeship. No one talked. All he heard was an occasional grunt or curse.

The noise and the dust were almost unbearable on that job. For the first time, Tim began to have doubts about becoming a miner. Often when the noon whistle blew he was almost too tired to open his dinner pail to eat the ham sandwiches his mother had made for him. Just the act of chewing was more hard labor until he learned to drink the cold tea with a lot of sugar in it before starting on the bread. Once he was so tired he lay down on the ground at the noon break, too tired to sit up, until the contempt of the rest of the crew made him do so. And there were times at the end of the day when after he washed up in the dry (the locker room), and changed from working clothes to those he'd come with, it was tough to walk home without having his knees buckle so much he staggered.

Just about the time he thought he'd be stuck at the crusher forever, Tim's father told him to report to the shaft mouth to go underground, that the log butchers building cribbing at the twelfth level needed a helper. Bill Plankey would be there to go with him. The steel cage in which they were to descend was not very large, just enough to hold two men in front, side by side, and two more behind them. It was open in front with only a bar across at waist level and had a V-shaped roof of steel above a heavy cross arm from which huge shackles and pulleys and cable were fastened. Above this cage was another cage of similar design, and it too was then empty. To Tim, the cable that suspended these cages looked very thin, though it was over an inch in diameter. He was very uneasy as he stepped aboard and Bill Plankey folded over the guard bar, but he really had no time to be afraid. Bells began to clang and then suddenly the floor beneath his feet seemed to drop from under them. Down, down they went with flashes of light showing where men were working at other levels. Then Tim felt his feet become heavy again as the cage slowed. He started breathing, but only for a moment. Suddenly the cage stopped, then bounced upward, then fell, and bounced again, before it became still. Bill Plankey was grinning as he unfastened the bar and they walked out into a large lighted room carved out of the rock. "Ah, you'll never forget it, will you, boy? I did it alone the first time and had the creepies all night, I did."

When his ears had stopped ringing and he had caught his breath, Tim could see the other two compartments of the shaft. The one on his left held nothing but some pipes and a stairway, not really a stairway, just ladders. "Them's where you go when you can't go anywhere else," Bill said. "And you goes up fast with the devil pullin' yer shirt tail, you do. I know!

The other larger compartment of the shaft was empty just then. "That's where the skip runs, where the ore and rock are pulled up." Bill said. "The skips probably down at Level Eleven getting filled. You'll hear it roar up when the bells ring again! Yah, you'll hear it and see it plenty before you're done. And feel it too."

After lighting both their carbide head lamps, he led Tim out of the station room into the drift, an eight foot high and five foot wide tunnel. "Pretty fancy, them lights," Bill said, pointing to an occasional light bulb on the ceiling. "In the old days, all we had was candles and these bulls-eye lanterns."

Following the narrow gauge rails on the floor of the drift, suddenly they entered a huge cavern, or stope. "This was the best pocket of ore we ever find in this here mine," Bill said. "We worked this stope for two year before she give out. Made ten ore piles on surface. They say they've hit a bigger one off the sump but I dunno. I seen the diamond drill cores and they sure look good."

After passing through more of the drift and several smaller stopes, Tim heard men working for the first time. "They're pushing up a couple of raises into the ore pocket above," Bill said. "One's the men's raise and the other's the ore chute. The men's raise is the one with the ladder in it. Don't get 'em mixed," These raises were smaller tunnels, only about four feet across, and up and down. They gradually angled upward, and weren't tall enough to stand in upright. The men Tim had heard were timbering the drift at the entrance to the raises, putting up rough supports for its roof. "They hit some soft ore here," Bill explained, "so they've got to crib it. We wouldn't do it in the old days, this being a hard rock mine, but all a man hears now is safety this, safety that. Ah, I guess it's all right. They's been too many a skull broken by a hunk of ore falling." He took Tim up to one of the men by the supports. "Here's yer new helper, Pete. Name's Tim." He left.

Pete looked Tim over up and down, then spat a huge glob of tobacco juice at his feet. "For Kee-rist sakes!" he roared disgustedly. "I ask for a man and they send me this. OK, haul up them four by fours here from the last stope and keep out of our way.

Tim worked three weeks with those log butchers and never heard a half-way kind word. No matter how hard he tried to please them, he couldn't. They gave him the hardest, dirtiest tasks they could devise and cussed him out whether he did them well or not. Once, when he was steadying a big tamarack pillar as Pete was spiking a cross beam to it on the other side, Tim had to cough and the big log shook. Furiously, Pete threw his twenty pound sledge at him, narrowly missing Tim's head. That night Tim told his father about it, not complaining at all, but just asking for advice as to how to handle the situation.

He didn't get any advice. "There's a lot of bastards in this world and you've got to put up with them if you're not the boss," his father said. But a few days later, Tim was shifted to a new job. He became an apprentice trammer, and an older man named Jim Engstrom was his partner. Their job was mainly to shepherd the heavy steel ore carts from the blasting sites to the ore raises, or chutes, down which the ore went to the skip. And then they had to push the carts back again. The job also meant some lifting and shoveling although there were other men too who helped fill the carts, or cars, as they were called. Often there were four or five filled cars joined together in a train waiting for them when Tim and Jim returned from a previous trip to the chute. Sure kept them humping.

Tim's new partner, Jim, however, was fun to be with although the work was terribly hard. He had a lot of old mining stories and mining songs, too. One of them he often sang as they pushed the trams:

"My sweetheart's a mule in the mine.
I drive her with only one line.
On the transom I sit and tobacco I spit.
All over my sweetheart's behind."

He told Tim that in some mines the tram cars were pulled by mules that spent all their lives underground and that he wished the Tioga mine had them too. Altogether, Tim enjoyed the two weeks he spent tramming. Perhaps his father became aware of this for soon Tim had a muck stick in his hand again, following the miners who were cleaning up the ore after the holes had been drilled and the rock blasted away from the head of the raise.

This work was not only hard, but danger was always in the air. It was interesting to see the drillers at work with their new compressed air equipment, boring deep holes into the front face of the rock with their long drills but it was so terribly noisy, Tim's ears rang for hours after he got home. And it was scary to see how casually the miners handled the round sticks of dynamite when they inserted them in the holes and put on the blasting caps. It was even scarier to see the men light the long white ropes of the fuses from around a corner and watch the red ash creep along the fuse before the big bang came and the blast deafened him. Even worse than the concussion was the cloud of dust and fragments that filled the raise almost to its juncture with the drift. Even before it had settled, he had to go in there and start mucking. Hard to breathe because every shovelful raised the dust again. No wonder most miners died young, their lungs full of the stuff.

There was danger as well as dust in the air. Always there was a chance that one of the rounds of dynamite had not gone off or was a sleeper that might go off late, or that a blasting cap was in the rubble. To watch one of the veteran miners listening intently to the blast, trying to guess whether it was as big as he thought it should have been was frightening in itself. Mucking fresh rock after a blast meant being extra careful too. More than one miner had been blown to hell in a handbasket when his pick or shovel set off a hidden stick that hadn't gone off.

Although by this time, Tim had got hardened to the hard labor, mucking new rock in a tunnel where one could never stand up straight almost killed him. His short handled shovel, his muck stick, sometimes didn't give him enough leverage to lift the heavy chunks over the edge of the tram car. Toward the end of the shift, it got harder and harder as he fatigued, and again, compared to the veteran miners, he felt weak as a baby.

Moreover, the rule was that no chunk of rock bigger than a man could lift was to be put in the tram car. Because Tim could never be sure that he could judge them right, he often did more sledging of the bigger chunks than the other miners did. This too took considerable skill. The older miners seemed to have an uncanny ability to know just where to hit a big chunk and have it split into handling size and they rarely had to hit it more than once. Not so, Tim. Often he'd wear himself out banging away at a rock with that fifty pound sledge only to have a smaller and older man laughingly whop it apart in one blow. Tim just couldn't hold his own and everyone knew it. Somehow their patience was worse than the cussing he'd had from the log butchers. He wasn't a man yet; he was just a kid.

Perhaps it was this realization, or perhaps seeing Jim, his old tram partner who'd been so kind, being hauled out on a makeshift stretcher after a chunk of ore from the ceiling of a stope had cracked his skull like an eggshell, but he wasn't so sure this was the life for him after all. He'd done a lot of thinking about everything, he told his father one night the end of August, and maybe he'd give college a try after all. He'd go to the College of Mines for a year anyway and see if being a mining engineer was for him. Tim's mother wept with joy and relief and his father almost did too.

The next week, Tim took the Duluth, South Shore and Atlantic train for Houghton, carrying a very heavy suitcase. But that evening, looking for Tim's work clothes to wash the next morning, his mother found that they were gone. So were his steel tipped shoes and carbide headlamp.

Thanksgiving

Come along, Cully," my father ordered. "I'm going to show you how to cut off the head of a chicken. You're eleven years old now and I was doing it at ten." He led me to the chicken yard back of his hospital. In one corner of it was the fattening pen containing two fat roosters that had fed so heavily on corn and table scraps for a month they could hardly crow.

"Now watch me catch one with the grabbing stick," Dad said. The stick was just a long pole with a bent over nail on its end. "You poke the stick out and grab a leg in the space between the nail and the pole and pull him off his feet. Like this." Dad deftly flopped one rooster over on its side and before it could get up, he had the rooster held upside down by the legs. "Now, I'll let it go so you can try it. But first, let's sharpen the axe. You'll find it in the woodshed. And put a pail of water into the trough under the grindstone, Cully. Don't bring the splitting axe. Bring the chopping one."

I turned the crank of the big grinding wheel while my father ground the axe to a fine edge, testing it against his fingernail until he was satisfied it was sharp. Finally, he said, "That's good enough, Cully. Not as sharp as the axes the Finn loggers use, though. Why, they can shave the hairs off their arms with their axes. But this one's all right now for chopping off a chicken's head. Go get me the bigger rooster and bring it to the chopping block over here."

I had some trouble getting it. Not so much in using the grabbing stick as in getting ahold of its thrashing legs once it was flopped over. It beat me pretty good with its wings before I had it under control and handed it to my father. He laid the big bird on the block and with one swift stroke, chopped the head off cleanly, then threw the rooster on the ground where it ran around grotesquely until it collapsed. "Just reflex action," Dad said. "It's good to have it run around like that and get the blood out of the carcass. That's a fine fat rooster. With the other one we'll have a real Thanksgiving feast. I have to go now, so you chop the other one's head off and bring both of them to your mother to pluck. Oh, one more thing. Cut off the wings at the first joint."

It was hard work but I managed it and was pretty proud when I brought mother the two big fowl. She already had two pails ready and after filling them with very hot water, put the roosters in to soak. "That loosens the feathers," she said.

I didn't hang around once she started pulling off the feathers fearing that she might teach me how to pluck. Besides, the smell of wet chicken feathers isn't too great. Instead, she had me go down to the cellar and get the cranberries we'd picked earlier that fall because they had to be sorted and all the bad ones removed.

Thanksgiving

I had enjoyed that cranberry picking. We had to walk out on the edge of the bog and it moved up and down under our feet. Sometimes our feet broke through and got wet. The cranberries on their short feathery bushes were easy to pick and the pail filled up fast. They were pretty too, all glossy red, with white sides underneath. No good to eat, though. Too sour. But they were sure fine when cooked for a Thanksgiving or Christmas table.

What a Thanksgiving meal that was! We ate at the big table in the dining room with goblets, silver, the Haviland china, and linen napkins. Besides the chicken and cranberries, there was sage stuffing, gravy with giblets, rutabagas, a huge dish of mashed potatoes, Waldorf salad in crescent dishes, wild strawberry jam for the home-made bread, chow chow, and, of course, both mince and pumpkin pie with cheese. All of us ate until we were glassy eyed with distention. Then we had to clear out so Dad could lie down on the couch in the living room and take a nap as he always did after one of those gigantic meals. I helped with the dishes and was about to go out to play when someone knocked at the back door.

When I opened it, I saw a stranger smiling at me. I knew immediately that he was a tramp because over his shoulder was a stick with a red bandanna bundle at the end of it but I told him to come into the kitchen.

"Ma'am," he said to my mother, "could you spare an old sailor down on his luck a bite to eat? The name's Sam Jones and I'm on my way back to my home port in Boston, Mass."

Mother hesitated only a minute. "Of course. Everyone should have a good meal on Thanksgiving Day, Mr. Jones. While I'm fixing it, why don't you go out to the barn and fill our woodbox. Cully will show you where the split wood is."

Sam Jones was a talking man. All I did was ask him if he had a family somewhere and his tongue never stopped. It was interesting talk, too. "Sonny," he said, "I've got a girl in every port and a port in every girl. The world is full of Joneses and old Sam here has scattered a few of them hisself. As for my home, well, here's my hat and I've lived in it in places like Amsterdam and Zoambanga and Hong Kong. For a sailor, my lad, his ship's his home." He had grabbed up a big load of wood and motioned for me to pile some more on it. He was strong! Didn't even grunt when he carried it in and filled the woodbox to overflowing.

When he saw what Mother had laid out on the table, his eyes popped and his mouth hung open. "Ma'am," he exclaimed. "I never seen so much food in my life. Hungry as I am, not having et anything for two days and that was a half can of pork and beans somewhere in Dakota, I wonder, Ma'am, if I might wash up first? A man gets dirty in them box cars and hobo jungles."

Mother nodded and put a washbasin in the sink. "Here's some soap, Mr. Jones, and there's hot water in the reservoir of the range here. You can use the roller towel on the pantry door. We always wash before we eat, too.

She was a bit shocked though when the sailor took off his shirt and, with a great spluttering and grunting, washed his face, neck and arms. Those arms were really something. Hairy below the elbows, above them a lot of blue-gray tattoos. One of them was of a girl in a hula shirt. Sam saw me admiring it. "Yea, sonny. Got that tattoo in the South Pacific. Want to see her dance?" he flexed his biceps rhythmically and sure enough, she did dance. Wow! Sure wiggled her hips.

For a man who hadn't eaten in three days, Sam Jones ate slowly, mainly because he kept talking all the time. We were fascinated to hear of the strange exotic places he'd been and of his adventures all over the world. To sit there in the kitchen of a wintry house in an isolated forest village and to listen to tales of the seven seas captivated us. Sam said he'd gone to sea first as a boy of fourteen, a cabin boy on a sailing schooner bound for Spain, but lately he'd been on steamers. The last one,

he said, was the worst of the lot with a mean captain and mates, lousy food, and rats as big as his foot that bit him at night. So when they took on cargo at Seattle to go back to the Philippines, Sam had jumped ship and was working his way across the country to Boston.

"Just wanted to see the country, Ma'am," he said between mouthfuls. "I seen the whole world but never my own land. Them Rocky Mountains sure are big, bigger than those in Australia even." Sam said that someone had stolen his purse shortly after he got ashore and that was why he was riding empty box cars across the country and having to beg for food.

When Sam got to his two kinds of pie, he was breathing hard and pausing once in a while. So I asked him if he"d ever been shipwrecked.

"That I have, sonny. That I have. The worst one was off the coast of Brazil where the Zambezi River enters the sea. Only five of us made it to shore and one died that first night. Jungle it was and full of crocodiles, great big critters looking like big logs with bumps on 'em till they opens their mouths like this." He spread his arms then snapped them shut. "And how they bellered at night. I seen one big she crocodile a-giving birth one afternoon on a sand bar and you never hear such a howling when she pushed out of her belly a whole string of little crocodiles, holding on to each others tails. Terrible noise, it was. Scared me, and old Sam Jones don't scare easy. No, sir!"

He crammed down the last bit of cheese and asked for another cup of coffee. "Ah, that was a bad time," he remembered. "Lots of snakes too, big around as me leg. And the natives in them parts are cannibals. They club you or shoot you with blowguns. Ever see a blowgun, Sonny?"

I said that I hadn't. "How did you get out of there" I asked.

"Ah, that's a long tale, me lad. We grabbed one of them Indians when he come ashore with a canoe and had him take us upstream to his village where we find another white man who could talk the lingo. A trapper he was, and a gold miner. Wanted me to go along with him and a native up to the rapids two days paddling upstream 'cause there was gold in the sand there. So I went with the two of them. But when we was one day upstream, some cannibals with bones in their noses caught us when we weren't looking and old Sam was in big trouble." He paused.

"Ma'am," he said. "That there was a fine meal and I've et all I can eat. You wouldn't be having a seegar in the house, would you now?" I ran down to the shelf in the cellarway and brought back one of Dad's undertaker cigars. The sailor smelled it appreciatively, then put it in his coat pocket. He got up from the table.

"But how did you escape, Sam?" I couldn't bear to have him leave.

"Easy it was," he answered. "Them cannibals, they like dark meat only, not white. They killed the Indian with us and sent us back downriver in the canoe. Never did find any gold. Not that time anyway but once in Africa…"

My father was in the kitchen doorway and he was biting his lower lip, like he always did when he was angry.

"Pete' Pete Fant! What the devil are you doing in my kitchen? Heard you were in prison."

"Just begging a bite to eat, Doc. On my way home, Doc. On my way…" The sailor grabbed up his stick and bundle and was out of the back door before you could spit.

"Sailor, hell!" Dad exclaimed when we told him the stories the tramp had recounted. "I'd bet Pete Fant never got any closer to the sea than Green Bay where he probably got that tattoo. A lot of loggers go there to have it done. He's a scoundrel, a bum, a no good! Got a girl pregnant, married her, then left as soon as the baby came to shack up with some Indian squaw up by L'anse. He's a cheat and a liar too. He bamboozled a widow up at Sidnaw out of all the money she had and he's been in jail lots of times. Last I heard, he'd been in a knife fight and had been sent to prison." Dad turned to mother. "Don't you ever let a stranger come in the house again. Good thing I was home." He was mad all over again that evening when he found there was no cold chicken for his supper.

Sure shook me up too, and it wasn't until I looked up the Zambezi River in the encyclopedia and found it was in Africa and that crocodiles laid eggs that I knew I'd been bamboozled good. Just the same, Sam's coming had sure made a fine Thanksgiving Day and I made a little vow that sometime I'd go to Green Bay and get a hula girl tattooed on my arm so I could make her dance.

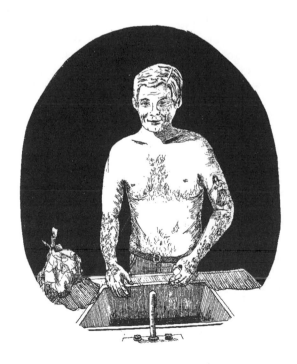

Wild Food

After the mine closed, the people of Tioga had some very hard times but they managed to eat despite the lack of biting money or any other kind. Sometimes toward the end of winter it was bare survival fare but we always made it somehow. I've been remembering the things we ate all through the year, the wild food that sustained us, not only in hard times, but in the easy ones too.

Meat was basic, of course, and fortunately deer were usually plentiful. Venison roasts, chops, steaks, in season or out, were staples in our diet. If we'd shot an old tough buck, we ground the deer meat into patties for our plates or we beat the hell out of it for our stews. We boiled it, fried it, roasted it, and sometimes fed the last remnants to our hounds. Few of our hunters shot big bucks if they could help it; the young spikehorns or does were much better eating. I ate so much venison when I was a boy I've never cared particularly for it since.

I guess I can say the same for rabbits, too. Some of those big snowshoes could also be pretty tough, especially those from a cedar swamp. After the snows came our rabbits were easier to snare than to shoot because they'd turned white. Often their brown eyes were all you could see before making out their contours in the snow. One year though, their winter change of color betrayed them. We'd had a big early snow, and then, when it turned very warm, we could walk along the south sides of our granite hills and spot them easily against the brown leaves. A lot of rabbits got canned that year.

Usually though, we got most of our rabbits by snaring. All we had to do was to find a well trodden runway, put little fences of twigs along its sides, then fasten a loop of picture wire in the middle of it. Five or six of those snares would almost always yield a rabbit or two overnight. There are old folks in the U.P. who still shudder at the thought of eating one more choked rabbit.

Deer and rabbits provided most of our meat but we ate other animals too. A young bear, shot in berry time or in the fall when it was still fat, could provide fine eating. The meat was very dark, almost black, and tasted like a combination of beef and pork. I liked it but some people didn't, probably because they hadn't dressed it out properly. Bears have to store up a lot of fat to hibernate, sometimes so much you have to parboil a bear steak before frying it.

We also ate groundhogs, beaver, squirrels and muskrat. I never cared much for muskrat. The meat tasted like the muck they stirred up smelled. The others were pretty palatable when you'd sickened of venison. I even ate, or tried to eat, an old porcupine once. Staying up at our old hunting cabin at the time, I worked over that old porky for three days and nights, boiling, baking, roasting and frying it. Never could stick a fork into that tough meat but I finally cut off a small slice and chewed on it for maybe an hour before quitting. I still don't know how it tasted.

Perhaps my trouble was that I killed that porky at the wrong time. I'd come across it and another one between our hunting cabin and the lake while they were mating. The only time I ever saw that happen! How do porcupines mate? Very carefully! And a bit nastily, too, as I found when I watched them do it. First, they touched noses, and then the male urinated on the female. She didn't like that particularly but I suppose he was just marking out his territory, like timber wolves did by urinating on certain stones atop our hills to mark theirs. Anyway, after the porkies touched noses again, the female lifted her quilted tail high and he came close and sat up on his haunches. Then she backed into him, with nary a quill shed. Yes, porcupines mate very carefully. I'm pretty sure it was the male that I clubbed and tried to eat. It waddled more slowly.

You couldn't find any better meat than a haunch of wolf, or coyote, broiled over maple coals. I don't know. He offered me a chunk of it once and I was tempted until I remembered that Old Man Salo's big hound was missing.

Fish, of course, were very plentiful in the old days. Rarely would a week go by in the summer without having at least one meal of brook trout, fried crisp in the pan and garnished with a sprig of parsley or a slice of lemon. I never got tired of them. Even ate the leftovers for breakfast. These were

native trout, their flesh firm and pink. Occasionally we'd also have a huge lake trout from Lake Superior and these Mother always baked so we could flake off big mouthfuls from the heavy white bones.

Northern pike were good too but you had to be careful of their forked bones. When we'd get one caught in our throat, we'd swallow a chunk of bread to carry it down our gullets. Early in the spring, even suckers were delicious though later they got soft and tasted muddy. Perch and walleyes always added variety and you didn't have to make your tongue feel around in your mouth for bones before swallowing. Many of our Finn families made fish soup with glazed fish eyes floating on top. I never cared much for it. Our French Canadians often boiled a mess of fish of every variety, even chubs, until the bones were soft, then ground the results up fine and baked them into a loaf. Very good! In the winter we rarely tried to fish through the ice. It was just too cold sitting there even after you'd built up a sweat chopping a hole through two or three feet of blue ice. No, winter was the time for the smoked fish that had been hanging from the ceiling of the summer kitchen, or for the marinated ones from the barrel. Oddly enough, our cats would never eat either. We sure did.

We also had fowl, and not just the extra rooster or broody hen from the chicken coop. Partridge was our main poultry dish, and it was excellent if you had a strip of fat bacon to cover it in the pan for otherwise it was rather dry. We shot a lot of partridge every fall but never tried to shoot them on the wing. Shells were too expensive. We'd walk along a deer trail or old logging road very slowly, looking and listening intently. Partridge weren't as wild then as they are now and they did a lot of clucking before they took off. Even then, if you set off an alarm clock in your pocket or had a good barking dog, they'd fly up onto a nearby limb and sit there, just waiting for you to shoot.

Occasionally, we'd get a spruce hen too. We called them "fool hens" because they sure were dumb, or perhaps just curious. They'd sit on a limb and watch you coming.

Sometimes you didn't even have to shoot, just club them if they were within reach. Their meat was very dark and I didn't care much for it. Partridge were much better. One old Frenchman downtown always hung his wild fowl in the barn after they were cleaned, until their heads fell off. "Takes away the gamey taste," he said. Perhaps it did but they sure smelled ripe before he got around to eating them.

During their migrations, we also shot a lot of ducks, mainly mallards, canvas backs and blue winged teal. The teal were the hardest to shoot on the wing but were the most flavorful. Coots or mudhens were miserable eating but the worst of the lot were the mergansers; they tasted like rotten fish. Once, when some of us boys were camping overnight, Mullu shot a sea gull and that was terrible too.

Sieur LaTour told us how to set up a fine meshed fish net on sticks, put chicken scratch feed under it, and then when blackbirds and robins collected to eat the grain, to pull down the holding stake with its rope and catch them. LaTour said he'd never used these bird traps himself but that his grand pere had done it in the old, old days. A lot of work, he said, but they made a good meat pie. Four and twenty blackbirds! It's hard for us now to understand how people ate almost anything when times were hard.

Our major vegetables were potatoes, carrots, cabbage, turnips and rutabagas but there were some years when the crop was small because of a wet spring or early frost. Then our people turned to collecting wild vegetables. They waded the shallow waters of a lake to dig up spatterdock roots to bake; they spaded to get the long roots of dandelions to boil. The pith of burdock roots was good in stews. Cattail roots were best boiled but they could be eaten raw too. Pete Halfshoes told us that his Ojibway mother used to boll Jack-in-the-pulpit bulbs so Fisheye and I tried them once. When they set our mouths on fire with their hot bitterness and we complained, old Pete said you always had to boil them three times in new water each time. Maybe so! Pete also suggested we try skunk cabbage but we weren't too interested. Most of us never ate any of these except experimentally but they were available and some of our poor families used them when they had to. We took some pride in being able to live off the land.

For greens we had wild lettuce, pursley (a garden weed that's hard to eliminate, hence the saying "mean as pussley"), lamb's quarters, young milkweed pods, wild onions (leeks), fiddlehead ferns and, of course, dandelion greens. Of these, I liked the fiddleheads best. You had to pick them in the spring of the year when the fronds were just beginning to unfold. They looked like clenched little green fists, when fresh, but after being canned, they turned darker. The Finns called them kuolema goru, (the hands of death). Our French Canadians canned a lot of fiddleheads and ate them all winter. A lot better than spinach, they were.

Somehow, when spring came, all of us hungered for green things, not only for our souls but also for our mouths. We chewed cuds of wintergreen leaves; we munched soursap, an acidic sorrel. We'd nibble the succulent bottom ends of timothy hay and wild oats after pulling them from their virginal sheaths. But best of all were wild red raspberry "tucks." These early shoots, when peeled of their fuzzy surface skin and dipped in a bit of salt, sure seemed to fill a basic need and we ate yards of them. Probably needed the vitamins they provided. Perhaps that same need also explains why we would often slice a raw potato and eat it with salt at break-up time or swipe a bit of sugar to put on the first green stalks of rhubarb. There were no salads in our houses when the snows were deep, nor for that matter, at any other time either. We were mainly meat and potato folk.

Most of us had sugar because it was fairly cheap. If you ran out, you could always borrow a cup from your neighbor provided that you returned it with a heap on. But our huge maple trees provided a bounty of sweet sap every spring that, when boiled down, would yield syrup, maple sugar, and maple wax. The latter was a very chewy delicacy created by throwing a ladle of thick hot syrup on clean snow. Sometimes maple wax glued your teeth together but it sure tasted good. We also sucked sap icicles when it froze overnight in sap time.

Occasionally, someone would find a honey tree by sighting the paths of bees as they went home. I never was successful though I sure tried hard and often got stung for my pains. I'd get a can and put it over a bumblebee on a dandelion or some other flower, wait a bit, then release it and try to see which way it went, then can another one and look again. Unfortunately, a lot of them got mad buzzing under the can and nailed me when I lifted it off. I did find a honeycomb of sorts in our garden once but the bees found me so thoroughly too that I never got any honey out of it.

Pierre Moreau got honey every year and Fisheye and I watched him do it one winter day when the temperature was way below zero. He'd spotted the tree and blazed it the summer before so he knew where to find it. As Pierre sawed it down, we could hear bees buzzing around inside and we kept away, much to Pierre's amusement. Finally, when the tree was down, the bees died immediately in the frigid air. Sometimes they popped. Pierre made another cut, then slabbed off a huge chunk to reveal a long comb along its hollow. He gave us each a piece full of honey and grubs and dead bees but I knew my mother wouldn't be interested so I threw mine away before getting home. Tasted like honey all right, but it took three days before my face and hands stopped feeling sticky.

We also ate mushrooms and nuts that we gathered in the woods. Morels, those wonderful wrinkled brown soldiers standing to attention in the spring woods, were hard to find but easy to eat when fried by themselves or better yet when used to smother a steak. We carefully guarded the places where we found our morels, making sure that no one else was following us, because they usually popped up in the same vicinity every year. The other mushroom that was commonly eaten was the white oyster mushroom. It appeared on dead logs a couple of times each summer, usually after a wet spell. Oyster mushrooms arranged themselves in layers on the log and you had to get them early or the insects and deer would eat them. We also ate the fairy ring mushrooms that came up in our pastures at night. All of these mushrooms were dried for winter soups and stews by threading them on fishline hung from the tops of our window for a week or more.

There were few nuts in the U.P. It was just too cold for such trees to grow there but, like the red squirrels and chipmunks, we sure stored up a lot of hazel nuts. They were small nuts, about the size of a fingernail, and they came in a greenish brown husk full of prickers that inserted themselves into the hands that picked them. We'd soak a burlap bag full of hazelnuts in the creek, bang it repeatedly on the ground to thresh them of their husks, then pick them out to put in mason jars for the winter. Or we'd crack them with our teeth to eat them on the spot. Hazelnuts got better as they aged, and on many a winter night, we munched upon hazelnuts by kerosene light until it was time to go to bed.

As I recall, my life as a boy in the U.P. at the turn of the century, I was always nibbling something. In the spring, I ate the little bulbs of spring beauty flowers, or violet leaves. In the summer, I munched on thistle shoots or young burdock stems. In the fall, I chewed wild rose hips, thornapples, wild rice and cranberries. Indeed, we sampled almost anything that grew. Once I dug up what I thought were ginseng roots and was sick for three days after eating them. If there were nothing better, I chewed maple twigs or straw or spruce gum. It took a lot of unpleasant work to get that spruce gum so it was free from pitch after we had scraped the globs of resin off the trees. Spruce gum was a grayish-pink in color but it chewed good. Sure made you spit!

For fruit, we had apples and berries. Many of our houses had old gnarled apple trees behind them, usually of the Dutchess or Yellow Transparent variety. They bore heavily every other year but always provided enough green apples for our bellyaches. Every dirt cellar in Tioga had many cans of applesauce on its shelves and also some boxes or barrels of eating apples, especially the Greenings which wouldn't begin to rot until March month. Also, up around the mine and in many little abandoned pastures, we could find a wild apple tree with good fruit. Most of the apples from these wild trees were poor eating without much flavor and only the deer fed from them, but there were a few that had excellent apples. I still remember one snow apple tree down by Maler's homestead that every year bore a good crop of bright red apples with streaks of pink threaded through the crisp white flesh. You'd bite into one of those snow apples and the juice would dribble from the corners of your mouth. Back then our apples had no scab or other disease and no one ever had to spray them with poison. We ate them baked, in sauce, in pies, or just in hand.

But our major fruit consisted of berries. Wild strawberries, red raspberries, blackberries, dewberries, thimble berries, blueberries, we picked them all in huge amounts each summer and they served as our desserts all winter. First in the season came the wild strawberries. Rarely could we pick enough to use them in pies or shortcake. They were mainly for jam or jelly. I remember that once my father insisted that no wild strawberry jam be served when a visitor from a city down below came to our table. "No one who's never picked a wild strawberry deserves to eat that jam," he said. Spread upon buttered home-made bread, fresh from the oven and washed down with cold milk, they were indeed ambrosia.

Unlike wild strawberries, which you picked while appropriately on your knees as if in prayer, our red raspberries could be gathered standing up. We found them everywhere along the edges of the old fields or rockpiles. Some of the best ones appeared along the logging roads a few years after hardwoods had been cut. They weren't hard to pick but you could never really get a heap on your pail of raspberries that would last more than a few minutes because they always settled. With the pails strapped to our belts, we could pick with both hands, the right one for the pail and the left hand for the mouth.

Our women canned hundreds of quarts of red raspberries each year. In season, every house had a little sugar sack fastened to the cupboard above the sink from which the scarlet juice dripped into a pan below so jelly could be made. Oh, those raspberry pies with the red juice coloring the latticed upper crust! My mouth wets with the remembering! Raspberry tarts, hot from the oven, steamed raspberry pudding with hard sauce, or just a dish of newly picked raspberries sprinkled with sugar and swimming in rich cream! Ah, we lived well up in the U.P. in berry time! And I must not forget the warm fruit soup the Finns and Swedes made with milk and eggs and raspberries. Just a bit of nutmeg dusted on top of the bowl was the final touch. I haven't tasted it for sixty-five wasted years.

Thimble berries were a lot bigger than raspberries, although not as flavorful, but your pail filled up fast. Some of us mixed them with rhubarb or apple or both to make a better jam. Gooseberries, once they got thoroughly brown or almost black, were very sweet but the green ones were so sour they'd turn your face into a dead man's skull. Gooseberry jam was excellent on heavily buttered toast and my father preferred goose-berry pie to all others except blackberry.

Anyone picking wild blackberries pays a price in scratched hands and faces or in torn clothing, but they're worth it. I had one special private patch of blackberries that surrounded a deep running spring which I visited every year to bring back the best blackberries known to our parts. Heavy with huge berries, the tall bushes drooped from their weight into the water. I could fill a ten quart pail in a hurry. Then came blackberry pies, blackberry cobbler, and, after straining the juice, the making of blackberry wines or cordials. Our French Canadians always stored up some blackberry juice for the treatment of constipation, but that was made from dewberries, a smaller, ground hugging variety of blackberry.

The great crops of blueberries, however, provided most of the fruit that covered our cellar shelves. We picked them by the gallon, whole families sometimes traveling miles to find the best patches. Every June we explored the plains and granite hills to make sure some late frost had not hurt the little white bells that were their flowers. A failure of the blueberry crop meant that the coming winter would be a deprived one for all of us.

There were two varieties, the blue ones and the black ones, and both could be found either on high bushes or low bushes. The black ones were not as tart or as good for pies but they were always sought after. The people who picked blueberries were of several kinds too: the sitters and the stoopers, and the clean and the unclean pickers. Clean pickers prided themselves on never letting a twig or green berry or stink bug enter their pails and, consequently, they often were slowed down by their persnicke-tiness. That one little green blueberry seemed to have an almost uncanny ability to bury itself the moment you tried to remove it. My Grampa Gage never bothered. He just stripped the bushes with both hands going at once, much to my grandmother's disgust when she had to clean them on the kitchen table afterwards. "Hell, Nettie," he'd say when she gave him the devil for it, "those green ones give character to the pie, and the twigs and leaves soak up the juice." Most of us were cleaners.

The monstrous tame blueberries of today that come from the grocery stores bear only a faint resemblance to the wild ones of the U.P., at least so far as flavor is concerned, and I will never eat another one. They lack being covered each morning with that Lake Superior dew; their color is comparatively dull; there is no reflection of our clean blue skies on their surfaces. They have no tang. I'd bet even the hungriest U.P. black bear would spurn them if it had a choice.

Our pancakes, muffins and cakes with wild blueberries sprinkled through their batter seemed to shorten our winters because they tasted of summertime. But, oh, those blueberry pies! I've never been able to decide whether blueberry pie is better hot or cold. With a piece of yellow cheese to restore the tastebuds of your tongue and palate to a new virginity after each bite or two, you'd always want more.

After the first fall frost, we'd find a lot of drunken robins staggering around under the chokecherry bushes. Before that time, chokecherries can pucker up your mouth so much you can't whistle, but not after they've been frozen and have started fermenting. Chokecherry wine is very good, much better than that we made of our black wild cherries or dandelions.

Enough! Surely by now you know that we managed to eat pretty well in the U.P. without spending any money. No wonder our kids come back from Detroit when times get hard down below! No wonder we lived long and triumphantly in that hard, but lovely land without vitamin pills! No wonder we had sisu! P.S. *If You want my recipe for sugarplum pie, let me know.*

Mustamaya

It was after supper and four or five men were belly-up to the bar in Higley's Saloon telling their fishing lies as usual. "You know that deep hole just below the Narrows?" one of them asked. "Well, I caught a twenty-one inches there yesterday. A sloib! Never caught a bigger brook trout."

"Aw hell, I caught one that went twenty-two in the Spruce River once," said another. "A big old spawner she was. You ought to see the eggs come out of her. Mighty nigh a pint of 'em."

Higley, the saloon keeper, couldn't stand it another minute. He smote the top of the polished bar with a mighty fist. "You're just a bunch of bloody liars." he roared. "I bet not a one of you ever caught a trout you had to cut to put in the frying pan.

The men were stunned. The unwritten law was that no matter how outrageous the fishing lie, you always nodded your head and then tried to tell a bigger one.

Higley was hotted up. "By God," he said. "I'm sick and tired of hearing all them fish lies. Tell you what I'll do. Any man that brings me a trout bigger than nineteen inches, I give him a ten dollar gold piece and keep the fish." He went to the back room and brought back a heavy leather purse. "And here's the gold piece. I'll glue it to the underside of the glass cigar counter so you can see it every time you come here. So put up or shut up!"

As you can imagine, news of Higley's offer swept through town like wildfire and the Tioga River and its tributaries sure caught hell. Most of us had never seen a ten dollar gold piece. A lot of money, those days. Higley's business sure boomed, so many came to look at it. "Yeah, he assured them. "You catch me a trout bigger than nineteen inches and the gold piece is yours. But no dynamiting!. If the eyes are popped out and its bladder busted, that don't count." Higley knew us.

The thing was, we all knew where there was a trout big enough to win that gold piece. It was Mustamaya, a huge hen trout that lived under the bank of the Tioga in the Pine Pool not half a mile from town. Many had seen her fleetingly and all of us had angled for her in vain. A monster trout. We knew it was a female because we'd seen her spawning at the head of the pool. How did she get that name? Well, "Mustamaya" is the Finn word for Queen of Spades and she sure looked black in the water.

The reason nobody could catch Mustamaya was that most of the time she stayed out of sight, feeding in the deep fast current that had undermined the south bank of Pine Pool. The water ran so fast under the bank there that you just couldn't get your bait to

---

161

her. It would be swept downstream in an instant. Besides, there were hidden snags down there to grab any hook that had a huge sinker tied above it.

Mustamaya was smart too, for a fish. She'd seen a thousand nightcrawlers and spoons go flashing by and probably preferred minnows or small trout anyway. Some of us had occasionally seen Mustamaya chase a school of those minnows out into the open pool, grab one and swirl back to safety under the river bank. No one doubted that she was big enough to merit the prize. When they looked at that gold piece under the glass of the cigar counter, they dreamed of Mustamaya.

Slimber Jim Vester, our town liar, didn't even try for Mustamaya at first. Just sat on the bank watching all the others trying to catch her and kidding them when they always failed. When Pete Fouchon waded up to his neck trying to poke his pole under the bank, and had to swim for it, old Slimber nigh to died from laughing so hard. When LaFontaine drove a big stake into the bottom of the pool above the swift run and tethered a heavy line with a five inch sucker on it so it would go under the bank, waited an hour, saw the line vibrate and waded in to haul out a five foot snag, Slimber said, "Damme! Mustamaya's so old she'd got petrified. Why don't you ask Higley to mount that snag over the bar?" Slimber wasn't there when Eino Rutilia fished all night on the theory that big fish fed then but he sure razzed Eino about it. Watching all those fools trying to sneak up on Mustamaya was good as a show, Slimber said.

I liked to go sit with him, watching the chunks of white foam from the rapids above ride down the fast current and disappear under the bank beneath us. Slimber liked any audience, even me. He sure told some good ones. They'd begin nice and easy and believable but then always ended with something outrageous. It wasn't that he varnished the truth. It was the lie that he varnished and polished. You almost had to believe Slimber, he looked so sincere and saintly with his white hair and whiskers.

I misremember most of the tales he told me there on the river bank but the one about the bullfrog comes to mind. We were sitting there in the sun half watching Sven Olson drowning a worm and dreaming of that gold piece when I said, "Hey, that's a pretty big frog down there at the water's edge. He'd better be careful or old Mustamaya will swallow him."

"Hell, boy, Slimber said. "That's only half a gulp for Mustamaya. Way too small! What I ought to have is that big bullfrog I tamed the summer I spent in a shack at Mud Lake where I crossed that heron with a duck. Named that frog Oscar, I did, and he'd eat bits of meat outta my hand. Great big old bullfrog, he was, maybe a foot tall sitting. You never hear such a croak as Oscar had. More like a boom. Sounded like a man beating on a bass drum, it did."

"How did you tame Oscar?" I asked.

"Twasn't easy," Slimber replied. "Couldn't get to him in the water, of course, but up on land he was almost helpless because he never had learned to jump. He'd just waddle, kind of. Oscar felt real bad he could not jump. Once I seen tears in his eyes when a little green grass frog goes hopping by him." Slimber took a long time filling and lighting his corncob pipe.

"But how could you teach a frog to jump?" I didn't believe him, Slimber being the town liar, but I had to see what he had to say.

"Well, I felt sorry for the critter," Slimber said. "So, I cotched him and put him in a box for a week or so, feeding and stroking him, and giving him a bath with a bucket of water now and then to keep 'im from a-drying out."

"But jumping? How'd you teach Oscar to jump?"

"Don't hurry me, boy. I'm a-coming to that," said Slimber. "After he was gentled, I took Oscar out of the box and squatted down just like he did and then jumped leap-frog way two or three times. Felt like a fool doing it but there wasn't no one around. I could see the big bullfrog a-looking at me, interested like, so I did it again. Then I pushed him down on his haunches and heaved him in the air like in jumping. I done that two or three times but the bugger still wouldn't jump. So I gets me one of them heron feathers and jabs it up his hind end. Goosed him good, and that worked. That old bullfrog, he took off like a grasshopper, a real good jump, maybe four feet high and ten feet long. Then I put Oscar back in the box to think it over."

Slimber liked the way I was listening. "Was that all you had to do?" I asked. "Just show him and goose him?"

"Well, no. And it wasn't easy as it sounds. Took Oscar a long time afore he'd jump without goosing. Once that heron feather got stuck up his hind end and Great Balls of Fire, he come back to me after the jump with the feather in his mouth-like a spaniel bringing back a duck."

"Another thing too," the old man continued. "Even after he learned to jump good, the critter never really used it for hopping, like a decent frog should. He'd still waddle clumsy-like. Jumping was something special, show-off stuff, and he never learned how to jump down off anything. Oh, he could sure jump up, though. Why, time after time, I'd have to get me a ladder to get him off the roof of my shack. No, Oscar never figured out how to jump down. Became a real trouble after a time, he did. Once I come near breaking my neck getting that old bullfrog down from a forty foot birch tree, so I heaved him in the lake, hoping to get rid of him. Nope, next morning there he was in his box a-croaking for meat. And he'd boom at night too, spoiling my sleep. Damned nuisance. Even thought of shooting him but couldn't bring myself to do it. Glad I didn't too, for Oscar, he took care of it hisself."

Slimber knocked out his corncob on a log and carefully filled it with Peerless smoking tobacco from a pouch. Then he tamped it, smelled it, and tamped it again before putting a match to the bowl.

"What happened? What happened, Slimber?" The old liar sure had me trapped.

"Waal," he said. "Old Oscar got better and better at jumping high in the air, even forty, fifty feet or more. He could do it without goosing too but he'd much rather have me do it, than have to jump by his lonesome. Anyway, one night about dark there was this big full moon over the lake when Oscar comes croaking up to me, wanting his bed-time play. Well, I give it to him but used the hot match I'd just lit my pipe with instead of the feather. Wow, did that bullfrog take off over the lake. Way up high until I couldn't see him no more. I never heard a splash and I never see Oscar again."

"What do you think happened?" I asked.

"I know, what happened, though I can't prove it." Slimber answered. "You just take a look at the man in the moon next time you see it."

I did take that look, and danged if I didn't see a frog there instead of a man's face. You'll see it too, if you look hard.

Maybe it was because I was such a good listener, or maybe it was because we had the straw stack, that I was there when Slimber caught Mustamaya. After about a week or ten days, no one was fishing for the big trout. No one had seen her or even felt her touch the line. They'd given up. Higley's gold piece would be under the glass of the cigar counter for a hundred years. Oh, it was said that one man tried to sew two fairly large trout together but couldn't do it, and another brought in a thirty-inch lake trout he'd caught in Lake Superior but he'd painted the spots on it so clumsily everybody laughed when he brought it to the saloon. No, Mustamaya was safe and snug in her hideaway under the bank. "She'll die of old age," they said.

Not Slimber! "Now that things have quieted down, I'll catch that trout," he told me. "Ask your pa if I can stir around in his straw stack and catch me a mouse or two? Mustamaya won't touch a worm but she might go for a baby mouse if I can get one."

I asked Dad and he said yes, so one afternoon Slimber came up to the house and stirred up the straw. Sure enough, he soon uncovered a mouse nest. The mother mouse scurried away with some little pink mouslings clinging to her teats but several dropped off and these Slimber put into his pocket, stuffing in a red bandanna to keep them from escaping. "Come along, Cully, if you want to,'" he invited.

I was glad to do so. But first we went to his cabin and Slimber came out carrying a posthole digger and some tackle. On our way down the street we met a couple of men who asked Slimber where he was going to build a fence. "No," Slimber replied. "I'm going fishing. I'm going to catch Mustamaya." Lord, how those men laughed.

But old Slimber knew what he was doing. First, he went down to the water's edge where the current cut under the bank and bounced up and down on the ground until he knew where the solid ground began. Then by squeezing the handles of the posthole diggers, and opening them wide after plunging the scoops into the earth, he soon had a round hole that went right down into the water. We could see and hear it flowing by.

"Now, boy, let's go up on the bank and cut us a government pole," Slimber said. He picked out a straight alder about two inches thick at the butt end and an inch at the top. "That'll do us," he said. "Hell, that pole would hold a horse." Then he attached a very heavy line to the end of it, tied on a hook big enough for a pike, looped a heavy chunk of lead around the line for a sinker, sat down and lit his pipe.

"Well, boy," Slimber said contentedly. "We'll just wait here ten minutes, then I'll tiptoe down to my hole in the ground, put on a mouse and catch that there fish."

And that's exactly what he did. No trouble at all. Slimber waited till the big trout swallowed the mouse, gave a great heave, and there she was, a nopping on the bank. He gave her a good tunk on the head with a stone, put her on a big crotch from a maple branch, and we headed for home. Nothing to it! I felt kind of disappointed.

We only met one person on the way up the hill. Boy, how his eyes bugged when he saw that great fish. "Mustamaya!" he yelled. "Slimber Jim's caught Mustamaya!" Within a half hour everybody in town knew it.

When Slimber Jim got back to his cabin, he put the great fish in a washtub full of water so it wouldn't dry out, had supper, and prepared for a big evening. For once, he'd get respect. And envy! And that ten dollar gold piece! He measured Mustamaya to be sure. Twenty-one inches and a little over. Nobody ever had caught a bigger trout. They'd be talking about this big one for years, and seeing it too, because Higley had said he'd have it stuffed and put above the bar if anyone could catch one big enough. Yeah, they'd listen to him tonight, they would.

The saloon was full of men when Slimber Jim arrived that evening and pulled the big fish out of his sack. Oh, what a hollering went up when he laid it out on the bar. "Mustamaya! By God, it's Mustamaya for sure. No, that trout's bigger than Mustamaya. Where'd you catch it, Slim? What kinda bait you use? She fight good, Slimber?" The questions and comments filled the air. "Measure it! Measure it Higley!" they demanded. Yes, it was plenty big enough. Twenty-one, maybe twenty-two inches. A sloib! "Ya got to get that mounted, Higley, like you said. And put 'er up there where we can see it every time we come in this joint." "How about drinks on the house, Higley?"

Without a word, Higley got out his jackknife and scraped the ten dollar gold piece from under the glass. "If you want to have drinks all around, I'll give you the change," he suggested. But Slimber would have none of that. "You keep the trout," he said, "but I keep the gold piece! Let them buy their own drinks."

After all the commotion and backslapping died down, someone again asked Slimber how he'd caught the monster. It was his moment of moments but he lit his pipe and took a snort of the whiskey Higley set out for him before he began.

"Well, boys, it was like this. I figured I wouldn't even try for Mustamaya until you quit thrashing around down there in the Pine Hole. And I figured, too, that I had to try something different. So I ups and made me this contraption." Slimber laid out on the bar the three foot length of hooks in tandem that he'd put together after supper. The men crowded around to see it. "Now, all of us know that big trout eat more minnows than worms," Slimber continued, "so I cotched me a little mess of chub minnows and strung them on these here hooks so they'd look like they was a-chasing each other when I pulled the line longside where the river goes under the bank. Every time I seen Mustamaya before, she was chasing minnows. Only thing as would get her out from under that overhang." All the men oh'd and ah'd. Made sense, that!

"How many minnow did she swaller, Slim?" a man asked.

"Not a damn one!" Slimber replied. "Twas a good idea but it didn't work. All I did was drown them minnows. Never seen hide or hair of Mustamaya when I was using it."

"Well, how did you catch her then, you old coot?" The men sounded mad but old Slimber was serene.

"I done some thinking," he said, "and I come up with the idear that old Mustamaya wasn't going to eat anything as had a hook in - it. No, sir! So I gets me an old bucket that had some holes in the bottom to let the water through, filled it with some dead frogs, and anchored it, on the bottom with a big rock so when she smelled 'em, she'd poke her nose into the bucket to eat." Slimber filled his pipe and lit it.

The crowd was impatient. "Go on! Go on!" someone shouted.

"Well," said Slimber, "I cut me a good sized government pole and hung a noose from it with wire like we use for snaring rabbits, and I put that loop in front of the opening of the pail so that when Mustamaya poked her nose in to get them frogs I'd give it a big yank and snocker her right up on the bank."

"So you snared Mustamaya? Never hear such a thing!"

"Nope," said Slimber. "She never went near that damned pail."

A groan of complete frustration went up from the crowd. "Quit yer stallin'. How'd you catch her?"

Slimber took a long time and he finished his drink before he answered. "Well, boys," he grinned. "If you want the truth, the real truth, so help me Cod, I got old Mustamaya with a post-hole digger!"

They picked him up and pitched him out of the saloon door and it was only part way open. Higley said later he'd never done such a good business with such a bunch of angry men. Slimber didn't mind it much. He had his ten dollar gold piece, and for once he'd told the truth, even if they hadn't believed him.

Ten years later, a traveling salesman from Chicago, saw Mustamaya, thoroughly stuffed, and a bit faded, hanging on the wall behind Higley's bar. He'd never heard of Slimber, of course, but what he said was appropriate: "Any man who caught a brook trout that big is a liar!"

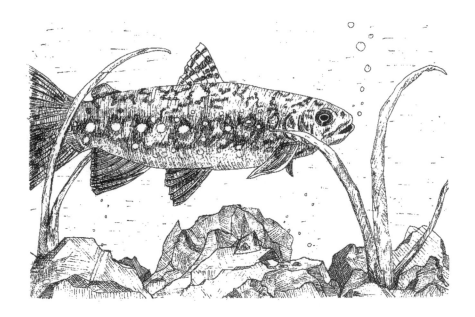

Lumberjack Days

Ibelieve I was about nine years old when I started building a tiny logging dam on the little creek at the far edge of the grove behind my father's hospital. The creek came out of the swamp where the first cowslips (marsh marigolds) always appeared and it dried up in August but in the spring it had a lot of water in it. Like all of us, I had heard many stories of the old logging days when they cut down the white pine forest and floated the great logs down the Tioga River to the sawmill at the edge of the lake. Sitting there, starting to build a dam, that tiny creek was to me a mighty river. I would be a lumberjack and riverman too, opening the dam to carry my stick-logs downstream. Yes, I might even make a little play sawmill with a paddle wheel run by a rubber band, I daydreamed, and maybe even a railroad to haul the boards away.

"Naw, boy, that's no place to put your dam. Put'er up by that big granite hill." The voice startled me but it was Jim Arnt, an old retired lumberjack with heart trouble, who couldn't do heavy work any more but was able to walk in the woods if he took it slowly. I knew Jim pretty well because my father had commissioned him to make me my first pair of skis and he'd let me watch him do it. Yes, Jim even let me help him lift the rock he used to weigh down the ski after boiling the tip of one end and anchoring it in the ladder to make the curve. He had quite a shop of woodworking tools in his summer kitchen and made cabinets and storm windows and such things. He even had a lathe in that shop, operated by a treadle just like that on my mother's sewing,machine. Yes, I knew Jim Arnt and liked him.

"Put 'er up by that big granite hill" he had said, but there wasn't any big granite hill there in the grove. I must have looked puzzled because Jim grinned and pointed to a smooth bald rock at the edge of the little creek downstream from where I had started. It was only about a foot high. Hey, I thought, delightedly, here's a grown-up who knows how to play!

"Yeah, Jim said. "I've helped build three logging dams in my time and I know. Always build them in the narrows between two rock hills if you can 'cause they got to hold back a heap of water if you want to float pine."

"Your first job, Cully," he said, "is to make another channel over here opposite the big hill so we can make a proper dam. Always make half a dam at a time." When I began to do it, he squatted down beside me and showed me how we had to begin scooping out the dirt with our hands from the lower end, not the top where the creek was. "Have a hell of a mess if we start upstream" he said. "Once we get the channel cut, then we'll open her up and we can build our dam on dry land."

While I was doing that, Jim got a lot of sticks and notched their ends. "Now, let's build the cribbing for the fill. You put these like you were building a cabin upside down with each big log's crotch fitting into the one below." Again, he showed me, but he sat on the log while I did it and sometimes Jim swallowed a little white pill from a small black bottle he took out of his vest pocket. Once he banged his chest hard. "Damme!" he said, "these big logs are too heavy for me now!" Finally, I had the cribbing done.

"Now, fill'er up with dirt," Jim ordered and, as I did so, he told me how, when they built Green's Dam on the West Branch of the Tioga, a horse that had been pulling earth in a scoop to make the fill had slipped off the embankment and fallen into some rocks below.

"Right here!" Jim said and pointed to the place where my cribbing joined the rock. "Broke both legs and we had to shoot it. Left it right there. The wolves cleaned it up in just three nights, bones and all. Lots of wolves around that Green's Dam in the old days. We'd hear them ahowling most every night when we were lying in our bunks. Say, come to think of it, Cully, we should have built the logging camp before we started the dam or where would the men be sleeping and eating? Well, no matter. We'll build it later."

That was the first of many delightful times when Jim and I relived the old logging days. I was so entranced by his stories and the things he showed me, I could hardly wait to get out of school to go to the grove. Jim seemed to enjoy it a lot, too.

The next afternoon Jim had gotten to the dam before I did and had spent the morning in his shop building a model of the sluice gate. He was down on his knees fitting it into place when I arrived. It was a little box open on top except for three bars across the opening and two spools with handles on them that acted as windlasses to pull up the gate. This gate slid up and down in side grooves when you turned the spools by the nails driven into the edges. It worked too. "Now you turn this winch, Cully, and I'll turn mine at the same time. That gate must weigh nigh half a ton but maybe we can lift it if we work together." He pretended to grunt with the effort. "Careful now!" he said. "If that handle slips out of your hand, it'll spin fast. Saw a man break an arm that way once." I held the nail tightly, he made it so real.

Most of the rest of that day was spent building the other half of the dam up to the bypass channel where the water flowed. When, at last we plugged it, we lowered the sluice gate and as we watched the water behind the dam gradually rise, Jim told me more stories of the old days.

"Reason for the dam is to back up a lot of water and let'er all roar down to carry the logs we'll have to stack at the rollways downstream. Then when the spring flood comes, we'll break out the logs there and let them roll into the river. If we log up above the dam too, we'll have to build some booms to funnel the logs through the sluiceway. Notice, Cully, that there's an apron coming out of the sluice." Jim pointed to a little board platform that did so. "You got to have that apron so the logs coming through won't hit the dead pool just below the sluice but will shoot out down into the current. I've seen some bad logjams, I have, but the worst one was right under Number Two Dam on the Yellow Dog River. They'd built too short an apron and the pine just buried their damn noses in the bottom. Looked like a mountain, that tangle did. Before they could repair the gate so they could lower it, there were logs piled up everywhere and every which ways, both below the dam and above it. Took 'em six days with a lot of dynamite before they got the mess undone. You think that apron's long enough, Cully?" He pretended to look worried.

When I tore down to the dam after school the next day, Jim was sitting on a log smoking an old pipe. "I made us a logging camp, Cully. What do you think of it?"

I was delighted. He'd built one out of little logs that was about two feet long and a foot wide. It had only one door but there was a sort of sky light and a little chimney pipe near the middle of the roof. After I had expressed my pleasure, Jim said, "The roof comes off. Look inside." The roof did come off just like the one on my sister's dollhouse. Inside Jim had built two rows of little sleeping bunks along each of the long sides.

"Yeah," he explained, "that's where we slept. No mattresses, just straw, but we were too tired at the end of a day to care. Some camps had two layers of bunks, one above the other, and some slept two men to a bunk, but the smaller logging camps were like this. Silver Jack Driscol ran a camp over by Seney that slept a hundred men, he did. I see you're looking at that bench that runs beside the bunks. That's the deacon's seat, so we called it. That's where we sat. Didn't have any chairs in the camp, though sometimes we'd make a table or two to play cards on and sit on nail kegs there on Sunday, our day off."

He apologized for the tiny stove which he had made from a condensed milk can. "The stove we usually had was a long cast-iron one that would hold four-foot maple logs. It would keep us warm all night after we banked it good. And look, Cully, see those racks hanging down from the inside of the roof above where the stove is. That's where we hung our socks or clothes to dry them out by morning time. Sure stank bad. That's why we opened that skylight to give us some fresh air. Mostly, it was too hot in there if it was closed."

"Didn't you have any windows?" I asked. "Sometimes, but not common," Jim answered. "No need for them. We were up before daylight and in bed by nine o'clock. Nothing to see outside but stumps anyway. Only time we might have missed windows was on Sunday. Those of us who could read - and most couldn't - used the kerosene lamps over there in the corners. And that's where we usually filed our saws and sharpened our axes for the next day's or week's work."

"Where did you eat, Jim? Don't see any long tables," I asked.

"Oh, not in the sleeping camp," he replied. "We ate in the big cookshack in another building. We'll have to build that some other time."

"I've heard that lumberjacks ate good," I said.

"Sure did in most camps. If a camp had a bum cook, the jacks soon left for a better one. For breakfast: dishpans full of pancakes, sausage, eggs, bread. All you could eat and then some! Noontime, we ate ham sandwiches out in the woods and washed them down with cold tea. Thick, homemade bread sandwiches so big you could hardly get your mouth around the ham in them. Then for supper we'd have meat, usually venison, beans, and potatoes. Turnips, too, with boiled onions and always cake or pie. All you could eat. They fed us good so they could work us hard. Never ate so good since." Jim tapped out his pipe and refilled it.

"One thing though," he said, "there was no talking at meals. You pointed for what you wanted - like butter or sugar. I remember one camp where some newcomer started talking and the cook came after him with a cleaver. Chased him right out of the shack, he did. Cook was king and if you felt like grumbling, you kept it to yourself."

That day Jim helped me build not only the dining shack with its attached kitchen and cook's living quarters, but also some smaller cabins for the camp boss and the scaler's office. Pretty crude, they were, but Jim had brought some shingles so they went up pretty fast.

"What did the scaler do, Jim?" I asked. "How come he had his own cabin?"

"He measures the logs and tallies how many board feet are in he replied. "He's the company's man and also keeps the accounts. We had a kind of store, see, where you could sign up for socks or mitts or chewing tobacco, and they'd deduct them from our wages when they come due. Some scalers were crooked, though, and sometimes we didn't get a fair shake. One time the men got so mad they threw the scaler in the river and wouldn't work until they got a new one."

"How about the camp bosses?" I asked. "I heard they had to be pretty tough."

"Tough but fair," Jim replied. "They had to be tough, handling a bunch of rough men like that. For instance, we had one up on the Baraga Plains name of Tom Haskins. Tom drove us hard, he did. Give you a sample how he was like. One of our teamsters, Pete Leary, come back from town one Saturday night with a bottle of red-eye. That's whiskey and no one was supposed ever to have any in camp. Well, we saw him a sucking at it and pretty soon someone had snatched the bottle away and it was passing hand to hand when there in the door was Tom. Probably heard the commotion and Pete hollering for the bottle. Anyway, Tom seen whose bottle it was and he grabbed Pete and beat the hell out of him even before he got up off the deacon seat. Dragged him to the door and kicked him out of it and told him not to come back. It was blizzarding terrible, it was that night and cold, too, and ten miles from town. Nobody said anything for fear he'd give it to us too, though we knew Pete could freeze to death out there without even a coat on. Pete didn't though. He snuck back and spent the night in the horse barn and come in for his things before we woke up. We seen his tracks. Guess he made it to town. Anyway, he didn't come back. That's how things was, them days. Hard men and hard bosses."

The next afternoon, Jim said it was time to start logging. First, he brought out a compass and we ran a line all around our forty acres of timber. Actually it was only about thirty feet square but he showed me how to spot the corner and then blaze the lines on the trees (Mainly poplar shoots). "You stand here, Cully," he said, "and sight along the compass needle until you find the tree in line with it which I'll blaze. Wave to your right or left until I locate it and then I'll put a slash on its bark. And then we'll change jobs and pace out the boundaries." That was fun and before long we had the tract surveyed.

Then Jim pulled from his pocket a little cross-cut saw he'd made out of a hacksaw blade. It had little handles on it just like a real one.

For almost an hour we cut down those poplar shoots, hollering *"Timberrrrrr!"* every time one was about to fall. The saw made the little bottom cut all right but Jim had to use his jackknife instead of an axe to open up the notch. I sure got the idea about how to fell a tree.

"You should of seen those pines in the old days," Jim said. "Four or five feet across at the butt they were and their tops so far up in the sky you couldn't see it. No underbrush. It was so dark and shady down below it was like being in a church," he said. "A good jack could chop down a tree so accurately it would drive a planted peg right into the ground. Shook the earth when it came down in a crash."

Jim told about some of the lumberjacks he'd known who were extra good sawyers. One of them was so fast, he said, no other man could keep up with him and two men were needed to spell each other on the other end of his saw. And Jim told me of the many accidents when a man got careless or was just unlucky. One of our little poplar shoots was leaning on another and Jim said not to cut it, that it was a widow-maker. "She'll kick back on you and it's hard to know which way it'll kick. And besides, you have to undercut 'em first." "Even with wedges, they're scary to cut," Jim said. Somehow the way Jim described what a falling pine could do to a man was so real I shuddered.

After we'd sawed down ten or twelve of the little poplars, we cut each of them into sticks, all of the same length, and took off any little leaves or branches. "Now, we've got to skid them out to the river road," Jim ordered. "We'll need horses or oxen for that but since we ain't got none, we'll just have to pretend we have. You make the river road first and then the skid trails up to where we've cut the pine." He showed me where to scrape out the road so it would be level. When I'd finished, Jim had carved a little horse out of a chunk of wood but it was time for supper again, so we had to quit for the day.

The next afternoon, we hitched Jim's little wooden horse to each of the logs and hauled them to the river road. "Now, we've got to wait for the cold weather," he said. "No, it's already winter and they've had the sprinkler making ice on the river road so let's haul our logs to the rollways below the dam." Then again, from his pocket, Jim brought out another toy tool, a cant hook, made of a stick with a curved wire hinged to its end. He showed me how a man with a cant hook could roll a log, one so big he could not possibly lift it, almost any place he wanted it to go. "With a cant hook or peavey, and a pike pole and an axe, a couple of strong men can make any log behave," he said. I asked him what the difference was between a cant hook and a peavey and he told me they were the same, that a peavey just had a sharp spike in its end.

Our rollways were on a little rise beside the creek bank. Below them we put three of our little logs to act as skids down which the logs could roll into the river when it was time to do so. Jim said that stacking the logs at the rollways (he called it decking) was always dangerous work and that breaking the piles was worse. He told me some harrowing tales about men being killed on these jobs.

I noticed that Jim was having a lot of trouble breathing, especially when he bent over, so I asked him if he were sick. "Naw," the old man answered. "Just the same old thing. My pump ain't what it used to be. Your father he examined me and said I had to take it easy, but old Jim's not bedding himself down yet. Being down here with you, Cully, helps me remember better days and feels good." He sure walked slowly going home.

Jim didn't show up the next afternoon and I sure missed him. The water behind the dam had backed up to form a little pond and soon it would be running over the top so I opened the sluice gate a little. When the flood of water rushed through the opening, I put a few little sticks in above the gate and watched with delight as they went through it and over the apron into the current below. It was time to break the rollways but somehow I couldn't do it without Jim being there so I went down to his house to see how he was.

The old man was in his bed with all his clothes on but he grinned when he saw my worried look. "Just taking the day off, boss," he said. He asked me how the logging operation was doing and I told him how I'd opened the sluice gate and how the logs had floated through fine. "Maybe I'll be feeling better tomorrow," the old man said, "and I'll tell you how us old river hogs used to drive the logs downstream." I was so concerned about Jim that when I got home I asked my father to go see him. Sure looked sick.

Dad wasn't too optimistic when he returned. "I listened to his heart with my stethoscope," he said, "and there's a lot of arrhythmia and skipping beats. I changed his medication to some stronger stuff and maybe that will help, but Jim's got to take it easy and never get excited. A few days in bed may help. I got Mrs. O'Canton to fix him something to eat and to look in on him several times a day. About all I could do."

Jim had reminded me that we hadn't built the horse barns or blacksmith shop so that's what I spent the next few afternoons doing. "Have a hayloft above with a hole to throw the bales down and make a stall on one end for the horses and on the other end for the oxen," he ordered. "Oxen always seem to do a better job of skidding than most horses. They're slow but strong." I did my best to follow his instructions but my barn didn't look as good as the men's cabin or cook shack that Jim had built.

I also cut a lot of other little logs but cheated a bit because I used a hatchet instead of the little cross-cut saw Jim had made for me. I did skid them out to the river road. It was a week before the old man appeared again, this time to bring me a miniature logging sleigh he had made. It even had strips of tin to serve as runners and a little yellow chain to hold the logs on it. Looked like a watch chain. Jim said he was feeling much better and knew that it was time to break the rollways. "I see that you've got the sluice gate part way open," he said. "That's good. She's a-building quite a head of water above our dam. Plenty to float the logs, I figure." He also admired my horse barn. Said he couldn't have built a better one himself. That wasn't true, but it made me feel proud anyway. Then he had me haul the logs in the new sleigh with the chain holding them down tight and pile them up along the others on the rollways.

"Well," he said. "Looks like it's about time for the log drive, boss. Get a crew of riverhogs and station them about a quarter mile apart along the river to watch for log jams. OK, break the first rollway!"

When I released them, the logs rolled down the three slanting skids and into the flooding creek. "Thar she goes!" he yelled. "All the way to Lake Tioga. Let her rip! Better open that sluice gate all the way and break another pile." He sure was enjoying himself and so was I.

Suddenly Jim let out the old riverhog's yell: "Ah-ee, Ah-ee. There's a jam a-coming down there at the bend," he shouted. He explained that when the rivermen above or below heard that cry, they passed it along and then came running. A little logjam was indeed forming at the bend and soon the logs were tangled in every direction, even piled up on each other. The water was backing up behind them.

"Got to get the key log out right away, boss," Jim yelled and he ran down with me to the bend. "There she is. That big one there on the angle, with its butt up in the air, is the key log." I tugged at it and when it finally came loose, the logjam unravelled itself and the sticks began to float downstream again, slick as a whistle.

"Boss, we got that just in time," Jim exclaimed. "A few hours more and there'd be logs backed up right to the rollways." He wiped his brow and breathed hard for a time. He'd got too excited, I guess, and he sat on our log for quite a spell saying nothing. Then he began telling stories of logjams and riverhogs in the old days.

"After the cutting was done and the logs were piled up at the rollways," he said, "most of the lumberjacks were laid off. Only ten or fifteen of the best of them, those that had experience driving logs, were kept on. A man was proud to be on those crews. Had to be a good man, one with cat feet, because riding those logs took a lot of jumping from one to another. We'd use our peaveys for balancing or to steady ourselves when we got a good rider log. Of course, we didn't just ride the logs except when we had to go out on them to keep them running straight, but there were times when you sure did and you had to be able to birl a log too."

"What's birling, Jim?" I asked.

"It means making the log turn around under you," he answered. "You jump up in the air and then when you come down, you stomp on it just off center and it'll start turning. You can steer a log some by birling and bring it closer to another log you might want to get on."

"I'd think you'd slip," I said.

"Yeah, and some did and paid a price for it," Jim answered. "Of course, we had corked boots, boots with sharp hobnails in their bottoms, and they helped plenty. We used to file them corks so their points were needle sharp. But even so, running across those fast floating logs was no Sunday School picnic. Never forget how a friend of mine, Jack Manning, slipped and fell between two big logs into the black water and then they rolled together. I can still hear how his skull popped. Never did find the body either! Almost every drive, some jack got killed or crippled but we got the logs down, we sure did. No job for a greenhorn." He was silent a long time remembering.

At last, Jim roused himself and lit his pipe. "Well, that's how it was in the old days, boss," he said. "Tomorrow, we'll start building the sawmill down there by the lake. Time to get back to camp, boss." We walked very slowly back up the path, resting often.

There was no tomorrow. Jim died that night and somehow I never could bring myself to go back to our little dam. Not until last summer, sixty-five years later, when I had a beard whiter than Jim's had ever been. Everything had disappeared except the rock against which we'd built our dam. At the place where our rollways had been, I found a glint of yellow watch chain half buried in the leaves.

Grampa Rebels

When a boy reaches the age of ten, he has many needs but the greatest of these is to have an adult male companion to be his hero. My Grampa Gage certainly fulfilled part of that requirement but he was so thoroughly hen-pecked by Grandma, I just couldn't worship him the way I wanted to. At the beginning of this century in the U.P. it was a man's world and any thought of women's lib would have been incomprehensible. Men were inherently superior to women, of course, and so were boys to girls. Rarely did a man and wife walk down the sidewalk together; she followed him. He made the basic decisions - or thought he did. It wasn't that he had any need to prove that he was macho; it was just the way things were, the way they'd been ordained.

That was why I always felt so bad when Grandma constantly humiliated the man I loved. You could see that she enjoyed doing it, ordering him around as though he were her slave, telling him, and everyone else, how stupid he was, bad mouthing him at every opportunity. Grampa wasn't a bit stupid. He'd been a lumberjack and a teamster as a youth before he went to a business college in Detroit to improve himself. Thereafter, he ran a successful grocery store, and then became a banker. Unfortunately, the bank failed when his friend, the cashier, absconded with all the bank's liquid assets and went to South America. Grandma never forgave her husband for the bank failure although he'd had the foresight to put the house in her name along with a considerable amount of his stock holdings. This left her rich and him poor, a situation about which she constantly reminded him with her nasty tongue. In his old age, he even had to ask her for tobacco money, and often went without smoking because he knew she'd give him hell all over again.

I probably should describe my Grandma Gage. She was a formidable looking woman, as tall as Grampa, always well dressed and very proud of her figure which she contained inside a whale bone corset that Grampa had to lace up each morning and unlace each night. Her gray hair was immaculately coiffed in a pompadour with never a strand out of place. When she was angry, which was her usual condition, her jaw stuck out and her blue yes blazed. A dowager!

Grampa was a slim, wiry man in his late seventies. He gave the impression of having great dignity but there was always the hint of a smile under his grey mustache and the corners of his eyes held memories of much laughter. Away from Grandma, and he stayed away all he could, he was the most joyous, imaginative person I've ever known. He not only knew how to play, but also how to pretend. Every day Grampa and I would assume new roles on our forays into the fields and woods or when we did our various projects. One day, we'd be Indians; another day antelopes, or trees, or beavers making a dam across a little creek. He gave me a new name every morning: Mr. McGillicuddy, Mr. O'hallahan, Julius Caeser or such and he would call me by it all day or else call me "Boy." Grampa, with me, was a little bit crazy, but then so was I. We sure had fun.

The day of Grampa's rebellion started like all of our lovely days together by my watching him shave at 5:30 a.m. As usual, he had managed to give me a noseful of lather despite my watchfulness and was just scraping the first bit of it off his own face when Grandma called from the bedroom. "Arzeee!" she screeched. (His name was Azra T. Gage.) "Fetch me a glass of water!"

"Be with it in a bit," he answered. "I'm shaving."

"Arzee! I want that water right now! Do you hear me? Right now!" Everyone else in the house could hear her, she screamed so loudly, and my little sister, Dorothy, aged three, began to cry in her bed. Grampa sighed, put down his long razor and was filling the glass when Grandma started yelling insults and just raising verbal hell loud enough for the neighbors to hear. And even after he brought her the glass of water, she didn't drink it until she'd laid him out in her usual nasty fashion. How I hated the old she-devil! How could he put up with her? Why didn't he hit her?

I asked him that when he returned to complete his shaving. "Well, Mister Hoogerhyde," he said. "I, sir, am a man of peace, as your grandmother knows well. There have been times in the forty-seven years since I married her when the temptation to smack her a good one in the kisser came to me but I fought it down, Mr. Hoogerhyde, but I always fought it down. For I am a Gage, sir, and a gentleman, God help me. It's *noblesse oblige*, you see. We Gages come from royalty and the king never slugs the queen. Repeat after me," he ordered. "A Gage and a Gage, and the son of a Gage, a Gage of the royal line. From every rugged feature, ancestral glories shine!"

I said it over and over until I had it memorized but somehow it didn't explain why Grampa always took her abuse so patiently without any protest at all, never fighting back.

That morning, after breakfast, Grampa said he wanted to be an ab-or-iginal prehistoric caveman. (He always sounded out the big words for me.) I was Ugo, he said, and he was Bugo and we'd better find us a cave right away before some dinosaur or other varmint got us. Well, the only place that resembled a cave near our town was a narrow passageway between two huge rocks up on Mount Baldy, so I led him up there, being careful to keep a sharp look-out for monsters all the way. We roofed over the space between the rocks and it really seemed like a cave.

"Now, we'd better make some weapons, Ugo!" Grampa commanded and before we were done, we had a stone axe made of a sharp rock bound with his shoelace between the ends of a cleft stick, two spears, and a pile of throwing rocks. That wasn't enough, Bugo said to me. "Homo sap must have fire to be safe!" He sent me out to gather some sticks and when I returned he had a little fire going. "Bugo make fire by twirling sticks," he growled but I knew he'd used the same match with which he'd lit his pipe. Then he ordered me to go out and kill a zebra and bring back a couple of leg bones to eat. When I returned with two knobby hunks of wood he praised me. "Ugo mighty hunter. When Bugo die, Ugo be chief!" We were toasting the wood chunks over the fire and pretending to gnaw them when suddenly Mullu's old hound appeared.

"A saber toothed tiger!" Grampa roared. "Build up the fire. Get your spear!" He sounded so fierce the old hound ran away. "Phew!" Grampa siad, wiping his brow. "Ugo, that was a close call!"

But somehow that old flea-bitten hound had shattered our fantasy and we came back to being ourselves again. "Something's bothering you, Boy. What's wrong?" Grampa asked.

I tried to tell him again how awful I felt when he let Grandma constantly insult him and treat him like a dog. I know I was half crying as I explained my need for him as a hero as well as a companion. I didn't ever say hen-pecked but he knew what I meant.

At first, he made a little joke about it, unbuttoning his vest and raising his shirt tail and underwear. "Ah, but you don't understand, Boy, that I have a secret weapon," he said. "When Grandma starts giving me hell, I just press this belly button and I don't hear a word she's saying." But somehow that didn't help at all and we went back to our house silently. It was time for dinner, anyway.

I'll never forget that meal as long as I live. Oh, it started out like every other noon meal with good food and conversation but before we had finished our apple pie, Grandma had completely spoiled it with another of her usual tantrums. She was just poisonous. She told my mother that the pot roast had been overcooked, and that the boiled onions were too hard. She snapped at my five-year old brother, Joe, for trying to talk with food in his mouth. She argued with my father about politics. She told me my hands were still dirty though I had washed them. She insisted that my sister sit up straight in her high chair. But most of all, she concentrated on Grampa's sins of commission and omission, even bringing up the bank failure again. She was just awful. I could see my father biting his lower lip, a sign that he was about to explode, but it was Grampa who did.

I've mercifully forgotten the last humiliating thing she said about him that made him rise from the table and go over to her on the opposite side of the table. "Henrietta!" he roared. "That's enough! I've borne your vicious tongue for forty-seven years. I've suffered your insults and tantrums too long. You have shamed me before my son and grandson too many times to count. But no more, Henrietta, no more! From now on, you will keep a civil tongue in your head, stop nagging me, and be the lady you profess to be, or I shall do to you *anywhere* what I'm going to do to you now!" Very calmly, he grabbed her hair and lifted it from her head and waved it high. We gasped to see that she was bald as an egg. None of us knew that Grandma wore a wig.

Grandma let out a shriek, covered her naked pate with her hands and fled upstairs to her bedroom, sobbing. Grampa knew that it was his finest hour because he ate the rest of his pie very slowly and had an extra piece of cheese. Then he arose, tucked Grandma's wig onto his belt, and motioned me to follow him. I couldn't help hugging his legs, I was so proud of him. We went out to the clothesreel and took turns dancing around it, playing Indian, and waving Grandma's scalp.

She never hen-pecked my hero again.

Golden Anniversary

Ya, that was a long time ago, Eino." Hilda said, looking up from her embroidering. "Fifty years ago, 1865." She knew what her husband was thinking about. Lately, the two of them almost always seemed to know. Tomorrow would be Midsummer's Day, their marrying day, their golden anniversary. She had put cedar branches all around the house and hung the green strings of groundpine over the kitchen windows. Eino had got them for her from the swamp so they were fresh and smelled good. He was a good man, Eino was, rough on the outside but tender in. They'd told her a Swede girl should never marry a Finn but they were wrong, fifty years wrong.

Her husband was sitting in the soft chair with his feet on the butter churn looking out of the open window, feeling the soft air blowing through the screen, and watching a few mosquitoes hunting for holes in it. "I was scared getting married," Eino said to her. "Only twenty, I was. Had job but no money and I was shamed to bring you to that shack I built. I got drunk fifty years ago tonight."

Hilda smiled. "Don't say that! We had good times there, Eino; raised babies there. I still miss old cabin sometimes, even though this big house better one. Old cabin always warm. You chink it good with swamp moss, Eino. You always take good care of me."

The old man grinned. "But lotsa mice in old cabin, Hilda, eh?" Hilda could never stand mice. They frightened her. Bears didn't. Like the time she shot a big bear trying to come through the summer kitchen window when she had little kids and he was away. And chased Salo's bull out of her garden! No, Hilda was no coward. Only for mice. He'd been lucky marrying Hilda that Midsummer's Day so long ago, in that new blue serge suit he'd sent the money order for. Didn't fit too good, but he sure felt dressed up there before the Justice of the Peace in Ishpeming. And Hilda in her new outfit too, holding his hand as the words were said. So pretty, she was. Yellow hair, like gold, in tight braids. Eino told her what he'd been remembering.

"Oh, no, Eino," she said. "You had brown suit, not blue. Blue suit you had for christening John and Olga. I know. I help you buy it in Ishpeming at Brastaad's. But you looked handsome in brown, Eino. And so strong. Big muscles." She smiled again. remembering how his hand had trembled in hers. Eino had really been scared that marriage day. He'd always been shy too, but when they got off the trail and started up the hill street, he'd insisted that she walk beside him, not after him like all the Finn women of that time did.

Then she also remembered that first supper in the old cabin. Mrs. Thompson, the woman she'd been the hired girl for, had given her a four-place setting of blue willow ware china for a wedding present, and knives, forks and spoons and a red and white plaid tablecloth, too. Hilda remembered how nice the homemade table looked when they sat down for their first meal together.

Eino turned from the window. He'd been remembering, too. "We had ham and eggs and potatoes," he said. "And coffee cake. Those dishes were best we ever had. Too bad they broken and gone." They'd eaten off them for fifty years, or almost. Maybe two plates and a chipped saucer were left, but the cat had broken the last blue cup only the month before. Somehow, coffee didn't taste as good any more. Those sure had been pretty dishes.

Getting out of his chair, the man groaned a bit. He got a stub of a pencil out of the button box he'd made for Hilda thirty, forty years ago, and began to do some figuring on the back of an old calendar. How many meals had they eaten on those dishes? Three hundred sixty-five times three made 1,095. Then, times 50, make it 54,750, about that. He told her the incredible figure.

"You cook me some 54,000 meals, Hilda," he said. "And all good ones too. You been good wife, Hilda."

"Yah," she answered. "And 54,000 washings of those dishes too. But sometimes you help, Eino. Not like other Finn men. You know when I too tired or sick. And you cook breakfast sometimes so I can sleep late. You good man, Eino. Always been good to me." She got up and put her bare arms around his neck. He always liked that.

Eino patted her hands. She had been a good helper too, Hilda had. He remembered how in the old days when they were very poor, she'd not only helped rake the swamp hay he'd cut with the scythe, but also carried her stick pole of it back up the long hill to the barn. Not as much hay as he could carry, but plenty at that. And hoeing the tough quack grass out of the new potato patch before he got back from the mine. And helping with the butchering of the pigs and steers and deer. And doing all that milking for years and years. Some women were lazy. Not Hilda. Her hands showed how much she had worked for him and the kids, hands that were gnarled and had swollen knuckles. They were beautiful hands. How many washings had they done? He didn't want to count.

Hilda was looking at Eino's hands too as he filled his pipe. She noticed that they trembled when he stuffed in the tobacco and that he couldn't straighten them out all the way any more. Too many years of hard shoveling up at the mine. But they were the hands that had brought her wild flowers, not only in the early years, but even that very day. She looked at the blue flags, the wild iris, in the white pitcher. Eino always knew that they were her favorite and he'd probably gone all the way to that swamp by Mud Lake to get them. Most Finn men never did that sort of thing. Eino liked to see flowers in the house: pink arbutus first thing in the spring, then yellow cowslips and pink ladys-lippers, then the blue flags and wild roses. In the summer, daisies and Indian paint-brush, and last in the fall the goldenrod, fireweed and blue asters. Eino had planted lots of them in the front yard by the porch too. Yes, Eino liked flowers as he liked her. Once he had called her his Swede blue gentian - because of her eyes, he'd said. That was why she soon must be starting slips from the old geranium so they could have cans of scar-let in the windows next winter.

As he lit his pipe, Eino glanced at her. "A fine looking woman still," he thought. "Always neat." Hilda sure looked pretty right now in that yellow dress. Not like the dull black and brown dresses most Finn women wore around the house. It was probably the Swede in her but Hilda always wore bright things, reds, and blues and yellows. They helped the winter go by. He'd never tired of looking at her - her braided hair, the way she dressed, the way she moved.

Eino grinned a little ruefully, remembering one other Midsummer's Day when he'd bought her some yard goods for a dress she could make. He'd known it was a mistake the moment she put eyes on it. She did make herself a skirt out of it and wore it just once because it looked terrible on her. Made her look like a gypsy woman. A color for hearses, that purple. He chuckled aloud.

When she asked him why, Eino told her and she laughed too. But then she reminded him of the mustache cup she'd bought for him one year because she thought he'd like it and wouldn't keep getting coffee stains under his nose when he drank from the blue willow ware cups. That too had been a mistake. Eino had tried valiantly to use that cup because it was a present from her, but he'd hated the damned thing so much he finally shaved off his mustache so he wouldn't have to use it. They both laughed, remembering how little Elsa hardly knew her father without that mustache.

That brought back the memory of Elsa's birthing. It had been a hard one. No doctor that time like she'd had with John. Just an old Finn midwife and the pains were long and fierce. Eino had stayed with her through all of it, holding her hand and squeezing it hard when the pains came. He'd given her the biting stick to sink her teeth in that he'd made out of soft basswood for her when John was born. It really helped, she said, or at least it helped her keep from screaming. She still had that biting stick somewhere among her private treasures.

Eino remembered that labor, too. That's why they'd had no more children. Two of them were plenty anyway. He just wished they lived closer so they could be there for this golden anniversary tomorrow. Hilda would like that. But John, his son, had a good job in Detroit, a white collar job. He was an engineer. It had been hard helping him get through college, but he'd worked most of his way and managed it somehow. Maybe John could come up later this summer on his vacation and bring the grandsons along. Little Eino was a good fisherman. He'd take him trolling in Lake Tioga for northerns.

Hilda was wishing, too. Elsa was married and expecting her third child so she couldn't come. It would have been a long trip on the train from Traverse City where she lived. Maybe two or three years from now Elsa could come home; she probably needed some babying herself. But, as always, it would cost lots of money and Elsa and her husband didn't have much of it. For that matter, Eino and she had never had much money either.

"Maybe if we had sent John enough for his ticket, he might have come," Eino thought. He and Hilda had talked it over but decided against it. John wouldn't take it anyway. He knew that his father's little mine pension didn't go very far even though they didn't need much except for eating money and the taxes. They had to save some out of each month's check for those taxes that came due in January. Probably he would have to tap Hilda's blue sugar bowl again. Eino smiled, remembering how they'd lived out of that sugar bowl for a month when the mine suddenly closed down. Hard times, back then, until he got a job on a railroad section gang, tamping ties. He'd even quit smoking to save money until one morning there was a can of Peerless on his blue willow ware breakfast plate. Hilda had bought it with her butter and egg money. Yes, Hilda had been a saver. She knew how to buy and keep. He told her so.

"But remember that big fight we had when I told you to take our bank savings and buy those forties?" she asked.

Yes, Eino remembered well. He and Hilda hadn't had many real fights or mean arguments. Oh, of course, there had been little ones, especially when they were first married. She liked her oatmeal soupy; he liked his hard and granular. She liked her bacon with the fat barely cooked; he wanted his bacon brown and crisp but limp. He liked thick pancakes like his mother had always made; Hilda preferred thin ones like those she'd had at home. But those were little arguments and they'd compromised. One of the big fights had been when Eino had been given a chance to go underground in the mine and was thinking about doing it. Paid much better than surface work, but Hilda said a big *No!* When he'd insisted that where a man worked was his decision, she answered that she would leave him if he did, and she meant it. He gave in finally, but got sick-drunk that night at Higley's Saloon, the only time he had done that since he got married. Good thing too that he hadn't gone underground because a week later they had a bad accident down there. Hilda was a smart woman, smarter in some ways than he was.

Hilda was remembering the other big fight. Reino Untilla had offered to sell Eino five forties of freshly cut-over land for three thousand dollars. At that time they had only about four thousand in the bank, their entire life savings. It was for their old age and funeral expenses. Hilda wanted Eino to buy the property. They were only in their thirties, she said. In twenty or thirty more years, there would be another crop of spruce and balsam to be cut and they'd have lots of money for their old age and the kids too. Eino didn't agree. He had no life insurance. The mine might close down again. That raha in the bank had been hard to save and with the kids, it would be harder still. They would have to pay taxes on those forties every year. It would be crazy to buy them.

"No," said Hilda. "It's a good buy. It's our one chance to get a lot of money for our old age and to leave some to our kids. We'll get along. I'll go back to being hired girl if I have to." They argued about it for weeks until Eino finally gave in and reluctantly bought the property after paying five hundred dollars more for a life insurance policy. That deal had been a sore between them for years but finally it had healed. Eino knew now that he was almost a rich man because a jobber had recently offered him three thousand for the stumpage of just one forty. Yes, Hilda had been smart about that timber. Once when he admitted it to a friend, he said, "Yah, I'm the head of the house but Hilda's the neck that turns the head'" It was true but it didn't matter anymore. The two old people sat there in the twilight among their memories until it was time to go to bed.

Next morning Hilda kissed him and baked up a storm: cookies, cake, cinnamon rolls, new bread, everything that Eino liked. He wandered around for a while, then went down to his boat at Lake Tioga to troll for northern pike. He caught two and they had them for supper. For a fiftieth golden anniversary, it had been a quiet day.

After supper, a very good one, Eino said, "I got present for you, Hilda. I hide it in loft." He got the ladder out and put it in place.

"Yah, Eino, I know," she said. "I got one for you up there too. You bring them both down.

Hilda opened her box first. It contained a six place setting of blue willow ware china. Eino had ordered it from Sears Roebuck after long thought and the perusing of many pages of the catalog.

When she finished unwrapping the last piece of china, Hilda was giggling so hard she almost dropped it. "Open your box, Eino!" she said.

In it was another identical six-place setting of blue willow ware. They had a hard time putting all the pieces out on the table. "We rich, Eino!" she cried. "We very rich! Look!"

Just then there came the damnedest yelling and banging of pans from outside the house. *Chivari! Chivari!"* people yelled, and pounded on the door. All the neighbors were there, celebrating their golden anniversary.

And so was John, their son, carrying four blue willow ware coffee mugs on a blue willow ware platter.

The New Cabin

Only one rich man lived in our little forest village. Perhaps, by modern standards, he wasn't really rich but he had raha (money) in the bank and since he'd retired, he'd been able to take his wife to Florida in February. That man was George Trelawny, but we always called him Captain Jarge because he'd been the mining captain in our town before they shut down the mine in 1912. Captain Jarge was a big, bluff man, rosy cheeked, and born to command. He'd made the most of his money buying and selling copper mining stocks on the basis of tips from the diamond drillers who, like him, were also Cousin Jacks, Cornishmen from the old country. Captain Jarge was also a very shrewd judge of men.

That was why the whole town buzzed when they heard that he had picked Billy Manton, of all people, to build a new cabin for his daughter near his own house on Easy Street. We called it Easy Street, not because it meant affluence, but because it was the only street in town without a hill. No, people just couldn't understand it. Everybody knew that old Billy was shiftless and lazy and not at all reliable. He'd had some experience, having helped Untilla build a cabin for some summer people, but Billy had to be supervised all the time, Untilla said.

We kids liked old Billy, not only because he told us interesting stories of the old logging days and river drives, but because he'd drop everything to go fishing with us, or to play mumbletypeg with our jackknives. Billy was sure good at mumbletypeg. He could go up the whole series of acts and his knife point went headfirst into the ground every time. Why, he could even hold the knife point on his scalp or tongue and then flip it with the other hand so it made exactly three somersaults before entering the earth. Billy could do that even on his knees or standing straight up with his eyes closed. That's something! Anyway Billy liked kids and we liked him. Not many big folks like to play.

Bill Manton's own house was a tar paper shack almost as disreputable as he was. Having been patched often, the big tin washers that held the nails were staggered all over the place and there were boards and sheets of tin at the craziest angles. A disgrace to the town, people said. In the winter though it was snug and warm because Billy covered it with huge heaps of snow. All of our houses in the winter had banks of snow over the foundations to keep them warmer but Billy's shack was more of an igloo than a house. Almost a cave in a huge mound of snow, only the stovepipe, the door and a small south window could be seen. Back of it was a woodshed and an outhouse, both of which were ramshackle. Nevertheless, we kids often dropped in to see Billy in his snow cave on our way back from skiing for it was always warm inside. He never gave us anything to eat, but he'd open up the front of his box stove and tell us stories by the flickering flames.

My father, the doctor, was up at Captain Jarge's house when Billy was asked to build the new cabin because Mrs. Trelawny was having another of her frequent ailments. So Dad couldn't help but overhear the conversation. "Billy," said Captain Jarge, "I want you to build me a good cabin, ten by twenty, one room, double bunk, three window and one door. It's for my daughter, Marian, who's lost her husband and may come up here to stay if I've got a place for her. If she doesn't, well I'll sell it. You know that lot I have, four houses down from here. That's where I want you to put it up. Make it like that cabin you and Untilla built. I've seen it and it's a good one."

Billy hesitated. Looked like a lot of work and would spoil his summer but he changed his mind when Captain Jarge pulled out a big roll of bills from his pocket and laid ten of them on the table. All hundred dollar bills! Billy's eyes popped. He'd never seen that much money in his life. Hell, he'd never seen anything larger than a fiver.

"Well, do you want the job or don't you?" Captain Jarge was getting irritated. "That's plenty of money, more than enough for a helluva good cabin, People will say that I oughtn't to trust you, especially since my wife and I are leaving tomorrow to spend the summer in Cornwall, in the old country, where I came from as a lad of thirteen. Ay, 'twill be good going back and 'aving a spot of they tansy tea, and kippered herring and kidney pie, and seeing tinkle bells on every cottage gate. And saffron buns and they real pasties." Captain Jarge interrupted himself. "Doctor, you sure the trip won't be too hard on the little woman, going by ship and all?"

"Be good for her," my father replied. "Good salt air and a real change of scenery can do wonders. Your wife isn't really sick. I promise you she'll be a new person once she gets out of the house."

All this time Billy had been looking at the money on the table. "Sure, Cap'n," he said at last. "I'll take the job. God knows I need some biting money. Had a hell of a time making it through this last winter. Anything else you want to tell me about it.?"

"No," said Captain Jarge. "Build it as good as you can - as if it were going to be your own house. And get it done before I come back the middle of September so you can hand me the key for the lock and say 'there she is' and say it proud. Well, man, don't diddle. Take the money and get going!" Billy left.

"It's none of my business, Jarge, but aren't you taking quite a gamble on that deal?" My father was still in shock.

"Not as much as you think, Doctor. I know what I'm doing. Besides, I owe old Billy something. Remember the time long ago when my boy Tim fell through the ice on the Beaver Dam and Billy pulled him out. Yes, and wrapped the kid in his own coat and brought him up the hill in that bitter cold? And wouldn't take a penny for it. But as you say, it's none of your business. It's mine. See you again when we get back from the old country."

All that money bothered Billy as he walked back to his shack. At first, he just carried the fat roll of bills in his hand but then he became afraid he'd meet someone so he crammed it into his side pants pocket. But as he walked, that loosened the roll and he looked down to see that a hundred dollar bill was half way out of the pocket. Finally, he put it inside his shirt. "A thousand bucks!" he said to himself. "What the hell will I do with it?"

Our town had no bank and the only honest money-keeper was Higley, the owner of our one saloon. Billy considered that recourse but he knew he'd start drinking if he went down there and besides it was kind of nice being able to feel all that folding money. Tired of thinking about the problem, he finally put the bills in an empty tobacco can and buried it behind the outhouse. Then that worried him too. A rain might wet those bills or someone might dig up the can when he wasn't home. Finally, he fastened the bills with a big safety pin to the inside of his long johns next to his chest. They rustled when he walked and he could pat them to know they were there. Even if one came loose, it would just fall down into his crotch. That took care of that!

Getting going on the cabin was more difficult. Billy went up to the Captain's lot and staked out the foundation area. Ten by twenty, Jarge had said, but was that inside or outside? Should he dig a trench all around and fill it with rocks from the mine and then pour cement to hold them in place so the bottom logs could rest solid and wouldn't rot? It tired Billy just to think of all that hard work. Shouldn't he scoop the surface dirt from the enclosure and replace it with sand so the floor joists wouldn't decay? Cabins sure got a mildew stink when they were built on ground. The answer again was yes, but when Billy started scraping, he hit some big roots and stones. To hell with that! Captain Jarge wouldn't know what was under the floor.

What kind of logs would he use and where would he get them? Cedar, white cedar, would be the best but they would be hell to get out of the swamp and besides they tapered too fast. Spruce? Yeah, that would be OK but there'd be a lot of branch cutting and knots. Perhaps he could get some spruce logs from some jobber who was putting up a carload of pulp wood. Decisions! Decisions! Billy was plumb worn out with all that thinking, and more miserable than he'd been for years. So he unpinned one of the hundred dollar bills from his undershirt, took it down to Higley's Saloon and went on a ten day drunk.

After he survived, and the hangover hemlock knot inside his skull had dissolved, Billy started building the cabin. He soon realized that he would have to hire help so he got Pierre Lafond to take his team and lumber wagon and cut and skid four big twenty-foot cedar logs out of the swamp and haul them to the site. That job also meant buying a new one-man cross-cut saw, a peavey and a chain and there went a lot of another hundred dollar bill! A lot of sweat and hard work! Billy went to Untilla's house and told him he'd pay him four dollars a day to help him on the cabin.

"No!" said the big Finn. "Me have you for a boss? You crazy. I no work for you for ten dollar a day. Got bellyful of you on other cabin. No!" Billy tried to get several other men but was again refused. Finally, he was able to hire several high school kids, including me, for two dollars a day.

Our first job was to lay the cedar foundation logs after peeling off their bark and smoothing off the top edges so they would lie level. That meant Billy had to buy a broad axe and a draw knife because, although he tried, no one would lend him any tools. They knew Billy Manton and besides there had always been an unwritten law in our town that you never asked to borrow a man's tools. Why, you'd might as well ask to borrow his wife.

The New Cabin

There were plenty of men in our village who owned spirit levels, those with the bubble in the viewing area that had to be right in the center if the log was truly level but no one would let Billy have the use of one. "Use a bread pan level," they told him. So Billy bought a bread pan, scribed a line around the inside an inch from the top, and filled it with water exactly to the line before he put it on the foundation log. It worked but it took a lot of time and some of the water was always spilling as he moved it from place to place as we hewed the log to even it up. Finally, he said, "To hell with it, boys. We'll just do it by eye from now on." Those bottom logs never were really level, nor, for that matter, were any of the other ones.

Our next job was to cut and haul the other logs that were needed: eighteen twenty-footers and eighteen more that were ten feet long. To the profound disgust of almost everybody in town, Billy cut them from a stand of poplar near the old stagecoach road. Poplar? Poplar for a cabin? Sure it was easy to cut and had few limbs and not much taper, but even well dried, poplar logs decayed fast. Wet green ones would show dry rot in just a year or two. Billy didn't give a damn about what people said. "Easy does it," was his motto. "I'll put up Jarge's cabin but I'm not going to kill myself doing it." He was already tired of the whole job.

Building a cabin out of poplar was bad enough but when the towns people saw that Billy was not going to notch or dovetail his logs, but instead was using the V-box and pole construction, they were outraged. That was only used when you were in a hurry or when the shelter was expected to be temporary - as in building a shack along a trap line. Sure, it was an easy way. You simply nailed two 2 x 6 inch boards together at right angles to form a V, then stood this trough upright in the corner, and as each log was set into place, you put a couple of spikes through the board into the end of the log.

Even with notches and seasoned logs, a cabin takes two or three years to really settle and it's good it does because it just makes the cabin tighter. Not so with Billy's method. Even if the spikes held, which often they would not if a heavy load of snow built up on the roof, it was certain that there would be big gaps between the logs in a short time. What was worse, Billy didn't use ten inch spikes. They were too hard to drive into the logs, he said. Instead, he used four inch nails, sometimes only two to a log. A crazy business! People made bets that the building would fall apart the first winter.

To get lumber for the roof, and the flooring, and to have windows and doors, Billy bought Mrs. Rameaux's old abandoned house. It was in bad shape and needed to be torn down anyway. We kids did most of the demolishing and salvaging. It wasn't worth the two hundred bucks Billy paid for it, because a lot of the boards were warped or cracked or split and all of them had hundreds of nails that we had to pull out or pound in. Pretty junky stuff, but after we painted them, it was hard to know how bad they were.

I'm not going to go into all the shoddy details of how that cabin was built. The floor joints were toe-nailed into the foundation logs, not inserted into notches that had to be chiseled. For chinking between the logs, Billy used ordinary cement mortar instead of wood fiber plaster. "Won't make any difference," he said. "As them poplar logs shrink, it'll fall out anyway and have to be done again, maybe in a year or two." The roof boards did not fit flush with each other and Billy didn't even cover them with tar paper before we put on the shingles. "No need to use two nails per shingle," Billy ordered. "One's enough."

"The hell it is!" roared Mullu's father when he saw what we were doing. "You got to have anyway two per shingle or they'll shift sidewise. And what the hell you doing overlapping them only two inches?" He was so mad, he made Mullu quit the job right then and there. "I no having you learn all wrong," he said. Billy just hired another kid and finally the job was done. We weren't proud. We had some money to buy school clothes and that was about all.

Even Billy wasn't too happy when he looked at the completed cabin and realized that Captain Jarge would be coming home soon. With only three left of the hundred dollar bills still pinned to his underwear, he thought for a long time before he bought a ten gallon pail of yellow paint and swabbed it all over the cabin, inside and out. He used two coats, and they really helped. Indeed, it really didn't look too bad sitting there in the sunshine. Of course, painting those peeled poplar logs would just make them rot all the faster because it would seal the moisture in. Billy didn't care. As he had said when we tried to argue him out of using green maple poles for the floor joists instead of seasoned two by eights, "What Jarge can't see, Jarge won't know."

Summer and potato picking time were over when Captain George Trelawny and his wife returned. Billy had to fortify himself down at Higley's Saloon before going up to confront him and he walked up the hill pretty slowly when he finally had to.

"Got the cabin done, Captain Jarge," he said. "And here's the key so you can go see it."

"No," said Jarge. "The key is yours and so is the house. Now you can move out of that crummy shack and have a decent place to live. And I no longer owe you for saving my son."

186

Stinker

Miss Feeney got to school early that morning and went directly to old Blue Ball's office. B. B. Donegal, our tough school superintendent, was already there, or course, but he didn't look up until she cleared her throat three times. "Well, Miss Feeney, what do you want? Speak up, woman! If it's more chalk, the answer is no! You've had your two pieces already this week."

"No, Mr. Donegal," she answered. "I come for some help and advice, sir. I have a problem and I just don't know how to handle it."

"Come to the point, Miss Feeney. Come to the point! The children will be arriving soon and I want you there when they do!" Old Blue Balls always sounded irritable.

"Well, it's because Theophilus Tissait, the boy the children call Fisheye, comes to school smelling very strong of... of cow manure and it's really causing some difficulties. The girls refuse to sit near him and they hold their noses and..." "I know that boy well," he interrupted. "I've had to thrash him more than once. Always into some trouble."

"But, Mr. Donegal, he's a good boy, really. And he's smart. A whiz at mathematics! He can do three place multiplication in his head and I've seen him working out algebra and geometry problems he got from the high school pupils. I don't think he should be punished for smelling the way he does, although at times it's awfully strong. I just want to know how I should handle the problem."

"I'll take care of it, Miss Feeney. I'll take care of it."

As she left, the teacher regretted having come to him. She liked Fisheye and she was worried about what old Blue Balls might do. A rough man, Mr. Donegal was.

About a half hour after our classes began, the classroom door opened and there he was in the flesh. All of us froze in our seats. "Continue! Continue!" he roared, "and Theophilus, come here, young man!" You could almost hear the sigh of relief from everyone but Fisheye. That unhappy boy got up from his desk and went over to the superintendent, who turned him around several times, sniffing as he did so, then led the boy out of the room. We looked at each other. Poor Fisheye, he'd been up to something and was going to get it good again. A slapping, or maybe the ruler across the hand? Or even the strap? Those of us who had known them ached for poor Fisheye!

But we were wrong. The superintendent merely marched the boy down the hill to his home, gave his mother bloody hell for not sending the boy to school clean, told her to give him a real bath and send him back in a change of clothes. That was all. Didn't hit him once.

When Fisheye didn't return either that morning or that afternoon, I went down to his home. He was my friend. We'd had a lot of good times together and he, with Mullu and me, had rung the schoolbell on that Halloween night when they declared the curfew. A good fishing and trapping partner too. We'd just built a live trap to catch spring rabbits and had planned to put it down in the swamp that very afternoon. And, of course, I wondered what had happened.

When I got there I went up to the back door. (In the U.P., no one ever entered the front door except when there was a funeral.) When his mother opened it, she told me Fisheye was in the cowbarn. "Wait a minute, Cully," she said. "Fisheye didn't eat anything this noon and he must be hungry. Take this piece of bread out to him." She smeared the slice with lard, then sprinkled some salt and a dusting of sugar over it.

I found my friend huddled on some hay, wrapped in a dirty old blanket, and naked. Although it was a fine spring day, it was still in the lower fifties, a mite cold to be that way without clothes. So I asked him how come. He explained what had happened and said that since he had no change of clothes and his mother had now washed his old ones and had them hanging on the line, he'd have to wait until they were dry. He also said that his mother told him he'd have to go back to sleeping on the hard kitchen floor at night like he did in winter time rather than in the soft hay, at least until school was finished for the year.

The Tissaits were dirt poor and they had a lot of kids, three girls and four boys, Fisheye being the oldest. The girls slept together in one corner of the loft and the younger three boys in the other, so Fisheye was odd man out. None of them ever had enough to eat either and maybe that was why Fisheye was the smallest boy in our class. But he was very strong and tough and not afraid of anything. A good fighter, too.

I, myself, had never noticed that he smelled bad though probably others did. Most of us by spring were pretty high in body odor anyway. I guess the tar oil or bear grease used on our boots to waterproof them during the break-up masked all other smells. I could understand though that Fisheye, if he slept in that cowbarn, would acquire an extra aroma because the cow's stall was still full of the winter's crap. I shoveled some of it out onto the pile behind the barn and wished there was something else I could do to help.

On my way home, I suddenly realized that unless Fisheye had another set of clothes, he'd soon be in trouble again. So when I got there, I went to my room and bundled up an old, but clean, shirt of mine and some pants, underwear and socks for him because I had extras. My mother, however, caught me sneaking down the back-stairs with them and wanted to know what I was up to. When I told her the whole story and how unfair it was, she agreed but she vetoed giving Fisheye my old clothes. "Let's get him some new ones," she said. "He's about your size, isn't he, Cully? But then she asked me if Fisheye or his mother would be sensitive about accepting them. You had to be very careful in the U.P. not to hurt a person's pride. We were a proud people. I told her about the bread smeared with lard and how Fisheye insisted on my having a piece of it before he'd eat any. Anyway, mother decided to go to Flinn's store immediately, buy a whole new outfit for Fisheye, get Father Hassel, their priest, to deliver it, and not to tell the Tissaits who had sent it.

Miss Feeney was delighted when Fisheye arrived in school the next morning in a new red plaid shirt, wool pants, new shoes and socks and even a real belt instead of the piece of clothesline that had previously held up his tattered overalls. He'd also been scrubbed until he shone and his hair had been cut. Altogether he looked pretty good and certainly the old cow smell was gone. No one said anything, of course.

I noticed though that at recess Fisheye didn't go down with us to the ditch of the little creek that flowed through the schoolyard into a culvert under our hill street. Playing lumberjacks, we were building logging dams and floating little sticks in the pond behind them. Fisheye watched us but said he didn't want to get dirty.

However, when school let out that afternoon, he got dirty anyway. It happened like this. Walter Donegal, old Blue Ball's youngest boy, started calling Fisheye names and picking a fight with him. "Hi, cowshit," he said. "Hi, stinker! So my old man had to take you out of school to get a bath, hey? Stinky, stinky, double stinky!" Walter had been a nice kid when he was younger and I used to play with him a lot even though he was one grade up from me. But he'd developed a cruel streak and was always bullying kids who were smaller than he was. Maybe it was because his father was also cruel and beat him up more than he should have done.

Anyway, after Fisheye took it for a while, he came out swinging. He was a pretty good fighter for his size, too, but this time he didn't have a chance, Walter being at least a head taller. He gave Fisheye a hard poke in the nose that set it bleeding. Fisheye didn't give up and tried to close in but Walter knocked him down. "Fight! Fight!" yelled the kids and soon there was a ring of us about the two of them, screaming and urging Fisheye on. It was no contest although Fisheye got in a couple of good licks to the body before he stayed down on the ground crying helplessly. Walter gave him one last hard kick and then everyone left but Fisheye and me. I'd sure wanted to join the scrap but the first rule of fighting in the U. P. was that it had to be one on one. No fair having anyone help you. The second rule was: No fair kicking in the crotch!

I sure felt sorry for Fisheye. His nose was still bleeding and one eye was swelling but the worst of it was that his fine new store clothes were a mess and he was afraid to go home. So I brought him up to our house and explained to Mother what had happened.

As always, she came through just the way she should have. She soaked one of Dad's gauze pads in cold water and had Fisheye hold it on his swellings. She washed off his face tenderly and kept talking to him nice and sweet as she took off the dirty shirt, sponged away the dirt and then ironed it. Then she gave each of us a big fat sugar cookie and a glass of milk as she brushed all the dirt from his pants. Pretty soon, Fisheye was cleaned up and except for his eye, no one would have known he'd been in a fight. Mother also gave him a little bag of chocolate candies, one for each of his brothers and sisters and two for his mother, and five for you, Fisheye, she said. So everything worked out all right.

Indeed, it did, for that next Sunday evening, Old Blue Balls smelled skunk coming up from his basement and found a big old striper in it with tail raised on high. Furious, he gave Walter a hard thrashing for not closing the cellar door as he'd been told to do, then ordered him to get the varmint out of there. We heard all about it from Mrs. Donegal when she came to ask my mother how to get the skunk smell out of clothing.

"You know my husband, Mrs. Gage," Walter's mother said. "He's got a terrible temper and when Walter refused to grab the skunk by the tail and carry it outside, I really feared for the boy, I did, Mrs. Gage, his father was beating him so hard. But Walter wouldn't do it and he claimed he'd shut that cellar door right after his father had told him to do it. Well, Mr. Donegal (she always referred to her husband in that formal way) tried to shoo the critter out but it wouldn't shoo and that made him so mad he got his shotgun and blasted the skunk to smithereens. But oh, Mrs. Gage, my house smells terrible and Walter does too because his father made him scoop up the remains and bury them in the garden. It's been a bad day, Mrs. Gage."

Mother told her she'd heard that it was wise to bury all the clothing in a hole and cover it with dirt and leave it there three days before trying to wash it, Mrs. Donegal said that she wished she could do the same with both Walter and Mr. Donegal. "I tried to tell them that if they'd just leave the cellar door open overnight, the skunk would go away, but no, Mr. Donegal just had to shoot it. It's awful to have to live with a man who has a temper like Mr. Donegal," she complained. She also asked to borrow one of Mother's copper boilers. "We'll have to have a lot of hot water for all the bathing as has to be done right away," she said as she departed.

The next morning it was evident that all the scrubbing hadn't helped Walter too much. He sure stank and the kids he couldn't lick began to call him "Stinky," a label he carried with him, without pleasure, all of his school days. And for a long time afterwards, whenever it rained, the Donegal's house stunk again of skunk and Walter got another thrashing from his father for not closing that cellar door.

Or perhaps he had closed it! All I know is that when Fisheye and I went down into the swamp below Company Field hill to put out the livetrap for spring rabbits, using an old carrot for bait, I noticed that the trap smelled pretty strong of skunk. Maybe that's why we never caught a rabbit in it.

The Rich Man

It was in the early summer that the rich man from Chicago came to town and asked my father, the village doctor and township supervisor, about buying Clear Lake. "I've made a pile of money," he said, "and I want to play with it. I want a lake with an island in it on which I can build a fine fishing and hunting lodge for myself and to entertain my business associates. I talked last month with Carter Harrison, the Mayor of Chicago, who, as you know, has such a retreat up on the Log Lake, and he was very enthusiastic about the fishing and hunting up here."

He'd already made a mistake, the first of many to come. Strangers were always supposed to give their names and identify themselves upon first encounter. We in the U.P. were always a bit suspicious about strangers, especially those from down below. Dad asked him his name.

"I'm James Daney, Chicago Board of Trade," the man answered impatiently and a bit arrogantly. "I've looked over these maps, (he spread two of them out on our dining table) and the lakes I've marked with a cross look like possibilities. What I want to know, my good man, is whether any of them have a two or three acre island in it."

My father stiffened. "I'm not your good man," he said curtly, "and you'll mind your manners, Sir or I'll show you the door!"

Mr. Daney apologized perfunctorily. "I'm used to doing business in a hurry, I guess, Doctor." he said, "but I'd appreciate it if you'd look at these maps. All I want to know is which of these lakes has an island in it.

Dad relented and looked at the maps. "The only one that might fit your requirements is this one, Clear Lake. It's about six miles north of here and about one mile from the nearest road."

"But look, Doctor, the map shows a road running right by the lake." Mr. Daney pointed to a faint dotted line.

"Oh, that's just an old logging road used in the days when they cut the big pine. It's all overgrown now, completely impassible. The closest you could get to the lake by horse and buggy is here at Lampi's Clearing. You'd have to hike in the rest of the way and it's rough going."

"But the island, Doctor, the island? Are you sure there's a good sized island in it?"

"Of course, I'm sure," Dad said irritably. "I've fished that lake and hunted around it for twenty years. The island's about maybe four acres in size and has some virgin cork pines on it."

"Good! I'll go see it. I presume your town has a livery stable?" Dad nodded. "Then, sir, can you find me a guide? I never buy a pig in a poke. Got to see it with my own eyes."

Dad was fed up with him. "No," he said, "I have to call on some patients. Find your own guide." He didn't want any rich man from Chicago buying Clear Lake. After all, he and B.B. Donegal had lugged a milk can full of tiny Northern Pike through that nasty country to plant the lake and it now had some real lunkers in it.

Marchand told my father later that he'd given the man old Maude and the oldest buggy he had in the barn. Marchand even had to tell him the difference between "Gee!" and "Haw!" and show him how to hold the reins. "Cette homme, he know nossing about horses," Marchand said. The stranger had tried to hire him to drive Maude up to Clear Lake and guide him in to it but the old Frenchman had refused. Nor did he know of anyone who could or would. This was haying time and the men who weren't making hay were cutting wood or fishing. Marchand told him he might find some loafer at Higley's Saloon who'd still be sober enough to take him up there.

So that was where Mr. Daney went first. The saloon was on the far side of the railroad tracks at the bottom of the hill, but, because he pulled the right rein when he had to make the left turn, he ended up at Paddy Feeny's blacksmith shop instead. There he blustered in, and explained what he wanted in some detail while Paddy was doing some rather delicate work on a broken chain hoist. Now, our blacksmith was something of an artist and we all knew that he wasn't to be interrupted when white hot iron from the forge was ready to be worked. We knew that, but the man from Chicago didn't. Impatiently, he began to repeat what he had said until Paddy grabbed his tongs and chased him out of the shop, roaring like only a mad Irishman can.

At the saloon, Higley wasn't much help either. "What the hell you want to buy that godforsaken pond in the hills for?" he asked. "There's no road into it and it'd cost a fortune to make one over those damned granite hills and through the swamps. Why don't you buy a piece on Lake Tioga?" No, he didn't know of anyone who'd guide him. The only one who might was Alphonse Moreau but he was down sick and if he had been well, he'd have laughed his head off at the idea of taking that city dude with the straw hat up in the bush. Besides, the fool hadn't even bought a beer. To hell with him!

Mr. Dancy was getting frustrated but he was so determined he began to stop at some of the houses to inquire. Unfortunately, he knocked at the front doors instead of going around to the back, as we always did in the U.P. Although several lace curtains fluttered, only old lady Bisset came to see who was there, and when she saw the straw hat and necktie and fancy clothes and pointed shoes, she let out a bunch of hostile French jargon, then slammed the door in his face.

Beginning to feel a bit hungry, Mr. Daney drove up the hill street looking for a restaurant or cafe and, of course, found nothing. When the mine was running many years before, he might have had a good meal at the Beacon House, but it was boarded up and decaying. As old Maude plodded up the hill, Mr. Daney met a bunch of kids going home to their dinner meal and he stopped the horse to ask where the restaurant was. The children milled around the buggy but they just shook their head. "Then is there a store up here?" he asked. As one kid nodded and pointed up the street, some angry woman came out of a nearby house and gave them hell in a torrent of half English, half Finnish, the children scattered. We watched over our children in the U.P.

The Rich Man

When Mr. Daney entered Flinn's General Store, Mr. Flinn took one look at his get up and told him in no uncertain terms that he didn't need any salesman trying to sell him a bill of goods, that he had his own suppliers. And when the man from Chicago asked about a cafe, he sold him a link of bologna, some cheese and crackers and a bottle of red pop. One dollar and seventy cents. No, Mr. Flinn didn't know anyone who might guide him to Clear Lake.

We'd had our noon meal when the stranger appeared again at our door. "Doctor," he said. "I've been unable to find a guide but I'm bound to see that lake. I have just one question: how will I know when I've got to Lampi's Clearing where the trail to Clear Lake starts?"

Dad tried to dissuade him. "You can't go in there by yourself. It's wild country. You'll get lost."

"Nonsense!" Mr. Daney replied. "I've got this map and it's only a mile. I tell you, Doctor, I'm going to see that lake."

"It's only a mile as a crow flies," Dad said. "But it's a lot longer by trail. The trail isn't easy to follow either and I have no urge to assemble a search crew to find some fool from Chicago up in that country. I'd bet you don't even have a compass and it's beginning to cloud up. You wouldn't have a chance, man. No!"

Mr. Daney was not to be deterred. "All right, sir. I'll have to take that chance. According to my map, that clearing must be about five miles up the road. I'll look for it and the trail. Good day, sir!"

Dad relented. "No, you mustn't do it!" he said. "You just don't understand what you're tackling." Then he turned to me.

"Cully," he said, "how about you taking him in to Clear Lake?" I nodded. "My son has been up there often, not only with me but with his friends. He knows the way as well as any man." I sure felt good to hear that praise.

Mr. Daney was relieved. "Fine, fine!" he said. "I'll pay him five dollars for guiding me."

"No," Dad replied. "That's a man's wages. Two dollars would be plenty."

So off we went in the old buggy with Maude plodding down the hill street, her head bobbing up and down with every step. But then I suddenly thought of something. "Mister," I said. "We'd better go back to Marchand's livery stable and get a halter and a rope. We'll have to leave Maude in the clearing for two or three hours and she can't graze good with the bridle on. We'll tie her to the back of the wagon. That's the way we always do it. Keeps them from straying, too."

The man from Chicago vetoed the suggestion. "Ah, hell," he said, "That decrepit old nag won't stray. We'll be lucky if she just gets us there and back." He yelled at Maude and slapped her back with the reins but the old horse didn't move any faster.

It seemed like a long trip even if it were only six miles and Mr. Daney didn't talk much except to cuss the horse for her slowness. When we got to the pool below the spring, Maude made for it, of course, and had a long drink despite his yelling. Once he got off the rig and walked alongside for a spell, then had to run to catch up, and was mad all over again.

Finally, we got to Lampi's Clearing and Mr. Daney marked it on the map. He couldn't wait to jump out of the buggy, and we left it right out in the open and where there wasn't any shade. Not much for the horse to eat where we stopped either.

C'mon! C'mon, boy. Let's go! Show me the trail!" The man from Chicago sure had burrs under his saddle. I led him to where the trail started behind the big rock but then he insisted on going first. Not for long, though, because he kept losing it and wandering off into the brush. Why he even argued with me when I refused to go down a well worn deer trail that crossed our route. A heavy man, Mr. Daney was soon sweating and so the deer flies began to bite him good. I offered him my extra red bandanna to put under his hat but he refused even though the back of his neck was getting bloody. He stumbled a lot too. Sure didn't know how to walk in the woods. Never looked at the ground or felt it with his feet like we did and he tried to plunge ahead too fast. I don't know how many times an alder branch knocked off that silly straw hat of his or how often a dry spruce limb raked his face. I do know that he fell heavily to the ground three times before we even hit the stream that flowed out of the lake.

Clear Creek, where the trail crossed it, is fairly good sized, maybe thirteen feet wide. The crossing comes at a place where the beavers once had a big dam, one that had washed out long ago, but there still was a deep muddy pool behind the part of it that remained. I knew of only two ways to handle it. One was to take a running jump to the big rock part way to the other side and then another jump to shallow water near the old dam. The other way was to go down below and wade across, fighting an immense tangle of windfalls and underbrush. I had no trouble getting across by jumping, but Mr. Daney didn't want to tackle it my way. It must have been ten or fifteen minutes later that he rejoined me and was glad to sit down. How he looked really worried me. Mr. Daney's face was beet red and the jowls on his jowls were purple. He was also breathing hard as he showed me how he had torn his coat and pants in that awful tangle.

But after a little rest, he was ready to go again, though he groaned when he got to his feet. "According to the map," he said, "we ought to be crossing that logging road soon. Even though it runs to the far end of the lake, I think we'll take it. Certainly, can't be any worse than this damned trail."

I tried to argue him out of it when we came to the old logging road although at that place it was fairly well defined. "The trail is a lot shorter," I said, "and pretty soon the old road turns into a swamp full of alders and almost disappears." But Mr. Daney would have none of it. Sure was a bull headed bugger.

Well, he got a good introduction to alder bushes when we hit that swamp. They knocked off his straw hat a million times; they tangled up his arms; they tripped him. When he tried by sheer force to bull his way through they knocked him down, and, of course, soon he had lost the old ruts completely. I followed and waited until he finally came to his senses, then led him out of the swamp up onto high ground and back to the trail again. There Mr. Daney had to sit down for a time. "How much further, boy? How much further?" he panted and he asked to borrow the bandanna he'd refused before. The mosquitoes had been pretty fierce down there in the swamp.

Nothing much happened from there to the lake except that he lost a shoe once in the muskeg and took a hard tumble coming down that last steep granite hill. Finally, I led him out onto Hedet Point, a big rocky ledge that jutted out into the lake with deep water on both sides.

For several minutes, Mr. Daney just stood there with his mouth open, taking it all in. "Lord, what a beautiful spot!" he said. "It's worth all that hell of getting in. And look at that island. Just perfect!" He sat down heavily on the stone on which hundreds of our men and kids had sat after heaving out a big bobber with a minnow on it. "Son," he said. "This is it! Just what I wanted. But is there a spring somewhere around so I can have a drink? I'm sure thirsty."

"No," I told him. "But the lake is spring fed, with spring water coming in under the surface. The water is good to drink. Here" I dipped in my felt hat and drank some to show him it was all right.

Mr. Daney was dubious about drinking out of my hat so I got some birch bark, made a cone of it, folded it in half and clinched it with a small branch slit lengthwise. He was surprised to see that it held water and he drank three dippers full before he had enough. Again he feasted his eyes on the lake.

Clear Lake is a pretty lake though there are hundreds as good or better in the U.P. It lies in a bowl of granite hills and on a quiet day like this one every feature of the skyline was reflected in the water, the spires of spruce, the taller pines, the white birch and the soft fluffy tops of cedars, everything.

Fifty shades of green could be seen in that blue lake and it seemed full to the brim under the labrador tea bushes that surrounded it. Then there was the island with its great pines only 150 yards off the point where we were sitting and white pond lilies on their flat green pads down below us. Yes, it was beautiful, all right.

Mr. Daney began talking to himself. "Yeah," he said. "That island is just right. We'll build a raft ferry to it with a long rope going over wheels at each end. And we'll have a big boathouse right here with the canoes and boats and fishing tackle. And behind us will be the men's and servants' quarters. And on the island, besides the master cabin, I'll have three or four guest cabins, a big dining kitchen cabin, and another big recreation cabin to hold the library and billiard table and grand piano. Lots of big windows looking over the lake…"

He fell silent and all I could think of was how he'd spoil it.

We sat there a long time as he talked to himself, making plans. "Yes, and we'll build a good road right to this point, and a bridge over that damned stream with a gate across it, and fence in the whole property…"

That was too much for me, so I interrupted his reverie. "Mister," I said, "I sure wouldn't put up any fence or gate if I were you."

"Why not? It'll be my property. Of course, I'll have the place fenced."

I tried to explain that in the U.P. we didn't like fences on land that we'd hunted and fished for years. "Just build your buildings," I said, and no one will bother you. But if you put up any gate or fence or no trespassing signs, they'll not only tear them down but burn your cabins and dynamite your bridge."

He looked at me as if I were stupid or crazy, so I didn't say anymore. Finally he looked at his watch. "My lord," he said. "It's half past four. We'd better be getting back if I'm to catch that train." Finally, he was willing to let me lead the way.

When we got to Clear Creek again, Mr. Daney decided not to tackle that awful tangle below the beaver dam, but to try jumping it like I did. Unfortunately, his leather shoes by that time were smooth as ice from the leaves and pine needles on which we'd been walking and so, with a wild waving of arms, he fell ass over appetite, plunk into the deep water. When he got to the other side Mr. Daney sure was a mess, muddy, wet to the bone, and sure stinking from the old beaver gunk. His straw hat had fallen off but I hooked it with a stick just before it went down the draw. Oh, how he cussed. I suggested that he take off his clothes and wring them out before we started walking but he just brushed himself off and refused. "Gad, if I ever take my shoes off, I'll never get them on again, my feet are so swollen," he said. He had to sit down several times before we came to the clearing, he was so tired. The last time he sat down, he talked about how good that bologna and rat cheese would taste when we got to the horse and buggy.

But when we finally got out of the bush into the clearing, there was no horse and buggy. The tracks showed that old Maude had decided to go home. I thought Mr. Daney would weep when he realized what had happened, but all he did was beat his head and swear. He lay on the ground for about ten minutes completely exhausted before he was able to start walking again.

We were fortunate enough to find Maude and the buggy three miles, and an hour and a half, down the road munching grass in a meadow. Although Mr. Daney was too tired to eat. I wasn't and as I drove the rest of the way, I munched the bologna, cheese and crackers as he nodded in the seat beside me. A long way back to town.

We heard the Chicago, Milwaukee and St. Paul train tooting for the cemetery crossing when we were still way up the pike. Mr. Daney looked at his watch, but it was so wet, it had stopped. He slumped in his seat. "I'll miss that train now for sure." he said. "And then what will I do? No hotel or anything else in that godforsaken town. Probably have to spend the night in the depot. Dammit, I could buy that whole town and I won't be able even to find a place to sleep!" I almost felt sorry for the man.

I got off at my house and he paid me five dollars, but didn't say thank you. Later we found out that he slept overnight in Marchand's hayloft under an old horse blanket before catching the South Shore to Negaunee and then the Northwestern Railroad back to Chicago.

For some reason or another, he never came back.

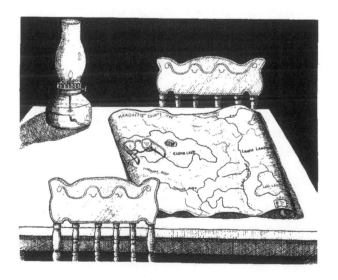

The Old, Old Days

In these tales of the old U.P., I have enjoyed remembering the people I knew as a youth in the early years of this century. But even when I was a child, I kept hearing stories of the real old days, of the strong men and gallant women who first migrated to our rough land, fought the elements and each other, and survived. Although the rock of the U.P. is the oldest in the world, the history of its inhabitants is very short. Indeed, most of it has occurred within two lifetimes - that of Sieur La Tour and my own.

La Tour was the oldest man in our forest village of Tioga, a wizened little man but still with black hair and good hearing. He was an uncle of a cousin of Fisheye's and that's how I got to be able to sit there by his cabin to hear him talk about old times. We'd bring him an apple, a half loaf of bread, or some cookies, and then ask him a question. That was all we had to do. He'd just start talking and we'd be there spellbound for hours.

Nobody knew exactly how old LaTour was. He probably didn't either but he was certainly in his late eighties or early nineties because he told us once that he was in his thirties when the Civil War was declared. The old man said according to what his mother had told him that he had been born in a birchbark canoe. His parents had been picking blueberries all day along the shore of Whitefish Bay just west of the Soo where they lived and were coming back when it happened. They weren't even able to make it to shore. That's all he knew about his birth but he did say that he remembered the cradle in which his mother rocked him and the brothers and sisters who came after him. It was made of a whiskey keg, sawed lengthwise so it would rock easily. They had painted it blue.

LaTour's father and grandfather had been trappers and voyageurs, couriers de bois. He recalled his father telling of almost drowning in Lake Superior off Tres Rivieres (Three Rivers) at the western edge of Lake Superior when the long bateau loaded with furs had capsized. One of his grandmothers had been an Ojibway Indian but she had died before he was born. Sieur La Tour had only a few things to tell about his early years. One spring afternoon we found him sitting on the bench beside his cabin door shaving thin strips from a chunk of white cedar. They were spills, he said. He used them instead of matches to light his pipe if a candle or a fire in the stove were burning. He couldn't forget how valuable matches had been when he was a boy in the Soo. Why, they were even used instead of money for small things.

Just about then a white throated sparrow began to sing in the lilac tree. "Ah, mes amis," the old man said. "Zat bird, she say 'Hard Times In Canady, Canady, Canady.'"

It really does sound like that. Then he went on to describe how it was to be poor in the old, old days in Sault St. Marie. His father was usually gone all summer hauling furs in the long canoes, and in the fall or spring he ran a trapline way back in the bush. So Sieur, as the eldest boy, had to play pere and feed the family. Fish was the main staple. There was an eddy in the river by Sugar Island where he fished almost everyday, mainly for trout. Sometimes he'd help the commercial fishermen dry their nets and be given a big lake trout or whitefish for his effort. And always, there were the many *lapin* (rabbits) he caught in snares or livetraps. No beef or pork ever, but venison, *mais certainment*, when his father was home to shoot a deer.

Suddenly the old man remembered a wild trip down the Sault rapids below the outlet of Lake Superior. In a birchbark canoe with an Indian and his father paddling, they had shot those terrible rapids. Sieur's job was to reach over the side of the canoe and scoop up, with a hand net, the whitefish that were swimming upstream. There were thousands of them there in the fast water and he recalled that he was half covered with flopping fish when they got to shore. That, too, was the year of the bad winter when the family almost starved and froze to death. "We fire all day and night and ze water she freeze in ze bucket by the stove."

LaTour remembered the Soo Canal being built because he had a job leading the oxen that dragged timbers to the site. He also recalled how, even before that, he had witnessed a sailing vessel being hauled over the plank and rail *portage* from Lake Huron to Lake Superior. He was "twenty or so" when the locks opened and the copper ore from the Keweenaw and the pig iron from Marquette no longer had to be brought over the portage by cart. With a wheelbarrow, he'd help unload the schooners that brought it to the Soo.

When the next son was old enough to take over his responsibilities, Sieur left home to make his own way in the world. He'd heard many rumors of the rich discoveries of iron, copper, yes, and even gold that were being made in the western part of the U.P. and that there were jobs for anyone who could work. He would go there and make his fortune.

Once, I asked the old man how he'd happened to come to Tioga and he answered that it was probably because of seasickness. He'd saved some money working on the Soo canal and had bought passage in a sailing vessel going to the Copper Country with a cargo of mules, hay bales, and bags of oats. At that time the early copper mines had to bring everything in, food and supplies of every kind. It was in late summer, LaTour said. After they sailed out of Whitefish Bay, they had encountered one storm after another. He was certain he was about to die, he was so sick.

They put in at the good harbor at Grand Marais and lay anchor for two days and then anchored again at Grand Island (Munising) for three more, waiting for calmer weather. When, instead of continuing to the Copper Country, the ship stopped at Marquette, again because of heavy seas, LaTour staggered ashore, hunted up a priest at the mission there and confessed his sins. He never got on a ship again.

For several years LaTour worked in Marquette or its vicinity but I'm not sure just what he did. He told of wheelbarrowing loads of couchons into the holds of sailing vessels at the ore docks. Very heavy work he said. These couchons (pig iron chunks about two feet long, also called 'blooms') had been smelted in the charcoal furnaces south of town.

Once, when we asked the old man how he became a lumberjack, LaTour answered that he started by cutting and hauling hardwood to the beehive kilns near the furnace, the kilns where the charcoal was made. He'd bought his first rifle then. Oh, yes, at another time the old man told us about helping build a plank railroad from the iron mines at Teal Lake to Marquette. Either my memory is faulty or the old man's was too, but this period in his life remains pretty vague.

Always wanting to go to the Copper Country, but unwilling ever to board ship again, LaTour had heard that there was a stagecoach route running from Green Bay to Houghton, so he started to work his way west to intercept it at a tiny settlement near Lake Tioga where they changed horses and had barns and sleeping cabins. It took him many years to do it, most of them spent working at the new iron mines at Negaunee and Ishpeming. He never went underground, though. "Me, I look in zat hole and say, 'Non, Non!' Ze grave, she is for LaTour not yet." There was plenty of hard labor to be done on the surface however and men were scarce.

When he got a chance to join a crew digging exploratory test pits for iron still further west, near Escanaba River, LaTour went along. He remembered vividly the great pine forest on the plains through which the Indian trail passed. Dark there even at noon, he said. No underbrush. No birds singing. When they came to the river and the granite hills, it was good to see the sun again.

But LaTour didn't like that test pit job. Too much down in the hole, he said. He had a mean boss and the food not only was poor, but there was little of it. After about a month, when he had to pack samples of rock back to Ishpeming for assay, he stayed there.

This time, however, he didn't work at the mines. He found he could make more money killing game for the boarding houses at the mining locations. Deer were plentiful and near enough so the dragging was not too bad. He'd get two or three dollars a deer and more if he butchered them. He also trapped a little. It was a good life, the old man said, except in the deep of winter when game got scarce. Then he cut wood.

Hearing that there would be good pay, LaTour also spent a year or two working for the railroads that were pushing into the wilderness. His first job was clearing the right-of-way and then laying track for the Peninsular Railroad which came up from the south to Ishpeming. He also worked on the Marquette, Houghton and Ontonagon Railroads that they were building west from Marquette. LaTour was there tamping railroad ties when the Civil War was declared. He was about thirty years old then.

We asked him if he'd thought of becoming a soldier in that war. No, he said. That war was far away and he was a Canadian. The main effect of the war on the old U.P. was just to increase the feverish demand for iron and copper. Jobs everywhere, the old man said. New mines were being built in every hill.

When the railroad got to the Escanaba River, they had trouble building the bridge and so for a month, he worked building kilns at Clarksburg. He didn't like that kind of work either and, when he almost got killed in the quarry, he quit to join a surveying crew heading westward along the edge of the granite hills. He was a chainman on that job and though it was easy enough compared to the hard labor he'd done before, he got bored doing the same thing over and over, and so again he quit, this time at the settlement that became Tioga, our town.

Already a lot of preliminary work was being done to build a new mine there: clearing the land, erecting cabins and a shaft house on top of our big hill. Down in the valley only a few stables, horse barns, and shacks marked the old stage coach stop but the stage was no longer being operated by the Welsh Brothers of Green Bay. Originally, the stage line had been started to bring mail and the payroll to the soldiers at Fort Wilkins at the end of the Keweenaw Peninsula. In the winter months, these were carried by dogsled. By the time LaTour got to Tioga, the stage coaches had been abandoned and only the winter sledges were still traveling up the old Military Road, as it was called, that skirted the south shore of our lake. Still intent on getting to the Copper Country of his dreams, LaTour once started to walk it but when he got to the big river that flowed out of Lake Tioga, it was a roaring flood. He tried to cross it, he said, but was carried downstream and so went back to Tioga. There he helped build a boarding house near the mine, and then later some of the company houses put up to house a constantly increasing number of miners, many from foreign lands: Cousin Jacks from Cornwall, Finns, Irish, French, and "Hunyaks" from Poland and other mid-eastern countries. Within a few years after the railroad came to Tioga in 1870, more than a thousand men were employed in the mines around the village. LaTour was one of them for a time, but he quit to become a market hunter again.

The demand for meat was so great that the mining company put LaTour and a couple of other men on its payroll to provide it. They also let them keep what other money they got from the boarding houses. He'd never made such good money before or since, the old man said, so he built a cabin down in the valley, and hid his pay of silver dollars in cans buried in the woods behind it. It was all spent now, he said, though perhaps he'd forgotten where he'd put some of the cans. Under his direction Fisheye and I dug around but didn't find any.

One afternoon, LaTour told us hunting stories for hours but I recall only a few of them. He said that when the railroad came with its telegraph wires, he and the other two market hunters cut sections of that wire and used them to snare deer. You had to find a good runway where there was a limber but stout young maple sapling. Then you'd make the loop, place it over the trail and anchor the tip of the sapling on the other side after climbing it to make it fall over. When a deer went into the loop, it would plunge ahead, release the sapling and be thrown. LaTour had caught many deer that way, he said.

He also described the pits he dug in the fall before the big migration. Back then our deer migrated south every fall once the first deep snow came and then in the spring, they'd return northwest to the hills. At that time these runways were old and over a foot deep, LaTour said. In the pits he drove heavy stakes with sharp points and then covered everything with thin balsam branches and leaves. When the snow came, the migrating deer fell into the pits and skewered themselves. Once he got a deer in each of fourteen pits in a single week, covered them up again, and after the next snow, got ten more. Meat for the winter, LaTour said, and no shells to buy that way.

His tale of passenger pigeons interested me most because at home we had a stuffed one in a glass case and they became completely extinct shortly after I was born. A big bird, the size of a barn pigeon, it had a reddish breast almost like that of a robin. There were tremendous flocks of them in the old days, LaTour said, sometimes thousands of birds in a flock. There were so many they'd often break the limbs of the trees they roosted in. "Wen zey come in zey sound lak tonnerre (thunder) and ze sky look lak night come." LaTour would hide in a blind under their favorite roosting trees and shoot them with a ten gauge shotgun, getting many with a single shot. Then the pigeons would circle around and come back and he'd shoot again. On one single day he got enough to fill a barrel with them, all skinned and cleaned. "They brought very good moneys," he said.

LaTour spent ten, twelve years doing this market hunting before the game got scarce and it was time to try something new. Having no urge to go back to the hard labor of the mines, he became a lumberjack, riverman and teamster. This was in the 1880's and he kept at it until Read and Company drove the Pesheekee for the last time in 1906 and all the virgin pine forest was gone.

The old man had many tales of his work in the woods, but I just can't remember them. He never was a sawyer for he said that he could make no sense of having to pull and push a saw all day for months at a time. Instead, because he had a way with oxen, he began by skidding the great logs down to the iced river roads with them, and then later he was promoted to be a teamster, hauling supplies from town to the camps. Then when spring came, he started driving logs down the rivers. That was dangerous work, but exciting, he said. He remembered one terrible logjam below Busch's Rapids that built up for days, and he told us of the horror that came when Brown's Dam let go. We heard about those several times but the one story he retold most often was the time they drove logs down the outlet of Lake Tioga right to Menominee and he had to walk back more than a hundred miles before he got home.

When our townspeople asked him to what he attributed his old age, he answered that it was because he had never drunk whiskey and had never got married. He'd had a good life, he said, without either of them.

LaTour finally did get to see the Copper Country, his lifelong dream. He was in his late eighties when he took the train to Houghton, looked around for an hour, then took the next train back to Tioga. Just some more mines, he said.

Those were the old, old days.

P. P. Polson

L ong before we entered sixth grade, we'd heard about the teacher we were going to get. "Just you wait till you get P. P. for a teacher," the older kids told us. "She's the meanest, toughest teacher in the whole school!" That was saying something too because back then in the old days, teachers were supposed to be hard nosed and they were. With a few exceptions, our teachers were the absolute monarchs of their classrooms, ruling the unruly by the threat or practice of corporal punishment. Parents never complained to the school board if a kid got a whipping in school; they just gave him another trimming after he got home. Uneducated, often illiterate themselves, they prized education as the one hope they had that their children might have better lives than their own. Teachers were looked up to in our town. Men took off their hats, and women curtsied when they met them on the sidewalks.

I'll never forget that first day of sixth grade. We filed in, took seats as far back in the classroom as we could, and covertly looked our teacher over. A big, strong Swede woman, P. P. Polson did not look up from the papers on her desk until the bell clanged. Then she went to the middle of the reciting platform in front of the blackboard, gave us a terrible glare, and said, "I'm Miss Polson, your teacher. You are my pupils, and don't forget it. I am determined that you will get an education whether you like it or not. I have rules and the first rule is that when I speak you will all sit up straight and pay attention." Whereupon she marched briskly down to where Arvo sat slumped in his seat, grabbed him up by the hair and dangled him at arm's length. He was a big kid, too. When Arvo let out a howl, she slapped him hard across the mouth with her other hand, put him down, and then calmly looked us over. "I trust, children," she said, "that from now on, you will remember Rule One." We sure did! When we didn't, our scalps regretted our forgetfulness.

She then called the roll. Rule Two was that the moment she said your name, you had to be out from behind your desk, stand stiffly erect beside it and say "Present, Miss Polson." Because those desks were sometimes too small for some of us bigger boys to extricate ourselves in time, we waited hair-trigger to jump out in a hurry. Miss Polson prowled about the room during roll call, occasionally examining us if we looked unkempt. "You're neck is dirty, young man. Go to the washroom!" she'd say. Or she'd look at our hands to see if they were clean. One time she kept Fisheye in at recess and combed his hair so hard he almost died. In calling the roll, Miss Polson always used our full names but she never was able to get Fisheye's right. She called him "Thissate" although it really was supposed to be pronounced Tisseye, which is where his nickname came from. French doesn't have any *th* and the final *t's* are omitted, but Miss Polson said it the way it was spelled - Thissate. She also had trouble on some of the Finn names, but no one argued with P. P. Polson. We just learned our new names.

Next, we pledged the oath of allegiance to the flag and not just by moving our lips either, as Lily Tomplin discovered to her sorrow. Miss Polson didn't lift her up by the hair; she merely cocked her second finger against the thumb and snapped it against Lily's ear. Although more than sixty years have passed, my own ears still tingle with the remembering.

In the morning sessions we had Grammar and Mathematics, then all too short recess of fifteen minutes, then History. Our afternoon classes were in Geography, Literature and Palmer Writing. No recess in the afternoon. The ones I hated most were Grammar and Palmer Writing. Miss Polson punished us not only for breaking her rules but also for not knowing our stuff. I remember one miserable experience up at the blackboard in front of the class when I had to diagram and phrase the sentence "*Only* Cully tried to fool Miss Polson and he *only* tried once." That word "only" was my undoing. Maybe the first *only* could be stretched enough to call it an adjective because it modified my name, a noun, but the second *only* came before "tried," a verb. How could that damned word be both an adjective and an adverb? My skull learned that it could when Miss Polson's hard knuckles impressed the fact upon it.

But the Palmer Writing was the worst. Gad, how I hated making those interminable ovals and push-pulls and never getting them right. No, that's not quite true. Once I made three perfect ovals in a row but when I tried to put the up and down push-pulls in them, I over filled the quill of my pen in the inkwell and plastered a huge glob of ink on the last one. Miss Polson did her best to motivate me but getting hit on the wrists with her ruler didn't help even though she did it five times before finally giving up on me.

At that, I was luckier than many of the other boys probably because I did well in the other subjects. Even so, I never once got a hundred on any report card. Miss Polson was a perfectionist and a hard grader. The best I ever got was a ninety-nine in history. Not in deportment! Though I tried to stay out of trouble, I never managed it. There were many opportunities.

Most of them came when Miss Polson had to go to the bathroom. They said she had weak kidneys-or maybe they were too strong. Anyway, two or three times each morning and afternoon she'd leave us alone in the classroom for a few minutes. (That's why, behind her back, we called her P. P. It wasn't because her full name was Paula Penelope Polson.) Sometimes we could see her getting restless, crossing and uncrossing her legs under her desk, and then she'd say, "Continue, children!" and make a dash for it. We rarely continued.

All hell would break loose. That's when the snakes or toads appeared to put the girls screaming atop their seats, Or the mice. Or Mullu eating a big worm. That's when the spitballs flew. That's when the snuff got put in the water cooler. That's when we hid her dreaded ruler or greased the end of her chalk so it wouldn't write. That's when someone put the egg in her snowboots.

Someone always kept an eye on that doorknob though, and when he saw it turn he'd say "Pssst!" and we'd be very good boys and girls studying hard again at our desks when P. P. returned, trying our utmost to keep from laughing. We had to be pretty careful, too, that P. P. wasn't faking it. Pipu Salmi sure got caught right in the act of putting a tack on her chair when she went out and came right back. For a long time, too, we couldn't figure out how she always was able to pick out the kid doing the devilment and punish him good until we found that she'd got Charley Olafson, our town marshall and school janitor, to bore a little peephole in the door.

Of course, we did some monkey business too even when she was right in the room but looking the other way. One favorite trick was to get a piece of rubber band, put it on the end of a pencil, pull it back and let fly. Gee, that sure hurt when you got it in the back of the neck. Our favorite target for rubber banding was Eva Thomas who had once tattled on us. She'd always yelp good. Even though Eva never tattled again after we soaked her pigtails in the inkwell, we never quite forgave her that one time. No tattling was *our* Rule One.

Not all of P. P.'s punishments were physical. She had a sarcastic tongue that could scrape the hide off our dirty little psyches. She also believed in making her punishment fit our crime. Any paper that contained even one spelling error had to be rewritten before you went home that night no matter how long you had to stay after school. Any grammatical mistake you happened to make in an oral recitation she wrote on the blackboard with your name beside it, and you had to write it correctly one hundred times, no matter how many recesses it took.

I don't know how P. P. did it, but she also had an uncanny ability to guess who'd done the mischief while she was in the bathroom. Once, when Untu had plastered a nice juicy spitball on the ceiling over her head by using a ruler as a catapult, and we waited for it to dry and fall down, she identified him immediately, picked him up by the ears, and shook him hard. Perhaps it was because he looked more innocent than the rest of us. That time, P. P. had to lift him by his ears instead of his hair because all of us boys had gotten our heads shaved. Shaved, not crew cut. I remember how unhappy my mother was when she saw me come home from the barber's, but I wasn't going to be the only boy with hair to pull out.

Speaking of spitballs, I got caught myself once because I wanted a supply ready when she left the room. I thought I was safe because I was chewing the paper pretty slyly and only when she wasn't looking. Later I figured out how she did it. P. P. really didn't have eyes in the back of her head. As she cleaned her glasses by covering one of them, it acted like a mirror. Anyway, she caught me, and that afternoon I had to stay after school and make spitballs until my tongue was hanging out, my mouth was so dry.

Yet there were times when P. P. did show a little mercy. When Untu, in geography class, said that capital was the turkey of Constantinople and we laughed, she punished us not him. She knew Untu always got his words mixed up and that only Finnish was spoken in his home. Another time, when Felix Poulet mispronounced some easy words, she didn't make him carry the baby nursing bottle all day like she did with others of us because his folks spoke French.

Much as we hated the old bugger, we had to admit that we sure learned a lot in that grade. I still remember how the Chinese made silk and that the British burned Buffalo in the War of 1812. I can still recite long passages from Shakespeare's Macbeth. To wit:

> "Round about the cauldron go,
> In the poisoned entrails throw.

Toad, that under cold stone,
Days and nights hast thirty-one.
Sweltered Venom sleeping got,
Boiled thou first in charmed pot.
Double, double, toil and trouble,
Burning fire and cauldron bubble."

Yes, Miss Polson sure made those witches of Endor come alive. She was one! Always too, we had to understand what we were reading because she checked up by having us paraphrase in our own words. Woe if we couldn't! P. P. also was a great one for mental multiplication. It disciplined our minds, she said, and by the end of that year we were doing three place numbers in our heads - or getting our tails disciplined. As you can imagine, our parents were much impressed. They agreed with old Blue Balls, our superintendent, that P. P. Polson sure knew how to teach.

Very rarely did she ever praise any one of us and when she did, you felt as though you'd been awarded the Congressional Medal of Honor or something. Just hearing her say, "Well done" was a real event. I suppose I remember her telling me once that I was a good thinker because the kids for days afterwards kept mimicking her, "Cully, you're a good stinker!" I got a bloody nose in a fight about that teasing.

I also remember how the days dragged that spring and how hard it was to sit still when the birds were singing outside the open window and the trout were waiting for me down in Beaver Dam Creek. At the end of each school day, we kids almost went crazy. We'd run around in circles, like young colts in their first pasture. We'd holler and scream all the way home and fight each other like maniacs.

Finally, at long last, our ordeal year with Miss Polson was almost over. We had a school picnic and then the next day returned for a brief hour to clean out our desks. On the playground before the bell rang, all of us were reciting, not Shakespeare but "Goodbye, P. P., Goodbye school! Goodbye, P. P. Damned old fool."

After calling the roll and hearing us pledge allegiance to the flag one last time, she made a little speech. "Children, (how we hated that term!), it has been my pleasure to have had you as my pupils for many months. I trust that you have profited! You will be glad to know that I have sought and been granted permission from our superintendent, Mr. Donegal, to be your next year's teacher too."

Geez! No fair!

WHAT? ANOTHER NORTHWOODS READER?

BOOK FIVE

The Man Who Killed Winter

John Kangas was worried about his wife Lena. It wasn't just that she'd stopped talking and spent the days sitting in the rocking chair with an unread bible in her lap. No, it was that she no longer kept the house neat and the food she put on the table was poorly prepared. How long had it been since she did a real washing to hang on the lines in the living room off the kitchen? "Aren't you feeling good, Lena?" he'd asked her. "Maybe you should go see Dr. Gage eh?" "No, I'm all right," she said with a sigh and she sighed often these wintry days. For the first time John noticed that Lena was looking old.

It's cabin fever, John thought. Lena had a right to feel depressed. Lord, this had been the worst winter of their lives. The first snow that had come in October was still there under the four or five feet of more snow that had covered it. Now it was the second week in March with little hope of spring because another great storm had swept down from Lake Superior building new big drifts and when it stopped a deep cold had settled in. Twenty, thirty below for days on end. For the first time in memory Silverthorn and Company had shut down their logging operations north of town because the horses and oxen, belly deep in the snow, couldn't skid out the logs and it was just too cold for man or beast. No one went outside unless they really had to. There was none of the usual visiting back and forth between neighbors for conversation and coffee. After you'd slogged your way to the outhouse and back you had to sit on a stool and plant your feet on the open door of the kitchen range for ten minutes before the cold began to leave your bones. Yes, it was a rough time.

Lena wasn't the only one in Tioga who was depressed. The whole town was in the dumps. My father, the doctor, said he'd never had so many calls from people who weren't really sick though they thought they were. "Sometimes I think they just want to see another human face, housebound as they are," he told my mother. "Of course I always give them a bottle of my special tonic which is half grain alcohol, strong enough to set their gullets afire. I tell them to take a teaspoonful every four hours. The old women especially swear by that tonic. Doesn't hurt 'em; just makes them feel better. All they really need is a thaw and to have the crows come back." When Father Hassel, our Catholic priest, came up for his weekly chess game, glass of whiskey and a cigar, he made the same diagnosis. "Their souls are snow-sick, Doctor. Only four people showed up for mass last Sunday."

One of the few people in our town who wasn't depressed was John Kangas. People called him the Happy Finn and he always seemed to be that way whatever the weather.

A big man with a big laugh, he made you feel good just to be around him. Always smiling, always joking, he often did zany things like the time on Midsummer's Day when he painted some crooked-neck gourds to look like penguins and put them up in his front yard when the temperature hit ninety.

John did his utmost to cheer his wife but his little jokes just turned her face to the wall. "Ah, Lena, it's March. Spring come. Sisu!" (Sisu is that lovely Finnish word that has no English equivalent. Roughly translated, it means enduring and coping gallantly. No matter what, you can triumph over any adversity. That word is why the Russians were never able to conquer Finland.)

But Lena wasn't having any sisu and John couldn't give it to her. She just sighed another long sigh. "Sounds like the suds going down the kitchen sink," John thought and grinned. If only they'd been able to have children all would be well. It was a deep sorrow between them. Perhaps he could get her a little puppy or a kitten. No, this wasn't puppy season and Lena had never liked cats. John went to the store and bought a pail of new coffee, a can of peaches, and some candy. That didn't help at all. He went down to the basement, sprouted all the potatoes, and even peeled a pot full of them so she wouldn't have to but Lena didn't even say thanks.

A bit discouraged, John shoveled a wide path through the big drift on the way to the outhouse, digging out three parallel trenches so they'd fill up first if it began to blow again. Lena didn't use the path, just used the slop jar. To make her comfortable, he banked snow around the house foundations to keep out the drafts, and he got up at midnight to put more wood in the kitchen stove, then got up again early to do it again so it would be warm when she arose. Lena didn't seem to notice.

Something had to be done. He'd go and get Dr. Gage to come see Lena. Maybe he'd give her some strong medicine. Suddenly, as John was putting on his boots, an idea hit him so hard it almost bowled him over. He'd make Lena smile. Yes, he'd make the whole town laugh. No more being down in the dumps. When he told Lena what he was going to do she said, "Oh Yonnie, you going crazy too now," but she smiled and patted his cheek. Whee! Full of exhilaration, John could hardly wait to begin.

But first he had to take down the stove pipe from the old pot bellied stove in the summer kitchen. John looked it over. Once that stove had heated their living room until the grates burned out because of too hot fires from anthracite coal. Then they had moved it into the summer kitchen to heat extra washing water but they'd only used it once. Lena had been after him for years to get it out of the house so she could have more room. Well now he'd kill two partridges with one stone.

Taking down stove pipes is always a dirty job. Even if you tap them first to shake down the soot always there'll be a cloud of it when you take off that first section. Lena appeared with an arm full of potato sacks from the cellar. At least she was out of that damned rocking chair, John thought. As she spread the sacks around the stove, Lena asked, "You not going move stove by yourself, Johnny?" "No," he replied, "I go get Okkari." He sure felt good now that Lena was talking again.

Okkari, his next door neighbor and good friend, was happy to have an excuse to get out of the house. "Yah, Johnny. I help. We use my big sledge with ski runners to take stove behind barn or where you want it."

By the time they returned Lena already had the stove pipes down, the cap in the chimney hole, and was shaking out the potato sacks by the back door. "First time for months she'd been out of the house," John thought. Cold as it was, a bit of fresh air would do her good. With a lot of grunting the two men finally got the big stove onto the sledge.

"Where we haul it? Back of barn?" Okkari asked.

"No we put stove in front of house, over there on little hill next to street."

"Why you put stove there, Johnny?"

John told him his wonderful wild idea as he was to tell many others later. "Too damned cold too long. I going kill winter. I going heat all outdoors. I keep fire going till spring come."

It took time for that to sink in before Okkari began to laugh and laugh and laugh. They kept laughing so hard they could hardly pull the sledge. Even through the walls, Lena heard them, pressed her face against the pane and they saw her laughing too.

After much effort the two men finally got the sledge up the little hill and then had to shovel a lot of snow before they hit solid ground. Taking an elbow off the stove pipe they erected a nine foot length of pipe straight up so they'd get a good draft.

"Now we build big fire, eh? Goodbye winter. Goodbye cold. Here come spring!" John went after birch bark and kindling and Okkari went to his house to get small wood and kindling, he said. When he returned, still laughing he held out a bottle of whiskey. "Here your kerosene, Johnny," he said, and they took turns tipping it until a column of white smoke rose up into the winter sky.

Entering the house, John was sure feeling good and he felt even better when he saw that a smiling Lena had cooked venison and mashed potatoes. Before they went to bed she insisted on putting some more wood in the stove outside. It was twenty three below zero.

The next morning John had pancakes with thin fried slices of salt pork just the way he liked it. "Get the fire going, Yonnie," Lena ordered. "There's no smoke coming out of the pipe." Then she giggled. Oh how John liked to hear that giggle. "Look, Yonnie. It's working. Thermometer says only nineteen below." It was the first time in a month it had been that warm.

So John built a new fire and had it going good by the time old man Marchand, our mail carrier, passed by, bringing up the morning mail pouch from the railroad station. "Whoa, Maude, whoa!" he commanded his old horse. Winding the reins around the whip, he came up to see what was going on. "For why you make fire in ze stove way out here?" he asked. When John told him the old man burst into laughter. "Ah, mon ami," he said, "I like zat. Ze winter, she's going to go now." He shook John's hand hard before he climbed back on his sleigh.

Okkari came next, then Reino, then some others. All of them had to put wood in the stove. "We make it through the winter now," one said as he tried to warm his hands. He almost had to touch the stove itself before he felt any real warmth. The men didn't care. They were warmed by their laughter.

That afternoon many others appeared to keep the fire going, so many that Okkari brought over some boards to serve as benches. When they got too cold, John invited them in for coffee and yakking. Lena didn't mind a bit.

The news of John Kangas' challenge to the gods of winter spread like wildfire through our forest village of Tioga. Somehow it twanged a universal chord: Make it through the winter. Make spring come. No more cold in the bones.

It's probably hard for people from Down Below to understand the deep hunger of our people to escape their yearly hibernation. John's gesture galvanized every soul in the village. They climbed our hill street to see his hot stove in the snow. They laughed themselves out of their gloom. Heat the whole outdoors! The notion was just so outrageous it was almost believable. Even if it weren't, it didn't matter. Just to get out of the dumps and laugh again was enough.

Lena had never before had so many visitors, nor had to make so much coffee. All her women friends and even others she didn't know so well came to see, to put a bit of wood in the stove, and to talk with her. Best of all were the children. Coming home from school, they milled around her front yard squealing, playing fox and geese. When one little girl, cold and shivering, knocked at the door to ask for a glass of water and to get warm, Lena melted, gave her a hug and a cookie too. It was a mistake. Soon many other kids were coming in and calling her "aiti (mother) Lena" and begging for cookies. Sometimes she even had to shoo them out so she could whip up another batch but it was so good to see happy little children in her home.

That night the fire never went out in the stove. Of course John had stoked it good before he went to bed but Charley Olafson, our constable and night watchman, filled it up again after making his midnight rounds, and Okkari, having to take a pee about three in the morning replenished it again. Then someone, no one knew who, put enough new wood in the stove so that it was burning fiercely when John arose next morning. Altar fires must not go out. That day the gifts came in. Pierre LaPoint brought up a load of dry maple poles on his logging sleigh behind the team, then helped John shovel out a place by the stove to put them. Reino Erickson brought two armloads of pine boards and split them for kindling. Okkari hauled over a sawbuck and bucksaw and every man who came sawed up some of the maple. Little chunks about eight inches long seemed to burn better. Soon there was quite a stack, enough so that everyone could have a piece to put on the fire.

Lena got plenty too. Mrs. Saarinen came with cinnamon rolls; Mrs. Oyalla with saffron bread and a tub of new churned butter; Mrs. Mattson with a plate of that delicious Finnish soft cheese that looks like custard pie. Several others brought big bags of korpua, that dry cinnamon toast for coffee slurping. All brought gaiety.

That afternoon Father Hassel stopped in on his way back from making a pastoral visit to Bridget Murphy and the beloved pig that she kept in the kitchen because it was too cold in the shed. Smiling, he too put a piece of wood in the stove and when he left, he said to John, "Bless you, my son. You have acquired merit," and the next Sunday he preached a sermon on the need to be joyous unto the Lord. "You have let winter defeat you, my children," he said. Then he told them about John Kangas and urged them to bring a stick of joy to put in his stove.

That sermon brought more French Canadians up our long hill street than ever before. You could almost feel the whole village coming together, all old animosities forgotten. Some even brought bottles of home-made wine: pincherry, chokecherry or wild raspberry. A festival it was. Lena invited them all in for coffee. For many of those French Canadians it was the first time they'd ever been in a Finlander's house.

Knowing the drain, someone brought up a huge five gallon coffee pot and five pounds of coffee along with four chipped lumber camp mugs to be used by anyone and soon the big pot was steaming on the stove. Someone else brought a box of Domino sugar lumps. When Arvo Mattila proposed that he'd bring over a big kettle of venison stew John said no. Enough was enough! The joke was getting out of hand. Too many people coming. It wasn't John's stove any longer. It was Tioga's.

Then the *Marquette Mining Journal* sent a reporter up on the train to interview John and Lena and take pictures. When it published a big article on the second page of the next edition, John and Lena were famous. Annie, the postmistress, posted the whole page on the bulletin board. More people came to see and take pictures too. Too much. John began to wish that he'd never gotten that crazy idea. What to do? He'd let the fire go out but our people kept it going despite his wishes.

I don't know what might have happened but the problem solved itself. A great thaw occurred. The sun shone; the great snowbanks melted into rivers that ran down the street. The crows came back. There was joy in Tioga beyond measuring. An early spring, thanks to John Kangas and all the people of our town who had put sticks in the stove. We once again had made it through the winter.

Valentine's Day

In the Upper Peninsula of Michigan, the U.P. February is the cruelest month. The wind roars down from the Arctic bringing one big snow after another. The pale sun has no warmth in it, not even enough to melt the hoarfrost on the windows. Yet, in our little forest village of Tioga there was one week in February that was full of gaiety and anticipation, the week before Valentine's Day.

Of course Valentine's Day wasn't as good as Christmas or the Fourth of July but it came close, perhaps because it came at half past winter. Flynn's Store always had a fine display of valentines on the front counter which we kids ogled but rarely bought. Only big people bought them to express their affections or their hatreds. Hatreds? Yes, some of the cards were terribly insulting. On the outside there might be a heart or flower but when you opened it up you'd see a picture of some old hag or devil with a bit of nasty sentiment. I remember one that said "Roses are red and violets are blue; I'm not so hard up I have to love you!" And another whose verse read: "I tell you true; I'm on the level; I hate your guts; Go to the Devil!" Oh there were a lot of them like that which found their way into the post-office boxes over which Annie Anderson presided. She said she never could understand why Old Blue Balls, our tough school superintendent, got so many valentines until she peeked in one that was unsealed and read the insults within.

But most of the valentines on the rack were nice ones, full of expressions of affection, pictures of pink cupids shooting yellow arrows into red hearts. Lots of pictures of flowers; lots of mush! Most of them cost five cents but there were some that cost a quarter. These had a lot of paper lace on them. And there was one that cost a dollar which had been in the valentine rack for many years. A bit soiled it was from the many hands that had opened it to see the accordion display of fifty little hearts, each containing the worlds "I love you." They say that Pete Ramos finally bought it one day when he was drunk, not because he had someone to give it to but just because it was so pretty. They say that someone who visited him one evening a year later found the old man opening and reopening that valentine by the light of his kerosene lamp and mumbling "I love you", words that he had probably never heard from the lips of a woman.

We kids never bought any of Flynn's store valentines; we made our own. Early in the week before Valentine's Day, our beloved teacher, Miss Feeley, had shown us how to make hearts by folding a sheet of paper in half, then with the school's snub-nosed scissors cutting the outline of half a heart on the outside edge of the fold. When unfolded, there was a perfect heart, a miracle. Fisheye, my friend, was so entranced he swiped one of those scissors and spent two hours in his outhouse making hearts of different sizes out of the Ladies Underwear section of the Sears Roebuck catalog.

I spent the week before The Day making some valentines. The first was for my mother. My attempt wasn't very good, mainly because I had only the stub of a red crayola to use in coloring the paper so I put the mess in the kitchen stove and looked for something already red. In the pantry I found an empty box of chocolates that was really scarlet so I asked mother if I could have it. When she said it was all right I traced a heart on it and began to try to cut it out but it was too hard so again when I asked for help, mother did it for me. I did cut out a smaller heart and pasted it in the middle of the larger one and printed on it these words:

"Roses are red and violets are blue
I try to be good but sometimes I'm bad
And that makes you sad
But I love you."

I wasn't very happy with the result. Too smeary. I'd put too much water in the flour to make the paste.

Then I made another smaller valentine for my little sister, Dorothy. She didn't get any poem - just a smiling face inside a traced heart - but she couldn't read yet anyway. That was enough work for one day, and time to get the paste out of my hair.

With only two days left before the big day, I began my major opus, a valentine for Amy Erickson, whom I had long adored secretly and from afar. Amy was a lovely little Swede girl with blonde curls I wanted to stick my fingers into. She was smart too, the only other person in my grade who made all A's like I did, but it was her up-tilted nose and wild giggle that really attracted me. Not that she knew it nor did anyone else, for I was very, very shy. Indeed I don't think she had ever looked at me or spoken to me.

For some time I'd been dreaming of a valentine for Amy that would make her notice me. I'd make the biggest valentine in the whole world, I would. Yes, I'd get some baling wire and shape it into a heart ten feet tall and cover it with cedar and ground pine and hang a red ribbon at the notch saying "Amy, be my valentine, yours, Cully Gage" and then I'd put it up against our classroom door so all the kids would have to step through it to enter. But we didn't have that much baling wire and the ground pine lay buried under six feet of snow and collecting all that cedar from the swamp, would take a week. No, that wouldn't work; I'd have to think of something else. All I knew was that Amy's valentine had to be a big one, bigger than others she might get.

After some thought an inspiration hit me. Up in the attic were some remnants of wall paper rolls from which I might be able to cut out a huge heart. Galloping up the stairs I found a dandy. It was blue mainly but covered with bright red roses. Using part of it to fold and cut a pattern, then tracing the huge heart on another piece, I had a valentine that must have been two feet across. This I pasted on a big sheet of cardboard to get the curl out. In its center I had another smaller heart of white on which I printed "Amy, please be my Valentine," but then I lost my nerve. I just couldn't write "From Cully." I could just see Fisheye and Mullu and all the other kids snickering. Finally, I just printed the letter "C" very small on the back side of the heart near its point. Maybe Amy would know I'd made it for her. Then I contrived a huge envelope for the valentine out of butcher's paper that my mother used to wrap packages and wrote Amy's name on the front of it.

I got to school very early on Valentine's Day to find that Miss Feeley already had the big valentine box on her table. It was a lovely thing, all covered with white tissue paper and red hearts. In its middle was a large slot into which the valentines were to be put but of course the slot wasn't big enough for mine so I just put it under the box, tingling with excitement, as I went out to play till the bell rang.

When it did ring and the room filled with kids waving their valentines, Miss Feeley called us sternly to order. "Here on the table is your Valentine box. Beginning with the first row, you will march up here and deposit (She then wrote the word 'deposit' on the blackboard) your valentines in the slot. We will then forget about them until after recess when we'll open the box and distribute (She spelled the word 'distribute' for us and wrote it on the board too) the valentines to each of you. Now let's forget about the box until after recess. Well, I hadn't expected that! My valentine to Amy was already up there under the box. My friend Mullu had told me on the playground that he hadn't made any damned mushy valentine for any damned girl or anyone else so I watched what he did when it was his turn. Mullu just marched up there scowling and pretended to drop something in the slot, so when I had to march up I pretended too. The sharp eyes of the other kids noticed of course and Mullu and I had to put on the macho act when teased at recess. Leo Belill overdid the teasing and I had to poke him a good one in the nose before he quit.

Finally it was time to open the box. "Now children, come to order. We'll do this efficiently and calmly. Each of you in turn will come to the box, reach in, pick up a valentine, read the name on it, and then bring it back to that person. There is no need to read the name aloud."

As she turned to the box she saw my big valentine to Amy under it. "Oh, here's one that was too big to fit in the box," she said. "It's for you, Amy, so come up and get it before the others take turns." Amy squealed with delight and tore the envelope off it before she got back to her seat, then waved it for all of us to see. "It's the biggest valentine I ever got," she said, with that wild giggle of hers.

As you can imagine, I was watching her very carefully as she read my valentine greeting, then turned the big heart over to see the tiny "C" I'd written down at its point. "Oh, it's from you, Carl. Oh thank you, thank you," she said as she turned to a boy, Carl Failla, who sat next to her. And she held his hand a long time. The dirty bugger didn't deny it and I almost died.

No one noticed my reaction. Then each of us, in turn, marched up to the valentine box, reached in, and delivered a valentine to the person to whom it was addressed and trying to read it on the way. The one I grabbed was for Mullu. It was a "You-know-who", a "From you know who." We all knew who. It was from Miss Feeley, our teacher, who always stuffed the box with valentine hearts for the children she thought wouldn't get any. All the "You-know-whos" were alike, just simple red hearts like the ones on the valentine box, and all saying, "Be my valentine."

Fisheye and Mullu got you-know-whos and some of the kids got a lot of valentines. I got none! I slumped down in my seat trying to hide my stricken face. Nobody noticed.

No one except Miss Feeley who came down and put her hand on my shoulder. "Didn't you get a valentine, Cully?" she asked. "Oh, I'm so sorry." "Yeah, I got one," I replied and pulled it out of my pocket to show her. It was a red heart with a bit of paper lace from the shelf paper in our kitchen pantry, and it said, "Be my valentine, Cully. From Amy."

Erick Niemi And The
Kangaroo Mouse

When I was a boy in he U.P. we had three kinds of mice, woods mice, house mice and kangaroo mice. Actually I think the woods mice and the house mice were the same species. Certainly they looked alike as they scampered across our floors. Every autumn some woods mice came into our houses to spend the winter with their house mouse cousins or they would hide in the hay and straw stacks. Rarely did they get completely out of control. Most of our families had cats and mouse traps and if all else failed Pete Half Shoes would let you put Mabel, his pet skunk and bed partner, down in your cellar for a small fee. Nothing better than a skunk to catch mice.

The third variety, the kangaroo mice, were much more rare. Seldom did we find them in our houses; they preferred our hunting cabins in the forest. I've only seen three of them in my whole life and that occurred when I spent a week alone up at our old hunting cabin just after Christmas one year.

My father who knew everything about everything said that their real name was jumping mice, not kangaroo mice, that the Latin term for them was *mus zapus*. Most mice can jump but the house and woods mice jump horizontally; kangaroo mice also jump vertically. They sit up on their haunches like a squirrel with their long tails behind them, then crouch down and leap straight up in the air, then do it again and again just for the hell of it. Maybe that's why some of our folk called them dancing mice. Oh, they don't always jump; usually they scamper like other mice when they are going some place. They seem to reserve their leaping for exhibition purposes, for jumping with joy.

But they also can jump horizontally if they have to. One of those I saw up at our old hunting cabin leaped from the corner of our table to the bench that holds our water pail, a distance of six feet. The furthest I could ever jump from a standing position was four feet and that kangaroo mouse did it sitting down. Of course I don't have a fat little tail to give me a boost. That tail, by the way, has a white tip while that of other mice does not.

Usually jumping mice hibernate the winter away except if they live in a warm cabin with plenty of crumbs. In the wild they subsist on an underground fungus, Dad said, called Endogone. which gives them both food and water but inside a cabin they'll eat anything any mouse would eat - which is everything.

I've had to tell you all this so you can understand what Erick Niemi had to tackle in order to tame and make a pet of a kangaroo mouse. Erick was one of Tioga's two hermits. The other one was old man Coon who had a gold mine up on the headwaters of the Tioga River. I've written about him and the three jugs of gold he had hidden in his spring in my first *Northwoods Reader* so I won't tell about him here except to say that he only came to town twice a year. Erick Niemi was different. He came to town twelve times a year, on the first of each month, to pick up his little pension check at the post office and buy his necessaries. Unlike Old Man Coon, Erick was always friendly. In the summers when some of us kids went to his little cabin by Horseshoe Lake at the edge of a huge cedar swamp, he was glad to see us, glad to have the company, and glad to have some of the little trout we caught in the shallow creek that ran through the swamp. We enjoyed seeing him cook them. First, he scraped the slime off with his hands, then he'd squeeze them. "Always squeeze them till they squeak" he'd say, then put them in a pan and fry them crisp brown. Never cleaned them. All the brook trout in that creek were small ones, six inches long or less and Erick ate them bones and all, head first, with some hardtack and tea or water for a chaser. Mullu and I tried them and they were very good. Sometimes we'd haul a pail of water for him from the spring at the edge of the hill near his little potato patch. No, Erick wasn't the kind of hermit who hates people. He just preferred living in that little cabin in the swamp. He didn't need people but enjoyed them when they came his way. Not many did because his shack was two miles from town and a half mile from Horseshoe Lake. Erick had been a miner and had a little pension which, with rabbits, deer, partridge, fish and potatoes, provided what he needed. He loved his swamp and the quiet, he said, and was never really lonely except sometimes in the long winter.

Erick's cabin was well made, though very small. So was its door; you bowed to enter. Inside, it was rather dark despite two little windows, one behind the small table, and the other behind the bench which held two water pails. On the west end Erick had his narrow bunk fastened to the wall and with its own roof of boards, the space above being a catch-all for tools, baskets, skis, snowshoes, oh, a lot of things. Nails on the logs held an assortment of clothing, blankets and cloths. Most unusual was Erick's stove. It was almost three feet square and two feet high. Fine both for cooking and warming. Erick said it had come from an old abandoned lumber camp.

Above the stove, suspended from the ceiling, was a long pole on which wet socks and other stuff hung. The only furniture was an old rocking chair with a seat of potato sack filled with grass, and an empty nail keg. Oh yes, there was also a table next to the south window with a dirty plate, cup, bowl and utensils. On the wall behind the table was one of M.C. Flynn's calendars, with many of the days crossed out. Erick explained that he crossed them so he'd know when he had to go to town for the mail. He had no clock or watch, just ate and slept when he wanted to do so. But all in all, the little cabin was fairly clean and on the table was a bean can with some fresh cedar in it. It was snug, and I guess that was the best you could say for it.

Outside the cabin there wasn't much to see except the swamp. Erick had a woodshed on the west side of the cabin that was filled one third with small wood and two thirds with chunks to keep the fire going overnight. Some kindling and birch bark filled one corner. Not too far from it was Erick's crapper consisting simply of a skinned log between two trees and a closed box holding a Sears Roebuck catalog. If it was awful cold at night, Erick said, rather than put on his boots, he just peed in an old Peerless tobacco pail and heaved it out the next morning. A simple life but it was good enough for Erick Niemi.

People wondered how Erick kept busy spending his days and nights in the swamp. "I don't have to keep busy," he answered. "That's the best part of it." Often in the winter he had a project or two. One winter he cleared and blazed trails all through the swamp so he could have easier walking. This particular year of 1915 he'd been making a snowshoe because the old left one was in such bad shape. Just held together with baling wire mainly. Anyway, making a snowshoe from scratch takes a bit of doing. Because he had cut them from a young ash tree the summer before he had the strips for the frame, and he also had the rawhide for the webbing. Boiling the woodstrips until they were supple enough to be curved around a snowshoe shaped path made of nails on a board wasn't too hard but it was patient work. Even more time consuming was making the holes for the rawhide with an old hand drill someone had given him. Since the bit wasn't the right size Erick had to burn out each hole with a nail heated in the stove until it was big enough to thread the rawhide through. Then he had to soak that rawhide and make pegs to hold it tight until he could make a new part of the webbing.

Just making a handle for his burning nail took a whole day. First he had to cut a length from a slender maple sapling, cut out a V-shaped groove to hold the nail, cut a little horizontal notch to hold the nail head, and replace the strip. To hold the nail tight, Erick cut a strip of tin from a pork and bean can, bound it around the handle and tacked it in place. It worked fine but holding the outfit in the coals burned his hands so he had to contrive a tin shield out of the can. That worked perfectly so he called it a day.

Erick never hurried. He didn't know what hurry was. He walked slowly, moved slowly, and talked slowly even when he was talking to himself. Rarely did he work at anything longer than a half hour at a time. Always there was something else to do if he wanted to do it. He could get a pail of water from the spring, or wander his trails in the swamp, or trim the wick of his kerosene lamp or lantern, or fill the woodbox or grease his boots. Usually he just smoked his old corncob pipe until he felt the urge to go back to his snowshoe. He ate when he was hungry and went to bed when it was dark, if he wanted to. Not such a bad way to live.

But when the snowshoe was finished about the middle of January, Erick found himself getting restless. Why he even went to town in the middle of the month, took coffee with the Pesolas and had a long sauna. After one sniff Mrs. Pesola offered to wash and iron his long underwear while he was in the sauna and he let her do it, then had more coffee and toast before he took the trail home. Why, she had even given him a new pair of socks. The new snowshoe worked fine.

Yet Erick still was restless. What he needed was another long time project for the rest of the winter. That evening it came to him in the shape of a little mouse. He was sitting in his rocking chair smoking his corncob pipe and watching the flames from the open door of the stove flicker on the logs when a mouse poked its head through the knothole in one of the boards of the cabin floor, came through it and began to dance in the firelight. Erick had never seen anything like it. The mouse would sit on its hindquarters looking around the room then suddenly take off in a series of leaps, sit down, then jump again. Finally, when Erick coughed, it made a long leap and disappeared down the knothole.

"I got company," Erick said to himself and the idea came to him that he'd spend the rest of the winter taming that crazy little critter. Climbing into his bunk he went to sleep trying to figure how to do it.

In the morning he remembered that this was soup day or rather soup week so he spent the time using his hacksaw to cut off a piece of bone from the hindquarter of venison that hung frozen in the woodshed. Putting this in his big cast iron pot along with some slices of salt pork, potatoes, an onion and a collection of rabbit and partridge bones, he dumped in part of a box of barley to thicken it. Barley? Hey the mouse might really go for that.

The cabin was too bright in the morning for mice because the sun came in through the windows on the south and east but by three o'clock in the afternoon it was really dusky, almost dark, almost time for his jumping mouse to appear. Realizing that he'd need to know what the mouse preferred to eat, Erick placed three little piles of food not far from the hole, the first of barley, the second of korpua crumbs, and the third of mashed hazelnut meats. Then, opening the door of the stove, Erick sat in his chair waiting.

It took only two pipes of tobacco before the kangaroo mouse popped out of the knothole. This time, however, it didn't jump or go for the food. Instead it scurried like any other mouse all along the base logs of the cabin, exploring, it seemed. It even entered an old boot before disappearing into its hole. Erick was disappointed. He spent some time trying to figure out an appropriate name for him. "Nikki," he said at last, "I'll call him Nikki." That made Erick grin because there was a man in our town, Nicholas Oland, whom we called Nikki and who really looked like a mouse with his receding chin, sloping forehead, big nose and large ears that stuck out from his head. Yes, Nikki Kangaroo it would be.

"Tulla Nikki," (Come, Nikki) Erick called softly and probably just by chance the mouse came out of his knothole. "A Finn mouse," Erick thought. "Already he understands Finnish." This time the mouse was hungry and it sniffed, then sampled each of the three tiny piles of food in turn. It ate several small bits of the smashed hazelnuts and, finding one whole nut among them, held it in his little paws and gnawed it round and round until it was gone. "Just like beavers." thought Erick. "They have to keep their teeth sharp." Nikki only ate a few crumbs of the korpua toast before trying the barley. That he loved. Made him squeak and dance. When it was devoured Nikki spurned the other food and disappeared down the knothole.

About every half hour that evening Nikki came back for more barley, Erick putting only five grains of it on the floor each time and moving the barley a little closer to his feet. Just before the man stoked the fire for the night and went to bed the mouse was eating barley off his boot. And the next night out of his hand by the boot. And the next evening Nikki allowed himself to be picked up and fondled as he ate out of Erick's hand.

I won't go into all the other details of the taming but soon Erick had a good little friend and companion. Often he'd come when called, run up Erick's leg and into the side pocket where the old hermit kept a few handfuls of barley. He never invaded Erick's bunk though and when Erick tucked him in his pocket to get wood or roam his trails Nikki just stayed there munching until they returned. Good company. Erick talked to him a lot and the old man was very content.

Then danger suddenly invaded Erick's little cabin. He'd been making the rounds of the trails in the swamp, had caught a mink by the creek and had snared a snowshoe rabbit. Nikki wasn't in his pocket this time; Nikki was a late sleeper. Rarely did he appear before three in the afternoon. By the time Erick had skinned the mink and rabbit, fleshed the mink skin, tacked it to the woodshed wall, and dressed the rabbit it was time for soup and a chunk of hardtack. Afterwards he was sitting in his chair enjoying his pipe when suddenly out of the knothole Nikki ran, squeaking in terror to climb up his leg and bury himself in the old man's pocket. What the devil had got into the mouse?

Soon he understood. A white sloping head appeared at the knothole, a weasel emerged, sniffed around a second or two, followed Nikki's trail scent up to Erick's foot, then began to climb his leg. Erick roared and brushed it off, tried to hit it with his stub of a broom, and finally the weasel went back down the knothole.

Few people nowadays know much about weasels, the most bloodthirsty animals on earth. Only about ten inches long, brown in summer and white in winter, they are absolutely fearless. And tenacious! Once on the trail of prey, they keep following it until finally they spring, clamp their long sharp teeth usually in the carotid artery behind the ear and suck blood until the victim expires. They feed on things much bigger than they are - rabbits, chickens, birds, and they especially like mice. They are killers, often killing many more than they need. Erick knew that Nikki didn't have a chance down there below the cabin floor so he emptied out an old cigar box full of things like scissors, needles and thread, bored air holes in the top of the box, lined it with an old sock and some barley, and after putting Nikki in it, tacked it shut. Now that the mouse was safe, Erick deliberated for some time where to put the box. At first he thought of putting it in his bunk but somehow he didn't fancy having a weasel prowling around his naked sleeping throat so he put it on the table instead. Day times he let Nikki out after plugging the knothole or he carried the mouse with him in his pocket as he roamed his swamp trails.

Weasels seldom stay in the same place long. They're roamers and so Erick hoped that this one would soon leave. But the bugger hung around day after day and night after night. Often when he'd poke his white head out of the knothole Erick would try to hit it with the stove poker but never came close. He tried to snare it with a little loop of picture wire surrounding the hole. Didn't work. He thought of suspending a large chunk of wood over the hole with a fish line over a nail that he could let go when the varmint appeared but decided instead to try to shoot it with his 22 calibre rifle. Erick hated to do it. Too much noise in his cabin. Too close quarters and the bugger, even when he emerged from the knothole, was always moving. Finally, after three misses, Erick got him. Not in the head but in the body and he had to club it with the poker before it finally succumbed.

I wish I could say that Erick and Nikki lived happily ever after but unfortunately one night a terrible windstorm tore through the swamp. Never had Erick heard the wind roar like that or so many trees going down. The next morning all his swamp trails were a tangle of windfalls. "Well, there's another year's project," Erick thought as he started out to see if he'd gotten any rabbits in his snares. Since the trails were hard packed because he had snowshoed them so often he just walked them in his boots. Just before he got to the place where he had put his first snare Erick was confronted by a huge windfall. Three big spruce trees had come down in the storm right across the path. Then the old hermit broke one of the unwritten laws of the woods: Never climb over anything you can walk around. Breaking off several of the stubby fir branches, Erick tried to make his way through the tangle but he slipped and fell hard. As he did so he heard or felt something crack in his right leg before a flood of excruciating pain engulfed him. Somehow he clambered back to the trail he'd come on but he had to drag himself. He could put no weight at all on that right leg. It shrieked with agony every time he tried to move it. How would he ever get back to the cabin, he thought as he lay there in the snow.

Though it really wasn't very far, it took Erick almost an hour of pain before he reached the cabin door. Trying to use a broken branch as a cane failed completely. Either it broke or the end of it sunk in the snow so far it couldn't support him. Eventually he fought the door open and slumped into his chair. If only he had a bottle of whiskey to kill some of the pain.

What to do? Trying to get to town for help was impossible. The chances of anyone visiting him were zero. There was enough soup to last for a few days more and he could put the rabbit in it with potatoes to make a stew. But could he keep warm? The wood-box was almost empty. Somehow he'd have to haul in some chunks and small wood and kindling. That meant he had to have a crutch of some sort. Maybe the old stub of a broom would do. Erick tried it out with the brush end in his armpit but the other end went too deeply into the snow to provide any support. Perhaps by crawling and then throwing the wood before him he could manage. Then Erick got the idea of nailing the cover of a coffee pail on the upper end of the broom. This meant sawing off the end of the handle. The pain was so fierce he could feel it behind his face but finally he got the crutch made so he could get in enough wood to last the night. Erick slept little that night. Spent most of it watching Nikki, now released from his box, dancing in the flickering light from the holes in the stove you use to lift the lids.

The next morning, when it finally came, was again full of pain. Once Erick had broken his arm trying to crank an old Model-T Ford and he remembered that Dr. Gage had set it and then put splints to hold the bones tightly together until it healed. Again in agony the old hermit hopped to the woodshed to bring back an armful of cedar kindling. Selecting some straight pieces and a strip of old blanket, he stood on that leg until he cried, then bound the leg first with the blanket tightly, then fastened the strips of kindling with fishline. Then he lay in his bunk only getting out of it when he had to do so. "Sisu!" he commanded himself. "All evils end!"

Many days passed before they did. They really ended when Annie Anderson, our postmistress, noticed that Erick hadn't picked up his pension check as he always did the first of the month. When John Pesola came for his mail one day, Annie told him about it. "I'm worried about old Erick," she said. "I know he sometimes has coffee with you when he comes to get his pension check the first of the month but it's been eight days after that now. Maybe you'd better go and check on him." In Tioga we took good care of our own, whoever they might be.

So one Saturday soon after that John Pesola snowshoed in to Erick's cabin in Horseshoe swamp, and then later snowshoed in again with Okkari and his sledge with ski runners to haul the old hermit back to town so Dr. Gage could treat him. Before they put Erick on the sledge he put all the barley and korpua he had left on the table for Nikki.

When my father examined Erick he told him he'd done a fine job of splinting, that he couldn't have done a better job himself. It was a simple fracture, he said, not a compound one, and the bones had already begun to knit. Dad put on a walking cast and told them to take Erick back to the swamp. He said it would hurt for a couple of weeks and to keep off it all he could.

So Erick came home again to his tight little cabin in the swamp and when he called "Tulla Nikki! Tulla Nikki" the little kangaroo mouse popped out of the knothole and did a wild dance of joy for him.

The Biggest Potato

Perhaps you remember Eino Tuomi and Emil Olsen, the Damon and Pythias of Tioga. They were the closest of friends, hunting, fishing and working together but each living in his own cabin separated from each other only by a garden. Eino had the cow and did the baking for both of them; Emil had the chickens, and did the canning of berries, applesauce and venison. He kept the marinating barrel of dynamited fish in his shed, while Eino had the smoked fish hanging from his. They dug and planted and harvested the garden together.

Sometimes it was hard to believe they were such good friends because they argued constantly, Emil, the old Norwegian, bellowing and Eino, the old Finn, just quietly and tenaciously repeating what he had just said over and over again until Emil gave up and listened. Perhaps you remember how Eino tapped the telephone pole on April Fool's Day or how Emil got skunked up at Pete Half-Shoes house or how Aunt Lizzie hornswoggled both of them into going to church for the first time in their lives and how they fled down our hill street clad only in their long winter underwear and their clompers.

Anyway, one April afternoon the two old buggers were down in Eino's basement sprouting the potatoes for the fourth and hopefully the last time. The two men stored all their vegetables there because it had stone walls and a dirt floor while Emil's had board walls and a board floor. It was dark down there despite the yellow light from a kerosene lamp and neither relished the miserable job because the spuds were already softening and most of them were small.

"Eino, dammit," Emil said, "Next year, no this year, let's grow bigger potatoes. These are not worth sprouting."

"Yah," said the old Finn, "but every time you come over for potatoes you take the big ones and leave the little ones."

"You're crazy, Eino, I take little ones too."

"No, you don't but I've hidden enough bigger ones for seed."

Well that was something to argue about again "Small ones can make big potatoes just as good as big ones can," said Emil. "In the old country, my mother used to save the peelings, and even they made big potatoes, and the small ones were just as good as the big ones. You just had to put four or five of them in a hill."

Eino said, "Big potatoes make big potatoes. Little potatoes make little potatoes. Big potatoes make big potatoes and little..."

Emil knew he didn't have a chance. "OK, OK!" he roared. "Maybe so, maybe so. All I want is we get more big potatoes this year. Tell you what I do. I bet you a bottle of Higley's whiskey I can grow a bigger potato than you can. I plant my row on one side of garden by my house and you plant yours on other side."

"And the one who grows the biggest potato gets the whiskey, yah," said Eino. The two men shook hands, knowing full well that the loser would share that whiskey as they had shared everything else for so many years. At least it was something to look forward to when the April snows still covered the land.

But those snows went swiftly and by the first of May they were gone. The first flowers, the marsh marigolds which we always called cow-slips, had lifted their yellow cups in the swamp pools. Then came the trailing arbutus, both white and pink, in which we could bury our noses and know it was truly spring. When its tiny flowers browned, the woods burst into bloom: wild iris (blue flags), Indian moccasin, lady slippers, pink, yellow and more rarely, pure white, adders tongues, blood root and Dutchman's Britches, jack-in-the pulpit, blankets of spring beauties, trilliums, and of course the violets. The white violets came first, then the blue and violet, and finally the yellow ones. Nowhere on earth can there be a spring as lovely as that which comes to the U.P. Almost worth the winter!

By the third week in May the ground was dry enough to plant the gardens and the potatoes. Oh the arguments that ensued! Eino generously brought out the big potatoes he'd hidden and offered to share them with Emil. "No!" said the big Norwegian. "Them Green Mountain potatoes we've been planting make too many small ones. I going plant Red Cobblers in my row."

"Red Cobblers don't keep so good and they full of bumps," objected Eino over and over again but Emil hiked up to Fred Longchamp's farm by the North Mine and came back with seven huge red ones. He offered one to Eino but the latter refused. "White potatoes best," he said, and that began another argument.

Then they argued about how to cut the seed pieces and how long they should dry and season in the sun before they were ready to plant. One good sprout on a piece, said Emil. No, at least two and better three, insisted Eino. Two days in the sun were enough to toughen the skin on the cut edge so they wouldn't rot? "No, three day, maybe four. In Finland always four," answered Eino.

As the cut potatoes dried, each man prepared his own row for planting. All Emil did was to dig a seven inch wide hole that was only about six inches deep, spacing the holes about two feet apart along the sixty feet of row where last year the peas had been planted. Eino thought that was too far apart, saying that only thirty hills apiece wouldn't yield enough to last the winter. One foot apart would be better, but in the end he gave up and used the same spacing.

However, Eino didn't make little individual holes for his potatoes, nor did he dig them in the old garden soil. Instead he began to dig a trench, one foot deep and one foot wide in new soil at his edge of the garden. "You crazy!" objected Emil. "Why so much work for nothing?"

"You'll see. You'll see," replied the little Finn, slicing off the sod and putting it on one side of the trench, then digging out the rest of the dirt to heap it up on the other side.

"You think you still mining, I guess," remarked Emil. "You nuts for dig so deep. Potatoes lie just under surface. Roots don't. Roots don't. And I put manure down deep, then put on sod, then more dirt from under cow manure pile, then surface dirt, then potato, then plain dirt."

"Oh, for dumb!" exclaimed Eino. "You think you plant roses, I guess. It's potatoes, not roses, you dumb Norwegian. Too much work!"

It was a lot of work and Eino was pooped when at noon he and Emil went into the Finn's house for a lunch of fresh baked bread, milk and a chunk of bologna. The butter was still pale, almost white. Cows needed green grass to make yellow cream and butter. Emil tore into the meal but Eino was too tired to eat. "Eino getting old," he said. "I go sleep a little before I finish."

By the time he awoke, finished his little meal and went to the garden, he found that Emil had dug all the rest of the trench and had enlarged his own potato holes. "You good friend, Emil," he said and the Norwegian answered, "Yah, you good friend too, Eino but you stupid dumb. Next time make holes like me."

The next argument had to do with what fertilizer to use. Now, back then in the early years of this century, there was no chemical fertilizer, just manure, but what kind was best for potatoes? Emil was for that from chickens. Eino insisted it was too strong, that it would burn and cook the potatoes right there in the ground or else it would produce big vines and few if any potatoes. He'd tried it once, he said. "Well, how about horse manure, then?" Emil asked. "We can get some from old man Marchand's pile..."

"No, no NO!" Emil was upset. "Horse manure burn too and full of weeds. Horse got only one stomach; cow have two to cook and kill weed seed. Garden pretty clean now; you put on horse crap and quack grass come right away all over."

"How come you know so much about horse shit?" Emil roared. "They got no horses in Finland - only reindeer. Maybe we go in woods and collect deer crap, eh?" So it went, on and on.

In the end, each man went his own way. Emil laid down a thin layer of chicken manure in his holes, covered it with two inches of garden dirt, covered that with an inch of humus from under the maple leaves, then made a shallow ring around each hole into which he put some more chicken manure. Also some pine needles for the seed potato chunk to sit on.

All afternoon the Finn labored hard with the wheelbarrow, bringing up cow manure from the oldest part of his pile to line the bottom of the trench. On this layer he then put the sod, grass side down, which he then covered with another layer of old cow manure. Next he covered that with about three inches of the new dirt he had dug from the trench. The trench was still six inches deep when he quit for the night but early next morning he covered the new dirt with a two inch layer of dirt, not manure, that he dug from under his manure pile. Black stuff, it was, and full of little red worms. Finally he shoveled in an inch of new dirt and called it a day. The trench was ready for planting at last.

The next morning they planted their seed potatoes, Emil his Red Cobblers and Eino his Green Mountains, but not until after another hot argument. The old Swede covered his with only two inches of soil but Eino used three or four. "Yours too shallow," Eino said. "They'll get burned by sun and turn green." Emil told him no, that all he had to do was put on more dirt and that Eino would be lucky if even two or three of his spuds ever saw the light of day.

Several weeks went by before Emil one early morning pounded on the Finn's door. "Wake up, Eino," he roared. "Come see!" A row of little green rosettes had appeared in Emil's row. "Yah, I tell you not to plant so deep. Norway forever!" Not a potato had come up in Eino's row, but Eino wasn't worried. "Mine come soon," he said, "and they have big roots and big roots make big potatoes, and whiskey for me." One week later his prediction came true. But then Eino did something that completely baffled Emil. He shoveled dirt over all those newly appeared potatoes.

"Why for you do that, you crazy Finn?" Emil asked. "Why you smother them when they need sun?"

"In old country we always cover new potatoes," Eino answered. "Makes them strong. You'll see!" Indeed they did break through the covering in a few days and looked very good. A few cold days ensued and there was a threat of frost one night. Emil took all his blankets off the bed, and all the old potato sacks, to cover his row. Had to build a hot fire and sleep in his clothes. Eino just covered his potatoes again with new dirt.

It tool almost a week before Emil's potatoes recovered from the flattening they got from the blankets he'd used and by that time Eino's had almost equalled them in height. Now it was time for hilling them up. When the old Finn saw how Emil was doing it, just hoeing heaps of dirt to mound them, he said, "No, Emil. You doing all wrong. You got loosen soil first before you heap." He took the hoe from Emil and demonstrated. "Big potatoes need soft dirt." After quite an argument Emil did the rest of his holes as Eino had told him. Eino banked his vines with dirt from under his manure pile.

Then came the potato bugs, the Colorado beetles. Now back then, in the early years of this century, there were few pests. No one ever sprayed an apple tree, for instance, because at harvest the apples were unblemished. Even today one can occasionally find a wild apple tree near an old lumber camp that still shows no signs of disease or codling moth damage. But we did have potato bugs galore. I remember being paid a penny for every ten of the yellowbellied, black striped adults, another penny for every twenty leaves whose undersides were covered with yellow eggs or pink and orange baby bugs. I'd drop them in a can half full of kerosene, then after my father had looked them over and paid me, I'd set fire to the can and cremate them.

Most of our people coped by just picking the bugs like I've described but some emptied out the cuspidors or soaked a can of snuff to make juice which, when much diluted, they could sprinkle over the leaves of the potato plants. Others who had more money bought a box of Paris Green to mix with rain water. That worked better than the tobacco juice and it left a shiny residue of poisonous looking green on the upper sides of the leaves. The trouble with both methods was that the undersides of the leaves where the eggs and young were deposited were left untouched, so you had to spray and spray again. No, I don't mean spray; we had no sprayers then; we used sprinkling cans.

As you can imagine, there was plenty of argument between Emil and Eino about which method to use. Neither had money for the Paris Green nor did either own a sprinkling can. So the Norwegian soaked half a package of Peerless smoking tobacco in a big pail of water, made a little broom of chicken feathers, and brushed the leaves with the brown liquid. Took Emil half a day but Eino spent a whole day picking off all the bugs and egg-filled leaves from his row, and then had to do it all over again several times because new bugs from Emil's row kept invading once they'd hatched from the underside of the leaves. He became so angry that he refused to go trout fishing with his friend one afternoon but the anger melted when Emil came back with six ten-inch brook trout, fried them crisp, and invited him over for supper. Eino noted that Emil had cut the heads off before cooking the fish which puzzled him. Always they'd been left on.

He found out why the next day when three of Emil's potato hills had little holes in them. "Yah, the old Norwegian grinned. "I bury two fish heads in each hill for extra fertilizer but skunk come last night and dig them out. All's fair for whiskey!"

Finally Eino's vines were just as tall as Emil's but the latter's blossomed first making a long row covered with pink-purple flowers. When they faded and dropped off, Eino's blossoms came, all white ones. Making a jar of sugar water, he patiently dipped a little of it on each blossom. Emil thought he was nuts and said so, but soon many bees were hovering over the patch. "Bees in flowers make big fruit," said Eino.

This coincided with one of the rare droughts that come to the U.P. For two weeks not a drop of rain fell. Knowing that blossom time and shortly thereafter is when the tubers are forming, both men hauled many pails of water from the well to soak the hills at this crucial time. One time Eino soaked his with manure tea after dumping some fresh cow manure in his rain barrel and stirring it up thoroughly. "That's crazy!" said Emil, observing. "How you going to get clean clothes now?" "I clean barrel," was the reply. Eino did one other thing too that made no sense to the old Norwegian. He got the rest of the swamp hay from the hay mow, now that the cow was in pasture, tucked it around the base of each of his potato plants, and then watered the hay too. "You dumb Finn," Emil roared. "Why you keep sun off? Potatoes need sun." But he had to keep watering more often than his friend did, and pulling more weeds.

One evening Emil saw Eino down on his knees, digging with his hands in a few hills, and pulling out some baby potatoes. Again he was sure the Finn had gone insane. "Let them grow! Let them get big!" he yelled.

"I get hungry for new potatoes," Eino answered. "Little ones the best." (And they are, too, especially when creamed.) But the real reason Eino was doing it was because he figured that if he pulled off the little ones and left the bigger ones, the latter would get more food and so grow bigger. "Yah," he chuckled to himself. "All's fair with love and potatoes."

July soon passed, and August month. No frost yet but Emil's vines had begun to shrivel and get brown. Not Eino's. They were thick and green and sturdy. "Give me two, three weeks and I get whiskey for sure," he said to himself. On September eleventh we got clobbered by a frost so heavy that even the grass was still white by noon. In the U.P. we call that the black frost because it blackens everything, everything except the forest which soon turns to a luminous symphony of scarlet and gold.

It was time to dig the potatoes. The first hill that Emil dug he got a potato so huge he pranced around hollering something like "Sittin de mai." It wasn't a pretty potato, being knobby, but it must have weighed a pound or more. Eino's first hill yielded about twelve large potatoes and two small ones but none of them came close to that first one of Emil's. The two men spaded very carefully, not wanting to slice any of them. A few potatoes always seem to lie beyond the hill in their own chambers and often they are big ones so the men always began spading far out before they lifted. I always loved to dig potatoes though I hated hoeing them. Earth's bounty. It was like digging for gold. To see how one little piece of potato could beget a lot of fat children always seemed miraculous. Sure was enjoyable.

Eino hit real gold on his third hole, one of those from which he'd stripped the small potatoes. It wasn't as big around as Emil's big Cobbler but it was almost a foot long and very wide. No scab. The eyes were flat and smooth. Almost the Perfect Potato. Eino stroked the dirt from its skin and showed it to Emil whose face fell when he saw it. But as he dug hill after hill, he turned up many other Red Cobblers almost as big as his first one. What a harvest! Those spuds lay there gleaming in the sun all along the row. Never had they had so many big potatoes for the winter. Almost worth the work even if they lost the whiskey. It was hard to say, until measuring, which man had the biggest. Each new hill gave promise that in it the biggest potato would appear. Yet they quit before they dug the last hill, as they'd agreed to do long before. That was their "hope hill", or "last hope hill." They'd dig that one tomorrow.

After lunch the two men sorted their potatoes, turning each one so the damp bottom side would also cure in the sun. One area held the really big ones, the monsters; another the ordinary big ones; and the third the few little ones. Then they had to choose which of the monsters was the biggest. Took a lot of time to decide. Once again a hot argument broke out, Emil holding that the biggest one in circumference was naturally the biggest. Not so, said Eino, the biggest is the longest. Or the heaviest? Worn out from arguing they selected the best potato monster they had and took it up to M.C. Flynn's store to be weighed on the meat scale. Emil's best weighed exactly one pound and fifteen and a half ounces. So did Eino's. Maybe one of their other monsters might weigh a bit more. They did some sorting but in the end, they agreed it was a tie. All depended on that last hill they'd dig tomorrow. Both felt that he might have a chance. Emil had peed on his every time he had to go out at night. Eino had given his hill extra manure and also cow milk in the water.

The next morning they dug their last hills. Emil sure worked carefully before he scooped out the monster of monsters, a twin potato so big that it was certain the whiskey was his. (I've grown a few twin potatoes though they are rare. They're two full grown potatoes joined by a common neck.) The twins on this monster, though, were as huge as the one Emil had brought up to be weighed at Flynn's store. Never had there been so big a potato!

"Yah," said Eino. "I think you win whiskey. I never see so big a potato, but I dig my own last hill first before I give up." He dug and he dug and finally unearthed a potato almost three feet long. Twenty smaller potatoes were strung along a peeled stick looking like a shish kabob. Then Eino took Emil's twin potato and showed that it also had been made by joining two big potatoes on a peeled stick.

They both began to laugh, helplessly. "OK, OK," Emil said. "How you know I make one of two?"

"Last night after I put out the light, I sit by window looking at moonlight," Eino replied. "I smoking pipe there long time when I see you digging in garden, then coming my house to cut branch from hazelnut bush by back door. So I go over your house and peek in window and see you putting potatoes together, then later planting them again. So I just make myself a bigger one yet. You got one more jar venison? We make a stew, eh?" A few hours later they washed it down with joint whiskey.

The Fortuneteller

I suppose that all villages have an amateur fortune teller or two who read Tarot cards or tea leaves to tell what's going to happen to you in the future. But Tioga had a pro, a real, genuine fortune teller, Madame Olga. She returned to our village, where she was born, at the age of 67 when she could no longer bear the rigors of the traveling circus and carnivals in which she had spent her life. Too much arthritis. She'd saved a few thousand dollars and hoped that they would be enough to last.

I got to know Madame Olga through my friend Fisheye who, for fifty cents a week, tended her garden and chickens, cut and hauled in her wood, watched over the old lady and listened to her wondrous tales. Every time I got the chance I'd help Fisheye with his chores so I could hear her stories. Madame Olga loved to talk and needed listeners so we really got an education about a fascinating world under the tents. Both of us were so impressed we decided we'd join the circus or carnival as soon as we could, and sometimes I'm sorry that I never did.

I'll try to piece together my memories of what she told us about her interesting life. Olga Beauvier, the only daughter of a French Canadian couple who had a good solid whitewashed log cabin down in Frenchtown in the valley, had always been an adventurer and rebel. After graduating from High School, she took the train for Milwaukee immediately and became a housekeeper for her uncle, a bachelor, who owned a hardware business there, so she could know what city life was like. Very beautiful and vivacious, she evidently had a ball on her off hours with a series of admirers whom she exploited to the utmost, but never loved. After two years with her uncle, Olga was taken by one of her admirers to the Ringling Brothers Circus and was immediately smitten by the bands, the acrobats, the rides, the sideshow freaks, the elephants and lions. On an impulse she applied for a job, any kind of a job, got one as a ticket taker, and began a new glamorous life that lasted forty years.

"Ah, my sons," she would reminisce. "The excitement! The color! The sounds! Never can I forget. The team work. The calliope. Everyone knew his job or jobs. Most of us had several. I had to learn to ride a horse bareback and stand up on it as we circled the ring with the band playing and me in spangled tights with a helmet covered with brilliants looking beautiful. And the applause! Sometimes I was a clown with heavy make-up hitting my partner with my broom to make little children laugh. One time I rode elephants for a month looking pretty way up there on the beasts. I sewed sequins on costumes. No two days alike. Then the long train rides to strange cities I'd never heard of. Pack and unpack, put on the show, take down the tents and do it again. Always excitement." I can still see Madame Olga in her rocking chair on the side porch talking to Fisheye and me on the steps. A white turban around her grey hair, a purple dress, and bright red slippers made quite a sight as she gestured animatedly. Once when she blew a kiss to the days that had passed she winced and cried out in pain, because of the arthritis I suppose, but she talked and talked while we listened entranced.

Fisheye asked her about the circus freaks. "Don't you call them freaks, mon petit," she commanded fiercely. "They had differences, yes, and made their living by them, but never have I known such gallant, fine people." Madame Olga told us a lot about them but I forgot most of it. At one time she thought she had fallen in love with the Human Skeleton, a tall man whose bones rattled in his skin. A very sweet man, she said, but not of the marrying kind. She told of the Wild Man from Borneo who scared the liver and lights out of the people who came to his tent to see his act. Really, a gentleman, she said, who, despite his ferocious appearance, was deathly afraid of mice, just like the elephants were. And the contortionist who practiced constantly and once got so tangled up, with his legs brought over his shoulders and crossed, that two roustabouts had all they could do to put him back in normal shape. Always the fraternity and comradeship. One big family.

Some of her tales were scary, too. Once a main spar holding up one side of the big tent broke during the lion act and that whole side of the tent came down. Screams and pandemonium. Another time they had a fire under the stands and the elephants panicked. Madame Olga had seen a black leopard go berserk and kill its trainer. Once the circus train had derailed in the night. At a time when there were no radios or television and only an occasional flickering movie Madame Olga's stories enthralled us. There was another magical world out there. Someday Fisheye and I would enter it.

One Saturday Madame Olga had a task for us. We were to set up her fortune-telling tent in the side yard by the raspberries. It needed airing lest the mildew spoil it and besides she was considering taking it to the Marquette County Fair the next month to make a few dollars which she badly needed. Perhaps she would hold a few fortunetelling seances right here in Tioga first to see if she could bear the arthritis and to polish up her old skills.

The tent was in her loft along with several worn trunks. It was very heavy but Fisheye and I finally managed to get it down the stairs and into the side yard. Madame Olga, using two canes, came down the steps to supervise. The poles were jointed and we had trouble fitting and locking them together as well as putting them up under the canvas but under her guidance we succeeded. About eight by ten feet and seven feet high, it sure looked good there in the yard with its black and white stripes. Madam Olga made sure we staked it properly and tightened up the guy ropes.

"Now bring down the green trunk," she ordered. Phew, that was a hard job too, it was so heavy, but we finally got it in the tent and opened it to find two collapsible chairs, a collapsible little table and a lot of black velvet coverings. Oh yes, and also a carved wooden box which, when opened, contained a beautiful black glass ball about four inches across. When you moved it, something swirled inside. Following the Madam Olga's directions we draped the table with the black velvet, put a white doily on top of it, and set the black ball on that. Then we placed an incense burner on each side of the ball. Madame Olga said she was ready for business but too tired just then to tell our fortunes but if we'd come back that afternoon, she'd do it. When she gave Fisheye his fifty cents she apologized for not being able to pay me too. "My money it is running out fast," she said. I told her I didn't want any pay, that I just liked hearing her circus stories.

That afternoon, when Fisheye and I returned, we found Madame Olga all dressed up in gypsy costume sipping some tea. I asked her how she became a fortuneteller and for more than an hour she regaled us with the tale.

It had all come about, she said, because once on her day off she had her own fortune told by no less than The Great Ozymandius, at that time perhaps the most famous fortuneteller in the land. She had been fascinated by the man and his uncanny knowledge of her life. She had been born in a log cabin, he told her, by a big lake. She had run away from home to seek her fortune in the city but had only found employment as a domestic servant for a man with a bald head. She had no brothers or sisters. She would soon be marrying an older man with a very black beard and would travel with him from ocean to ocean. She would have no children.

"It was all true," Madame Olga said, and in three weeks she had married The Great Ozymandius whose beard was black as tar.

He needed an assistant as well as a wife so he trained her and imparted to her all of his secrets. At first, she spent many weeks listening behind the other compartment of their tent as her husband told fortunes, or she served as a shill or barker to get the gullible to seek his services. The Great Ozymandius insisted that he had no special powers to foresee the future but that he'd learned how to read the body language of his clients and how to hypnotize some of them, and also himself. There were two parts to fortunetelling, he told her. First, you had to tell them things about themselves that only they, could know. This was done by scrutinizing the clients to see how they agreed or disagreed with any statement made by the seer. Sometimes it would be as obvious as the shake or nod of the head but usually it was the way they held their mouth or breath or other little signs meant yea or nay. Once he had learned these signs, he then started his patter, making tentative statements that could be completed in different ways, depending on whether the client showed signs of agreeing or not. if he agreed, then you continued guessing along the same line; if not, you took a new tack.

Fisheye and I didn't understand and Madame Olga knew it, so she gave a simple example. "Suppose I've already found out that the man is married but want to tell him how many children he has. I would watch him carefully as I said, 'As for children...' and if I see the sign for no, I would tell him that he didn't have any. But if I see the sign for yes, than I would say, 'You have one... two... three' and keep going till I get a yes response, and then I'd tell him how many he had. You follow up your leads, always watching for the yeas and nays. It's not easy to do but I learned from a master and became very good myself. One of the hard things for me was pretending to read their palms when I was really reading their face and body looking for positives or negatives."

Madame Olga told us some almost unbelievable things that she had discovered during the sessions, that one man had killed his wife, that a woman had tried to commit suicide three times and was planning another attempt. "Sometimes it almost scared me," she said. "They tell their own fortunes by their sign language. I just put it into words," she insisted.

"But how do you predict the future, Madam Olga?" I asked.

"Oh that's the easy part," she answered. "Much easier than telling them who they are. For one thing, they can't know what's going to happen, and I'm far away before they find out. By the time I go to the crystal ball for my trance to read their future, I already know quite a lot about them so I just guess what will occur."

"What's a trance?" asked Fisheye.

"I don't know," said Madame Olga. "The Great Ozymandius called it self-hypnosis. Sometimes I have to fake it, but usually I can go into a fortunetelling trance by looking into the black ball, prolonging the end of my breath and saying 'Oom' over and over again to myself. Then, when I get the feeling I'm half conscious, I start my mouth going and say almost anything that comes into my head in a strange voice until I run out of things to say. Then I wake up or pretend to and ask them what I've told them. Often the things they remember are the things they want to happen or are scared might happen. It's not easy work; it drains you because you have to be so alert. Haven't done any of it for three years now and perhaps I've lost my skill. That's why I want to tell your fortunes. But now a little wine."

Fisheye was the first to have his fortune told while I waited outside the tent. He came out radiant. "She told me I was going to be a soldier," he said, "and fight way over the ocean in a strange land. And that I would be an officer in command of many men." (Fifty years later he retired from the army with the rank of colonel.)

When I entered and sat down across the table from Madame Olga the smell of incense was overpowering. She took my hand and in a strange voice told me all about myself as she traced the lines and bumps. Nothing new; nothing that anyone in Tioga wouldn't have known. But then, after a long silence when she stared into the black crystal ball, Madame Olga came out with a torrent of words about my future. Her black eyes seemed glazed as sentence after sentence flowed from her lips. Finally, she shook herself and came out of the trance. "Tell me what I said," she commanded.

Lord, I couldn't remember half what she had told me. I would fly on a silver bird to lands far beyond the ocean. (This was in the days when the Wright Brothers had just made their first flights and I doubt that Madame Olga even knew about them. But she spoke truly. I have flown to many foreign lands, from Australia to the tip of Scandinavia and between.) Also she had said, "I see a great audience in a great hall and you are speaking to them. And when you are finished they all stand up and applaud." (This too has happened.) In that black crystal ball she had also seen me in a white suit being married. (A self-fulfilling prophecy? I did wear a white suit. Was it because of her prediction?) I would have three children, two girls and a son, and many grandchildren, (True!) In the swirls of that ball she had seen me on a great white ship on a sea surrounded by great mountains. (I have been on a white ship going up the inland Passage to Alaska.) But the most amazing thing, one which at the time seemed absolutely nonsense, was this. "I see you at the piano playing on the keys while many sheets of music keep unrolling from it. I see a room with many books. I see your name on a blue book." (Madame Olga couldn't have known about typewriters or that here in my book lined study are thirty-two that I have written.) I'm sure that there were other predictions that haven't come true. At least not yet. (One of them was that I would have three wives and a red dog.)

The Fortuneteller

Madame Olga seemed very tired when the seance was over and we had to help her get back to the house. "I don't know," she said. "Maybe I'm too old." She seemed exhausted.

Although she had planned to put up a sign in the post office advertising her fortunetelling services, she did not do so. Instead she went to bed for a week, finally sending up word to have my father, Dr. Gage, come to see her. After a thorough examination, he told her that her heart was fine and she'd probably live a long time. "But I can't, Doctor," Madame Olga said. "My savings are about gone. I am ready to die. Living in pain is no life." Dad gave her some of his purple aspirins and told her she must eat more, that she was badly malnourished, and would have to regain her strength before trying to earn a little money telling fortunes. Then he went to her neighbors asking them to visit her and help her. In Tioga we took care of each other.

Life was better for Madame Olga after that. The priest, Father Hassel, visited her, and mobilized his parishioners to bring her soup and food and gay conversation. Fisheye refused his weekly fifty cents but did all her chores and more. He and I often dropped in to get her talking about the old days but it was obvious that she was depressed and failing. Only Fisheye's Tante (Aunt) Cherie, an old childhood friend, seemed to be able to cheer her up, and discovering this, she came every day for conversation and to do the dishes and make the bed.

Later that month Fisheye's aunt had brought a bottle of chokecherry wine, a hunk of cheese, and a loaf of crusty French bread and the two old ladies were feeling the wine when Tante Cherie proposed that Madame Olga read her own fortune in the crystal ball. Madame Olga objected at first. "How can I do that?" she asked. Cherie suggested that she put the long mirror on the chair so she could see herself across the table. "But how will I know what I have said when in my trance?" she objected. "I will sit in the corner and tell you," her friend replied.

So, after the bottle was emptied and she had put on her gypsy clothing, the ball was brought out. It was very difficult for Madame Olga to get into the trance. Too many giggles at first. But at last her eyes began to glaze and her breathing slowed down. She swirled the ball and began to speak in that strange voice. Suddenly she shook herself and giggled again. "What did I say, Cherie? What did I say?" she asked.

"You say that you will soon be travelling again. On a train. And that you will be very rich."

"Ah, Cherie. It is as the Great Ozymadius, my husband, used to say. It's all humbug. hocus pocus. You tell the suckers what they want to hear. Oui, I want to travel again. I want to stop worrying about money. That is all impossible, of course, except in dreams."

But the very next day Annie, the postmistress, brought down a registered letter to Madame Olga. It was from Johnson, Beeman and Jones, Attorneys at Law, Milwaukee, Wisconsin, telling her that she had just inherited her uncle's estate of $342,000 but would have to come there to sign the necessary papers.

The Great Ozymandius was wrong. Madame Olga took the next train for Milwaukee and never returned to Tioga. Fisheye's aunt had a card from her from Arizona and that was all. It said, "Having a fine time spending money. Arthritis isn't bad. Dreams come true."

My Friend Rudy

Shortly after supper on December the first, 1905, two babies were born in Tioga. I was one of them and Rudoph Salmi was the other. Fortunately our homes were right across the street so my father was able to deliver both of us without difficulty though it kept him humping, he said, because both of us arrived within the same hour.

Back then all babies were born at home but Rudy was born in a hospital, my father's hospital. This occurred because the Salmis lived in its west wing, his father being the hospital's male nurse and his mother the housekeeper, who kept it spotless. They were first generation Finns who had come to this country in the late 1890's. Unable to speak a word of English, Saul and Vilma Salmi were met in New York by a cousin who helped them buy a ticket for Tioga, gave them a bag of food and taught them the English phrase "Where toilet?" He also pinned a card on each of them that said "Tioga Michigan." Another cousin met them at our village station, took them in and found Saul Salmi a job. They were only nineteen.

In 1900 when my parents came to Tioga it was not the little sleepy village it is today but a thriving town jumping with energy. Over a thousand men worked in its three mines and half again as many in the woods cutting the great white pine that covered the land. Tioga had been built from scratch in the forest and at that time was considered to be a model mining town. The Oliver Iron Mining Company which owned all the land had built a town hall, a clubhouse, a hotel (the Beacon House), a large boarding house, a three story school, many company houses all painted red and all identical, and a company-owned store to keep the people in debt. It built big frame houses for the mining superintendent, the mining captains, the school superintendent and the doctor, all of which were painted yellow. A few whitewashed log cabins built on rent-free land filled up the rest of our long hill street and there were many more of them on the side roads. Four churches took care of the souls of the inhabitants and three whorehouses and Higley's saloon handled their other needs. The mining company wasn't being altruistic in providing all these amenities; it just wanted to keep the men reasonably happy so they'd work twelve-hour-day and night shifts for a dollar.

When my parents arrived in Tioga the Beacon House was full so they were given a suite above the operating room in the hospital consisting of a bedroom and a living room. They took all their meals at the hotel, a block away but living in that suite wasn't too pleasant for my mother to put it mildly. The only child of fairly wealthy parents, she had been reared in a city in lower Michigan and had attended finishing school to acquire all the social graces. To suddenly be plunged into a totally different and rough culture where more than half the people couldn't even speak English was very traumatic. - Nevertheless she made the best of it.

My father, fresh out of medical school, loved the primitive land and its people. Dr. Beech, the company doctor, who had been overworked for a long time appreciated his services, taught him a lot about medicine, and gave him much responsibility. After my father had shot his first deer and caught his first trout he was hooked forever.

As she told the story to me many years later, those first months in Tioga were very difficult for my mother. She was very lonely and my father was absent most of the day and sometimes at night on a baby case. The groans and moans of the patients in the ward next to their suite were hard to bear and the screams of those in the operating room below her were worse. Desperate for female companionship she decided to hold a tea party for some of the young wives of the mining engineers and school teachers that she had met during their meals at the Beacon House. Fortunately she brought with her a complete tea service of Haviland china and she knew how to make tea though she'd never baked anything in her life. Since one had to have teacakes, she went up to the company store and bought tea and sugar, cream and two bags of different cookies, one of ginger snaps and the other of chocolate-covered cookies covered by gooey coconut. Unfortunately the cookies were so stale they were inedible.

Her mother had also given her a book of recipes and in it she found a cookie recipe that read as follows: 1 c butter; 1-1/2 c sugar; 3 eggs; 1 tsp baking soda diss. in 1-1/2 T hot water; 3-1/4 c flour; 1/2 c chopped raisins; 1/2 c chopped nuts; 1/2 c currants. Drop on buttered tin and bake at 350 degrees for 15 minutes.

Purchasing the ingredients, she went downstairs to the hospital kitchen where Vilma was doing the dishes from the noon meal for the patients.

"Paiva, Vilma," she said. (My father had taught her two Finnish words, *paiva* for hello, and *kituksia* for thank you.) "I'm going to have a tea party for some of my friends this afternoon and I wonder if you would show me how to bake some cookies." Vilma gestured helplessly and mother realized she hadn't understood a word. She tried again speaking very slowly and got the same response. When mother pantomimed stirring something in a bowl and pointed to the oven of the big hospital range, Vilma looked puzzled and said something in Finnish that left my mother helpless too. They looked at each other and laughed.

Then mother had an inspiration. "Come with me, Vilma," she said beckoning the Finn woman to follow her upstairs to the suite where she had already set the table with linens and fine china for the five women she'd invited. Vilma nodded her head with understanding. Then mother pretended to put some oolong tea in the silver teapot and to pour it into the cups. Again Vilma nodded. Opening the two bags of stale cookies she had purchased at the store, mother pretended to taste one, made a face of disgust, an put the bags in the wastebasket before pointing to ingredients for the cookies she wanted to make. Again she acted out putting them in a bowl and stirring. Vilma's face lit up. "Yo, yo (yes), she exclaimed pointing to herself and stirring in the invisible bowl. She understood. After the two had brought the cookie stuff downstairs to the kitchen mother again pantomimed stirring and putting the batter in the oven. Vilma nodded but, when mother picked up a towel to help dry the huge mound of dishes on the sink Vilma took it away from her. "Ei ei (No), she said, "Doktori vaino (wife) ei, ei." She made it clear that the doctor's wife wasn't to do any dishes by almost pushing her to the base of the stairs. Mother opened her little gold watch and pointed to the number four. Vilma nodded.

The tea party was a great success with good talk and merriment even though there were no cookies. Instead Vilma had baked a *pullaa*, a Finnish coffee cake. Never had they had such a marvelous coffee cake, mother's guests said, "so full of nuts, currants and raisins." Afterward, when mother went downstairs, she used the only other Finnish word she knew. "Kituksia, Vilma. Kituksia, Kituksia. Thank you so much," and kissed Vilma on the cheek, getting a big hug in return. They were friends.

That evening she told my father, "John, I've needed a project to keep me from being lonely and I think I have one. I'm going to learn how to speak Finnish and at the same time I'm going to teach Vilma how to speak English. I like her very much. Do you think it's possible?"

Dad was very supportive. "Of course," he replied. "You learned French and German in finishing school. Finnish won't be any harder. Just wish I could speak it. The only things I can say are "Where does it hurt?" and "How are your bowels?"

So thereafter each morning at ten o'clock Mother would go downstairs to have coffee with Vilma and the latter would come up to the suite every afternoon for tea about three. They began by building what a linguist would call a corpus, a basic vocabulary of terms for the things around them. Mother would write out the words she wanted to learn on a sheet of paper and Vilma would write down their Finnish equivalents. Chair was *tuoli*; oven was *yvni*; hot was *kuuna*; match was *tullitikku* (Mother often had to borrow one to light the little alcohol stove on which she made her tea); fork was *hanko* and knife was *puuko* or *veitsi* and so on. They would practice saying them until they got the pronunciation right. Mother had trouble with the Finnish *y* as in *hyvasti* (Goodbye) and Vilma had trouble with the English *th* sounds. Fortunately, Finnish is a very phonetic language, each written letter always representing the same sound, and she mastered them more quickly than did Vilma because in English the written spelling is often very unphonetic. Since they only learned about ten words a day both made headway.

Then came the problem of putting words together in phrases and sentences. Mother solved that by writing out the sentences she wished to speak and then going across the road to Dr. Beech's house where they had a hired girl who spoke both English and Finnish. She wrote them down and coached her on how they should be spoken. That helped a lot.

By the end of three months the two women were able to understand each other part of the time; at the end of the year they had only a little difficulty. Mother had sent away for three books, a history of Finland, an English-Finnish, Finnish-English Dictionary and a copy of the Kalevala, the great Finnish epic which they began to translate into English. The two women by this time were very close friends.

Then Dr. Beech left for softer climes and the Oliver Mining Company gave his big house to my father, rent-free, together with all of its furnishings, two horses, a buckboard, a surrey with an actual fringe on top, and a cutter for winter driving. The move meant that mother had to learn to cook and do a lot of other things. Vilma's help was invaluable.

When, two years later, Vilma and my mother discovered about the same time that they were pregnant, they were delighted, at least until the morning sickness hit them.

My Friend Rudy

Nothing in my father's dispensary seemed to help so one day Vilma made a brew of some wintergreen berries "like they did in the old country," she said. Mother asked Dad if she should try it.

"Why not?" he replied. "Who knows? Some of these old folk remedies really work. I used one the other day on a woman with a stubborn urinary problem, two drops of turpentine on a spoonful of sugar. Heard about it from an old French Canadian woman. Anyway, it cleared up the problem." So mother drank the wintergreen brew and had no more morning sickness.

From the first, the lives of Rudy and me were closely intertwined. Each of us had two mothers. As soon as the winter abated, Mother would bring me over to the Salmis when she came for coffee and to speak Finnish. In the afternoon when Vilma came to our house to speak only English, she brought Rudy with her. Somewhere there are some old snapshots of Rudy and me in my playpen with our arms around each other but with blank expressions on our faces, and of the two babies in the Salmi's big crib sleeping peacefully together. The two friends loved to hold each other's baby and once when I was very restless Vilma put me to her breast to suckle. This shocked Mother but she did the same to Rudy. When my mother found that Vilma was dusting flour on Rudy's bottom she gave her a big can of talcum powder. In return, when Vilma found mother's diaper pail overflowing she took it home and returned it not only clean but with the diapers ironed. There also are pictures of the two of us crawling on the Salmi's rag rugs and on the Gage's carpets.

At first Rudy and I could play together only during our mothers' visits but as soon as we learned to walk and could be trusted to cross the street we were in each other's houses and yards all day, in his every morning and in mine every afternoon.

I don't really remember how we learned to talk but soon both of us were speaking each other's languages, always speaking Finnish in his home and English in mine. I dimly recall a game we played called *mita* which means "what?" We'd take turns pointing to something and if I correctly identified the big kerosene lamp with the red roses on its globe as lamppu after Rudy said *mita*, or a chair as *tuoli*, Rudy would hug me and then we'd roll around on the floor. If I got it wrong, he'd say "ei, ei" and correct me. Counting in Finnish was hard for me but I finally learned to say "yksi, kaksi, kolme, nelja," and so on. I never learned to read or write Finnish so I hope the Finns who read this book will forgive my mistakes.

My *äiti* (Yes, I thought of her as my mother) always called me *Kalle*, the Finnish equivalent of Carl or Charles. Charles is my real first name but I was known all my childhood and youth as "Cully" and even my wife called me that for fifty years, hence the pen name I've used as the author of these Northwoods Readers.

I wish I could find words to describe our relationship. Rudy and I were not just the best of friends. We were much closer than brothers, perhaps as close as identical twins. We could play in my sand pile all afternoon making mines and never have an argument. Though often we wrestled and chased each other like bear cubs, we never once fought. We shared everything. If we went to pick wild strawberries or flowers for our mothers, we made sure that neither of us had a bigger handful. If we played marbles the winner always gave the marbles back to the loser at the end of the game. If one of us were hurt, the other cried too. I remember once that äiti caught us chasing chickens, a no no, gave Rudy a hard swat on the behind, and called him a "paha poika! (bad boy), which made him howl. I howled too and took her hand and made it hit me. She marched us back to her home, put us on the warm wide lap I loved so well, gave us a sugar lump to suck and sang us a Finnish lullaby till our tears were gone.

Rudy and I always helped each other do our little chores. We collected the eggs and fed the chickens and hauled in kindling and small wood to our mothers' kitchens. We put the potato bugs in a can that held some kerosene, then asked for a *tulitikku* (match) to set them afire and hear them sizzle.

But mostly we just played. In the winter we made snow forts but never threw a snowball at each other. In the spring we made snow dams in the wagon ruts and whooped when Mr. Marchand, our mail carrier's sledge broke them to let the water loose, or we sailed little shingle boats on the snow melt ponds in our yards. When summer came, we'd climb little saplings in the grove behind the hospital until they bent and let us down. We built crude little shacks in that grove and often would sit close together there in sheer happiness.

When occasionally we got permission Rudy and I would walk up to the mine, always hand in hand, to see the great wheels on the shaft houses bringing up the ore and the little tram cars hauling it out to dump on the huge ore piles. In the evenings when the bats circled overhead we'd try to catch one by flinging up our caps. Never caught one but we tried. Or we'd play aunty-eye- over, throwing a rag ball over the shed then running around to see who could find it first because whoever did could be the thrower, Sometimes we'd give each other the ball when we found it. Often at lunchtime we'd eat in each other's homes. Äiti cooked a dish consisting of creamed smoked fish on mashed potatoes which I dearly loved and there was a soft cheese called juusto that was delicious. But best of all were her hot cinnamon rolls, huge brown things with thin spirals of dough which we unwound slowly to get to the delectable heart. When Rudy ate at our house mother always played the piano afterwards and he and I, holding hands, would prance and dance wildly to the music.

When I was half past three my parents decided to enroll me in kindergarten because I was already reading children's' books and perhaps they felt I needed playmates other than Rudy. It was a disaster. I hated every moment of school. Every morning I fought my mother when she insisted I go. There was a lot of anxiety too, wondering if Rudy would be there when I returned. Finally, after a month of it, the kindergarten teacher told my folks that I was still too young to profit from school so Rudy and I were together again.

A year later when both of us went to school, everything was fine. Rudy had a harder time than I because he was then learning how to read and write in both languages so I often helped him with his homework. I remember that when he misspelled a word and had to sit down, I misspelled my word on purpose so I could sit down too. At recess we played with each other, not with the other kids, and we protected each other. Once, when Pipu Viirta, a big kid, teased and hit me, Rudy swarmed all over him and together we got him down rubbing his nose in the dust until he fled away crying. Triumphant, we hugged each other all the way home.

Our seventh year was a delight. My father commissioned an old Finn to make a set of skis for both of us so the winter went swiftly. That summer we both learned to swim, or rather dog-paddle in the shallow water of Fish Lake. We hunted birds and chipmunks with slingshots but never killed any. We hiked down to the beaver pond and caught trout. We explored the edges of the forest. Comrades!

That fall a very virulent type of scarlet fever hit Tioga and Rudy and I contracted it on the same day. We were both very sick. I still remember the hallucinations I had, the cold cloths they kept putting on my forehead, the burning of the fever, the cool hands of my äiti and my mother. This happened long before there were any sulpha drugs or antibiotics and despite my father's heroic efforts several of his patients died.

Rudy was one of them.

When, after two weeks of very serious illness, I recovered enough to walk about, my mother told me. "Rudy was very sick too," she said weeping, "but he died and is in heaven." I could not believe it. "No!" I said. "No! No! He's right across the street." She tried to hold me but I broke away. When äiti saw me she too began to cry. *"Missa* (where) Rudy?" I asked her. "Can he come out to play?" äiti picked me up, hugged me hard, and rocked me in her arms as she weepingly told me that yes Rudy was dead, that he was in heaven, and that I'd never see him again, I wept inconsolably for a long time. It was impossible. Missa Rudy? Missa Rudy? Because every night I prayed hard to God that Rudy would be at his home when I went there, I said the same thing to äiti morning after morning: "Missa Rudy? Can he come out to play?" but he wasn't there. Finally one day she took me to his little grave in the hill cemetery, showed me the small rock slab that said "Rudolph Salmi 1905-1912". We wept together and I wept again seventy years later when I saw that marker so hard to read.

I remember praying to God that he would take me up to heaven too so I could be with my friend. "Now I lay me down to sleep/I pray the Lord my soul will keep/If I should die before I wake..." Yes, dear lord, let me die before I wake so I can be with Rudy in your heaven. But He didn't take me and for weeks I felt guilty just for being alive, for just being able to walk or to move a finger.

Few adults can comprehend the intensity of a child's grief when he has lost a loved one but I do. My world was empty. Half of me was gone. I had uncontrollable crying spells even in school. At home I would sit for hours pretending to be reading a book. Often I had fits of uncontrollable rage. It wasn't fair! It wasn't fair!

Then I had a period in which I couldn't bear to go across the road to see my äiti because it hurt too much. Instead I developed a fantasy life. Rudolph and I were the sons of Captain January, a lighthouse keeper. Day after day we would climb the circular stairs to fill the lamps with kerosene or to polish the big lenses. We'd sit for hours on the sand watching the big waves roll in. We'd put our arms around each other and talk. Sometimes when I was living this fantasy at home my parents worried because they couldn't get through to me.

Just as I was partially healing there came another blow. Suddenly one afternoon a great cave-in at the mine occurred, breaking the sidewalks and smothering the sun with a huge cloud of dust. The next morning officials of the mining company came down from Duluth, looked the situation over and decided to close the mine, close it forever. All the employees were dismissed, the hospital was closed, and the Salmis moved to Ishpeming.

I had lost my äiti too.

To Bed, To Bed,
You Sleepy Head!

When Alf Jensen and Helga Svenson got married the whole town of Tioga as delighted. Never such a fine young couple. Made for each other, they were. Both were Scandehoovians. Alf was Norwegian and Helga was Swedish which might possibly cause some trouble but they had been sweethearts since grade school and never had any fights. No, it was a good match. Alf had inherited a fine house from his parents with a hayfield and barn and chickenyard. Helga had worked as a hired girl and cook for a rich family in Marquette for a year so she knew how to keep house. Alf had a good steady job as a section hand on the railroad. Yes, they'd have a good marriage and lots of kids.

The wedding in the Swedish Lutheran Church cost five dollars for rent, fifteen for the preacher who had to come up on the train from Ishpeming, two dollars for a license, and five more for the chivaree they knew would be forthcoming. Because all of us liked them it came mercifully early in the evening before they'd gone to bed and only lasted an hour or so. Helga made Alf a good snack before they retired and the loving was very good too. It had been a long day so Alf promptly fell asleep. Helga did not.

As Helga looked lovingly at that strong young man beside her in bed, she felt both happy and lucky. But not for long. Suddenly from his open mouth came a sort of catch, then a sudden throbbing inhalation. It was very loud and those that followed were louder yet. Then came a snort and a whistling noise and finally a bit of merciful silence. Helga closed her eyes seeking sleep but almost jumped out of bed when a whole series of snorts, gurgles, and nose grunts built up into a crescendo that rattled the rafters. Helga, with great effort, finally shook him awake.

"What's a matter?" Alf asked sleepily.

"You snore so loud I can't sleep." replied Helga. "Turn over on your side." Alf did but he turned facing her and soon was snoring in her ear. She tried to turn him over the other way but he was too heavy to move and he was snoring even worse, if that were possible. Finally she gave up and went into the kitchen to sit in the rocking chair by the stove.

Her thoughts were not pleasant ones. She had married a monster. She would never be able to get a night's sleep again. Did Alf know how awfully he snored? He should have told her. Could she ever get used to it? Maybe in fifty years. Without sleep she'd turn into an old hag. Self-pity and anger flooded over her. Was there any way to stop such terrible snoring?

240

To Bed, To Bed, You Sleepy Head!

Finally she went back to bed, pulling the covers over her head but that didn't help much. Then she tried to go to sleep with her fingers in her ears to block out the wheezes, croaking, sizzles and loud fluttering snorts but to no avail. She wanted to hit him in the mouth, to cork that open mouth with a dishrag. It infuriated her to see him sleeping so deeply and happily while filling the bedroom with bedlam. Her wedding night! And thousands more to go!

Helga probably did sleep a few winks or two but in the morning when Alf became amorous she refused his advances, telling him in no uncertain terms that she hadn't slept a bit all night because of his snoring. She did get up to stagger around the kitchen getting his breakfast but she told Alf he'd have to pack his own dinner pail, that she was so exhausted she was going back to bed. This she did and slept until noon.

That afternoon, revived, Helga baked bread and rolls and made a fine pot roast supper to welcome Alf when he returned from work. Everything seemed perfect and the loving that night did too. After it was over Alf suggested that she go to sleep first, that he'd sit in the kitchen for an hour before coming back to bed. Ah, he was a good man, Helga thought, a kind one. They'd have a fine marriage after all. But she couldn't go to sleep, try as hard as she could, and was still wide awake when he came, lay down and started snoring immediately. It was another long, utterly miserable night for the new bride. Something had to be done.

The next day, Sunday, Alf didn't have to work so eventually they had the time for some straight talk. Helga asked him if he knew he snored so loudly before he proposed.

After long thought Alf answered. "Yah, I guess I knew but I never think of it. All I could think of was you, Helga. I don't ever hear myself snore so I don't know how it sounds. Last year, though, Iggy and Reino and Sven asked me to spend a week with them hunting deer by their cabin on the South Fork and after the first night in camp they kicked me out. Said I snored so loud none of them could sleep. So I guess I knew but didn't think to tell you. Would you have married me if you had known?"

Helga got up and put her arms around his neck from behind his chair. "Oh yah, Alfie. I marry you no matter what. I'll get used to it." But she asked him to make her some ear plugs. He spent most of the afternoon whittling them out of basswood. Little tiny things they were, fitted carefully to her ears with many kisses and wrapped in cloth saturated with beeswax. When she tried them out, Olga could barely hear what he said to her. They worked!

After more wonderful loving that night she put in the ear plugs and waited for that first horrible snore. It came soon enough but it was muted. She could hear it but it wasn't really very loud so Helga yawned and closed her eyes. Unfortunately she found that every time she yawned, or sometimes even if she swallowed, her ears ached and, being so tired, she yawned a lot. It's hard to keep from yawning or swallowing so, despite a few brief catnaps, Helga got up, took out the ear plugs, and tried to sleep in the rocking chair again. Another very long, miserable night, but by morning Alf found it hard to waken her when it was time to make coffee, probably because the ear plugs were in place. When Helga told him that again she had slept very little, he found it hard to believe her.

That evening before they went to bed Alf asked her to tell him or show him how he snored so he could understand what she had to put up with. Somehow she couldn't so she spent much of that studying his snorings and making a list and practicing. Some were very hard to describe in words and a few she just couldn't imitate but the list she showed him the next morning and demonstrated went like this "catch, throat flutter, snort, whistle, gurgle and gargle, nose grunts, three kinds of moans, sizzle, sudden hoots or yelps." Alf was shocked. "No wonder you can't sleep," he said. "I didn't know it was so bad. You think you can ever get used to it?"

"I must," Helga replied. "But it's harder because you snore so many different ways. If you did it only one way it would be easy to blot out. But, Alf, I noticed too that you never snore if your mouth is shut - only when it hangs open. Maybe you got a crooked bone in your nose so you can't push much air out of it?"

"I'll try tonight to keep my mouth shut and breathe through my nose" said Alf, "and if that doesn't work I'll go see Dr. Gage and have him take a look. OK?" Helga nodded.

Helga almost felt sorry for her husband when that night he kept saying to himself over and over again, first aloud, then in a whisper and finally with only his lips moving, "Breathe nose; no breathe mouth." He really tried, Alf did, but tired from the days heavy labor he was soon asleep with the jaw hanging down and snoring hard and loud. Helga tried to get used to it, to ignore it, to think of other things or to try to bear the ear plugs longer but she was back in the chair again at midnight. Alf roused, found her gone, and sleepily staggered into the kitchen. "Oh Helga, I'm so sorry. I tried to keep my mouth shut but when I sleep I forget, I guess. Tie a scarf over my head and jaw so I won't open it." She was very touched by his concern and hugged him hard as she put on the scarf. He was a sweet man. But it didn't work. Kept slipping off.

True to his word, Alf went to see my father, the doctor, the next day and explained the situation. Dad was sympathetic and said snoring could be a real problem - especially in a new marriage. Then he cooled a little mirror with a long handle under a faucet and placed it under each nostril as he compressed the side of Alf's nose, first on one side, then the other. "'No," he said, "there's no blockage." Putting on his headband with the big round mirror with a hole in it, Dad focussed some light on each opening to see if they were clear, and then had Alf open his mouth wide so the throat could be examined. "Your uvula, (that's the little thing that hangs down between your tonsils) is a bit long but not enough to cause the trouble. No, Alf" he said, "there's nothing organically wrong with you; there's no drug that can help either. Modern medicine has a lot of problems with no solutions and snoring is one of them. You don't have to feel guilt about it. Some men snore and some don't. There's no cure. Oh, I've heard that the old Finns have a cure but I don't know what it is. Probably just nonsense." Dad didn't charge Alf anything for the examination.

The next day Helga went to see our town's Wise Woman, Mrs. Matson, to ask if she knew the Finnish cure for snoring. "Yah," said the wise woman. "You get some limburger cheese or better yet the Norwegian gammelost which they ripen in a manure pile over the winter. Limburger stinks like hell and gammelost even worse. What you do is wait till he's in deep sleep and snoring, then you smear some of it just below the nose. Don't let him see you doing it or he'll hit you." The wise woman lit her corncob pipe. "Yah, works fine every time."

When Helga, desperate enough to try anything, went to Flynn's store, Mr. Flynn said he didn't carry any limburger or gammelost cheese. Never had and never would.

They stank too much. But he told her that he'd heard the Leif Backe family still made gammelost in old country way and perhaps she could beg some from them. "Be sure to have them wrap it good," Mr. Flynn said, "or you'll stink up the whole town. Why you want that awful stuff?"

Helga didn't tell him but she did get a little jar of gammelost from the Backes. "Best to eat only a little of it on a lot of crackers and wash it down with aquavit fast," they advised her.

Helga didn't feel good about the whole thing but, desperate after having no sleep until three in the morning, she dipped her finger in the jar and gingerly smeared some of the soft cheese above his upper lip when he was snoring something awful. She was seared. Maybe Alf would hit her and, if he did, she wouldn't blame him. In just a moment, Alf's snoring stopped dead in its tracks. He snorted three times, then, without opening his eyes, he said, "Helga! Move down! Move down!"

"Move down!" The implication hit her like a rock. Helga wanted to kill him right there in bed but all she did was slap him hard across the face, sweep the deena (the goose down comforter) off her sleeping and again snoring husband, and weeping went to the kitchen to roll up in it by the stove. Her finger stank. She resolved that she would move out in the morning though she knew her family would not let her come home. No, not for a little thing like snoring. They would tell her she had made her bed and would have to lie in it. Divorce? No, that was impossible. No one got divorced in Tioga. She had no money.

Helga was still sobbing in the deena when Alf appeared. "Helga," he said, "You no stink. I stink. I make fire in sauna."

She got up and put her arms around him to confess what she had done and through her tears to beg forgiveness. No, he didn't hit her; he just picked her up in his big arms, took her to the bedroom and laid her gently down on the bed. Then he returned to the kitchen to sleep under the deena by the stove despite her protests. Too exhausted to argue, Helga fell immediately into a deep sleep from which she awakened at daylight to the smell of coffee and the stroking of a finger under her nose. When she opened her eyes there was Alf with a big grin on his face. "You snore so loud I can't sleep," he said.

He took the day off work, went to Ishpeming on the train, and brought back in the baggage car a single bed with mattress and springs. When Marchand our mailman couldn't fit them on his litter, Alf borrowed some rope and lugged them up the hill on his back. It took him three trips. Tioga wasn't at all surprised. All of us knew why he'd been kicked out of deer camp and it just made sense to have two beds when he snored like that.

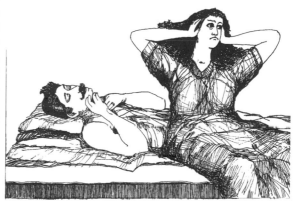

So Alf and Helga slept happily ever after.

Grampa Gage

Every nine or ten year old should have a grandfather like mine. Grampa Gage, who lived with us two summers when I was at that impressionable age, probably shaped me more than any other individual and not always for the better, may I say. At seventy-four, Grandpa was a short, wiry man with white hair and mustache who'd been a teamster in a logging camp, a grocer, and a bank president. Around our home and in public, he was very self-possessed and dignified but once he and I were alone that picture changed dramatically. A wild, zany companion he suddenly became, sometimes an Indian on the warpath, a hunter of lions in Africa, a bird, even a he-flea hunting for a she-flea and that's hard because as he said, "the flea is wee and mercy me, you cannot tell a he from she, but she knows well and so does he." Never have I known anyone with such a freewheeling imagination. It was contagious.

Each morning Grampa and I shaved, then did our exercises before anyone else was up. He'd lather up both our faces, then shave himself with the gleaming edge of his long razor, then mine with the back of it. Always he kept saying, "I'm the mildest mannered man that ever cut a throat" so ferociously he almost scared me. His calisthenics were equally wild and varied. He'd put his old head between his legs to make faces and insist I do the same. He'd alternate swinging his arms over his head then wiggle his fingers with his thumbs in the opposite ear, or do his Dance of the Wild Cucumber. "Limber up the old bones, Mr. Bones!" he'd chant. Really quite a workout. Then he'd build a fire in the kitchen stove, put a pot of coffee on to boil, and we'd sit for a spell on the back steps enjoying the early morning sunshine.

That was when he gave me my name for the day. No, he never once called me Cully. I was either "Boy" or "Mr. Finnegan" or "Mr. O'Rourke" or had some other name. Once, after I'd been in a fist fight the evening before and had gotten a black eye, he dubbed me "Joshua" and all that wonderful morning Grampa and I fought the "Battle of Jerico When the Walls Came Tumbling Down." We climbed up on Mount Baldy, got stick swords and spears, and fought the Philistines all over that cliff, ending the battle by rolling big rocks over the edge and listening to them crash in the woods below. "Take that, Belshazzar," Grampa would roar. "Watch out, Joshua!" he'd yell. "There's four Philistines right behind you. Smite them, Joshua!" and then he'd come to my aid, walloping the trees and bushes and yelling war cries. Finally, when we were tired out, we counted the enemy dead and Grampa looked me over. "Only one walking wounded. That's not bad. Only one black eye!"

Grandpa Gage had found the secret of childhood: Let's Pretend! Most of us, as we grow up to get clobbered by reality, forget that secret and our lives are the worse off because of that forgetting. Only a few of us are lucky enough to have retained it. "All those who believe in fairies, clap their hands!" I clap mine and I hope you do yours. Certainly Grampa did. One morning he said to me, "Mister Hogan, I've a mind to find a big raven today, climb on its back, and take an aerial voyage. Will you join me, sir?" Again we went up on Mount Baldy and searched around until he found a long black boulder. "Ah," said he. "Here's our raven. Shall we board, Mr. Hogan?" We climbed on the rock and Grampa put his arm around me as we soared off into space, flying first over Lake Tioga, then back over the village with its tiny houses so far below. Grampa kept up a running commentary all the way and soon I was doing it too. Finally we flew back to Mount Baldy in a big circle. "Now, Boy," Grampa roared, "We're a coming down, so hold tight. And keep your head up high. Boy. It may be a rough landing."

I remembered those words once when many years later I was on a plane going to Nashville to make a speech. Over the intercom came the Captain's voice. "Folks," he said cheerily. "We're having a little problem getting the landing gear down. The co-pilot with the help of one of you strong men will try to auger it down manually." The co-pilot appeared with a large device looking like a brace and bit and he and one of the passengers tried in vain to turn it. "I guess, folks, that we'll have to skip Nashville this time and go on to Atlanta for our belly landing. They have better foam and firefighting equipment and a longer runway. We'll make it."

At Atlanta we circled around and around for a long time, ditching fuel, before he told us to put our heads between our knees and against the seat in front of us and to remember where the exits were. How deathly silent that plane was except for the murmur of people praying. Crouched in that fetal position, I remembered Grampa's command to hold my head high and when I did so, I felt a lot better. If I were going to die. I'd die proud, not craven. Ride ,em cowboy! The plane came down with a crash and skidded in sparks and foam almost to the end of the runway. Thanks to Grampa, I felt proud of myself even though I had a sore neck for a week afterwards.

Among the many things Grampa taught me was to know and appreciate many of the facets of that jewel, the Upper Peninsula of Michigan. Each of our "ex-pe-dit-ions" (He always sounded out big words) was a journey of discovery. Let me give you just one example. One morning Grampa was carrying a little pail when we set out for our walk, first through the Grove, then through Company Field, and finally down to the big beaver dam swamp. "No, Mr. McGillicuddy," he said when I asked him if the pail was for coffee. "I'm all out of shaving lotion so I thought I'd brew up a batch of my own, if you will kindly help me, sir, to pro-cure some of the ingredients." He gave me a bag to hold them.

That whole morning was a delight. Tips of balsam fir which we squeezed and sniffed were the first to go in the bag, then some sassafras bark. Grampa apologized to the bush for slicing the strip and gave me some to chew. Then we found some sweet grass, the kind Pete Half Shoes used in the aromatic baskets he occasionally wove. In the field we also plucked some sour-sap, a weed with a tangy taste almost like vinegar. Down by the Beaver Dam we found wintergreen berries, wild mint and Labrador tea leaves. Grampa picked a big leaf of skunk cabbage and asked me my opinion as to its suitability before throwing it away and washing his hands in the creek. Lord, we must have smelled and tasted fifty kinds of bark and leaves before he said, "There's only one more thing we need for our concoction, Mr. McGillicuddy - some witch hazel." Finally we found that bush and Grampa and I picked a lot of little flowers off the tips of its branches. We boiled the stuff in a pail over the campfire and next morning anointed ourselves with it.

Day after day we went on other expeditions, all of which opened my eyes and ears and mind to the wonders of the U.P. One time we went on an orn-i-thological expedition, collecting birds or rather writing their names down. Grampa Gage knew his birds and taught me all he knew-and a bit more. For example, once he stopped suddenly and held up a finger. "Hear that gurgle, Mr. Grogan? Over there in those pine trees." I listened hard but couldn't hear anything but the wind in their branches. "There it is again," he said. "That's a double-breasted drib. Very rare. It's the only bird that flies backwards to see where it's been." Hey, only now as I type this do I realize that drib is bird spelled backwards. Oh Grampa, you lovely crazy old bugger! But I've been a bird watcher ever since, to the enrichment of my days.

One day when we went trout fishing the flies were terrible: mosquitoes, black flies, deer flies, gnats and no-see-ums. It also was very warm and the sweat poured off our faces while not a trout rose to our flies. Suddenly Grampa let out a yell. "Enough!" he hollered. "Boy! Remember this: We don't have to endure the unbearable. Let's get the hell out!" We did! And that command got me into trouble in Australia. Let me explain.

When I became thirty I made a life plan for myself. During my thirties I would explore new human relationships. I did. I got married. My forties I would spend in creativity. I did. I fathered three fine children and wrote ten textbooks in the new field of speech therapy. My fifties I would spend in becoming wise; my sixties in folly; and my seventies in becoming resigned. The only trouble was that in my fifties my new found wisdom made it clear that if I postponed my follies for ten more years I probably wouldn't be able to enjoy them so I switched and made that decade my age of foolishness. I soon discovered that the basic prescription for folly was just to say yes.

Thus it was that when someone called me from New York and asked me if I would go as this country's representative in speech therapy to a Pan Pacific Conference on the Disabled in Sidney, Australia, all expenses paid, I said yes, immediately and automatically. I didn't want to go to Australia but these were my years of folly so I said yes.

So after a grueling eighteen hour flight in a propeller driven plane from San Francisco via Hawaii and the Fiji Islands I found myself completely exhausted in the Hotel Australia. Shortly after I'd gone to bed the phone rang. "I am Joyce Johnson. your hostess," she said in a stiff very British accent.

There will be a reception for all the delegates to the conference at the governor's palace this evening at eight and I will be in the lobby to take you there at that time."

I tried to beg off but she wouldn't hear of it. Thus it was that I, a child of Lake Superior and its forests, under the tutelage of Miss Joyce, became a part of a crowd of people milling around in the huge reception hall under the chandeliers, making polite conversation that no one could hear, and nursing champagne and hors d'oeuvres proffered endlessly by butlers or such. After the first hour of making fake faces and small nonsense talk, I was in a daze. After two hours of the hullabaloo I remembered Grampa's words: "You don't have to endure the unbearable. Get the hell out!"

When I told Miss Joyce I was leaving, she had a polite British fit. "No," she said. "That's completely indefensible. We haven't even gone through the reception line yet. You just cahn't." But I did. I fled out of the door, crawled in one of the waiting cabs and told the driver to get me the hell out of there, to show me the seamy side of Sidney, its pubs, and famous beaches. A gay rascal and fine storyteller, the cabbie sure followed my instructions. But Miss Joyce Johnson never forgave me.

One afternoon Grandpa found me encircling items in a Sears Roebuck catalog. "Why are you doing that?" he asked. I told him that I was picking out all the things I would buy when I grew up and had a lot of money. "Fool!" he roared. "The more stuff you buy, the poorer you are." And then he took me down to Lake Tioga, gave me a five dollar gold piece, and insisted I throw it way out into the lake. "The only nice thing about having money is that you can despise it," he said. "And the more possessions you have, the more they possess you." I learned a lot from Grampa Gage.

On another expedition when we were collecting "rep-tiles" I spied a toad but wouldn't pick it up, fearing that I'd get warts from the ugly creature. "Nonsense!" exclaimed Grampa. Then he told me the story of the prince who had been turned into a toad by a sorcerer and how he stayed a toad until kissed by a beautiful maiden. "Let's see if we can make a princess out of this one," he said. He picked up the toad, showed me the beautiful jewel that was its eye, then kissed it. Nothing happened but he taught me that, if you looked closely enough, nothing was really ugly.

I remember vividly one morning when I didn't get up to have Grampa shave me. It had rained hard for three days and was raining again. "Why get up?" I asked him when he came to my bedroom to see what was wrong. "Raining again. Another lousy day," I said as I pulled the covers over my head. Grampa pulled them back and marched me to the bathroom, then took my hand and put it inside his shirt.

"What does it feel like?" he demanded.

"It feels warm," I replied.

Grandpa grinned. "Yes," he said. "You're feeling the sunshine inside my skin sack. It's not the weather outside but the weather inside that counts. Now let's go down and have some breakfast."

I've remembered those words often in my long life and always felt better because I did. Once when I was in Ireland I made arrangements to go fly fishing for trout on one of their lovely lakes but when my ghillie (guide) called for me at six thirty in the morning I almost backed out. A nasty day, cold, and drizzling. I put a bottle of whiskey in my coat to make sure I'd have some of Grampa's sunshine in my skin sack.

Paddy McMullan, my ghillie, was a very old man, bewhiskered and disreputable, and the old Ford he drove was almost as old as he was. We rattled along a bumpy back road to the ruins of an ancient castle at the edge of a large lake. The boat, hidden in the bushes, leaked. The ancient bamboo fly rod was heavy and stiff but I finally was able to master it enough to make some good casts.

"Begging yer pardon, sorr," Paddy said. "You'll niver catch an Irish trout that way - except in a river. You have to dap, not let the fly sit on the water. I'll show ye." Paddy was a master fly fisherman and caught a trout on his first dap. The moment the fly hit the water, he'd quickly retrieve it, then flick it out again, over and over again, sometimes skittering the fly along a foot of the surface thereby creating the illusion of a hatch. Very difficult to do, it took me some time before I got the hang of it and to celebrate the accomplishment I brought out the bottle of whiskey. The old man's rheumy eyes sure lit up when he saw that bottle and he took a huge swallow from it.

I swear that Paddy knew where every fish was in that lovely lake. He'd row me over to a patch of reeds and say, "Ah, there's a good one here, sorr." And there almost always was. At each new location Paddy usually tied on a new trout fly. About mid-morning the action slowed down: "May I have that bottle, sorr?" the old man asked. When I gave it to him, Paddy dipped a new fly in the whiskey, handed me the rod, and said. "Here's one for the gintlman! We Irish like whiskey, that we do, trout or man." As I cast, I noticed out of the corner of my eye that he took a big gulp from the brown bottle. Again I began to catch trout, Paddy dipping the fly in the whiskey and sneaking a snort of it with each cast. Perhaps I managed to get two or three swallows of liquid sunshine before the bottle was empty but no matter. Thanks to Grampa and Paddy McMullan it was one of the best mornings of my life.

On another occasion Grampa and I went hunting for gold in the granite hills north of Tioga. We didn't find any though once after he had distracted me by asking me to look over there at a pileated peewee I found a silver dollar where I had been digging. What I remember most about that trip though was what happened on our way back. Suddenly I got so utterly fatigued I couldn't stand up let alone walk any more. Grandpa was both concerned and sympathetic. "You old fool," he said to himself. "You forget the boy is only nine." Finally, after I'd lain in the grass a long time with him sitting beside me, he said, "Well, Mr. O'Connor, it's time for us to be hiking home again."

I began to cry. "I can't, Grampa." I wailed. "I'm too tired to move."

He stood me up then gave me a little talk about how all of us have a tank of reserve strength within us that we can use when all our other strength is gone. "I shall now turn on that tank, Boy," he said as he turned his finger in my navel. "Now forward march! You're a member of Sousa's famous band." Then he sang a song I'd never heard before, one that set me laughing, and down the path we went strutting like drum majors. Here's his song and the tune was that of one of Sousa's marches:

Do yer balls hang high? Do yer balls hang low?
Can you tie 'em in a knot? Can you tie 'em in a bow?
Can you throw them o'er yer shoulder like a European soldier?
Do yer balls hang low?

There have been several times in my life when I had to call upon that tank of reserve strength behind my navel. Once was when my heart stopped as my wife was driving me to the Emergency room of our hospital but another came when I'd shot a goose on a little muskeg lake near my cabin at Bitely. It was almost dark and the dead goose was floating about ten feet from the edge of the matted muskeg. I knew better but this was in my decade of folly so, leaving my gun on the shore, I picked up a pole and tiptoed my way out on that swaying muskeg, hoping to be able to bring the goose within reach. Suddenly all the matted growth gave way and into the icy water I went. There was no solid bottom, just ooze, and my soaked heavy clothing so weighted me down that swimming was almost impossible. No one knew where I was. After struggling in the muck for some time I became exhausted and almost gave up until I remembered Grandpa's insistence that I owned a tank of reserve strength. So I turned it on and finally managed to make my way to solid ground. I still don't know how I ever was able to do it.

But the most important thing that Grandpa Gage ever said to me was the word "Enjoy!" Let me tell you about it. We had walked the two miles down the old railroad track to the bridge, really a trestle, high above the Escanaba, a tributary of the Tioga River. When we got there, I began to cross on my hands and knees, always having had the fear of heights and those spaces between the railroad ties looked very big. Grandpa was outraged. "Walk like a man!" he commanded but I couldn't do it. It had rained earlier that morning and the ties were still wet but Grandpa began to skip across the outside edge of the ties to show me I had nothing to fear. Alas, he slipped and fell into the big pool below the bridge but not until I heard him shout, still in mid-air and before the splash, "Enjoy! Enjoy!" He came up snorting and escorted me across the bridge hand in hand and skipping too. I have never forgotten that admonition. "Enjoy! Enjoy!" has been the mandate of my days. I hope it will be yours, too.

The Strap

This is an account of how Fisheye stole Old Blue Balls' strap and the consequences thereof. But first, so that you can understand, let me forsake my usual happy nostalgia about my homeland, the Upper Peninsula of Michigan in the early days of this century, to give another side of the picture. It was a hard, harsh land, very primitive, first settled only a few decades earlier by miners, loggers or a few farmers, most of them immigrants from countries over the seas.

The climate was fierce, especially in the winter, the long winter from October until May, when the winds blew down from Lake Superior to bury the countryside in huge drifts of snow. For months on end the temperature was always below zero, sometimes as bitter as forty or fifty below. There were a few summers when frost occurred every month, and a lot of them when terrible thunderstorms crashed their lightning bolts all about us day or night. Forest fires swept through the slashings, filling our little village of Tioga with so much smoke it was hard to breathe.

Above all, there was always that feeling of isolation from the rest of the world. No radio, no TV, no real roads between towns, just two wagon ruts. No automobiles or planes. Only four people in Tioga got newspapers and these were passed on from family to family until they were shredded or plastered against the inside walls of the cabins to keep out the wind. Only the railroads linked us with the outside world and tickets cost biting money to get away. Tioga was our world, our tiny world.

Hard lands breed or make hard people. Ours had to be tough to survive. Our men in the mines worked ten or twelve hour shifts for a dollar a day, came home to eat and fall asleep, and then spent their Sundays fishing, hunting for food, or making hay and wood for the winter to come. It was dangerous work. I recall Henry Thompson, our mining superintendent telling my father that he had to go to Duluth to catch hell from headquarters because seven men had already died that year, two more than the quota allowed. "They don't give a damn about the men," Thompson said, "but they'd budgeted for only five for the year and there are still two months to go." Many others got maimed or crippled. No one sued the mining companies because all the local lawyers had accepted retainer fees from them. If the families got a hundred dollars in death benefits and a tiny pension, they felt lucky. At least they could keep their houses or cabins unless they caused trouble because all the land was owned by the mining company. Eviction without mercy was swift and sure. It was hard to save money because again the company owned the store, charged high prices and gave credit, so any paycheck didn't last long. Most of our miners stayed in debt all their working lives.

The logging business was equally dangerous. No, not quite, but men were killed every year in the woods. When a tree is felled but lodges its branches in a nearby tree, it is still called a "widow-maker" in the U.P. Some trees when almost sawed through suddenly "kick back" wiping out the men who are sawing. Loading the huge logs on sleighs or railroad cars, riding the logs on the river drive took their toll of human lives and led to many personal tragedies. A harsh life and a very dangerous one.

Our women had to be tough too. They bore many children not just because sex is the poetry of the poor but so the family could have cheap labor until the kids grew up and went away and perhaps because they might have one of them who could tend them in their old age. Our women were always tired. They milked the cows and churned the butter. They tended the garden, did the interminable washings with nothing but a blue faced scrubbing board and the sad irons heated on the kitchen woodstove. They did the baking and canning and cooking, hauled the water from the well, read their bibles and prayed. Prayed to a cruel and fearful God not only for forgiveness from their current little sinnings but for the original sin bequeathed to them at birth from Adam and Eve. Every Sunday they were reminded of the hell and brimstone and damnation that might await them in the hereafter.

Like the sound made by the rat that gnaws at the cellar steps at night, fears gnawed at their lives, fear that the woodpile or the cans of berries and venison would run out, fear that the well would run dry, fear of the always encroaching forest, fears of illness or accidents, fear of losing one's job. No, the good old days weren't all that good.

When fear and danger and drudgery are mixed together the resulting brew has anger in it. There was a lot of brutality in our lives. The camp boss ruled his men with his fists. You did what he said without protest or complaining or he knocked you down. The mining captain was king and the foremen down to the straw bosses had absolute power. No one ever argued with the man above him.

In turn, the father was king of his cabin too. His word was law; you disobeyed at your peril. Punishment was swift and very harsh, even brutal. I recall once driving with my father as he made house calls on some patients down in French Town at the bottom of the hill and seeing a man beating a tied up horse. He was hitting it over and over again with a two-by-four with terribly hard blows. Awful!

When I asked my father why he didn't stop it, he said, "Cully, that's his business, not mine. If I'd gotten out of the buggy and protested he'd have hit me with that two-by-four too. Life is cruel, as you'll find out some day." I thought of some of the thrashings, he'd given me and felt that I'd already found out. My father was a decent man but when he became furious with me for something I had or hadn't done, he beat me up pretty badly. I recall once refusing my mother's request that I take a bath because I knew she'd see the terrible purple bruises he'd given me. When I lost the argument and she did see them I just said I'd had a bad fight in school. I wasn't the only one who got thrashed severely by a father. All of my friends had too. We felt we had it coming. We also learned the art of taking a licking. You didn't shed any tears. Men and boys were never ever to cry. You just yelped loudly after each blow until they stopped, and then you could go off by yourself and weep. Spare the rod and spoil the child. There weren't many spoiled boys in Tioga.

Our schools of course reflected the cultural practices of the time. Along with blackboards each room was furnished with birch switches, often well worn with the white bark long gone. Only in first and fourth grades had they never been used, the grades taught by Margaret and Nellie Feeley whom we loved too much to cause any trouble. By the time we were in the sixth grade most of us were too big to switch (we just laughed defiantly if the teacher used the birch or we brought her some new bigger switches) so for serious infractions we were sent up to Old Blue Balls' office.

That was big trouble! Mr. Donegal, Old Blue Balls as we called him behind his back, was a disciplinarian of the old school. A short but powerful man, he ruled our school by fear. Not only us kids but all of the teachers were terrified of him and with good reason. He would invade our classrooms, watch the teaching and criticize it, or take over the teaching himself. He patrolled the hallways and schoolyard, sometimes actually hauling a boy by his hair up to his dreaded office. Old Blue Balls would even go to a boy's home if he suspected the latter was playing hookey and look under the bed. And his bite was worse than his bark, which is saying a lot.

Mr. Donegal had three favorite methods of corporal punishment - the ruler across the wrists for minor devilment, THE HAND, (we always capitalized it), and The Strap. Most of us who had known all three claimed that The Strap was the worst. Old Blue Balls would have you get on all fours on his office floor, then whop you as many hard ones as he deemed you deserved, then, after a pause, one terribly hard one so you'd never, never do it again. It sure was difficult to sit down after you'd had The Strap. I remember doing my duty under a bush rather than sit on the outhouse hole.

Mr. Donegal had ruled his school long enough that there were in it children whose fathers he had thrashed in their time. But times were changing. Almost unheard of earlier, parents began to complain to my father, who was also secretary of the school board, that Old Blue Balls' punishments were too severe, that as he had grown older he had become more brutal. But, because my father and Mr. Donegal were the closest of friends and hunting and fishing partners, he never mentioned it to his friend. "Whatever his methods, he runs a fine school," my father told them, "the best one in the county. We have more students going on to college than from any school around. They're getting a fine education."

One autumn afternoon just before school was to be dismissed my close friend Fisheye dipped Amy Erickson's pigtails that hung over his desk into his inkwell, turning the ends of those pigtails from blonde to black brunette. She had it coming. She'd been teasing him about his broken shoes which were all he had. One of our unwritten laws, was the boys shouldn't hit girls no matter what the provocation so he had to get even somehow. Well, Amy tattled and raised cain and our teacher sent Fisheye up to Old Blue Balls' office with a note explaining what had happened.

But Mr. Donegal had sneaked out early so he could go partridge hunting and Fisheye waited and waited until finally he said to hell with it, and left the school himself. But not before he stole THE STRAP. He'd been looking at it for some time with dread even though he knew it well, and on an impulse at the last moment he just tucked it under his shirt and ran down the stairs. The ultimate crime, the great revenge! God knows what Old Blue Balls would do if he found out who had swiped it! At the moment Fisheye didn't care. He felt ten feet tall.

Of course he had to share The Strap with us after swearing us to secrecy, Mullu and me, anyway. It was the trophy of trophies but not one to parade around so we hung it from the roof of a decrepit little shack we'd built some time before in Beaver Dam

Swamp. Better than a set of deer antlers, it was. We used to take it down to feel it and give each other a few light licks, then run around bellowing. Fisheye was our hero. He had chopped off our dragon's tail. Afternoon after afternoon we went down to that shack to admire The Strap, tell tales about the lickings we'd had, and eat slices of raw potato with salt or sticks of rhubarb with sugar.

Somehow Old Blue Balls never discovered who had stolen his strap but that didn't phase him in the slightest. What he did was to get some ironwood shoots about four feet long and about an inch thick at the base. Now ironwood is the toughest wood in the whole U.P., almost impossible to cut with a knife. We kids used to make bows of it for our arrows and it was always hard to bend, even after we peeled off its black wrinkled bark. Mullu was the first of our trio to get trimmed by Old Blue Balls with those ironwood shoots and when we saw his behind we were scared crazy. Great purple and black welts ran across his butt and his back at least a quarter of an inch wide. Some bleeding too. No licking we'd ever had had looked like that. The ruler was bad enough; THE HAND was worse; The Strap was awful but none of them left their mark on the flesh as deeply as did those ironwood shoots. We sure resolved to be on our best behavior. When another kid, a grade beyond ours, suffered the same thrashing and wasn't able to come back to school for two days, we held a pow wow down at our shack and decided that Fisheye should somehow return The Strap to Old Blue Balls' office. I don't know how he managed it but he did for I saw it hanging in its familiar place on the desk. I also saw the group of black ironwood sticks. No, I didn't get thrashed that time; I just had to take a message from our teacher. I think she just wanted some extra chalk, but I saw those sticks and wanted no part of them. Of course the whole school heard of them too and for some time there were few disciplinary problems.

But boys will be hellions when the urge comes over them and Sulu made the mistake of hitting the teacher with a short strip of rubber band. They could really hurt if you fastened one end over a sharp pencil, aimed it right, pulled it back and then let go. Sulu's aim was accurate and he hit her right behind the ear. Sure made her holler! Now that, of course, was a major infraction so Old Blue Balls again passed by The Strap for the ironwood sticks.

That evening after supper Sulu's father came down to Mr. Donegal's house carrying a black stick which he placed on the railing of the porch before knocking at the door. "Won't you please come in?" Mrs. Donegal asked. "No, I'd like to talk to your husband out here," Sulu's father replied.

When Mr. Donegal came onto his porch he failed to notice the grey-white look on Sulu's father's face. Finns rarely show much emotion but when their faces turn that color they are furious and you'd better watch out.

"What can I do for you?" asked Mr. Donegal. "You interrupted my supper."

Fighting down his anger. Sulu's father began slowly and carefully. "You beat my boy, Sulu, today pretty bad but I make you a bargain. If he do bad things, you tell me and I punish, not you. You hurt him bad."

Old Blue Balls was enraged. No one had ever challenged his authority before. He put his face close to Sulu's father's and roared, "I'll have you know that I run my school the way it ought to be run. When you were a boy I had to punish you. No to your bargain! No, no, no! If Sulu was dumb enough to hit one of our teachers with a rubber band, he got what he had coming, and if he does it again he'll get it worse."

Sulu's father pole-axed old Blue Balls right there on the porch with a right upper-cut to the jaw. And then he took that black ironwood cane and beat the prone superintendent again and again on his back and hind end as hard as he could. Then he placed the ironwood cane against the porch railing and left.

When Mr. Donegal recovered enough to go to my father for help, Dad put ointment on his welts and a bit of bandage on cuts. "You've sure taken a hard beating, Fred," he said. "How did it happen?"

Our superintendent told him the whole story, even about the ironwood canes, and swore that next morning he'd press charges for assault and battery and have the bastard put in jail.

"Well," said Dad. "Perhaps you can make a case for yourself if the prosecutor down in Marquette would agree, which might not be certain if he sees Sulu's back. Fred, I hate to say it, for we've been friends for so many years and had such good companionship which I would miss greatly, but don't you think it's about time you retire? Times have changed. I've had a lot of complaints from our people about your brutality and cruelty and have protected you because of our friendship. Go to bed for two days and think it over." My father always told it straight. I remember him telling a man, "Pete, you have at most only six months to live. Make the most of them." Mr. Donegal said he'd go to bed and think it over.

And he did retire. He went back to the family farm in Indiana and raised cantaloupes and watermelons until he died. All that just because Fisheye stole The Strap!

Lice Aren't Nice

"John," my mother asked, "Will you look at my scalp? It's been itching a lot lately. I suppose it's just the usual lack of humidity that always comes in January when the house has been closed so long. I'll probably have to put some steaming teakettles on all the stoves."

Dad looked her over. "No, Edyth," he said. "You've got head lice. See, here's a big grayback." He plucked it off her collar before knicking it with his thumbnail.

"No! No! Oh dear no! Don't tell me!" She was almost in tears.

Dad had been prowling around in her hair. "Yes, Edyth," he replied. "Your hair is full of them, and a lot of nits too. Nits are their eggs. Can happen to anyone up in this country especially in the winter. Well, I'll go over to the dispensary and bring back some oil of myrrh so you can rub it in before and after you wash your hair. Have you one of those fine tooth combs, the kind you used on Cully about three years ago when he got lousy?" She nodded. "If you use the myrrh and comb hard and long, you'll get the nits. They're little gray or white things, almost specks. May take a week of combing and washing your hair before they're gone. And don't scratch! No use getting a scalp infection too. I also suggest that you put a heavy towel around your neck to catch those that fall out when you comb, and to wipe the comb with. Then put it outside in the snow so they'll freeze to death."

When Dad returned from the hospital, Mother already had her hair down and a towel around her neck. He poured some of the oil of myrrh in a saucer and put the bottle beside it. "Now be sure to comb hard right near the scalp," he said. "That's where the little buggers hang out. And if you find any lice or its on the comb put it in the basin before you wipe it on the towel. And, before you begin, take a look at my scalp. I suppose I'm getting them too."

Mother looked hard but couldn't find any. "Oh, I've just got too tough a skin," my father said. "Smoking Granger tobacco in my pipes keeps the insects away. Mosquitoes don't bother me, as you know, and probably lice don't like the flavor. If I were a louse I'd prefer your pretty head to mine anytime. Anyway, it's no great catastrophe. As David Harum said, 'A certain amount of fleas is good for a dog: it keeps him from brooding on being a dog.'" Mother almost threw the bottle at him. As he left, he asked to be sure to check the boys' heads when they got back from school. "And Dorothy's too," he said. "Even if she's not old enough yet to go to school, you might have given some of yours to her."

That afternoon Dad was holding his office hours in the old hospital across the street when Fred Donegal, our tough school superintendent, the one we kids called Old

Blue Balls, came to see him. "Doctor," he said, "I'm afraid the school's coming down with an epidemic of head lice and I'd like your advice about what to do. Odd thing, though, only the kindergarten, the second grade, and the fifth grade kids are lousy, and of course not all of them are. Can't figure out why only those grades are infested, but I know that soon all of them will be."

"Yes," said my father. "Head lice sure can spread fast. Haven't had an epidemic for three years now so I suppose it was bound to come. Some father probably came back from a lumber camp and gave them to his kids. I suggest that you tell all your teachers to keep in from recess any kid who's scratching his head, look him over and send him home if he has lice. It's hard to understand, though, why the outbreak is confined to just those grades."

"How do you treat an infestation of head lice?" Mr. Donegal asked. "What should I tell them to do?"

"The Finns have an old remedy," my father replied. "They either shave off or clip off all the hair on the head or soak the scalp with kerosene. Others just shave the scalps bare. That works though the kids will have some pretty cold heads in this winter weather, and the girls won't stand for it."

"But the kerosene?"

"Yes," my father replied. "Rubbing kerosene in the scalp will get rid of the lice and some of the nits but it burns the scalp. The best treatment is oil of myrrh and hard combing. I fear many will feel they can't afford the myrrh. I have a quart of it and you can tell them I'll give them a bottle of myrrh free until it's all gone. May stink up your schoolrooms. And be sure to tell them to comb hard with a fine tooth comb so they can get the nits. I just hope they have one or that they can get one up at Flynn's store."

"Will going to the sauna do any good, Doctor?" Mr. Donegal asked.

"Those head lice are tough," my father answered. "I doubt it. I've heard tell that some of the old Finns first go to the sauna, then wet their heads, and roll in the snowbank afterwards to get rid of them. One Finn told me once that he got rid of his lice by rubbing his dog over his head. I doubt that too. Human lice prefer human heads just as chicken lice prefer feathers. Probably all that really happened was that he added some dog fleas which are not so particular."

When Dad got home he asked if any of us had lice. "No," my mother said. "I've gone over their heads with the fine toothed comb thoroughly and didn't find a single nit nor louse. John, how did I get them?" she wailed. "I haven't been out of the house for weeks except to go to church and then I keep my hat on like the other women do, although I think it's silly."

"Well I don't know where you got them either," Dad replied. There's a good chance the two boys will be getting them later." He told her about Mr. Donegal's conversation. "Cully in the fifth grade and Joe is in kindergarten two of the three grades where they've appeared. You be sure to check them every day."

Mother sure did. I got so I almost hated to get up in the morning because I got combed before breakfast, again when I came from school at noon, and again before supper. This went on day after day even though she never found a louse or nit. Then one afternoon before supper she found two. I knew what had happened. Fisheye and I were the only boys in our grade that still had hair. All the others had heads that were clipped or shaved. And we'd been wrestling. Well, finding those two lice sure raised cain. Mother redoubled her efforts, scraping my scalp rather then just combing, and rubbing that stinky myrrh stuff all over my head. Oh how I hated the smell of it, not only on me but even on her, for she was still using it as well as combing and washing her own hair daily. Each morning before I went to school I had to fill the big copper boiler with packed snow so she could have soft water to do her hair. The water from our well was full of iron and left orange stains on the sink that only Zud could remove. In the summer she used soft water from the rain barrel outside under the eaves but only melted snow could provide it in January.

I just couldn't understand why she was making such a big deal of a few pesky lice. My head wasn't itching even if it was sore from the combing. "Lice aren't nice," she told me. "A louse in the house is almost as bad as having bedbugs." Oh how she battled them, boiling the brushes and combs, scouring the hats and caps with wood alcohol, then putting them outside to freeze. Twice a day she ran the carpet sweeper not only over the floor but even on the upholstered chairs and couch. I sure got tired of having her examine the collar of my jackets or sweaters and always parting and peering at my hair.

Finally, at school I was the only boy with hair, Fisheye's uncle having shaved his head so close he was bald as an onion. How the schoolroom stank of kerosene and myrrh so I decided I'd have my head shaved too. When I brought the subject up to mother, she vetoed it immediately. "No, you don't, Cully. You have such nice thick hair like your father. I don't want you looking like a convict in prison."

But I was determined. If I got my head shaved there'd be no more combing agony two or three times a day and besides I didn't want to be different from the other boys. So one afternoon after school I went upstairs to my bedroom and tried to open my piggy bank to get money for the barber, Mr. Rich. It really wasn't a piggy bank. It looked like a little banker sitting in a cast iron chair. When you lifted up his iron arm and put a coin in the hand, the arm would come down and slip the coin into the banker's pocket. Real neat! It worked every time. But getting money out of that banker bank was hard going. Underneath the chair was the opening, covered by a plate that was screwed down so tight I just couldn't turn it. I had quite a lot of money in that bank, so much that it hardly rattled any more when you shook it. Yes, there were even two ten dollar gold pieces in it that my beloved Grampa Gage had given me. I sure wished he hadn't tightened that screw so tightly. Finally, by holding the bank upside down between my knees and turning the screwdriver with a pair of pliers, I got it open at last. Wow, what a pile of money there was! I was rich! Taking only a quarter for the haircut and a dime for candy. I put the rest of the coins back, replaced the plate and made sure not to tighten the screw too tight. Then I went to the barber shop.

When I told Mr. Rich that I wanted my head shaved, he said no, that he'd only shave it if I brought a note from my mother. He'd clip it short, though, if I wanted. So that's what I had him do. It was quite an ordeal. Mr. Rich was an ex-miner who had lost a leg in a mining accident and the wooden leg he wore often hurt him so he left it in a corner as he hopped around the barber chair. Since he chewed snuff, his heavy breath was full of that smell but his clippers were the worst. They were hand operated because we had no electricity back then and they were very dull, often yanking out the hair rather than cutting it. After what seemed like an eternity of torture, the barber turned the chair around so I could see what he had done. I hardly recognized myself. Paying him the quarter I then bought two strips of black licorice and went home to face my mother.

She wept when she saw me but the deed was done. She did insist on taking my picture as I held a piece of cardboard with the number 1729 on it and for a week she called me Convict 1729 instead of Cully. My father approved not only my head but my gumption but he also confiscated my bank. "When you want money ask me for it," he said. "A savings bank is to put money in not take out."

"Well everything has an end and a woman has two," as my Grampa Gage often remarked. Finally my mother stopped scraping my scalp, the kerosene smell in school faded, and we no longer were afraid to scratch our heads. Even mother stopped smelling of myrrh. Dad told us why. "All epidemics are self limiting," he said. "Our people are generally a clean folk and can't abide lice. Besides, the life cycle of a louse is only thirty days from the first tiny nit to maturity and most adult lice only live three days. They can do a lot of blood sucking in that time and that's what makes the itch. Once you get rid of the eggs, the nits, the problem solves itself. I just wish I knew how this epidemic got started."

I think it was about the end of March when he found out. One evening after supper Dad was sitting in his Morris chair very content. He'd had venison chops, mashed potatoes, rutabagas, and blueberry pie with a piece of store cheese and he had read the Chicago Tribune. I hovered around knowing that this was the time he tended to share with my mother accounts of his practice. We kids weren't supposed to listen but I did, knowing well that if I ever told them to anyone else I would probably be beheaded. I'd heard a lot of dandy ones over the years like the one about the lumberjack who slashed his leg with an axe, got drunk, and lay in the sun for two days before they brought him to my father. "And you know what?" Dad would say. "When I squeezed that leg a whole procession of maggots promenaded out of the wound in single file. And that wound was clean as a whistle. No pus, no proud flesh, no nothing. All I had to do was put in a few stitches. We ought to have flies and maggots in our pharmacopoeia."

But on this particular night, Dad wasn't telling any tales. Instead, he said to mother, "You know, Edyth, medicine is not only an art but a science. A scientist knows that there is always a solution to any problem; he abhors unknowns. Well, I've been troubled for more than a month trying to figure out how our louse epidemic got started. The essential facts are these: you and the kindergarten, second grade and fifth grade kids all came down with lice at the same time. What then could be the common source? It must have been their teachers. Now I vaguely recall that you had those teachers here for tea one Saturday afternoon early in January, had a hilarious time, and then went up to Flynn's store. Well, I went up to Flynn's store too this afternoon and looked at some of those silly women's hats Flynn has had up there for years."

"Oh no," mother moaned. "Of course that's where we got the lice. The four of us had a lark trying on those crazy hats. Of course, that's what happened. Oh dear, we started all this trouble."

"Looks like you did." said my father. "Anyway, when I looked inside those hats I found plenty of lice so I bought the whole batch of them for five dollars and brought them home. I thought you might like to try them on again."

"John, you didn't!" mother screamed. "Where are they? Where are they?" Dad grinned. "I burned them up in the burning barrel."

U.P. Cussing

At the beginning of this century the U.P. was a rough crude land. Its men were a hard working, hard fighting, hard drinking lot. In that harsh environment they almost had to be. Their speech was rough too; they were a hard cussing crew.

My first experience with profanity came when I was an innocent four year old. It was Sunday morning and, watching the people going to church, I saw Mr. Koski, clad in his very best Sunday suit, slip on a cow pasty (which is what we called those circular platters of manure), and sit down right in the middle of it. As he picked himself up and started back home he gave vent to some angry cussing, repeating it over and over again until he was out of sight.

Somehow his words had a good ring to them and so it was that my horrified mother found me marching around our dining room table chanting over and over again:

"Sonza bits,
Sonza bits,
Sonza, sonza, Sonzabits."

Emerging from the kitchen a moment later with a cake of Fels Naphtha soap in one hand and a wet washcloth in the other, she bade me stick out my tongue which she then anointed. When I began to cry, she took me on her lap, wiped away my tears, and gave me a little talking-to.

"Now Cully," she said. "I put that soap on your tongue so you would remember that we Gages do not swear nor talk dirty. I know you'll hear a lot of bad language before you grow up but it isn't nice to talk that way, and I don't want you to curse and swear and use dirty words. You'll never hear me doing it, nor your father either. Please don't ever do it again!!"

What she said about my father was true. All the time I was growing up I never heard a bit of profanity come from his lips. Except once! When I was fifteen my father, and his crony, Jim Olson, took me with them on a trout fishing trip. To escape the mosquitoes we made our night fire on a bald granite hill above Brown's Dam. On one side of the fire was some thick moss and grass; on the other was just bare rock. They put their blankets on the moss while I was given the rock for a mattress. Fair enough! A boy knew his place. Men first!

Well, suddenly all hell broke loose. My father and Jim began to yell and swear, tearing off their clothes, dancing around and swatting themselves. They had bedded down on a red ant's nest. I pulled the blanket over my head to stifle my laughter but I recall vividly the torrent of cussing my father pemitted. Never repeated himself once. I had to admire his repertoire. Later, when he was in his nineties and I reminded him of the experience, he laughed. "Yes, Cully. I haven't sworn very much ever since your mother made me promise, while I was courting her, that I'd break myself of swearing, drinking, and chewing tobacco, three nasty habits I'd contracted in Medical School. Well, as you know, I don't mind taking a nip or two on occasion but I did give up swearing and chewing tobacco. I started chewing tobacco when I was in Medical School and had to dissect cadavers. For some reason I've never been able to tolerate the smell of formaldehyde. Chewing tobacco took some of the stench out of my nose and mouth. The other students could go to the cold room, take a cadaver off the hook and dance her to the dissecting table, singing, "Waltz me around, Mamie; Waltz me around," but I never could because of the smell. So I backslid on only one of the three promises. Not bad!"

The almost universal proclivity to swearing is one that has existed since earliest times. My mother also swore, although I'm sure she never knew she did. When the cake collapsed in the oven as she tested it with a toothpick, she said, "Oh Drat!" the equivalent of "Oh Damn!" When the hired girl dropped and broke one of her Haviland china cups she said, "Oh, Dear! Oh, Dear Me!" When the knitting slipped off her needle in a tangle, she said "Fiddlesticks!" with an intonation that meant "Dammit to hell!" My mother never took the name of the Lord in vain and never uttered a dirty word but she did her share of cussing too.

I never heard my Grandma Gage do any cussing. She didn't need to, her tongue being razor sharp, as my beloved Grandpa Gage knew all his married days. "Arza," she would say. "You're as stupid as a newborn louse!" She, like my mother, was a Lady. My Grandma Van, on the other hand, was not. She was just a sweet old woman but when she forgot where she had hidden her false teeth or Civil War pension check (They were always under her pillow!) she would say "Scats!" and "Dang it!" Or call someone she didn't like a "danged copperhead!"

If I recall correctly, most of the swearing in Tioga was done by the men, not the women. Nevertheless, upon real provocation, the women would cuss too. We had only one German family in Tioga, the Rhinelanders, and I often played with their son, Fritz. Mrs. Rhinelander was a huge, powerful woman who beat up her husband and son. Once, when I was playing in their kitchen with Fritz, a cat jumped up on the table, whereupon Mrs. Rhinelander swept it off with a heavy blow, and with it a glass spoon holder that broke into many pieces. Fritz fled and I with him but not before I heard her exclaim, "Donder und Blitzen!" I put that in my collection.

Fisheye's mother and father were French Canadians and so their profane expressions were always in French. Once, when Fisheye's mother had just hung out a new washing, the clothes pole broke and the clean clothes sagged into the mud. "Nom de norn de, norn de chien."" she roared. That only meant name of a dog, but it sure sounded like cursing. And was!

Mullu was Finnish and he taught me some of their choicest swear words. So did his mother one day when the cream she was churning just wouldn't turn into butter. "Saatana!" she said. Mrs. Salo also used that word when we put molasses around the hole of her outhouse. "Saatana! Saatana pelikeda!"

U.P. Cussing

The most frequently used cusswords in Tioga were "hell" and, of course, "damn." The latter is an ancient word derived from the Latin "damnare" which means to injure or punish. It occurs at least 145 times in Shakespeare's plays and was spoken a thousand times each day in Tioga when I was a boy.

But not usually in anger. It usually meant "very" as in "That's a damned fine buck you got, Eino!" "You're still a damn good looking woman, Lempi," or "the best damn pasty I ever ate," "Yah, it's damned cold outside. Almost froze my bollix coming up the hill."

My friend Emerick tells a tale of his tough old Cornish grandfather who, on his wedding night, took off his pants and commanded his bride to put them on. "But they're too big for me," she protested. "Yes," the man replied, "and you better damned well never forget it, woman!"

The word hell was often used in the same way. "Hell no, Sulu. I no going to Polka with you in them clompers." Or, "That's a helluva big trout, Slimber. How in hell you snag him?" Or, "You did a helluva good job skinning that skunk, Arvo, but you sure stink like hell. Better go sauna!"

A lot of so-called swearing consists of exclamations rather than curses and the words damn and hell were often used in this sense. When Sven Olson was shingling his house, he put down the hammer to get some more nails from his pouch and inadvertently moved his hammer which fell to the ground. "Oh damn!" he exclaimed. "Oh hell! Oh Double hell!" He didn't mean to say anything profane. He was just venting his frustration which is a good thing. Or so we felt. When his neighbor, Felix De Forrest, was lowering a pail of butter, eggs and milk down his well to keep them cool on a warm summer's day and the rope broke we didn't condemn him for saying, "Mon Dieu! Oh hell and dammit!" Better to let the emotion out than keep it in.

Of course, there were times when the usual hells and damns were used as epithets, as curses, and so were a lot of other words. The appeals to the Deity for help in attacking other individuals or inanimate objects or even the curser himself were commonly heard. "God damn you, you so and so!" was not unusual nor was the appeal to the Virgin Mary from the French Canadians. The so-and-so's included a wide variety of vilifying phrases such as the sonovas: son of a bitch, of a whore, of a couchon (pig), of a gun! Oh there were many more that are unprintable. These were fighting words unless you said them with the preface "You old" and smiled as you said them. I remember thinking that a couple of lumberjacks were going to have a fight down at the railroad station because they were thumping each other and calling each other names but no, they had not seen each other for a long time and were just happy to meet again. "Ah Francoise, you Goddamn old bastard, where you been? Haven't seen you since we cleaned out that saloon at Big Bay'"

I never heard anyone ever commit blasphemy or curse God but I sure heard a lot of name-calling that occasionally included dirty words. Indeed name-calling was a part of the experience of growing up and I early learned to chant "Sticks and stones may break my bones but names will never hurt me!" But they did! Many of them included references to paternity: "You son of a pissant," "You son of a cur!" "You son of a skunk!" Others just described you in unpleasant terms: "You crooked, lop eared, dog-faced toad!" "You horse's ass! "You dog!" "You bag of snot!"

Some years ago I read a fat, scholarly book by Montague entitled "The Anatomy of Swearing" which traced the history of the art from the Greeks and Egyptians to the present day. It listed all the four letter words (and others) that should never be spoken by civilized human beings, the words for intercourse, urination, defecation, and genitalia. They are well known so I don't have to put them down, remembering my mother's soap.

However one of them, shit, should be mentioned because back then it did not seem vulgar at all. It was just the regularly used word for excrement, just another word, standard usage. It merely meant manure, and, Lord knows, there was plenty of it in Tioga where the cows and horses regularly roamed the streets and sidewalks. My mother never used it, being a lady, but she never said "manure" either. Her equivalent was the phrase "big dirty," as in "Did you do a big dirty, Cully?" Though casually used in our communication, the word was unpleasant enough to find its way into many of our profane expressions such as the Finnish "Buskan hosu" (shit pants!) or as an old Dutchman put it, "You're a big bag of skiet."

Another word that Montague had on his list was the word "bloody!" Abhorred then in England as one of the dirtiest words in the language, it was brought to the U.P. by the Cornish miners along with their wonderful pasties and saffron bread. "You bloody bastard!" "You bloody bugger!" were common components in U.P. swearing, but, like shit, the word bloody was not felt to be unutterably vulgar.

For the most part, though, the bulk of U.P. cussing did not use these dirty words. They were reserved for situations involving extreme anger or frustration. I remember old man Trevarthan's swearing as he tried to split a big chunk of elm. Now elm has a diabolically twisted grain that grabs an axe and holds it stone-tight. If you put a wedge in the crack, that gets stuck too. Well, old man Trevarthan cursed for ten minutes straight before giving up and he never used a single really dirty word. It went something like this: "Damn my eyes if I won't chop you, you bloody bullheaded bugger, you dog, you blasted son of the swamp. Great balls of fire! Holy Hokey Pokey! Take that! and that! you crooked rotten devil" and so on.

It was said in Tioga, that old man Marchand, our delivery man and mail carrier, owned the record for continuous swearing. It happened when he bought a new Model-T Ford without really learning how to drive it. He tried to steer it by yelling "Gee" and "Haw," as he did to his horses; he pulled up on the steering wheel shouting "Whoa!" when he wanted to stop; and he cursed that mechanical monster all the way up and down our steep hill street. Alas, he swore in French so I can't replicate it here but people who knew the language told me he never repeated himself. A two mile curse.

Pierre Trude was repairing the trim on the Catholic church with Father Hassel, our wise old priest, steadying the ladder, when he hit his thumb hard with the hammer. His face purpling, Pierre just mumbled something. Then he hit the thumb again. "Father," he said. "May I please use your outhouses" "Of course, my son." When Pierre emerged, there was Father Hassel with the holy water. He knew the weaknesses of the flesh.

Yes, there was a lot of swearing done in the U.P. when I was a boy but most of it was pretty innocent, just an occasional damn or hell. There was little profanity or vulgarity, certainly not as much as I hear today. It never soared to artistic heights such as Shakespeare's: "The devil damn thee black, thou cream-faced loon. Where gottest thou that goose look?" Nor did it have the wit of the famous 18th century scholar, Dr. Samuel Johnson, who went down to a fishmarket to buy a fresh fish. Evidently he was pretty indecisive for the fishwife clerk called him every dirty name in the book. Dr. Johnson looked her in the eye. "And you, Madame, are a parallelogram!" Stopped her in her tracks! Yes, it isn't the words you use but how you say them that counts.

But I weary of my topic and, sensing a faint taste of Fels Naphtha in my mouth, I bring this little piece to a close with the song "Sammy Hall." When the old Cornish miner, Tim Squires, got snockered up sufficiently in Higley's saloon, and upon request, he would sing it loud and strong, with all the other customers joining in the chorus. And then he would sing it over and over again as he staggered up our hill street. I learned it by following him. Here we go!

> *Oh, my name is Sammy Hall, Sammy Hall, Sammy Hall,*
> *Oh my name is Sammy Hall and I hate you one and all.*
> *You're a gang of muckers all, Damn yer hide!*
> *Oh I killed a man, 'tis said, that I hit hint on the head,*
> *And I left him there for dead. Damn his hide!*
> *To the gallows I must go. I must go. I must go.*
> *To the gallows I must go with my friends all down below*
> *Saying Sam, I told you so. Damn their hides!*
> *Oh the preacher he did come; he did come; he did come.*
> *Oh the preacher he did come and he looked so very glum*
> *As he talked of kingdom come. Damn his hide!*

Then Tim would shift to a falsetto as he sang the final verse:

> *There was Nellie in the crowd, in the crowd, in the crowd.*
> *There was Nellie in the crowd, and she looked so very proud*
> *That I told her right out loud: Damn yer hide!"*

Widows 'N Orphans

Old Man McGee had had a hard night. The heart pains had been bad, especially those where the elephant stepped on his chest, or so it felt. Hard to breathe. Oh, he'd taken several spoonsful of the medicine that Doctor Gage had given him and they helped cut down the pains that rose up and ran down his arm but the old pump just wasn't working right. Kept stopping and then galloping. He'd sat up in the chair all night and was sure pooped when dawn came.

"Well, McGee," he said aloud to himself as he built a fire in the cookstove. "Might as well face it. Yer on yer last legs, McGee. You're gonna die, and damned near did last night. Just a matter of time. The old man sure craved a cup of strong coffee but he was all out of coffee and wouldn't have any until his pension check came the end of the week. He dumped the coffee grounds from the blackened pot onto a plate. Naw, they were gray. He'd boiled them three days in a row and the last time it was just like drinking warm water. Of course he still had tea but somehow it's not too good in the morning when you need a bracer for the day. What his old gullet thirsted for was a mug of black java, strong enough to coat the fur of the tongue so you could taste it after the mug was empty. "Well, how about some swamp coffee?" the old man asked himself. "Just a snort of whiskey in enough hot water to soak the korpua so I kin chew it. Yea, that'll do, McGee. That'll do! But easy on the water, McGee! Easy on the water."

The old Scotsman felt better after breakfast but he was still thinking about dying. It had been a close call last night. No, he wasn't scared of dying but he did have some concern about what might happen in the hereafter. He knew it would be heaven or hell and the way the revivalist preachers painted the latter with fire and brimstone, McGee wanted no part of that.

"What are yer chances, McGee?" he asked aloud. "You ain't done any sinning to account for anything much since you were a young buck so that's in yer favor. But maybe St. Peter, he's kept track of them early doings. Got 'em down on a marble tablet, mebbe."

That worried the old man. Without his morning coffee it was hard to think straight but the thought came to him that maybe if he could do some good deeds he'd have a better chance of playing a golden harp on those heavenly stairs. "Yea, McGee. That's what you gotta do to cancel them early sinnings. Do some good deeds to widows 'n orphans, mebbe. Wasn't there something in the Bible about helping widows 'n orphans?"

McGee knew his Bible, the one his old mother had given him when he left Scotland a million years ago. He read it every day. Widows and orphans and doing good deeds. Where would it be? Not in the first part, maybe in Psalms or Proverbs. These he thumbed through but found nothing except a lot of wisdom. Perhaps the New Testament would be a better bet. All morning he read Matthew, Mark, Luke and John without avail. Then he skipped to the apoerypra and by chance stumbled on I Esdras, II 20: "Do right to the widow, judge for the fatherless, give to the poor, defend the orphan, clothe the naked." Well, that wasn't just what he was hunting for but it would do. "Somehow, McGee," he said to himself. "You've got to do some good deeds for widows 'n orphans."

Unfortunately there weren't any orphans in Tioga. If other family members existed, they took the kids in. If not, then some other family did. For example, when Mr. and Mrs. Pelkie died of food poisoning from eating badly smoked fish at a neighbor's house leaving seven children ranging in age from two to twelve, they had all been adopted within three days, two of them by the neighbors who'd been deathly sick but recovered. In Tioga we took care of our own.

But there were some widow women, usually older ones who might need a man to do some things they found hard to do by themselves. Old man McGee could think of three right away who'd been without a man around the house for some time: Katy Flanagan, Helen Johnson, and Aunt Lizzie. Actually Katy Flanagan wasn't really a widow for she had a widely wandering husband who showed up every year or two for perhaps a week, then took off after he learned again he couldn't stand the rasp of her Irish tongue. But she might need help. Mrs. Johnson, a nice woman, had lost her husband only two years before. A logging accident. As for Aunt Lizzie, she'd had a lot of husbands who'd died on her but none recently.

After a lunch of bologna, cheese, hardtack and tea, McGee was so sleepy he lay in the bunk for a time, falling fast asleep and not awakening until almost dark. No time to do any good deeds and get stars in his crown until tomorrow. The old pump was thumping along nice and regular. "No, McGee," he said, "You ain't going to die tonight. You kin start kerlecting your good deeds tomorrow."

The next morning McGee was feeling much better so after arming himself with a file, a hone, and an axe he started up our hill street. By the time he got to the Catholic Church he was out of breath so he rested a while on its steps. "Dang street!" old man McGee said. "Keeps tilting on me and getting steeper every year."

Soon, however, he was on his way again, axe in hand. Mrs. Flanagan was sweeping her front porch viciously when he opened her gate and approached. "Ma'am," he said politely, doffing his old hat, "Have you some chores I might do for you? Split some wood or kindling? Sharpen your knives; fix something?"

Katy Flanagan thought that he was asking for work for pay. "No," she said. "I got no extra money, taking in washing and ironing as I do." McGee tried to explain that he didn't want any pay, that he just wanted to do some good deeds for "widows 'n orphans."

Wow! That sure turned her hot tongue loose. "I'm no widow, and I'm no orphan and I make me own way. Nothing a low-down man can do that I can't". She accused McGee of trying to get on the best side of her so he could take her to bed but she'd have him know she was an honest woman who'd been cursed by a shiftless man, and you couldn't trust a one of the blaggards, and anyway her man would be back one of these days or years and she'd tell him what she thought of him, she would. On and on she went, getting madder by the minute, as McGee backed up to the gate, fearing that if he turned around he'd get clobbered by that broom. He could still hear her ranting when he was four doors up the street.

When he got to Mrs. Johnson's house he saw her coming out of her barn with a load of small wood in her arms. Hurrying to her, he took the wood into the kitchen woodbox, then went after another load. Helen Johnson was most appreciative. Her grandchildren were coming that weekend, she said, and she was baking up a storm. She offered him a cup of tea, explaining that she was out of coffee. McGee told her he was out of coffee too and then explained his mission. "I figure I'm going to die pretty soon, Miz Johnson," he said, "and I'm a-trying to do some good deeds so I won't be going to hellfire and damnation. You got some other things I could do for you, sharpen some knives or anything else?"

Mrs. Johnson was a nice lady. Yes, she had some knives that needed sharpening and a pair of scissors too and perhaps he could fix that hinge on the cellar door. As he worked on the tasks, they had some pleasant conversation. Leaving, McGee told her he'd drop in every so often to see if she needed some help. No, he wouldn't take any pay. He was just doing a good deed.

His next stop was at Aunt Lizzie's house. When he explained why he wanted to do good deeds, her eyes lit up. Yes, she could sure use a man around the house. She had a lot of things that ought to be done but would he start by chopping her some small wood and kindling. She had a lot of it in the shed. McGee noticed that there was a coffeepot on the range and thought of asking for a cup but thought it might be wise to wait until he'd done some work. After he had quite a pile, he went back to the kitchen and asked her if he'd done enough. And he smelled the coffee. No, Aunt Lizzie said, after she'd examined the pile he'd cut. Just a mite more.

After he'd split a lot more, he asked Aunt Lizzie if she had any more he could do, noticing that she was drinking a cup of the coffee and eating a cinnamon roll. She didn't offer any of either but asked him to bring down a mattress from the bedroom to air it out and then to haul out the rugs and beat them and the mattress with the carpet beater after he hung them on the clothesline. Now mattresses are mean critters to bring down narrow stairs. You just can't get a decent hold on them. They flop around and stick and jam but somehow McGee got them out in the yard, thinking that it would have been a lot easier if Aunt Lizzie had helped a bit. Beating those damned rugs wasn't any fun either. A dirty dusty job but he got it done.

It seemed that the instant he finished one job, Aunt Lizzie came up with another. She had a kerosene lamp in which the wick had fallen into the bowl. Could he snake it out and rethread it? There was a barrel in the cellar full of trash and rotten apples. Would Mr. McGee please haul it up and put it behind the shed? Would he please climb up on the roof to see if the chimney needed cleaning? Did the chicken coop need cleaning? McGee took a look at it and was sure that it did but he said no. He was getting very tired. Needed a cup of coffee or something. Finally when Aunt Lizzie proposed that he clean her attic, McGee rebelled. "I'll haul that damned mattress back up to your bedroom," he said, "but that's it." Again she didn't help him and wrestling the thing up those narrow stairs almost did him in. Exhausted, he sat down in a chair in the kitchen trying to catch his breath.

Eyeing the coffee pot on the range, it being past noon, McGee finally asked Aunt Lizzie if she might spare a cup. "No." she said. "There's only about one cup left in it and I always like to have a cup after my nap." She didn't even thank him for all his work.

On his way back to his cabin Old Man McGee was figuring out how many good deeds he'd done. "Let's see," he said aloud as he walked down the hill street. "At Miz Johnson's I hauled two loads of wood, sharpened three knives and those damned scissors and fixed the cellar door. That makes seven. And up at Aunt Lizzie's - hell, I can't even count how many. Make it thirteen and that makes twenty. Not a bad day's work, McGee. Hope old Saint Peter is a-counting."

But there was still another good deed to come. As he passed Mrs. Johnson's house, she came out to the gate holding a dollar bill. "Mr. McGee, would you do one more good deed for me? Will you take this up to Flynn's store and get two pound bags of coffee? I'm in the middle of baking and can't get away and I'm just dying for a cup of coffee. Have them grind it on the big red coffee grinder." McGee was sure tired but did the errand and enjoyed the aroma of the coffee beans being ground. When he returned with the two bags and eleven cents, Mrs. Johnson gave him one bag of coffee for himself and told him to keep the change.

Old Man McGee went home, brewed himself a fat cup of coffee, and went to bed, unafraid of the hereafter.

Aunt Lizzie's Mulled Cider

The U.P. has always been known for its hard drinkers. So was Tioga. It wasn't just the cold winters and hard labor that made our men hit the bottle; it was mainly because the only place where they could gather together and have male companionship was Higley's Saloon. Few of them ever got really drunk (they didn't have the money) so they nursed their beers until closing time. Oh, there were one or two who might be considered real drunks, Billy Bones and Pete Ramos for instance, but for the most part our men just drank a little and went home to bed. None of our women ever went to Higley's Saloon but they often sipped some of their chokecherry wine. A few bought Lydia Pinkham's Vegetable Compound, which was half alcohol, to taste when life got too tough for them. There were few teetotalers in Tioga.

Every year or two a wandering temperance preacher came to town to raise a little hell. Our people listened politely but when church was over they returned home for a little nip to pass the winter away. One of those preachers, however, the Reverend Zachariah Smith, once caused a lot of trouble in our town mainly because he enlisted Aunt Lizzie to help the cause. He was a good hellfire preacher but unlike the others who claimed we were committing all sorts of sins, the Reverend Zachariah had boiled them all down into one: the imbibing of alcohol.

Lord, how he raised Cain about drinking. It was EVIL, he shouted. "The Turks, Mohammedans, they prohibit any use of Al Kohol (He spelled it out) because their word for the Devil is Al Kohol. Don't tell me that them infidels have a better religion than us Christians, but at least they know that beer and whiskey and wine are the devil's work. It's the curse of our nation!"

From there he went on to tell what alcohol did to your system, and he showed two lantern slides to illustrate. The first showed a normal stomach nice and clean; the second, a decrepit organ riddled with red and green abnormalities. Sure was scary! "But it's your liver," he roared, "that takes the real beating. It shrivels when alcohol comes into it, and sooner or later you'll die and go to hell." He showed us a livid liver that no one would want to have. I was so scared I resolved that I would never take a nip of anything alcoholic again. I remembered that my beloved Grampa Gage often took a slug from the black bottle he carried in his hip pocket and so I worried about him. And I myself had sneaked a little snort from the bottle of brandy and also from the bottle of Scotch whiskey my father kept in the cellar way. They tasted terrible, especially the Scotch, more like medicine than castor oil did. No, I'd never take another taste of The Devil so long as I lived.

Aunt Lizzie's Mulled Cider

Alas, I must confess I broke that resolution and gradually worked my way through beer and wine and bourbon to Scotch whiskey. In my college years, those when Prohibition ruled the land, I drank bathtub gin and moonshine on occasion, and once after Homecoming at the University of Iowa a policeman intercepted me as I was walking down an empty street with a flashlight. I told him I was Diogenes, looking for an honest man. "Well, you've found him," he said, "Come with me; Diogenes." It was the only night I ever spent in jail. So I made that early resolution all over again and promptly broke it. In my old age, I find that two fingers of whiskey at Happy Hour gives me a nice feeling of mellowness and serenity while one finger (or perhaps a thumb) helps me to have sweet dreams. But I never get drunken and I feel sorry for those who compulsively use the lovely poison to escape their troubles. Nor do I take my whiskey straight. "A little bit of water makes the whiskey go down, the whiskey go down, the whiskey go down. Oh, a little bit of water helps the whiskey go down, in a most delightful way." It helps me forget my aching old bones and makes me feel young again.

But back to my story. After painting our liquor-riddled organs scarlet and black, the Reverend Zachariah ranted about what liquor did to the families of boozers. "Al Kohol, the devil, wrecks families," he shouted. "Women and children starve when the wage earner wastes his pay on liquor." He lost us there. None of our women or children starved because of the money spent on a few beers at Higley's saloon. They always had potatoes in the cellar and illegal venison or fish in the shed. Sensing our negative response, the preacher became evangelical. "In this congregation," he insisted, "there are one or more persons who can be my hands, who can carry out my mission to rid this village of the curse of Al Kohol. Just one person can make all the difference. If any one of you feel that you can carry the torch of temperance, please see me after the service."

The only one who did was Aunt Lizzie. She told the Reverend Zachariah how impressed she was with his presentation and that she knew firsthand of the evils of drink because all of her husbands had imbibed and died. As a poor widow she would be glad to carry the torch of temperance and be his hands, but she didn't know how to begin. The Reverend Zachariah sold her two hundred copies of a tract on the evils of Al Kohol for ten dollars and told her to make a survey of the homes in Tioga and to leave a copy in each of them, and to try to persuade the saloon keeper to mend his ways. He also gave her free fifty copies of a card that read "Lips that touch liquor shall never touch mine" to distribute to the young girls of Tioga. They were to sign it, he said, as a perpetual pledge.

For his purposes, the Reverend Zachariah couldn't have picked a better person. Aunt Lizzie was our town gossip. Each day she walked our hill street from home to home collecting and spreading the rumors and tidbits of the day, especially those that could cause trouble. Some called her The Raven, the huge black bird that flies over the land searching for carrion. She was the nosiest person in town. Completely insensitive to criticism or rejection, and very tenacious, she roamed Tioga leaving a lot of hurt feelings in her wake. I suppose she served a useful purpose as our town's newspaper, helping us to know what had happened to each other. When the Catholic Church bell failed one morning to ring Angeles, Aunt Lizzie soon found out why. Old Francoise Pitu had been having an argument with the priest and besides his arthritis was acting up again. Lempi Salo had been kicked in the head by the cow she was milking. Dr. Gage had to put in five stitches. Pete Ramos was in jail again up at the town hall. Charlie Olafson had found him passed out in Mrs. Carlson's petunias. One of the high-school girls had told her that the new English teacher didn't wear any panties under her skirts. Pete Hemel's horse got in a clover patch and foundered. All bloated up and like to die. "They say that the priest is about to discharge his old ugly housekeeper and get a pretty younger one." So it went day after day as Aunt Lizzie made her rounds.

But now she had a cause and a calling. The Reverend Zachariah had asked her to be his hands, and the Lord's hands, in the battle against Al Kohol, the Devil. She had to take a survey to identify all those who had fallen from grace by way of the bottle. She had 200 temperance tracts to hand out and pledge cards to give to the girls. Aunt Lizzie was in full glory. She couldn't wait to get started.

Having memorized some selections from the temperance booklet, and never being at a loss for words anyway, Aunt Lizzie sure gave Tioga a good working over. Oh there were doors slammed in her face when the news of her crusade preceded her but she just tucked a copy of the tract under the door, jotted down the name of the householder in her notebook as a probable sinner and went on to the next home. When she was able to get inside, she gave her spiel, tried to get them to pay ten cents for the tract to recoup her investment, and if they refused she left it with them free. Many just told her to her face that it was none of her business if any one in the family drank. Didn't faze Aunt Lizzie in the least. She just preached a little harder, loving every moment of it. Altogether she became the worst nuisance our town had known since 1915, the Year of the Mouse, when hordes of them invaded our village. So far as we could tell, Aunt Lizzie converted few if any of us to the cause of temperance. Probably we just imbibed a bit more.

God-fearing, but fearing nothing else, one evening she even had the guts to enter Higley's Saloon where no woman or child had ever set foot to leave a handful of her temperance tracts. Higley leaped over the bar, picked her up in his, arms, took her outside and sat her down carefully in a snowbank. "You try that one more time and I'll throw you over the fence," he roared fiercely. Aunt Lizzie didn't try it again but it gave her the nice feeling of being a Christian martyr. Altogether she was having a ball.

For some reason, she had not visited our home until one bitterly cold winter after-noon. Perhaps she remembered how our cat, Puuko, had clawed her when she insisted on sitting in his chair, or perhaps it was because she knew my father was openly hostile to her. He'd told her outright that she was a nasty old busybody always stirring up trouble and that she was unwelcome in his house. It was a good thing that he was out making calls on his patients when she came to the door.

"May I come in, Mrs. Gage?" Aunt Lizzie said to my mother. "I'm about friz to death and fancy I'd better warm up before I go the rest of the way home." Of course mother had her come in and sat her in the chair next to our big baseburner, the hard coal stove. Aunt Lizzie was sure shivering, really shaking. "I've been preaching the temperance gospel over in Finn Town back of the mine and only one of them, Mrs. Rautila, the Holy Jumper, invited me inside. That wind, Mrs. Gage, is terrible today but the Lord's work must be done." Her shivering had begun to subside.

I knew mother was worrying that Dad might come home any minute and wanted her out of there before he did but, always the lady, she had to find ways of being hospitable. "I have some sweet cider heating on the kitchen stove," she said. "My husband always likes a mug of hot mulled cider when he comes home on such a cold day. Would you like some, Mrs. Campton? It will really warm you."

Aunt Lizzie was suspicious. "What's mulled cider?" she asked. "If it's the same as hard cider, thank you, no!"

"Oh no, it's sweet cider. We heat it first, then Cully gets a poker white hot in the dining room wood stove and puts it into the cider mug where it hisses. Mulling cider gives it a special flavor. Do try some." Mother motioned to me to get the Toby mugs and put the poker in the stove. Just then my father entered the back door off the kitchen. He was frozen too. "Good!" he said when he saw the cider heating on the kitchen stove. "I've been thinking of hot mulled cider all the way home. Oh, it's cold out there!"

Mother hurriedly explained about Aunt Lizzie and begged him to be pleasant. "I couldn't turn that poor old woman away, John," she insisted. "After she's warmed up and had a mug of hot cider I'll find some way to get rid of her." Dad growled but gave in. "Cully," he said, "You be sure to put the usual three fingers of brandy in my mug after you put the poker in it." Then he stalked into the living room, gave Aunt Lizzie a curt nod and started to read his Chicago Tribune.

I got the brandy from the cellar way, put the poker in the woodstove and turned up the draft lever on the stovepipe to get a hot fire, then fetched four Toby mugs (those with the funny faces baked into the clay) and put them side by side by the stove. Mother and Aunt Lizzie were chatting in the living room and being studiously ignored by my father. I'd planned to bring the hot cider from the kitchen stove to fill the mugs but the handle was too hot so I brought back the mugs to the kitchen putting Dad's brandy in one of them. After it was filled and ready for the white hot poker, I brought them back to the dining room stove and had fun with the mulling.

Proudly I bore the first two mugs, one for Aunt Lizzie and the other to my father, then went back to mull some for Mother and me. In just a few moments my father stomped past me into the kitchen to get more brandy. He was angry. "I told you to put three fingers of brandy in the cider, not one," he said to me as he passed. "Might as well be drinking hot swamp water." I couldn't argue with him because I was busy with the steaming poker but I really had put brandy in the mug. Yes, I had!

Then the thought came to me that somehow I'd mixed up the mugs and had given his to Aunt Lizzie. Oh, oh! I brought mother her cider and sat where I could watch the effects, if any. They were soon forthcoming. "My, my!" Aunt Lizzie exclaimed, "That's the best cider I ever drank in my life. It sure warms my innards!" Soon she was so warm she had to move her chair further from the stove and a bit later she began to giggle. No one in Tioga had ever heard Aunt Lizzie giggle. Mother couldn't believe her ears but kept a patter of conversation going only to find that whatever she said was greeted by that giggle. Yes, I must have given her the mug with the brandy in it. Her speech began to get a bit slurred by the time her mug was emptied and when she suggested she might like a bit more of that mulled cider if there were any left, my father, who had also made his own diagnosis, spoke for the first time, "No," he said firmly. "It's all gone and I'll have Cully hitch up the horse to the sleigh and take you home."

When I returned for Aunt Lizzie she had a helluva time putting on her coat even with mother's help and I had to support her as she staggered to the cutter. Getting her out of it when I reached her house was even more difficult but finally I got her through the door and into a chair.

I fully expected to catch bloody hell when I entered our back door where mother was waiting for me. "Is she all right?" mother asked anxiously. I reassured her. "Now, Cully, remember this: you are not to tell a living soul about what happened," she commanded.

"But I already have," I responded. "Aunt Lizzie begged me to tell her what was wrong with her so I did. I told her she was drunk." Mother moaned. "Suddenly my father was there in the kitchen with us. "All I want to know is if you did it on purpose?" he asked sternly.

"No," I replied. "I just got those two mugs mixed up. I don't know how it happened. Honest!"

Dad grinned his crooked grin. "Here," he said, giving me a new silver quarter. "If you'd done it on purpose, it would have been a half dollar instead. That old buzzard will think twice before she stops in here again."

I don't know just what impact the experience had on Aunt Lizzie. I do know that her crusade sort of seemed to peter out and peace again returned to Tioga.

The Honey Tree

Pete Half Shoes, our resident full-blooded Ojibway Indian, was one of my favorite people in Tioga, and with the other boys I often visited him and Mabel, his pet skunk, to while away a few hours before supper time. Pete liked kids, and dogs and kids always know when a man does or doesn't. Not that he ever really showed his feelings. His copper brown face seemed carved in red granite and we often did our utmost to get him to laugh or smile, making silly faces, doing silly things, saying nutty stuff, but he never batted an eye. Just sat there on the porch of his cabin smoking his pipe, petting Mabel, and watching our antics with complete impassivity.

Pete Half Shoes didn't talk much either. If you asked him a question, he'd consider it for a long time before answering, and when he did reply it was usually a single word or phrase. But he would willingly walk quite a ways in the woods to identify a strange animal track we had discovered. "Marten," he said, "Pine marten." A wonderful carver, he could whittle out a tiny canoe, or a frog, or squirrel in only a few minutes. Most of the kids who lived uptown in Tioga had something Pete Half Shoes had carved for them. Being with him in the woods was a revelation and an education. He taught us what was good to eat and what was not. He showed us to see with strange eyes, noticing things like the trail of a pine snake on the forest floor or the very high-pitched song of the grasshopper sparrow. "Indian bandage," he would say, pointing to the leaf of a hairy plantain. "Put on cut; no more bleed."

Unfortunately, most of the people in our town didn't appreciate old Pete Half Shoes the way we kids did. He didn't have a job nor want one, spending most of his time wandering in the woods, fishing and hunting, or every evening just before the St. Paul train pulled in he'd be in the corner of his favorite booth at Higley's Saloon drinking. It was always beer and rarely more than three bottles and he nursed them carefully so he wouldn't have to go home before ten o'clock. Only once had he ever got really drunk and that was when he tried to enlist in the army at the beginning of World War I and was told he was too old. That was a beauty, a ten day drunk, but he recovered and went the rhythm of his days thereafter.

But I think it was because of Mabel that most of our people didn't approve of Pete Half Shoes. He'd found the baby skunk and descented it when it was just a baby, made a pet of it, and often carried Mabel on his shoulder even when he went to Flynn's store to buy groceries. I liked Mabel. She was fun to play with; she liked being stroked; she liked kids to pick her up. People said that she was old Pete's bed partner but what was wrong with that? I've slept with a lot of cats in my day though my mother never knew

---

273

it. When they howled outside my back bedroom window on a cold or rainy night I just had to let them in. People said that Pete Half Shoes probably lived in filth because of that skunk but that wasn't true.

Once, when I hadn't seen him around for several days and the door was open I went in timorously to find him sitting in a chair reading. "Are you all right, Pete?" I asked. "I've been worrying about you." "Old Pete, OK," he replied, gave me a bit of maple sugar, then sat with me on his porch for a long time. I put my head against his leg, as a spaniel does to his master's knee and said, "I, I like you, Pete." After a moment he put his old hand on my head and said, "You good boy, Cully." And incredibly, he smiled. I felt anointed. Old Pete Half Shoes had smiled.

Shortly after this had happened I overheard a conversation, or rather an argument between my mother and father. "John," she said to him. "I want you to forbid Cully's going up to Pete Half Shoes' place so often. I don't think it's good for him to be around that shiftless drunken old Indian so much."

"No, damned if I will," replied my father, "and you mustn't either. Pete's no shiftless Indian and though he's a regular down at Higley's Saloon every evening, he never gets drunk. I respect Pete Half Shoes. He was an Indian Scout in the regular army for many years, took part in the campaign against Geronimo and the Apaches, fought with Roosevelt in the Spanish American War, and gets a good enough pension so he doesn't have to work."

"But that skunk? And he never goes to the sauna?" Mother interjected. "You don't either, Edyth," said my father. "He's a clean man and a proud man. You know how he marches with the other few veterans in our Fourth of July parades and he puts up an American flag in his window every morning and takes it down every night. He pays his bills at Flynn's store and never causes any trouble. I'm glad to have Cully have a chance to be with him. He may learn more from old Pete than he does in school."

So I had no trouble being with the old Indian any time I wanted to. I helped him pick berries and was fascinated to see how he dried them, sometimes in a pan on the stove, sometimes on his roof, blueberries, raspberries, thimbleberries and even cranberries. Pete never canned them as our people always did. He didn't have a garden either. When I asked him why not, he just grunted, "Squaw work. Pete got no squaw." He bought his winter potatoes from his neighbors or traded them for the venison he'd shot in season or out. Every spring he made a batch of maple syrup and boiled it down to maple sugar and I helped him gather wood for the boiling down.

He had another source of sweetening too as I found out one summer's day. One hot afternoon in July Fisheye, Mullu and I were planning to take a swim in Lake Tioga. As we took the shortcut through the grove to go down Company Field hill, we saw Pete Half Shoes putting a pork and bean can in the clover. Curious of course, we had to go over to see what he was doing. "Old Pete hunting for honey tree," he said after a long silence. "Sugar for winter." Suddenly he plopped the can down, then slipped a bit of birch bark under its opening. We could hear the bee buzzing inside. Then, standing upright, he let the bee go, watching where it went, and placing some poplar shoots to line its path toward the grove. You couldn't see that honey bee very long, so Pete had to catch several before he was sure of the line. Of course we begged to catch some honeybees too, and he let us but when Mullu caught a big bumblebee in the can, Pete said, "No. Bumblebee no good for honey. Get little one like so." He had me go to the fence line of the grove and waved me to the right or left as he let the bees go until he had the direction right. Then he moved over to one side about fifty feet and started getting bee lines again with other bees. Tiring of it, we kids headed for the lake.

One bitter morning the next winter I swiped some new cookies from the jar in the pantry and with Mullu brought them up to Pete Half Shoes. He thanked me and asked if we wanted to go with him to cut down a honey tree to get some honey. We were overjoyed, of course. Pete had located it by triangulation the summer before and when we put our ears to the trunk of the basswood tree we could hear humming inside.

"But won't the bees sting us?" Fisheye asked. Pete thought a long time, then said "No!" I'd carried his one man cross-cut saw and Mullu had Pete's ax and Pete had two water pails. Soon they were put to use. First Pete chopped the kerf so the tree would fall on its back opposite the little slit through which the bees had entered and left. A few bees zoomed out but when they hit the cold air, it just zapped them and they fell dead in the snow below. Then Mullu and I took turns sawing and finally the big tree fell with more bees getting zapped. We never got stung once though we sure expected it. Then Pete made two half cuts above and below the entrance hole or slit, let more bees swarm out to die, and then with the axe cut out a slab to reveal the honeycomb inside.

Lord there was a lot of honey in that basswood tree. Taking off his mittens Pete just scooped the stuff into the pails, honeycomb, larvae, bees and all. Didn't look too appetizing but Pete dug out a handful of honey and frozen bees from the trunk to stuff it in his mouth. "Bees best of all," he said. So, of course we had to try it too. Incredibly sweet it was, and very sticky. I couldn't help but spit out some of the honey-coated grubs or whatever they were and soon I'd had enough honey. But Pete Half Shoes insisted we each take a big chunk of it home with us, something we eventually regretted for our mittens never lost their stickiness till April.

Then suddenly Mullu who had been chomping on his hunk of bee mess gave a howl, a scream, and ran around in circles, alternately holding his mouth and sticking his tongue out as far as he could. Must have got a live bee. And then, for the first time we heard the old Indian laugh. Oh how he cackled! A rusty sort of cackle and laugh. With his tongue hanging out, Mullu said he had to get home so I went with him, carrying the axe and saw, and letting Pete to carry the pails of honey back later.

When we reached the grove, I asked Mullu if it still hurt awfully badly. "Naw," he said. "I didn't get stung at all. I just wanted to make old Pete Half Shoes laugh. And I did!"

But I had made him smile.

Slimber Tells The Truth

It all happened because Sally Griggs, our third grade teacher, invited her father and sister from Chicago to see the town where she had taught the year before and would again this year. They'd arrive on the morning train and leave on the evening one.

Sally's letters about Tioga and its people and the forest had intrigued them greatly and they hoped to see as much as they could in the short time at their disposal. Now really there's not much to see in Tioga so Sally arranged with old man Marchand who owned the livery stable to provide her with a horse and a two seated buckboard so they could drive up along the Tioga River to the Haysheds where the stream broke through a big chain of granite hills in a spectacular waterfall and rapids. "Oh yes," she told Marchand, "and please find me a good driver, one who knows the land and its history and who's a good storyteller. I'll pack lunch for the lot of us. Leave at ten and be back here about four in the afternoon."

Marchand knew just the man to be the driver, he said, Slimber Jim Vester. Knew horses and the country and sure could tell stories. Sally vaguely recalled the name. "Is he the one they tell about who caught a trout with a posthole digger, the one who crossed a blue heron with a duck? The one they call the biggest liar in Tioga?" "Oui, ma femme, Slimber he the man," answered Marchand. "He tell you stories for sure, oui!"

Slimber was glad to see that Marchand not only gave him the new buckboard with two seats and cushions but also Celeste, the big brown horse, to pull it. He'd been afraid he'd get old Maude, notoriously the slowest horse in town, whose back legs were said to walk backward when the front ones went forward. Celeste clopped along smartly and soon Slimber was at the door of the boarding house. Jumping down and doffing his cap politely to reveal that saintly face of his framed in white whiskers, he introduced himself and Celeste. Sally greeted him warmly and presented her sister, June, and her father Mr. William Griggs. A lawyer from Chicago, she said, who also wrote articles about the many places he traveled. "So don't tell us any of your little fibs," she added.

Slimber felt insulted. "I don't tell fibs," he said. "I tell only big fancy lies and them only to those bums down at the saloon. I'll tell you only the truth, the whole truth, and nothing but the truth, so help me."

"God!" said the lawyer from Chicago.

As Slimber was handing up the girls to the rear seats and the father to his, Sally asked him to drive first past the old mine and then down the back road to Lake Tioga before they went up the road alongside the river. "My father and sister just must see that lovely lake," she said. "There are fifteen pine-covered Islands in it and..."

"Begging your pardon, Ma'am," interrupted Slimber. "There's only fourteen of 'em and Flat Island doesn't have a tree on it since it burnt off six, no seven years ago." A stickler for the truth was Slimber Vester.

Of course they had to stop at the mine to see the cave-in and Slimber filled them in with some of its history. "At one time this was the deepest iron mine in the world," he said proudly. "One of its shafts went down a mile. Even when it was twenty below zero on the surface it was so warm down there the men only worked short shifts, ten hours a day rather than the usual twelve. Hard to believe now," he said waving around at the abandoned buildings and desolate rock piles, "but when I was a young man we had a thousand men working here."

"Were you a miner?" asked June.

"Well, yes and no," said the old man. "I worked on surface, carpenter work and such. Never wanted to go underground though the pay was better. Saw too many men come up with their heads cracked open like hazelnuts and their brains leaking down over their ears. Rocks fall from ceiling of the stopes, them's the big rooms where they've taken out the ore. This here cave-in come because the Mining Company robbed too much ore off the pillars that supported the ceiling." Slimber for a moment almost started telling the story of how August Keski, riding the skip down with two cases of dynamite, saved himself when the hoisting cable broke by jumping up in the air just before the cage hit bottom but he resisted the temptation. Too bad! It was a good story the way he could tell it but no sir, he wasn't going to tell a single lie all day. No sir!

Instead he told them about the blue snow they had when the mine was working. That raised some eyebrows until he explained that this was a hard ore mine, with specular hematite, silvery blue in color, not red like the ordinary hematite in most mines. "When the big crusher was working hard, grinding up the chunks of ore that came up from the bowels of the earth, the dust covered everything including the snow with a light blue color." Noting that they were doubting, Slimber found a little piece of specular hematite to show them. As its fine scales glistened in the sun it looked more silver than blue. "Just the same, snow looks blue when crusher working," insisted Slimber.

To change the subject Slimber pointed out the tall stone smoke stack that still stood above the stone walls of the engine room building. "Every night about sundown thousands of swallows circle around that stack and ever so often one of them folds its wings and drops down into the chimney like a rock. Don't know how they stop or find their nest but every morning they come out at sunrise again. Worth seeing. Ever see that, Miss Sally?" he asked. She said no, but that she'd sure be looking now.

Back on the buckboard it was pleasant being out of the sun and under the tall trees that arched over the sandy ruts of the road. Very quiet and very peaceful with only the sounds of Celeste's hooves breaking the silence. At one of the turns a little road branched off to the left. "That's the old stagecoach road," Slimber said. "Tioga in the old, old days, was just a stagecoach stop where they changed horses and drivers, just barns and a sleeping shack or two. The road really was a military road, running from Green Bay in Wisconsin up to Fort Wilkins on the Keewenaw peninsula where they kept a garrison of soldiers, I dunno why, mebbe to fight the Indians. Anyway, once a week in the summer a stage coach was hauled along this old military road, bringing up mail, some supplies, and the payroll for the soldiers. No railroads back then."

"They say that once some highway bandits tried to shanghai that there payroll but the drivers whipped up their horses and the paymaster inside the coach threw out the money bags in a narrow part of the road where them men a-chasing them couldn't pass. I dunno if the story is true. I hunted all along that old road when I was a boy and never found any gold pieces. That's what they paid them with in the old days."

Out of the corner of his eye, Slimber noticed that Mr. Griggs had been writing in his notebook, things like: "Mine, one mile deep?" "Blue snow?" "Thousand swallows drop in chimney like rocks?" and now "Stagecoach money sacks?" Slimber didn't like those question marks one bit. Hell, he'd been telling the truth all the time.

When they got to the shores of Lake Tioga, Slimber stopped the horse, and the four people went down to the sandy beach to get a better look at it. A beautiful lake, a large one, seven miles long and a mile wide, Slimber told them. It seemed brim full, with the waters lapping the base of the labrador tea bushes at its edge. It had rocky points too and the first of the pine-crowned islands were clearly visible. The water was so clear every pebble could be seen. High hills, mostly granite, surrounded the lake as far as one could see.

"How's the fishing?" asked Mr. Griggs.

Slimber paused a bit before answering, remembering what a bad time he'd had when he caught Old Lunker, that great northern pike, and the bear stole it from him just before he reached town. He was tempted to tell the tale because, after all it was God's truth, but if his own townspeople never believed him, these foreigners from down below wouldn't either. So all he said was that there were bass, walleye and the biggest Northern pike you could find in any lake in the U.P. His arms ached to show them how big Old Lunker really was, but he resisted.

He did tell them that once in the old days there had been a steamboat on the lake. That raised their eyebrows. Why would you need a steamboat on a lake that was only seven miles long and a mile wide? "Well," said Slimber defensively, "It was really only a tugboat they'd hauled up on the plank road from Marquette, but it had a real steam engine that burned wood. They used it to haul rafts of hardwood from the hills across the lake to fuel the big boilers at the mine before the railroad came to town." Slimber could see Mr. Griggs writing "Steamboat????" (But it was true. I, Cully, played on the tug's wreckage when I was a boy and still remember the rusty smokestack that emerged from the lake at the place it had been beached.)

As they drove along the south side of Lake Tioga to its end, Slimber pointed out some depressions in the ground. "Those are the deer pits," he said. "In the old days, the first settlers and Indians used to dig deep pits in the deer trail that deer then used to migrate when the deep snows came. Then they planted deeply in them some very sharp stakes before covering the pits with a light layer of branches. The deer would fall into these pits and skewer themselves. Bullets cost too much those days," Slimber said. "Men had to eat. No, they don't migrate like they used to. Now they yard up in a cedar swamp to make it through the winter." Mr. Griggs made an entry in his notebook. Slimber couldn't see if it had the usual question mark.

"How did they know where to put the deer pits?" Mr. Griggs asked. It was a challenge. "There's miles and miles of forest here."

"That's easy explained," replied Slimber, slapping the reins on Celeste's rump. "Deer form runways, travel the same path often enough so you can see it. They usually travel single file. Down here as they had to go around the lake on their migration south they'd trod down the path for centuries. Hard to see now because they don't do it any more but when I was a boy that migrating path was about a foot deep still. So the old-timers just put their staked pits in the deep ruts." Mr. Griggs erased something in his notebook.

Soon they were trotting along the road that ran beside the Tioga River. Sally saw a big bird flying overhead. "What a big crow!" she exclaimed, pointing. "Naw, that's no crow. That's a raven" said Slimber. "Hear him a croakin'? Ravens don't caw like crows. They croak. They got a bell sound too that they make. Not many people ever hear that bell sound. Ravens don't fly south; they stay up here with us all winter."

"Quoth the raven 'Nevermore'," said June.

"Naw, ravens can't talk," said Slimber, "but crows can." He told them the story about Nikki Sippola's pet crow that almost broke up their marriage by saying, "I come back." It was a true story but Slimber knew none of the three would believe a word of it.

The Tioga is a beautiful river running thirty-forty feet wide through the forest but in summertime it is usually only about three or four feet deep at most. Many rocks lift their heads above the current. Slimber had been regaling his passengers with stories of the old logging days and the river drives of the spring when thousands of huge logs were floated down the river to Lake Tioga.

"It's hard for me to believe that the kind of logs you describe could ever be floated down such a shallow stream," Mr. Griggs said. "I think you told us some of them were five or six feet across at the butt. A big log like that would weigh a ton. Surely, sir, you have been exaggerating a little. Weren't those logs really smaller, say about two feet across?"

That irritated Slimber. "Just look at those old stumps alongside the road," he said. "They're five to seven feet across. These were cork pine, Mister. Virgin pine, sometimes one hundred fifty to two hundred feet tall. You saw one down and when it crash it sounds like thunder."

"I still don't see how they could be floated down this stream," Mr. Griggs objected.

"Ah hell, Mister," Slimber said. "This is summer low water. In spring flood the Tioga is six, eight feet deeper. And then they had logging dams upstream, holding back lakes of water that they released through the sluice gates to send a wall of water down that could float any log any size." Then Slimber told them of the log-jams and how the rivermen with their pikes and peavies would have to tease out the key log, or sometimes dynamite it, to get the river of logs flowing again. He told them how the men would ride the logs, birling, rolling them with their caulked boots to steer them a mite when they had to. He told them about some of the tragic deaths and miraculous rescues that had occurred. Completely fascinated by his stories, the passengers often also showed little signs of skepticism.

Mr. Griggs pulled out a big gold watch from his vest pocket and opened the lid. "Oh, half past noon already," he said. "I'm hungry. Is there somewhere near here where we can have our picnic lunch? I know the girls must have something good in that hamper you put behind the seats."

"Yeah, there's a fine place just around the next bend," Slimber replied. "A fine spring there and a little clearing right above the river."

It was indeed a lovely spot. Taking off Celeste's bridle, he gave her a half pail of oats and some hay from the buckboard, then showed the Griggs around.

"There's the big spring," Slimber pointed, "and there's the little one. Best water south of Lake Superior." The girls opened the hamper, spread out a tablecloth with four cups and plates. "Oh, I brung my own grub," said Slimber, pulling out of the pocket of his coat in the buckboard a big onion, a chunk of bologna and some korpua, but they insisted he share their food. The bottle of milk, however, was warm, so as it cooled in the lower spring, Slimber made them a birch bark cup, peeling a piece of bark from a nearby tree, rolling it into a cone, folding the lower half up to the brim and then fastening that with a cleft stick. All of them had to try it and agreed that they'd never had such ice-cold delicious water.

"You kin boil water in a birch bark basket," Slimber said. "I've made lots of coffee and tea that way in my day." Mr. Griggs made a mental note: "Boil water in birch bark???????"

The girls had been prowling around the edges of the clearing and brought back some berries. Slimber took one look and plucked out three big blue ones. "Good thing you didn't try to eat these," he said. "Them's aconite-bad poison. Four of 'em would put you in a casket. The other's are all right: blueberries, thimbleberries, one red raspberry, and some wintergreen berries." He ate one of each in the interest of eternal truth and was glad to see that for once they believed him because they tasted them.

Their doubts began again, however, when he found a Venus fly trap, the pitcher plant, and told them it ate flies. It was old and dried up and so didn't have any of the flies and bugs it usually contains. Then he found a ladyslipper, also long out of bloom and a bit bedraggled. "Educated fella told me once this lady slipper, they also call it an Indian moccasin, is the only North American orchid," he said, "but I don't know what's an orchid." They explained but said it didn't look like any orchid they'd ever viewed.

Packing up their stuff after the meal and with a last drink of spring water from the birch bark cup, they resumed their journey and soon were at the Haysheds. Tying Celeste to a tree, Slimber led them first by way of the upper trail to where the river had broken through the huge granite hills and where in the old days a logging dam had been constructed. (It has always been one of my favorite spots in the U.P.) Above the remnants of the old dam there's a great marsh where you can see for miles. "Yeah, they could store plenty of water there for floating the logs," Slimber said. "It was a lake a third as big as Tioga." He led the way to where they could peer over the granite cliff to see the water plunging fifty feet in a series of cascades around a huge waterworn granite hillock in the middle. Not much of the old dam remained but Slimber showed them where the sluice gate had been located and the log apron and flume were. "You ought to see it in the spring flood," said Slimber. "Then it's just one big waterfall."

The Griggs were impressed. "This is one of the most beautiful spots I've ever seen," said Sally.

"Let's take the lower trail," said Slimber. "It'll give you a better view," but as they did so, they found a dead porcupine in the path. Slimber looked it over carefully. "I'd say it was killed either by a bobcat or lynx. See, the bottom's all eaten out. Them wildcats are the only thing will kill a porcupine. They flip them over and chew out their insides." As they made their way to the bottom of the falls and oohed and aahed about them, Slimber showed them some of the quills he'd plucked off the porky, pointing out the sharp barbs on their ends. "Why they look like a crochet needle," June said, "only much sharper."

"Sure are sharp," Slimber agreed. "Hard to pull out even with pliers. And if they break off, they work their way all through the flesh. A Finn man over by Halfway got one in his foot and it traveled all the way up to his knee before it come out. And I know of a dog that had a quill go to his heart and kill him." Slimber could just see Mr. Griggs putting down more question marks in that damned notebook of his but he gave each of them a big quill to take home for a souvenir.

Slimber was kind of quiet on the way home. They had to have another drink from the birch bark cup at the spring and June asked if she could keep it. Then Mr. Griggs asked Slimber about what fish were in the river.

"Mainly brook trout," Slimber replied. "Range from six to twelve inches mainly. Good eating though, any size. Also there's chubs and shiners and hornadays and a few big suckers."

"How do you fish for trout?" asked Mr. Griggs. Maybe he couldn't stand the silence.

"Oh usually with a government pole-that's an alder branch, a fishline and hook and worm. Not hard to catch. Once in a while we just tickle them." Slimber knew immediately that he should have had more sense than say that even if it were true.

"Tickle trout?" Mr. Griggs' voice was incredulous. Slimber explained how it was done but the more he talked the more they doubted him. Dammit, he'd have to show them. If he could! Trout were scarier this time of season. Tickling was better in the spring. But when they got to a plank culvert where a little stream crossed the road, Slimber saw a likely place, a little pool just below a new beaver dam, not far from the river. "Well, let me give her a try here," he said. "I don't guarantee it but I might just be able to show you how it's done anyway." He took off his shirt and lowered his arm very carefully into the pool and waited some time as the Griggs people watched. Then suddenly the arm came up with a big fish that he flung on the bank. "Ah hell!" exclaimed Slimber. "Just a big red horse sucker but that's how we tickle trout, Mister. Let yer hand lie there quiet till a fish swims over it, then slowly stroke it till you feel the gills, then heave 'em out on the bank."

"Well, I'll be damned!" said Mr. Griggs.

They stopped only one other time on the way home to give the horse a drink at a little pond that lapped the side of the road. Beside it was a big birch tree that had been girdled deeply by a beaver. Although Slimber told them that beavers have two three-inch long curved brown teeth sharp as a razor, they found it hard to believe they could have gnawed such large chips from such a big tree. While they waited, Slimber picked some chokecherries from a nearby bush and gave them a few for tasting. Then as they winced from the puckering of their lips he said that chokecherries made the best wine in the U.P. They doubted that too. An overturned pine stump showed signs, Slimber said, that it had been done by a bear eating ants. "Them ants, they're the bear's salt and pepper," said Slimber and out came Mr. Griggs' notebook again.

Only one other occurrence happened on the way back. Suddenly, Celeste snorted, then balked, then tore down the road as fast as she could while the girls screamed and clung to their seats. "Bear smell!" said Slimber holding tight to the reins. "I smelled it. Didn't you folks?" They hadn't.

Driving home in a horse and buggy always seems to take a lot longer than going some place. Finally, to break the silence Mr. Griggs asked Slimber if he hunted as well as fished.

"Why sure," said Slimber, surprised at the question. "Everybody hunts up here in the U.P., in season and out. Except for bacon and salt pork not many of our families ever buy store meat. Oh, some raise and butcher a steer or have a few pigs, but it's the game as feeds us through the winter till the fish come. I get me a deer or two each year and lots of rabbits, ducks, and partridge. I like partridge hunting best."

"How do you hunt partridge?" Mr. Griggs was passing time.

"Well, some shoot them on the wing but they use too many shells. Me, I like to spot them on the ground and shoot 'em before they cackle and fly off. Walk slow and shoot fast. Sometimes they'll fly up in a tree and then it's easy pickings."

"I thought you used a pointer dog to locate them," Mr. Griggs interjected.

"Naw, not me. Oh the dudes from down below do bring up some of them fancy dogs to point pat and then retrieve, but as for me if I had a dog I'd want a barker. Had one long ago, and he sure was good. Soon as he'd see a partridge he start yapping like crazy and the pat would fly up into the nearest tree every time and I'd shoot him easy. Only had him one season. He got chewed up all to hell by another dog and died. Then I used an alarm clock for a season or two…"

"An alarm clock?" Griggs was fumbling for his notebook.

"Yah," said Slimber. "That works too, just like the barking. You wind it up and then when you think you see a pat, you turn it on ringing, and the bird goes up in the nearest tree." Slimber was about to tell of his old horse Joshua who used to point partridge with his left front leg but, seeing the skeptical expression on the lawyer's face, he skipped it. Too bad. Joshua did point partridge.

At last they had left the hills and were back on the long plains bordering the river. They were beautiful with white daisies, orange indian paint brush, some early goldenrod and a few splotches of pink fireweed. And, of course, blueberry bushes.

"Slimber, why aren't there any trees here on the plain?" asked Sally. "Did they use to farm this land?"

"No Ma'am," the old man replied. "This land been burned over so many times, couldn't even grow hay. Pete Ramos' pappy, he used to burn it over every other year to make bigger blueberries. Sure did, too. Something about ashes that makes fine blueberries. We used to fill pailfuls here but one year old man Ramos he let his fire get away from him and we sure had a godawful forest fire and they put him jail for setting it. Still some good blueberries here but not like it was."

"You mean that someone would set a forest fire just to get blueberries?" Mr. Griggs asked. Slim didn't even answer, just slapped Celeste's butt with the reins to get her a moving.

Finally, when they got back to Sally's boarding house, the two girls thanked Slimber profusely for his "entertaining stories" and the porcupine quills and the birch bark cup but Mr. Griggs said he'd ride down to the livery stable with him to pay "the fees".

"Entertaining stories," they'd said, thought Slimber. Hells bells, he'd told the truth, the whole truth and nothing but the truth, so help me, all day long. Well, if they didn't believe him, they could go to the devil. And if that lawyer buzzard asked him a question on the way down to the livery stable, he'd really tell him a whopper-if he could think of one.

The question was forthcoming. "I understand you have some deep snows here in the winter, Slimber," Mr. Griggs said. "How deep do they get?"

The old man's eyes lit up. "Well, Mister," he said. "Some years worse than others. On a good year, maybe six feet on the level; bad years twice as much. That's not counting drifts that can be thirty feet high. People quit shoveling and just make tunnels to their gates. Not as bad here though, as in the Copper Country up the road. There they have snow so deep they have to keep crews working to keep the telephone wires from being buried."

Mr. Griggs pulled out the notebook and made an entry. "How do you keep the roads open?" he asked.

"We don't," said Slimber. "We just ski or snowshoe on top. We take the runners off our cutters and just slide along, toboggan-like behind the horse."

"But how do the horses ever get along in such deep snow?"

"On snowshoes, too, like us. Special round ones big around as this." Slimber made a big circle with his arms. "They soon learn how to spraddle their legs and walk on 'em easy as a man can. Course their legs are further apart anyway."

Mr. Griggs was gulping. "And the cold? It must get pretty cold up here," he said.

"Cold? That's God's truth," Slimber answered. "Stays in the twenty and thirty belows for months. That's why we make firewood all summer to keep from shivering all winter. And it gets colder than that, sometimes forty, fifty below. That's cold, Mister. If you spit when it's fifty below it pops in the air from freezing."

Mr. Griggs was impressed but thoughtful. "I don't know quite how to say it, but how do you er relieve yourself when the cold is so intense?"

"Well", said Slimber. "You just fill yer pants if you can't get to an outhouse. And if you can't wait to pee, you just let the tip of yer pecker out of your pants and hold it in both hands to keep it from freezing. Had a bad accident that way a year or two ago. Arnie Pelkle was in the bush on snowshoes when he couldn't hang on for another minute. Fifty-two below, it was, and with a strong wind, so Arnie straddles close behind a big tree to take his leak. Should have let it go down his leg inside his pants but he didn't, and you know what, his stream froze in the air and chained him to that there tree. If Okkari hadn't happened to come by to chop that icicle with his hand axe, Arnie would have been there till spring. He never did have any more kids after that."

A saintly smile came over Slimber's face. "Not bad," he said to himself. "Not bad."

The Artist

One fine morning in July I was cutting across lots to see if I could persuade Mullu to explore Goochee Swamp with me. I wanted to know if it was true that a compass went crazy in that area. Just something to do when it was too bright for trout fishing. As I went through Marchand's barnyard I saw the old Frenchman talking to a stranger who had a suitcase beside him. "Ah, Cully", he called. "You come here, eh? Zis man, he come from Chicago and need driver. You want to drive him, oui? He want find place for a cabin to build." I accepted eagerly. Might make a few dollars and it was better than fighting windfalls in that swamp. "How long will we be gone?" I asked the man.

"I don't know," he replied. "Perhaps just the morning. Perhaps all day. I plan to catch the evening train for Chicago but may stay a few days if I find what I want." I looked him over. A man about thirty, he was very stylishly dressed and topped by a straw hat. Every thing about him spelled city. While Marchand was hitching up old Maude to the buckboard I ran home to tell mother I might not be back for lunch, stuffed some cookies in my pocket, and returned.

As old Maude plodded down the hill, the man introduced himself. "I'm Carl Forster," he said. "I'm an artist, a painter. Up to now I've mainly done portraits and am sick of doing them. Want to try landscapes and such. Woodlands and water. But really what I want to do is to escape from the city and try a new life."

"How did you happen to pick Tioga?" I asked.

The man grinned. "Well I got a map," he said, "and decided to go as far north as the railroad would take me. So here I am riding behind an old horse along one of the most beautiful rivers I've ever seen and I've traveled widely both here and in Europe. Now all you have to do is to find me a Walden Pond so I can build a cabin and live a simple life free from all my past."

When I told him I'd read Thoreau's *Walden* and also his *A Week on the Concord and Merrimac River*, the artist was surprised and delighted. "Then you'll know what I'm seeking," he said. "But who are you? I've told you a bit about myself so it's your turn."

I answered that I was Cully Gage, the son of the town doctor, that I was sixteen years old and that my dad wanted me to go away to college but that I didn't want to at all. The thought that I might have to leave the forest and lakes and streams was hard to bear. Books were fine and I'd read a lot of them but going away to spend four years in classrooms and libraries didn't appeal to me a bit. Maybe I'd just take off, build me a shack up by Lake Superior and live off the land, hunting, fishing, and trapping.

"You are a kindred spirit, Cully, my friend, and I was lucky to find you," he said. "You probably know much that I must discover. All I know is that I've got to shed my old life as a snake sheds its skin. What was it Thoreau said? 'Simplicity, simplicity, simplicity. I've never known that.'" Out of his pocket he pulled a well-worn copy of Thoreau's *Walden*, hunting for a passage he'd underlined, then read it to me: "I went to the woods because I wished to live deliberately, to confront only the essential facts of life and see if I could learn what it had to teach, and not, when I came to die, discover I had not lived. I wanted to live deep and suck out all the marrow of life."

I interrupted. "He also said somewhere that most men live lives of quiet desperation. I don't want to live like that. I don't want to be famous or be rich. I just want to wander in the forest like a courier du bois or a mountain man living by my skills and wits." I felt a bit embarrassed talking that way to a grown man but found that he hadn't even been listening.

"Stop the horse!" he demanded. "Look at that! Look at that!" he exclaimed. We were in the middle of the plains where the forest fires had swept years before, in the center of a vast sea of white daisies, yellow buttercups, and orange paint brush with a few dark blueberry bushes thrown in. Mr. Forster cupped his hands, framed them, then peered out at the panorama. "Breathtaking! I must paint that. No more damned portraits. If I can…" He picked an Indian paintbrush to riffle its petals. "Burnt umber and…" He was talking to himself. Almost seemed to forget that Maude and I were there. Suddenly, after he had bent over and peered at the scene from between his legs, he snapped out of it. "I suppose you think I'm crazy doing that," he said, "But when I was in France studying painting, the master told me that only by looking at a landscape upside down could you see the true colors."

We stopped two more times, once so he could view a single white birch sapling from various distances, and then again when we came to Hansen's pool where the great granite hill plunges straight down into the river. There's a diagonal strip of red feldspar on the face of the cliff that contrasts with the blue-gray of the granite.

"Spectacular!" said Mr. Forster. "Spectacular! That I must paint too." He studied it for the longest time before noticing that Maude and I were getting restless. When finally he climbed back on the buckboard, he said, "Yes. This is where I live and paint. All I need is a Walden Pond where I can build a cabin."

I told him that up the road a little ways might be the place, that there was a little pond, maybe about five acres of it, on the south side of the road. It was spring fed, I told him, and its outlet was a little stream that ran under a culvert into the Tioga. There were a few trout in it too, I added, and asked him if he were a fisherman or hunter. No, he replied. He'd never caught a fish or fired a gun in his life. I wondered how the hell he'd ever make it through the winter.

When we got there, I took off Maude's bridle and put the halter on so the old gal could munch the grass along the road while we explored. It sure was a pretty place all right with a little clearing that overlooked both the pond and the river and a good view of the granite hills. Lots of spruce and balsam surrounded the opening and you could hear the gurgle of the stream down in the ravine. I sat on a rock in the clearing and ate a cookie as the artist prowled around exclaiming. When he returned he was ecstatic. "This is it. This is where I'll have my cabin. This is where I'll live the rest of my life! Let's see how big a cabin Thoreau built." He pulled out the book.

"If I remember right," I said, "It was ten by fifteen and cost him only twenty-eight dollars, but that was almost a hundred years ago. And he scrounged a lot of his building material including a thousand old bricks." Yes, I knew my *Walden*. After all I'd read it three times.

Mr. Forster had found the passage and corroborated the size and cost. He picked up a few rocks and placed them to show where the corners of a cabin about that size would be. "Yes," he said to himself. "A log cabin with a big window on this side overlooking the river and another big window from which I can see my pond." I raised my eyebrows. "That would be OK for a summer cabin," I said, "but with all that glass you'd freeze to death in the winter. Thoreau didn't have that many windows in his cabin. And that will make it expensive too even if you'd build it yourself."

The artist laughed. "Oh no, I couldn't build anything. Surely there are men in Tioga who could. As for the expense, I don't care how much it costs. I inherited more money than I can ever use. Maybe that was my curse. Do you know of someone who could build it for me?"

I thought immediately of Mullu's father and told Mr. Forster about him. He was one of the best log butchers in the county. He'd built his own cabin, a fine one, two story and three bedrooms, and also several other cabins. At the moment too he was out of work and the haying was done so perhaps he might take the job. Not cheap but a real craftsman and absolutely honest. It would be hard to find a better person. "But how about the land?" I asked. "You'll have to buy it from the owner."

"Of course," the artist replied. "I hadn't thought of that. How would I find the owner?" I suggested that the best way was to ask my father who was our township supervisor. "He keeps the tax rolls and would have the information on the ledger," I said.

"Good!" replied the artist. "Wouldn't it be wonderful if I could buy the land and get someone to build the cabin before I go back to Chicago." I asked him if he wouldn't like to go further along the river road to see some other possible places but he said no, that he'd found the place where he'd spend the rest of his life. We did stop at The Narrows where the river goes through a little gorge so he could watch the roaring rapids and the little islands of foam tumbling over the rocks.

"How can I capture that? How can I possibly?" he asked himself. Then opening his suitcase from under the seat he brought out a pad of heavy paper and some fat charcoal pencils to sketch me and Maude and the buckboard. He was a real artist all right. Just a few swift strokes and he had us right there on paper. Amazing! I hoped he might let me have it but no; he put the sketch back in the suitcase. Said he wanted to show it to someone in Chicago. When we got back to Tioga, Mr. Forster asked me to take him to a restaurant and was shocked to find that we had none. "But where will I eat?" he asked. I thought of asking my mother to feed him but it was way past noon so I told him I'd drive him to Flynn's store where he could buy something for a picnic on the shore of Lake Tioga. Then we'd go back to find out from my father who owned the land and to see if Mr. Untilla would build the cabin.

Well, when he came out of the store, he'd bought bread, a pound of butter, a circle of bologna, cheese, milk, a can of peaches and a jackknife. I knew that jackknife well - I'd ogled it often because of all the little tools that were built into it, even scissors and a can opener. The latter would come in handy to open the peaches. We drove down to Lake Tioga and had our picnic on the rocky point where Beaver Dam Creek enters the big lake.

The Artist

Again the artist was impressed by the beauty of our land, the long sandy beach on the east end of the lake, the islands in the distance, the huge hills that surrounded it. "I have found the place," he said over and over again. "Oh dear," he exclaimed, "I forgot to buy any cups or spoons or plates." No problem! From some poplar shoots I whittled out the utensils and then stripped some birch bark for plates and cups. That impressed him. "I have so much to learn," he said. He sure did. Why, I even had to tell him he could use his handkerchief for a napkin. How could he possibly make it through the winter living alone?

When we drove back to town, I took him to my father's hospital. Dad was there and since there were no patients in the waiting room, I told him about the artist's needing to know who owned the land by the pond on the river road above the flats, because he was planning to build a cabin there to live in over the winter and beyond.

"Yes, I think I can find the owner," Dad said. "It's probably some big logging company but let's see." He opened up the big tax roll ledger and scrutinized a map. "No," he said. "That forty, the South 1/4 of the Southeast 1/4 of Section 32, Town 16 North, Range 14 West is owned by Pierre Rambeaux and the taxes haven't been paid for two years. He's probably planning on letting it revert to the state. You might be able to buy it for a song though you'll have to pay the back taxes. Cully, drive Mr. Forster down to Pierre's house and after the dickering is done, bring him up here so I can notarize the bill of sale."

Old Pierre was so surprised he almost forgot to dicker at all but they settled for five hundred dollars which Mr. Forster paid him in cash as soon as the sale had been witnessed by my mother and our hired girl. Mother was so charmed by the artist and his dream that she invited him for supper so he could stay with us until train time.

Now that the artist had his land, he had to find a builder. I took him over to see Mullu Untilla's father. When Mr. Forster described the cabin he wanted built, it was pretty evident that he didn't know much about cabins. Finally he pulled out his sketch pad and drew it. "Cully will show you where I want it built," he said. "I'll pay you whatever you charge and here's a thousand dollars earnest money." He pulled out ten one hundred dollar bills from a fat wallet.

Mullu's father hesitated. It sounded too good to be true. The man from Chicago wanted it done in two months which was really pushing it. He also wanted it furnished with table, chairs, bunk, and two stoves, one for cooking and one for heating.

"You'll also need a woodshed, an outhouse, and well. And storm windows or you'll never be able to stand the cold no matter how you fire up." Mullu's father was busy figuring costs. "And cut wood for the winter. What kind of logs you want for the walls? Cedar's best but cutting it would slow up work by a month. I've got seasoned red pine logs on a forty I own not far from your place. They make good cabin."

The artist said that red pine would be fine.

"What kind of roof? What kind of floor? Single or double bunk? You want cellar with trap door to keep potatoes and stuff from freezing?"

There were so many questions of that sort that finally the artist said, "Mr. Untilla, I know nothing of these things. You just build it as if it were your own and as if you were going to spend the rest of your life in it. I will pay you generously. I just want a cabin I can move into next September or October and start living and painting there. The two men shook hands.

I didn't have much chance to fish with Mullu that summer because he was always helping his father build the cabin and I was in school when Mr. Forster arrived about the middle of September. Mr. Untilla drove the artist with two trunks and a suitcase up to see the cabin. Utterly delighted with it, the artist paid Mullu's father five hundred dollars more than he asked. After the artist had been shown the outhouse and woodshed Mullu's father took him over to see the spring. He'd been unable to dig a well, he said, because two feet down there was only solid granite. Spring water was better anyway. It wouldn't freeze over like a well often did. If he needed more water for washing, he could haul it from the pond or the river. Mullu's mother had made pasties for them with an extra one for the artist's evening meal. The two men ate them, then Mr. Untilla left.

The cabin looked very bare after he was gone. The artist told me later that suddenly he felt catastrophically alone, completely helpless and overwhelmed. Most of the afternoon he just sat outside on one of the kitchen chairs reading Thoreau or walking down to the river to watch it flow by. As the shadows began to lengthen, he realized he should build a fire in the box stove and make up his bed. Never having built a fire before, he put the split wood on the bottom, then the kindling, and on top of them the birch bark. Untilla had given him a handful of matches and he used most of them before he got a blaze that would last.

Then the new stove and stovepipe smoked as they always do when the surface olish burns off and it took some time before he could figure out how to open the upper windows to let the smoke out. It was almost dark when the artist ate half of the other pasty down by the spring, drinking from it face down because he had no cup. When he returned, the cabin was black dark so he opened the door of the box stove to get enough light to make his bed with the silk sheets and cotton blanket from his trunk. No pillow. No mattress. Just hard boards. It was a long night.

When Mullu told me the artist had returned I hiked up the river road to visit him early the next morning. He was sure glad to see me. He had a notebook and was writing some things in it. "I'm making out a list of things I have to buy to furnish my cabin," he said. I looked at his list and there were only three items: a pail, a cup, and a mattress. "Look, Cully," he said handing me his worn copy of *Walden*. "Thoreau had a bed, a table, a desk, a kettle, a skillet and a frying pan, three chairs, a wash bowl, two knives and forks, three plates, one cup, one spoon, a jug for oil and a japanned lamp. I'm sure I'll need a lot more but I can't figure out what they might be. Can you help me?"

I took his list and added these items: a dish pan, a tea kettle, coffee pot, frying pan, big saucepan for boiling potatoes, a kerosene lamp and oil for it, silverware for three.

"Why three?" he asked. "Thoreau says to simplify, simplify."

"Because you may have visitors drop in and you have to give them coffee and korpua or they'll think you're stuck up." I replied. "You'll also need some haywire, hammer and nails, and an axe, and shovel," I added. "There's always a need for haywire, if only to make a hanger over the stove so you can dry your clothes, and you'll need a shovel to dig a garbage pit and to clean out the spring."

"Yes, one about four feet deep and square, so the bears won't raid the cabin. Keep the stuff covered with dirt. And three cups and a paring knife and a butcher knife and maybe a pancake turner. You can turn a pancake with two knives but a pancake turner is better," I explained.

"I've never turned a pancake in my life," the artist said. "Indeed I've never cooked a meal for myself in my life." He explained that his family always had a cook and servants, and that after he was on his own he always ate in restaurants or had room service sent up. "I find myself really helpless, Cully," he said, "and I'm scared. Nothing in my life has prepared me for this. Graduating from Harvard cum laude never taught me how to make coffee…"

I interrupted. "Yes, you'll have to buy a coffee pot, a teapot. Oh, I've already got those down on the list. What else? Some bowls for soup though you could use a cup. Better get two pails, not just one. And some towels. And soap."

"How about clothing and bedding? I asked. Explaining that one trunk contained only his artist's supplies, he opened the other. It held three changes of underwear but no long johns, a sweater, two fine linen shirts, some fine handkerchiefs, some books and candles. Mr. Forster pointed to the bunk. "All the blankets and sheets are there but they sure didn't keep me warm last night," he said. "I'll need to buy some more but what should I get?" I told him he needed two woolen blankets, a heavy comforter, some winter underwear, heavy woolen pants and socks, and a mackinaw. Oh, yes, also a slicker or some other kind of rain gear. And boots, I added, looking at his fancy store shoes. He'd need some clompers like I wore, with rubber bottoms.

"But what I need most, after that terrible night," the artist said, "is a good mattress. My bones still ache. Do you think we could find one down at Flynn's store?" I doubted it. He might have to take the train to Ishpeming to get some of the things.

"What food supplies will I need to buy?" he asked. "Thoreau had a list of the food he lived on for eight months. Oh yes, here it is on page 57: 'rice, molasses, rye meal, Indian meal, pork, flour, sugar, lard, apples, potatoes, one pumpkin, one watermelon, salt.' Of course he also had a garden."

"Well, let's make a list," I said. "What do you usually have for breakfast in Chicago?"

"Oh, nothing much," he replied. "Always fruit juice or fruit in season-melon, grapefruit, strawberries. Then a croissant and coddled egg. Perhaps a rasher of bacon, toast and marmalade.

Fruit in season? I wrote "apples" on my list. "What's a coddled egg?" I asked. "How do you coddle an egg? Fondle it?"

He grinned. "I don't really know," he answered. "It comes in its own little cup and you have to unscrew the lid. Then you salt and pepper it and dip it out with a small spoon."

"And what's a croissant? You won't find any at Flynn's store."

It was a kind of French pastry, he explained, crescent shaped. I told him the closest he could come to that was a chunk of korpua. I didn't query him further, just made up the list myself. "Apples, bread, butter, korpua, eggs, slab of bacon, coffee." The artist said that he preferred coffee au lait with a spoonful of sugar. OK. "Milk, condensed milk, sugar, salt and pepper." Lunch? He liked consomme, a salad, asparagus spears on toast or a sandwich. "Pea soup, two cans," I wrote. "Butter, lard, pork and beans, corned beef, cheese, potatoes, a rutabaga, a cabbage, ketchup, pancake flour, syrup, corn meal, yeast and baking powder. Oh yes, some toilet paper too."

We added two items on our way back to town. A strong wind kept blowing the straw hat off his head and after a mile or two he began to limp a bit. "You need a cap with ear laps," I told him, "and some boots or clompers like I wear. Those shoes will never hold up on these stones and gravel." He agreed but forgot to write them down on the list.

"How far is my cabin from Tioga?" he asked. "Thoreau had his about two miles from town." I told him three or four miles.

When we got to Marchand's livery stable I asked the old man if we could have his dray wagon with the long box because Mr. Forster had to haul a lot of supplies. Sure, the old man said, but we'd have to have Maude again. While they were hitching up I ran home to ask Dad if we could have two of the old hospital mattresses he had stored in the back room after the mine closed. "They won't be very, soft," Dad replied. "They're filled with wooden shavings. Be sure to get ones without any mouseholes in the ticking." We picked them up on our way to the store and they fit just right in the wagon box. Smelled a little musty though.

When Mr. Forster gave Mr. Flynn the list, the storekeeper gasped. "That'll cost you over a hundred dollars," he said. The artist didn't bat an eye so Flynn and his clerk and I went to work collecting the stuff. No, Mr. Flynn didn't have any comforters or candle holders but he had everything else. Quite a load! The artist also bought some steaks for supper since I'd told him that after I'd brought the horse and wagon back I'd hike to the cabin to spend the night with him and help him get organized. He was very grateful.

When we got to the cabin I helped him unload by the road and showed him where to dig a hole below the spring where he could put a pail to keep the milk and butter cold, then drove Maude back to Tioga.

When I told mother I was going back to spend the night she wasn't sure it was a good idea. I tried to explain how helpless the man was. Dad came in while I was telling her and said, "He'll never make it. He'll be out of here by Christmas." I had the same thought but hoped it was wrong. "Anyway," I said, "He's paying me five dollars a day for helping him and that's not hay." Dad thought it was too much. I put a woolen blanket and a sweater in my packsack, took a bunch of cookies from the pantry and was on my way.

When I got to the new cabin I figured it was about four thirty or five o'clock. Maybe I'd have time to make him a balsam bed to put under that hard mattress. The artist was sitting outside in a chair sketching a big spruce and when I entered the cabin, I knew why. Lord, I could hardly enter it. Mr. Forster had hauled all the stuff from the road but had just piled it at random in the cabin. He said again that he'd felt overwhelmed. Didn't know where to put the stuff. Well, I got the two trunks, put them side by side under the east window, and put a mattress on top. That cleared out enough space to walk around in. When I told the artist to put the potatoes and rutabaga and cabbage in the cellar, he had to be shown where the ring to the trap door was. He'd forgotten he had a cellar. I set him to work driving nails into the logs behind the cookstove to hold the skillets, pans and stuff but then had to show him how to hold a hammer and how to start the nail with short taps before driving it in. Lord, he was clumsy. I also had to straighten most of his nails so the pans wouldn't slip off. To keep him out of my hair while I built some shelves from boards I found in the woodshed, I asked him to peel some potatoes for supper. He didn't know how to peel a potato as I discovered later. He'd cut the potatoes in little chunks first and was whittling away the skin. So I showed him.

Finally I got the place organized so you could move around with the canned stuff on the shelves, and the clothing hung up on the nails. To keep him busy while I made him a balsam bed, I told the artist how to make a cooking fire outside between two logs so we could have coals for the steaks and to start boiling the potatoes and to make a potato masher out of one of the split wood in the woodshed. I figured he'd never get done peeling those little chunks of potatoes so we might as well mash them skins and all.

Between loads of balsam tips, I supervised his fire building. At least he'd learned to put the birch bark on the bottom and the kindling above it but the split wood he'd brought from the woodshed was way too large so I had to show him how to split them in finer lengths. He'd never used an ax. Didn't even know how to put the stick of wood upright against a chunk. Didn't know how to hit it so the blade would angle just at the moment of contact. Didn't know how to extricate the axe when it got stuck. But he learned and by the time I had his balsam bed done and the mattress atop it he had some good coals between the two logs with potatoes boiling and apples cooking in the other pan. I had to make the potato masher myself and teach him how to sear the steaks and salt them. He wanted to eat by candlelight but since Mr. Flynn had no candleholders, I got a couple of Indian slates (a lichen) from a yellow birch, made holes in them, showed him how to turn the lighted candle upside down to fill the hole with hot wax, then put it in the hole until it was held firm. It was dark when the food was done but we had a fine meal by candlelight before going to bed. Even then, I had to show him how to roll up his sweater to make the pillow that Flynn didn't have. I slept on the mattress on top of the trunks and he in the bunk after demonstrating how to blow out a candle or a kerosene lamp by cupping your hands over the chimney or flame. He sure slept well and so did I.

The next morning we had applesauce (fruit in season), pancakes, bacon and coffee. No croissants! I had to show him how to make boiled coffee, how to have it turn over, pull it aside, let it come to a boil again, then put a dollop of water to settle the grounds. The artist sure had trouble slicing the bacon off the slab. Until I showed him how to slice along the rind, then cut, he had been sawing on that rind with the butcher knife in vain. He didn't know that you had to pierce two holes in the condensed milk can before it would pour. He didn't know that when you stirred pancake batter you always left a few small lumps. Hell, he didn't even know how to crack an egg. Harvard cum laude! The first pancakes he cooked were terrible but with some instruction about watching for the bubbles he finally managed to flip them without getting them in his hair. It was a good breakfast. Mr. Forster said he'd never had a better cup of coffee even in the Waldorf Astoria.

The water was hot in the teakettle and in the reservoir of the wood range so we did the dishes. The man didn't know that you rinsed them in fresh water afterwards before drying. Drying? No towels. Again he was helpless. I got one of his five bath towels from the trunk and cut it to make two dishtowels and two dish rags. Where should he put the dishwater? "Throw it out the door," I said. Before I left I told him how to make a salad dressing for his cabbage: Mix some ketchup with a beaten egg and a little milk, then salt and pepper. And cut the cabbage fine. I had him practice using the little can opener on his jackknife so he could have soup for lunch, then demonstrated how he would have to turn the key to unwind the top of the corn beef cans. "Cut the slices about this thick and fry them slowly till they're brown on top," I told him.

He hated to see me go after he paid me ten dollars and I started out of the door, "I hope you'll come back to see me when you can, Cully," he said. I told him I might be able to make it after school the next Thursday if we didn't have basketball practice but I would be sure to come up Saturday to see how he was doing. He walked with me about a mile down the river road before turning back.

I was able to get away that next Thursday afternoon after school and found the artist frying some ham and sliced potatoes for supper even though I got there about five o'clock, Very glad to see me, he seemed to have a terrible urge to talk. He was all right. He'd dug the garbage pit and had to show me both it and his blisters. Would I stay for supper? He'd cooked enough for both, on the chance I might show up. He'd had a little accident, pouring kerosene on a slow-starting fire in the cookstove. Singed his arm when it blew off the lids. He was now eating when he felt like it and had forgotten to have lunch that day. The balsam bed was heavenly. He'd slept soundly except when something gnawed at the door early one morning. (I told him it was probably a porcupine.) Some creature had been chewing the toilet paper in the outhouse. (Probably a mouse.) He'd taken a swim off the sandy beach east of where he got the wash water, soaped good, and swam again. Terribly cold but exhilarating. How do you cut a rutabaga? (With an ax, first.) The salad dressing on the cabbage was fine but he hungered for vinegar or pickle juice and also for sweets. Bread and butter with sugar on it was excellent.

I asked him if he'd done any painting. "No," he replied, "I did try some water colors trying to get the green for that pine out in front of the cabin."

"It's a spruce, a white spruce," I said.

"Whatever it is, I am determined to capture it. I'll probably have to use oils."

On the way up the river road I'd noticed that the trees were beginning to show the color changes, the reds and scarlets of fall. "Why not paint them."' I asked.

"Too garish. Too overwhelming. If I can capture that pine, I mean spruce tree, that would be a supreme achievement. But I'm really too busy just surviving to have time to paint. By the time I've made my bed, had my breakfast, done the dishes and tried to clean the place it's time for lunch. I walked around the pond yesterday and it took all afternoon. Oh, Cully, do you think you could clear a path around it? It's awfully hard walking in all that brush and broken trees except in the marsh on the far side."

We went down to see the pond. It sure was beautiful but the brush around it and the windfalls, especially among the cedars, made it in spots almost impenetrable. So I told him, no that I alone couldn't do it on a weekend or two but that if he would hire two of my friends, Mullu and Fisheye, we might be able to clear a good path in two days. That was fine, he said. He didn't care how much it cost. Just wanted to be able to walk around his Walden pond and bathe himself in beauty.

After we had our early supper, I said it was time to go if I were to get home before dark. This time he gave me, not only a five dollar bill, but a hundred dollar one with a list of things he said he needed. "Bring your friends up and the supplies on the buckboard Saturday and pay Marchand whatever he asks." After I looked at the list I told him I thought we could pack it in.

Mullu and Fisheye were tickled pink when I told them they could get five dollars a day for cutting brush up at the artist's cabin and after they saw the list they agreed to help bring it in their packsacks too. Here was the artist's list after only five days in camp: clothesline, vinegar, dipper, ladle, scissors, needles and thread, tablespoons, broom. (I told the artist he could make a broom like the Finns always did but he said no, he wanted a real broom, oh yes, and a dustpan too), something to sharpen the knife and axe, a serrated knife to cut bread, more bread and milk, four steaks and a pasty if I could buy one (I told him no, that all our families made them but not for sale.) More soup, a different kind if possible. Cookies and maybe candy; another pail and another bigger frying pan. Some pickles. And especially a pillow if I could get one. And some wine. A knitted cap he could pull over his ears.

No wine, I said. Higley only sold beer and whiskey and he wouldn't let a kid like me inside the door of his saloon. As for the knitted cap, I didn't think Flynn would have one. Put a bandanna handkerchief over your head. Your straw hat looks silly up here. I might be able to find a cap but I don't know your size. He said it was 7 1/4.

Well we got all the stuff although I had to get the pillow from my mother, and Mullu got a pasty from his. Up the river road we went carrying our heavy packs and me holding a broom. Sure looked silly in bird season. Oh yes, Fisheye had also swiped a bottle of wild black cherry wine from his cellar, so we had everything on the artist's list.

We found him outside with his easel set up sketching the outline of that spruce tree but he dropped everything and helped us unpack and went with us to the pond where we started clearing the path. Mullu had brought up an axe and a bucksaw and Fisheye had a hatchet so the work went swiftly. Mr. Forster was so fascinated by the bucksaw and how it went so easily through one of the cedar windfalls, we let him try it. It took him some time to learn to hold the saw frame straight and not to keep pressing down. Also he was surprised to find that by bending over a bush it was easier to cut off at the base. By five o'clock we were finished and, because we hadn't eaten anything since morning, those steaks and potatoes sure were good. Afterward, the artist sketched the three of us sitting on a log, paid us each ten dollars and bought Mullu's bucksaw for another ten because a new one only cost eight dollars. We felt so rich we built him a sawbuck behind the cabin and hauled some cedar logs up from the swamp so he could make kindling. Again I'd had to show him how to split off the slabs and make the fine stuff. Again he walked part way home with us.

I only visited the artist two or three times the last of October and early in November. He was doing all right. Seemed happy and content. The only trouble he'd had was keeping the fire going all night in the box stove. He said that usually he had to get up four or five times so I showed him how to bank the fire with ashes before he went to bed and to be sure he had a green log on top. He'd been doing a lot of painting as well as sketching and had a wonderful picture of the big spruce on canvas. When I told him it was magnificent, he disagreed. "No, Cully, it's not right. I haven't been able to capture that glint on the needles, that sheen." He showed me a pencil sketch of a deer and a half-grown fawn that had posed for him one evening at the edge of the clearing. He sure could draw.

When I visited him again in early November after I'd had my belly full of hunting partridge, ducks and rabbits, he was working on a canvas, trying to paint a spruce branch with some cones on it. "Too cold to paint outside," he said. He'd done a washing which hung kitty-corner from one end of the cabin to the other. He'd hung it outside the day before but it froze overnight. He said he had washed the clothes, underwear, shirts and socks, in the river but wouldn't do it again. Too cold. He told me that Fisheye and Mullu had been up to cut some more wood for the winter and showed me proudly how much kindling he'd sawed and split. No, he didn't need anything. I refused to take any money for checking on him. When I left I felt that he might really make it through the winter.

We did see him in town occasionally because he usually walked in to buy groceries or to take a sauna at Mullu's house on Saturday afternoons, or to get or post his mail.

Once, while he was waiting for the mail to be disturbed (distributed), among the men there was old Pete Ramos. The artist became fascinated by the old bugger's craggy face, he paid him five dollars to let him sketch it. A perfect likeness, it even showed the wart on the west side of the old drunk's nose. Then he posted it up on the bulletin board along with the other posters of men wanted for murder and other crimes. Our people in Tioga got a kick out of that and were proud to have a real artist in town - even if he did live way out in the bush. As for old Pete, he was proud too. I don't know how many days he came to the post office to see his picture.

Once the artist went to Ishpeming on the train and when he returned with a comforter, more socks and some wine, he asked me to teach him how to drive old Maude up to the cabin. No problem! He did everything wrong at first, trying to steer the old horse by pulling on the reins when he didn't need to. Finally Maude stopped and looked back to see what the hell was going wrong, so I showed him to let her go with the reins limp, how to slap her rump when she slowed down too much, and how to swear at her in French like old Marchand did.

I guess the last time I went to his cabin was about the middle of November, just before deer season. Mother had invited him to stay for supper. She liked the artist a lot. Said he was a real gentleman. By that time it was dark even at five o'clock but the artist said he'd love to have a home cooked meal and wouldn't have any trouble walking back under the stars.

But there weren't any stars by the time we finished supper. Instead a real blinger of a blizzard hit us. High wind and snow coming down so thick you couldn't see a foot in front of you. We get sudden storms like that in the U.P. Anyway Dad insisted he spend the night with us. He could sleep with me in the big brass bed and head for camp in the morning. It was a very pleasant evening. Mother played Chopin on the piano; Dad told some of his gory medical tales; and the artist described his experiences living alone. No he wasn't at all lonely. A raven flew over his clearing twice a day; a red squirrel was always around; he'd tamed a couple of Canadian Jays to eat bread out of his hand; occasionally a hunter would drop in for coffee and korpua. No, he wasn't lonely a bit. Thoreau was right!

His only problem, he said, was that he was having a hard time doing landscapes, especially trying to capture a big spruce tree in front of the cabin. He was a pretty good portrait painter, he said, and had studied landscapes in Italy, but that spruce tree was sure hard to get right.

Dad told him that it would be a different spruce tree when he saw it again, that it would be loaded with snow. Oh, I forget most of the conversation but it was fun to listen to. The artist told us he was thirty years old, the same age that Thoreau had been when he went to Walden Pond. He said that it was difficult to live as Thoreau did. He'd been trying to bake bread his way but the results were disastrous. Mother gave him her recipe, the one using potato water. Finally we went to bed with the wind howling in the shutters. Mr. Forster was not a very good bed partner. Kept tossing around probably because he missed that balsam bed and the hard hospital mattress.

The next morning we had over a foot of snow on the level and it was still snowing so Dad told me to hitch old Billy to the cutter, and drive the artist back to the cabin. He gave him a pair of our snowshoes and told me to teach him how to walk on them - I put a lot of Dad's Chicago Tribunes in the packsack so he could read them or use them for a fire if the birch bark ran out or to clean his lamp chimney.

The Artist

On the way I let Mr. Forster drive and he did fine although Billy was feeling his morning oats. The cabin was very cold, of course, and the artist couldn't understand why, after we built a fire in both stoves, I insisted on keeping the door open for awhile. Fresh air always warms better than stale air, I told him. I helped him haul water from the pond and said that if it froze over he could make a hole with the axe or get water from the river or spring. He was sure having a hard time on the snowshoes but finally learned how to swing his legs so one of them wouldn't sit on top of the other. It was still snowing hard when I drove home.

After that I didn't go up again but saw him several times when he walked to town. He was fortunate because Silverthorn and Company were logging way up at the headquarters of the Tioga and kept the river road plowed out that winter. Anyway he came to town every week for his necessaries or mail and sometimes he dropped in at our house. Once he gave my father the sketch he'd drawn of the deer and fawn, and he told me he thought that at last he'd really captured that spruce tree covered with snow. He never said paint, always capture.

Annie, our postmistress, let the word leak out that when he'd first come to Tioga all the mail he got or sent were letters to or from a law firm but that lately he'd been sending letters, sometimes two at a time, to a Simone Bouregard in Chicago. Never a Miss or Mrs., just the name, and he'd also been getting mail from someone in a woman's writing on very fancy stationary. Romance? I sure didn't know. The artist had never said a word about any of his past relationships.

But we were surprised when we learned that on a December morning a beautiful tall woman dressed in expensive furs had got off the morning train from Chicago, to be greeted by the artist, and whisked away in Marchand's cutter pulled by old Maude. "Why there must have been thirty or forty mink skins in that coat," someone said who had seen her. "And she had a fur cap and tall boots with fur on them too." All we really knew is that he brought her back that afternoon and she took the evening train for Chicago.

Two days later the artist also took that train and we never saw him again. After the breakup next spring I hiked up to his cabin and found it just as he'd left it. No one had been there so far as I could see. There was even old coffee in the pot. No note of explanation. His paintings were still there but the fine one of the spruce tree was smeared and crisscrossed with paint. That was all.

We hoped that he might return that spring or summer but he never did, then or ever. Was it that he had to go back to that beautiful woman and an easier, less lonely life? Or was it that he finally realized he would never be able to capture the spruce tree? There are a lot of mysteries in the U.P. and that was one of them. Anyway, Tioga had an artist once.

To My Grandson

Dear Jim: Your Uncle Tim and I will pick you up at six-thirty Thursday morning for the long trip north so you'd better have your breakfast and have your stuff ready to go by that time. I'm sorry your father couldn't make it this year but I'm glad you can take his place. You will be the fourth generation of Gage men to hunt deer in the forest around the lakes that bear our name. I say "men" because, although you're only sixteen, we will treat you like a man, not a boy, and will expect that you'll act like one.

For example, when we get there the cabin will probably be cold and damp. We'll build a big fire in the fireplace while you chop a hole in the ice of the lake to get two pails of water for drinking, dishes, or priming the pump. You may wonder why we will open the door and windows when we build the fire. We do so because fresh air heats up faster than stale air. That's just one of the many things you'll learn at deer camp. After getting the water, chop a lot of cedar kindling and some small wood. Put these beside the big woodbox, not in it. Then haul in the big chunks of hard maple until the woodbox is full and has a heap on it. During our stay at the cabin, getting wood and water will be your primary chores.

But there will be others too. When the alarm clock goes off at five-thirty you will hop out of your sleeping bag pronto, build up the fire and make the coffee. To do the latter, you put in eight level tablespoons of coffee along with eight cups of water into the pot. Watch it closely when it begins to boil, let the grounds turn over, then take it off the fire for a minute, then put it back on the fire for a second short boiling. After that, plunge in a half cup of water to settle the grounds and set the pot on the back of the stove. We'll drink a lot of coffee up here and it's your job to make sure there's always coffee in the pot when we come in from hunting. Your final job is to wash and rinse the dishes. We'll dry them and put them away, do the camp cleaning, keep the fire going all night, and occasionally help you with your duties.

Why do so many men feel that ancient urge to go deer hunting each year? According to the papers there will be more than 700,000 of us in the woods on opening day. It is certainly no longer just for meat though when I was a boy in the U.P. venison was vital in our making it through the winter. Not now! For the money I will spend on this expedition I could fill my freezer to overflowing with the best cuts of choice beef or pork. Venison is good, but not that good and I sure had my fill of it when I was growing up.

No, there must be some other reason that impels us to leave all the conveniences of home to freeze on a stump or shiver on the trails for hours on end. In part we hunt deer for the escape from all responsibility, from our wives and work. It provides an opportunity to share man talk and male companionship, a chance to play and be carefree.

But there is something more. Deep in our genes, or whatever, there is a primeval urge to hunt and kill which has been transmitted since the earliest times in the human race. Men have always been hunters. Certainly we Gages have been. The first Gage came to America in the late 1600's when the land was all wilderness. Successive generations of Gages moved gradually westward, always at the edge of the forest, until the 1850's when they made a long hard trek by covered wagon and on foot to southwestern Michigan. I remember my grandfather, Arza Gage, telling about how on that journey his Aunt Patience and mother cooked pancakes for some Indians until the men came back from hunting, dragging a deer. He said that the women made the pancakes small so they could gain time. He also told me that when he was a teamster in the logging camps up by Saginaw, he always carried a rifle in his wagon to shoot any deer he could get because that was the only meat the lumberjacks ever had except salt pork. So he was a deer hunter too, like you.

My own father, your great grandfather, Dr. John Gage, never missed a deer season until late in his eighties and he always got a deer or two or three others for his hunting cronies who didn't hunt as hard or long as he did. Arising before daybreak and with only an apple and a sandwich in his pocket for lunch, he'd hunt until dark. I understand from your father that you will be using my father's rifle. That's good. Your great grandfather would have liked that. Take good care of it.

As for me, in my own eighties, I have no urge any more to shoot another deer. I've shot my share. Indeed I felt bad when I shot the last one and every footstep I took when dragging it back to camp was a penance. But I still have that primitive urge to hunt even though I won't shoot. I love the feel of a gun under my arm as I walk this forest I know so well with every sense on immediate alert. I love to read the animal tracks in the clean snow. The woods in winter is another world from that in summer. When the sun lightens up the openings between firs shaggy with white snow it can be like walking in a fairyland. Even as I write this I feel the old excitement welling up within me. Yes, I sure have the ancient urge.

On the first morning after we've had a fine breakfast I'll take you up the camp road a ways, then to your first sitting place just a bit north of a good deer trail. It will still be too dark to see to shoot and you should sit there watching the trail until it's light and you can't bear sitting another moment. Then you should start walking east and roughly parallel to the trail until you hit an old logging road. I suggest that you turn right (south) on it for about a quarter of a mile, then circle back by going west until you hit our camp road again. This area is my favorite deer hunting territory as it was my father's and I don't think you can get very lost unless you go north. Don't go north! If you do you'll come out on Lake Superior thirty or more miles away. If you go east far enough, you'll finally come out on the new road along Dishno Creek. If you go south, you'll also hit that road eventually, and if you go west, you'll come out on our camp road. So you shouldn't get lost even if you can't backtrack because the wind has covered your tracks.

Just go east, or south or preferably west and you'll get back to camp. It's wise, however, to occasionally check your compass to see which way you're going or to know which way you've been coming from.

As you sit or stand watching for deer, don't take quick glances but rather let your eyes sweep across the terrain, almost as though you were using binoculars. If you see anything that looks remotely like a deer or deer head focus on that until you're sure it isn't. Also, look back on your trail because sometimes a curious deer may follow it. Above all, try to see the lay of the land, the hills, gulleys, swamps and little streams. Look for landmarks that you can recognize again. There's a lone big hemlock on a steep hill that you should spot, a large arch made by a maple sapling, a cascade of big boulders where a bear once made its den. On the north side of one of the hills is a large stand of beautiful white birch. Maybe you'll find my throne, a big hollow pine stump at the end of a ridge. I shot a deer once from that throne.

Let me suggest before you move from you spot that you practice targeting your rifle. Pick out some target, a stump, or sapling, then bring up your rifle, aim at it and squeeze the trigger. I hope I don't have to tell you that you should have the safety on. It really helps your coordination when you actually see a buck. If you don't practice you may have trouble lining up the sights.

And remember to listen. At times the sharp crack of a broken branch may mean that a deer has broken it. That's why you should step over, not on such a branch as you walk. But listen too to all the other sounds, to the croak of ravens flapping overhead, to the sliver cats. That's what we call trees that groan as they rub together. If you hear a deer snort, freeze. He's got your scent and will be circling you.

Most of the winter birds, except the ravens, are silent creatures. Even the blue jays rarely screech. I like the Canadian jays best because they're curious and friendly and very appreciative of a crumb of korpua or bit of apple as they show by twittering. I once had one perch on my gun barrel. People of the U.P. call them whiskey jacks and claim that they are the reincarnation of dead lumberjacks.

Red squirrels can be a nuisance when you're hunting. It's not bad if they are merely using their single ratchety calls but when they sit in a tree above where you're standing and chatter excitedly, you'd better move on. Every deer within a mile will be able to locate you.

As you follow a trail or cut cross-country note the various animal tracks you encounter so you can tell us about them at Happy Hour. I'd guess that you'd better put a pad of paper and pencil in your pocket with the apple and korpua so we can help you identify your sketches. Fox tracks go in a straight line usually; the Y-shaped rabbit tracks show they are leaping. A partridge leaves a thick trail of webbed marks. A bobcat has the padded prints of a house cat, only larger. A bear track looks like a stubby human hand. You may even come across a moose track, three times as large as any deer. If you see a moose, don't even point your rifle at it. Any man from the U.P. would beat you senseless if you shot one. They airlifted a lot of them from Canada and let them go not four miles from our lake and we want the herd to get established. I've not seen any moose yet but I've seen their tracks by the beaver dam.

You may hear some far-away shots. Remember to tell us about them and when they occurred because they usually mean that the deer are moving at that time. Generally speaking, the best times to see a deer are from early in the morning until about ten o'clock, then again from four until dark but once I shot a buck at noon. Tim and I usually come back to camp about ten o'clock for coffee and I take a nap in the afternoon until two. I don't think you'll see any hunter in your territory. Most of them prefer to hunt the plains south of Ishpeming or Republic where there are many more deer. To put it bluntly, there aren't very many deer around our lakes. That's why they planted the moose so near us, to keep them from catching the brain worm that deer have but are invulnerable to. Nevertheless, as you will discover, there are deer near our lakes and their relative scarcity just makes the challenge all the greater. You'll see fresh tracks every day. Actually I'm always amazed when I've shot a buck. The odds are all in its favor. This is big country and the chances that you and the buck will have your trails intersect at exactly the same instant at a particular spot in that vast expanse of forest are really very low. Yet most years we get our bucks. If we don't, no matter. We'll get one next year. The fun is in the hunting, not the kill.

I suppose you're wondering if you might get buck-fever. I would doubt it. You've hunted before and shot pheasants and rabbits. When that buck is in your sights you'll shoot straight. And be back at the cabin by five o'clock so we won't worry.

No I don't think there's any real possibility that you'll get really lost but if you do or if you are injured so you can't walk, then give the following signal. Shoot twice in quick succession, then count slowly to sixty, then fire two more shots, then wait about a minute more, then fire two more. We'll find you, so sit on a log until we get there. By the way, be sure to take a small plastic garbage bag in your pocket to serve as a dry-ass. Even though you scrape the snow off a sitting log you'll get a band of wetness across your rump unless you have one.

Now to the deer hunting itself. My father repeatedly told me to try to walk as slowly as possible and either to sit quietly without moving or to stand alongside a tree. And never to make a quick movement! Once he walloped me for moving my head before moving my eyes and told me if I saw a walking deer to bring my rifle up slowly not quickly. Deer can see movement though their eyesight is not as keen as their senses of smell or hearing. He also insisted that I always try to keep upwind when I chose a sitting or standing place. Usually the wind up here is from the west or northwest but not always, so check it. Deer tend to travel upwind.

None of us Gages have ever been long sitters even though we know that this is the best way to get a deer. Most of the Finns up here can sit all day along a deer trail until one comes along. I just can't sit so long and never could even when I was younger. Fifteen minutes or perhaps half an hour is all I can stand or rather sit and then I have to get moving, always wanting to see what's over the next hill. My main method of hunting is to prowl through the woods looking and listening until I find a fresh track. This I follow, not right on the trail because deer often keep looking back at where they've been, but some distance parallel with it, first on one side of the trail, then on the opposite side. If the deer is making long leaps (I once measured one that was nineteen feet) I don't bother because it will be half a mile away before I catch up to him but it the deer is feeding as evidenced by its wandering around and nipping off the tips of maple brush and I don't cross its trail again, I sit or stand in wait, and have often gotten my buck that way.

How can I tell if the track is a buck or doe? I really haven't been able to determine this except that very large bucks seem to leave sharper points in their hoofprints than do the does. Usually it doesn't matter because often a buck will be following the doe anyway, so if you see a doe be sure to wait ten or fifteen minutes. And look for fresh beds or scrapes on saplings that seem new, or for oval black deer turds that are still steaming. The deer will be very near. How can you tell a fresh track from an old one? I know but it's hard to put into words. I'll have to show you. If there are granular bits of snow in the track it's not new.

You've seen deer in the summer when fishing up here but their rich brown coats are replaced in the winter by gray ones, so look for gray, not brown. Often they'll appear - like grey ghosts, so quietly do they present themselves. In thick brush all you may see is a head and neck so look for these too. Most of the deer you'll see will be walking, or running with their white tails held high. Sometimes if you whistle sharply a running deer will stop, trying to see where the sound comes from. Only rarely will you see a deer standing still. If you do he will be watching you.

Of course, the first thing you do when you see a deer is to look for horns. We Gages have never shot a doe or fawn and you'd better not be the first one to do so. Any deer with antlers is fair game. This holds true for spikehorns too but the prongs must be at least three inches long to be legal. These prongs are often hard to see but if you have any smidgen of doubt don't shoot. Better to have a spikehorn get away than to shoot a doe.

Where should you aim? If the buck is sideways to you, aim for a spot right behind the upper front shoulder. Some beginners after that first shot will lower their rifles waiting for the deer to fall. A veteran hunter will shoot again as quickly as possible. If the buck has not dropped in its tracks, go immediately to where you saw it and look for blood spots. If you find some substantial ones, wait about fifteen minutes before following the trail so it will lie down. Most deer, even if mortally wounded, will run a short distance before they fall. If, when you find it, and it is still living but unable to move, shoot it again in the neck to end its suffering. You may not want to do this but you must.

If you find occasional blood spots but no dead deer you must follow the trail. We Gages always stay on the trail of a wounded deer until no more blood signs are seen and we know that the wound was superficial. Your great Grandfather once kept trailing a wounded deer until dark, came back to camp for a flashlight and a blanket and returned after midnight but he got his buck.

Where do you shoot if the buck is coming right toward you? You aim for the upper part of the chest, just below the neck. Some hunters will shoot randomly at a running deer or shoot it in the side or hind end. We Gages don't because there's too much chance of merely wounding it and a lot of the meat will be spoiled anyway. The best way to get a running buck is to note which way it's going and then aim ahead of it. When it comes into your sights, squeeze the trigger. Yes, squeeze it; don't pull it. And after you've shot, put the safety back on.

If the buck is on a hillside higher than you, there's always a tendency to under-shoot, so hold your rifle so that all of your front sight is in view. Conversely, if the buck is downhill from you, draw a fine bead on the front sight so you won't overshoot.

After you've killed your first deer, you'd better come - right back to camp. We will have heard you shoot and will be ready to help you clean it, or rather to tell you what to do. It's a bloody business and not difficult but there's a knack to it. First you must lay the deer on its back with its head higher than the legs. Then you'll have to slit around the balls, then up the belly to the sternum, the bottom of the rib cage. After that you'll cut the-windpipe and diaphragm and spill the entrails on the ground, saving the liver. Then we'll help you drag your buck back to the cabin and hoist it up to hang from the buck pole on the woodshed for all to admire.

That evening during Happy Hour while supper's cooking the three of us will be sitting in the big chairs before the fire munching on crackers covered with the smoked whitefish we picked up at Naubinway. We may even give you a shot glass containing diluted whiskey which will taste awful and we will raise our glasses to the latest member of the clan to get his buck. We will want to know every minute detail about what happened, where you first saw the buck, your feelings, how you targeted it, how it reacted, oh, everything. It is a tale you will tell many times so get it straight. Some day you will tell it to the next Gage, your son.

My Island

For almost sixty years I had an island on a hidden unnamed lake in the U.P. I discovered it when I was nineteen while roaming the granite hills north of Tioga in search of gold. Yes, there is gold in them thar hills, gold as well as hundreds of other minerals including uranium. Today just west of Ishpeming a gold mine is still going full tilt on a site where, long ago, the Ropes and Michigan gold mines yielded millions of dollars worth of gold—and even more from the pockets of their shareholders.

Over and over again, as a boy, I had heard the tales. Jim Bedford, station agent at Humboldt, on his day off had gone trout fishing on a creek that empties into the Escanaba River. On his way back he cut cross-country and got lost. As he came over one of the big granite knobs he slipped and dislodged a mat of turf which revealed a long seam of white quartz threaded with little yellow veins. Bedford broke off a chunk and had it assayed. Yes, it was gold, so rich that a ton of it would be worth sixty thousand dollars.

Bedford hunted for that hill and that seam of quartz until he died but never found it again. One summer he even hired an experienced prospector from out west but he couldn't find it either. I know the tale is true because I held that heavy chunk in my own hands when my father took me to the station and while he played chess with Bedford. You could see the gold in it clearly. Dad said that chunk was probably worth more than a hundred dollars.

Then there was the tale told by Jim Olson, one of Dad's hunting cronies, who was the caretaker of the mining properties after the mines closed down. On the hills surrounding Silver Lake Jim had found an old iron door on a side slope that was so firmly fixed he could not budge it. Below that iron door in the swamp were chunks of blasted quartz, some of which had fine threads of gold in them.

And, of course, all of us knew of Old Man Coon, the hermit, who had spent thirty years putting shafts in the hills near the upper reaches of the Escanaba. I've been to his place and was impressed by the long piles of rock that he'd dug out of those shafts. Thirty years of hard, solitary labor. He must have found some gold.

So that is why, on a warm afternoon, I was roaming the hills with a frying pan and little prospector's pickaxe in my knapsack. I'd panned for gold, swirling gravel around in the frying pan, in two little creeks but had found nothing. I'd found two seams of quartz next to greenstone that might possibly be promising and hacked out chunks that I could scrutinize later with a magnifying glass. I did find a fine sample of fool's gold, iron pyrites, with its little cubes of yellow. Absolutely worthless, of course. Always there was that dream of striking it rich. If I did, I wouldn't have to go Down Below to go to college and get a job and maybe never see my beloved U.P. again. I'd be another Old Man Coon, fishing, hunting and prospecting the rest of a wonderful life in the land I loved.

I came to a notch, a gulch, which I had to cross, and as I was working my way through it I heard water gurgling. Looking down I saw a little stream barely a foot wide flowing out of the earth below a fallen spruce. A spring! A spring! It had been a warm August day and I was perspiring, so I lay down to drink from a little pool. Waugh! It was no spring. The water was not ice cold but warm. I drank anyway but curious about its origin I walked up the gulch and found the stream again. What was the source? I had to know so I followed it upwards through a terrible tangle of alders and windfalls until suddenly I came out on the short of a narrow little lake.

A beautiful lake, it was, cradled in the granite hills, but what hit me immediately was the island. Right in the middle of the shimmering blue water was a narrow island with huge pines, virgin pines. Evidently the loggers who cut the pine in the old days had overlooked it. I could hardly wait to take off my clothes and swim the fifty yards to its shore, to a little sand and gravel beach. As I stood there dripping and naked, a strange feeling came over me, one that alas I cannot recapture. Sort of like Adam when he first entered the Garden of Eden, I suppose. I sat down on a log by the beach for a long time, then got up to explore. Actually there weren't many of those huge pines, perhaps only eight or ten of them, but they towered far into the sky. No underbrush, just a bed of pine needles so thick it was like walking on cushions. One old tree had fallen but beside it were several tiny pine saplings hunting for the sun.

I roamed the shoreline, most of which was covered by Labrador tea bushes or Michigan holly. The latter's berries were full formed but not as scarlet as they would be once frost came. The north shore was a great slab of granite and red feldspar which sloped then plunged into deep water. I ran down it and dived into the lake yelling Hallelujah, and felt ashamed because I'd broken its silence. Then I hugged one of those great pines, went back to the little beach, and swam to the other shore where my clothes were awaiting me. I remember hating to leave my island, wanting to stay there forever. I hadn't found any gold but I had found something infinitely better.

That was in 1926 and I revisited my little lake and island almost every year thereafter. Twice I slept overnight under the great pines, once completely naked, but covered by heaps of the brown needles. It wasn't good; the covering was too prickly though warm enough. The second time I floated over my clothes, a blanket, a coffee can and some food on a little raft, caught a trout and a perch, and spent the night on some moss just back from the beach. I remember that my little cooking fire seemed to desecrate the place and spoil the night so I put it out as soon as the fish were done, then cleaned up the site so that no one could ever know anyone had ever been there. Not that there was much chance of that.

Only once did I try to share my lake and island with another person, my newly wedded wife, Milove. She had heard me tell of my island sometimes at night when I held her in my arms but when we got to the base of the hills and she saw what she would have to go through to get to the lake she balked. I didn't blame her; indeed I felt relieved. Much as I loved my new bride I selfishly did not want her or anyone else to know my own secret place.

My island? It was not mine. It was owned by a big logging company as I discovered when I later tried to buy it and was refused. But in a larger sense I never felt that it was mine; rather that it possessed me. I was not an intruder; I was a part of that lovely island, as much a part as were those great pine trees. The moment I stepped ashore, dripping, it put its arms around me and I was safe, safe as being in Abraham's bosom.

Most of the people who have lived on an island tell me that they know that feeling well. They say that the water barrier creates a sense of sanctuary. Perhaps that's why castles had moats. Anyway, one of the vivid feelings I had on the island was that of complete safety. Not that I had any fears of wolves or bears; only those from Down Below fear them. Oh, we're leery when a bear has cubs and drives us away but that doesn't count. No, it's the safety from all evils, even from the personal demons that haunt all of us.

But there were other feelings too, some too deep to put into words. Up there on the island I felt cleansed both inside and out. After just a few hours there I always felt a sense of renewal, of new vigor, of potential for further growth. Hard to explain but the experience was vivid. Also there came an increased alertness. I saw things with strange eyes: three kinds of mosses and five varieties of ferns, to give but one example. My hearing seemed more acute: I actually heard two grasshoppers making love.

My sense of smell, long dormant due to pipe tobacco, awakened to fragrances and aromas I'd never known. One afternoon on the island I put my nose to everything I could find. Many of the scents were old friends but there were some new ones too. The best came from three white water lilies floating in a little bay by the point. No, I didn't pick them. There's nothing so sad as a wilted water lily - except perhaps the last drop of whiskey in the glass. Instead I joined them with just my floating face turned to the sun. Four water lilies! Some people claim that our wild white water lilies have no fragrance. They are wrong.

Then there was that delicious feeling of freedom. I could do any damned fool thing I wanted to do. No one could see or hear me or touch me - not even with their voices. No one could make demands. I had left all the pollution of civilization on the other side of many lovely hills. I felt primal, uncivilized, and beat my bare chest to assure myself that it was true. Drinking deeply of the solitude and isolation, that freedom almost intoxicated me.

But best of all was the feeling of peace, the peace that passeth understanding. All my little or big worries just vanished. Part of that was due to the deep quiet on my island. Oh, occasionally I became aware of the soft rustle of wind in the pine branches far above me, or the lapping of little waves on the shore, but these were murmurs, not noises. Lying there on a bed of moss, with the sunshine on my face and body, all I heard was the utter silence. No one can describe that sort of peacefulness, but one of its elements seemed to be that time had stopped. No hurry, no urgency, no concern for what I should do next. That freedom from the tyranny of the clock that hassles our everyday lives was part of the peace I felt. But hell's bells, I'm almost talking like a preacher, a role that does not fit me.

Year after year I returned to my island, usually just once or twice, lest it lose its magical impact on me. It never did. Never was there any sign that any other human had been on its shores. Always felt that serene safety, cleansing, renewal, alertness, freedom and peace. Always I was reborn.

I missed going there only two years, once during World War II and once after I suffered my first heart attack. "Never get out of breath. Never overexert," the doctors told me and getting to my island would have been too dangerous. A few years later, though, I started visiting my island again and kept it up annually until about nine years ago when more heart troubles and other betrayals of the flesh said no.

I have not seen it since. No, that is not true. I've seen it in the ambulance, in the hospital bed, at night here at home when I thought I might die. Always the vision has given me peace. At eighty-one I have no hope of ever going there again but that doesn't matter now. I had my island once and I have it still. May you find an island of your own.

A Marriage Of Convenience

When John Sivola came into the house after feeding and watering his horses he swore. The coffee had boiled over on the wood range and the bacon was burned again. Another lousy breakfast! He'd had a lot of them as well as other bad meals ever since his wife Siiri had died.

Stirring an egg into the charred bacon and straining the coffee through a square of window screen into a dirty cup John ate the mess right out of the frying pan. No way to live, he thought. A man needed a woman.

He looked around the house. It was a fine house, a frame house, not a log cabin. He had built it with his own hands for Siiri but oh it was so dirty now. The hardwood floors that she had kept scrubbed until they shone had barn dirt ground into them because he forgot to put on the barn boots when he took care of the horses. Siiri never let him forget. And the windows were so dirty it was hard to see out of them. And all those dishes piled in the sink. It would take an hour to clean them and then they'd soon be dirty again. He thought of the bedroom with the bed that hadn't been made for months and the, pile of dirty sheets and blankets in the corner. He'd done a washing several times, a long nasty job, and tried some ironing as the big brown spot on one of the sheets testified. And his own clothes were so bad he hated to put them on in the morning. He needed a woman to take care of those things.

As he fixed a ham sandwich for his lunch in the woods where he was cutting pulp off one of the three forties he owned John hated the store bread that he smeared with mustard. Weak stuff if was. Siiri's homemade bread had always clung to the ribs and made him feel full. No, he wasn't eating right and he knew it. Too much bacon, pork and beans, and bologna and store soup. It wasn't that he lacked for money. No, he had plenty of raha in the bank but he hated to go to Flynn's store for groceries. Siiri had always done the shopping. When he did go now he always forgot something and had to go back again and again. The cellar shelves, once filled with canned venison and berries and applesauce, were empty now and in the summer there always were fresh vegetables from the garden she tended. John had planted a garden last year after she died but got little from it because of the weeds. The kitchen no longer had that fine smell of cinnamon rolls or pies baking in the oven. Indeed it smelled faintly of horse manure. "And so do I!" he said to himself. It had been fun to go sauna with Siiri; not much fun to go alone. Something had to be done. He couldn't keep on living this way.

John took a big wad of Peerless and put it in his pipe. It was time to do some hard thinking, and the first thought was that he'd have to get married again. Filled with guilt, he rejected it at first. This was Siiri's house. How could he bear to have another woman in it? A flood of memories of her returned but again and again it became clear that he could no longer live alone. He would have to find another wife.

But who? At sixty-three years of age, no young girl would look at him and besides he didn't think he could handle the sex business if he did find one. No, the best bet would be a widow. There were three of them in town, Aunt Lizzie, hell no!, and Mrs. Belanger but she was French Canadian and Catholic and that was out. The third was Helmi Teikkenen whose husband had been killed two years before when a beam fell on him in the railroad roundhouse. John didn't know her very well. He'd seen her at church before he stopped going there. A plump woman, fairly good looking, and easy to talk to, she lived in a log cabin up by Sliding Rock. A real possibility. Maybe she needed a man as much as he needed a woman.

But how to go about courting her? How to find out if she might be interested? It had been easy with Siiri. He'd carried her books home from high school and they had walked many miles down the railroad tracks after church talking up a storm. John didn't know how it came about but suddenly they were married. Eighteen she was, and he nineteen. They'd lived together happily until the scarlet fever killed her. John knew that he couldn't just up and tell Helmi Heikkenen that he needed a wife to do the cleaning and washing and cooking. No, he would have to court her. But how? There was nothing to do in Tioga, no place to go except to church. Each evening at nine the kerosene lamps of the village winked out except for those in Higley's saloon and the railroad station. Maybe, after they got acquainted, he could hitch up one of his draft horses to the buckboard and go for a ride down to Lake Tioga some afternoon if she were willing. Yes, getting acquainted was the first step.

So John Sivola shaved, put on the cleanest shirt, and drove his team and lumber wagon up to Flynn's store, bought some hamburger and a chicken and some cookies, then took the back road home past Helmi's log cabin hoping to see her in the yard. She wasn't but John noticed that the smoke coming out of her chimney was not emerging from its top but rather from its base where the bricks joined the roof. That's a dangerous business so John knocked on the cabin door. When Helmi opened it he told her what he had seen.

"Helmi, going by I see smoke coming out at bottom of your chimney. You could have bad fire that way. You want me to fix it?"

She thanked him warmly for his concern but said that she had no money to pay him. John smiled. "Oh, that's OK," he said. "I do it for free. I got bricks and cement at home. I go get them. But can I come in to see if bottom of chimney is bad too?"

The cabin was spotless, the windows sparkling clean, and there were good cooking smells. Helmi's hands were floured from bread making. "I give you cup of coffee, John," she said, "but coffee is all gone until next week when pension check comes. You want some maitua (milk)? I got lots of milk now that my cow just freshened and eggs and butter, and soon have fresh bread. I give you new bread with butter and wild strawberry jam when you come back." John could tell that she was feeling bad that she couldn't offer coffee. In the U.P. you always "give coffee" when someone drops in.

John returned that afternoon with the wagon filled with bricks, a mixing box, sand and cement. The cement and bricks were left over from the outhouse he'd built for Siiri when she got tired of the boys dumping it over every Halloween; the sand he got from the beach at Lake Tioga. The job took him all afternoon but it was done right and Helmi sure appreciated it. As they sat across the kitchen table afterward eating fresh bread smeared heavily with butter and wild strawberry jam she told him so.

"It's hard without a man in the house," she said. "Most things I can do but big things no. Hard for you too, John, I think, now that Siiri is gone. I do washing tomorrow and if you bring me basket of your dirty clothes I wash them for you, eh? We help each other." Though sorely tempted, John refused her offer. "My clothes too dirty." As he left, she gave him a piece of blueberry pie for his supper.

The next day he had to work in the woods and there was plenty of time to think. Yah, they would hit it off. Yah, she needed him as he needed her. How soon should he wait before asking her? Being acquainted only one day not long enough. Was he ready yet to go to bed with another woman? No! Would he ever be? Maybe so, but not yet. Meanwhile he should try to see her often. Her cabin needed new wood plaster chinking; a bottom log was rotten and needed replacing; her barn and chicken coop were in bad shape. No point to fixing up those because he'd have to build some new ones for her when she moved into his house. But to have some excuse for seeing her now, he'd fix that bottom log and do the chinking. John cut down a fine cedar that he could use.

The second day of his courting John brought her a pail of coffee beans and when he found that her coffee grinder was broken and she was trying to grind them with a hammer in a dish, he repaired it. All it needed was a shim around the axle of the little cog wheel. Taking most of the afternoon to replace the rotten log and chink the other logs, he was rewarded by a fine supper of maijuka (venison stew), Helmi having found in her cellar one last jar of the canned deer meat. And coffee and applesauce for dessert. Sitting there across from her at the red checkered table cloth, John felt not only full but more at peace than he had been for many months. Twice he almost broached the subject of marriage but it seemed too soon. Instead he asked her if she would be willing to come see his house the next day and show him how to wash his sheets. No matter how hard he boiled them, they were always grey.

"Did you put bleach or blueing in the wash water?" Helmi asked.

"No. I don't know if I have them," he replied. "I use plenty of soap though. I buy some if you show me. And kituksia (thanks) for the fine meal. I sure love your leipa (bread)." Helmi agreed.

So the next afternoon he came for her after cleaning up his house and washing the dishes and making the bed. The sheets were still hanging out on the line and he had the copper boiler steaming on the stove. Helmi brought in the sheets, poured some of the bleach and blueing she had brought with her into the boiler, put in the sheets and then went with him all over the house and to his barn and even to his pasture and hayfields. Then she rinsed and put the sheets through the wringer and hung them on the clothesline outside, singing as she did so. Soon they were white-white and despite his protests, she ironed them in his kitchen, folded them and placed them on his bed. Before she left she also cleaned his sink, using some of the bleach. John was over-whelmed. "Oh, kituskia (thanks) Helmi," he said. "You good woman. Now I know how to do it. But he hoped he wouldn't ever have to do it again.

The next day, lacking anything else he could do to help her, John split a lot of firewood and kindling. When he came in for coffee and coffeecake, he finally popped the question. "Helmi, will you marry me" he said. "You and I have hard time living alone. We need each other. You poor. I have lots of raha in the bank. I make good money and give you all you need. I need someone to cook for me, and wash, and clean. I lonesome and maybe you are too. Only bad thing is that I don't want any love stuff. Too close to Siiri yet." Helmi lifted an eyebrow at that and said that she'd think it over.

The next day when he brought her a box of chocolates from Flynn's store she gave John her answer and with it a bombshell. Yes, she would marry him. It was a business bargain with no love stuff as he had made clear. But she wouldn't move into his house; she would stay right here in her own. He could eat his meals here and she would pack his lunch pail. She would do his washing when he brought it to her, and once each week she would go to his house to clean it up. He would give her money for food or anything else she wanted to buy. He would do chores for her like splitting wood and kindling. She would feed him good. But she was staying in her own cabin not moving into his house. No love stuff. He would sleep in his own bed, not in hers. A business bargain.

Well, that sure surprised John Sivola so much his mouth hung open. Yet it made sense. The people in town would do a lot of tongue wagging once they found out but nuts to them. When Helmi brought out some coffee and hot cinnamon rolls it took only one bit to convince him. "Yah," he said. "Tomorrow we take afternoon train to Ishpeming and get married by Justice of Peace."

So that is what they did. John got two copies of the marriage license, one for him and one for her, and had them framed in a little shop next door. Then he insisted on buying her a new dress and shoes and a bright new huivi (head scarf) with lace on it before he took her to the Chocolate Shop for the biggest banana split they had. That was their honeymoon.

When they got off the evening train and walked up our long hill street, John leading the way and Helmi following, as was the custom for married but not unmarried Finns, they met Aunt Lizzie on her gossip rounds. "Helmi, you and John get married?" she asked. "I see that he fixed your house and they say that you went to Ishpeming to get married."

John stepped in. "Yah, we get married though none of your business. I marry fine woman." By the time they climbed the hill and were at Helmi's house, the whole town knew. And approved. Two nice people should not live alone.

When they got there Helmi told John to go to his house to feed and water his horses while she fixed his supper. Before he left, however, he put her copy of the marriage certificate on the shelf above the kitchen stove and left under the coffee grinder a wad of green money. "This for you, Helmi," he said, "and you can have all you want anytime." It was an awkward moment, almost as though he was buying a wife, but she smiled on him as he left. He liked that smile. Things would work out.

When John returned, they had supper. Not much of a wedding feast but very good. The rest of the venison stew and a piece of yesterday's pie and some more cinnamon rolls. Helmi apologized. "I make you good meal tomorrow, John, after I go store."

Smoking his pipe afterwards, he heard her singing softly as she did the dishes. Was it the Finn Marrying Song? No, it was Kuopia, a song about a lonesome wanderer who had finally come home. "Miksi tau tu sineh o Lempia, miksi tau tu raukusta." His mother had sung it to him when he was a child. John lit pipe after pipe, hating to go home to an empty house. So warm, so full fed and happy he was he could hardly bear to leave. Ah, she was a fine woman, Helmi was, and a happy woman. So he dallied.

It was a good thing that he did for suddenly outside there came a hullabaloo of yelling and the banging on pans. "Oh, oh," Helmi cried, "They give us chivari, I think. How they find out so soon?"

We let them make noise for a while, then I pay them." John responded.

Finally came the knocks on the door and shouts of "Chivari, Chivari!" John went out to confront the twenty young men and boys. "We go to your house first," one of them said, "but you no there. We find you anyway. Pay!" John grinned. "OK," he replied. "Here four bucks, three for your keg of beer and one for boys' candy. You go away now and leave us alone." When they departed, John said to Helmi, "Well I guess we married now, eh? And I must go my house. I don't want to go." He looked at her but saw no sign of protest. "Good night, John," she said, "I have breakfast for you at seven."

It was a short winter for the U.P. that year with ice out by the end of March. John shot a deer much of which Helmi canned and many rabbits and partridge so they ate well. He also shot two geese which Helmi plucked, using the down to make him a pillow for his bed. "So you will think of me" she said. Think of her? She was always in his thoughts.

As the winter wore on, the business bargain arrangement began to seem not right to John. Almost always the fire was out in the stove when he returned to his empty house each night. He got tired of having to bring her his clothes to wash. It was hard too for Helmi to go to his house each week to keep it clean, having to go down our long hill street, then up Keystone Hill, then back again. John usually came to her house the back way on his skis and so feeling sorry for her, he brought over Siiri's old skis so she could do the same. Made him feel silly but not too much. Helmi was a good skier and once the two of them skied cross-country over to Big Rock on Fish Lake and had a pot of coffee over a campfire just as though they were courting.

Only once in that long time did Helmi show him some real affection. He had brought her a perfect little spruce Christmas tree one morning before going to the woods and when he returned she had it all decorated with colored chains of paper, and popcorn strung on threads, yes, even with a bright star on top that she had painfully cut from the top of a tin can. Sure looked pretty and when he told her so and said that she did too she patted his check. That was all but he felt her soft hand for weeks.

Yet once, when impulsively he swept her onto his lap, she fought back like a wild cat, hitting and slashing him till he let her go. And didn't cook a bite for him for a day. "Don't you forget. Business-bargain, business-bargain, no love stuff," she shouted. John went back to his house early that night.

But spring came, the miraculously lovely U.P. spring. The snow melted and, hoping one day that Helmi might too, John brought her a great armful of blue flags (wild iris) from a swamp that had soaked him over his knees. She was overcome with delight and showed it.

"Why you bring me flowers, John?" she asked.

He swallowed twice, then said, "Because I love you, Helmi."

She cupped a hand to her ear. "Say again!" she ordered, "and again and again!"

Then Helmi put her arms around his neck and kissed him. "Oh Johnny, why you no say that before?" But after supper she insisted again that he go back to his own house.

As he lay there with his head on the goosedown pillow John wondered about the inscrutable ways of women. Why did she send him home? Maybe spring thaw had come to her but deep ice doesn't melt all at once. Remembering her bare arms around his neck, he slept deeply.

The next morning all was the same except that Helmi had made blueberry pancakes with store sausage and had put a hot pasty in his dinner pail. As they ate across from each other the blue flags in a big bowl separated yet joined them and when he left for the woods she patted his cheek again. Yes, the ice was melting.

That afternoon as he returned from cutting spruce John drove his team to Flynn's store to pick up another box of chocolates but when he entered Helmi's house she was not there. Probably having coffee with the neighbors. Too early for supper yet, so he drove the team to his barn, fed and watered it, then entered his house to wash up. Helmi met him at the door. "Oh, Johnny," she exclaimed as she put her arms around his, neck. "Meet Helmi Sivola, your new bride. This is my house too now. I move in to stay." There was meat cooking on the stove and the blue flags were on the kitchen table so John said it again. "I love you, Helmi." And they lived happily ever after.

The other volumes of the
Northwoods Reader series by Cully Gage:

- *The Northwoods Reader, Volume 2
  Northern Love Affair*
  The original book 4 *(The Last Northwoods
  Reader)*, book 8 *(Tioga Tales)* and *A Love
  Affair With The U.P.*

- *The Northwoods Reader, Volume 3
  Northern Memories*
  The original book 2 *(Tales Of The Old
  U.P.)*, book 6 *(Still Another Northwoods
  Reader)* and book 7 *(Old Bones And
  Northern Memories)*.

Avery Color Studios, Inc. has a full line of Great Lakes
oriented books, puzzles, cookbooks, shipwreck and lighthouse
maps, lighthouse posters and Fresnel lens model.

For a full color catalog call:
1-800-722-9925

Avery Color Studios, Inc. products are
available at gift shops and bookstores
throughout the Great Lakes region.